Sowing the Wind

Sowing the Wind

The Mississippi Constitutional Convention of 1890

Dorothy Overstreet Pratt

University Press of Mississippi / Jackson

www.upress.state.ms.us

The University Press of Mississippi is a member
of the Association of American University Presses.

Copyright © 2018 by University Press of Mississippi
All rights reserved

First printing 2018

∞

Library of Congress Cataloging-in-Publication Data

Names: Pratt, Dorothy O., 1949– author.
Title: Sowing the wind : the Mississippi constitutional convention of 1890 /
Dorothy Overstreet Pratt.
Description: Jackson : University Press of Mississippi, [2018] | Includes
bibliographical references and index. |
Identifiers: LCCN 2017026732 (print) | LCCN 2017027884 (ebook) | ISBN
9781496815477 (epub single) | ISBN 9781496815484 (epub institutional) |
ISBN 9781496815491 (pdf single) | ISBN 9781496815507 (pdf institutional)
| ISBN 9781496815460 (hardcover : alk. paper)
Subjects: LCSH: Mississippi. Constitutional Convention (1890) |
Constitutional conventions—Mississippi. | Constitutional
history—Mississippi. | Mississippi—Politics and government—1865–1950.
Classification: LCC KFM7001 1890.A29 (ebook) | LCC KFM7001 1890.A29 P73 2018
(print) | DDC 342.76202/92—dc23
LC record available at https://lccn.loc.gov/2017026732

British Library Cataloging-in-Publication Data available

Contents

Prologue　vii

Chapter 1　Introduction and Overview　3

Chapter 2　The Bourbon Elites　10

Chapter 3　Opposition to the Bourbons　27

Chapter 4　Calling the Convention　47

Chapter 5　The Convention Debates the Franchise　69

Chapter 6　The Convention Adopts the Understanding Clause　87

Chapter 7　The Convention Considers Reform Agendas　105

Chapter 8　The Convention Exposes Class Divisions　125

Chapter 9　Defending the New Constitution in Congress　144

Chapter 10　Defending the New Constitution in the Federal Courts　168

Chapter 11　Conclusion　193

Notes　211

Bibliography　273

Index　285

Prologue

This has been, hands down, the most complex project I have ever undertaken. The difficulty came not because it was a lengthy project (although it was), or because the sources were hard to find (they were), but rather because the production of the book has been emotionally draining. This is not an uplifting narrative. No one is a hero. No one comes off well. It is an American tragedy.

I thought I knew the story. Having been raised in Mississippi by parents born in the state, and with three of four grandparents who were natives, I thought I understood the history, with all its flaws and triumphs. Like many historians before me, I had simplified this period by believing that the constitutional convention, as well as its subsequent document, was a reform effort—absolutely misguided and based on bigotry, but a reform nonetheless. In fact, a letter to the *Clarion-Ledger*, of Jackson, Mississippi, in 1890 argued that "old men of the present generation can't afford to die and leave their children and grandchildren with shot-guns in their hands, a lie in their mouth and perjury on their lips in order to defeat the negroes."[1] That statement appeared to confirm my initial interpretation. But as I did the research and unpeeled the layers of argument, cynicism, and corruption, I was left with little of the good. The story had to be rewritten.

The simple fact that this is not a nice story makes its acceptance problematic. Mississippi deserved better leaders than it had, and the consequence was a state mired in a slough of economic despondency and governmental malaise. Yet these leaders should not be assumed to have been stupid or without sophistication; in fact, their ability to manipulate the law was extraordinary. Unfortunately, while often intelligent and well-informed, they were wrongheaded about so much. Histories of the state often emphasize, with some justification, that narrow-mindedness and the problems it caused. Yet since the 1970s the state has moved far beyond the days of Jim Crow. This does not mean there are not problems even yet. There are. But the state of Mississippi in 1963 is not that of 2017. Understandably people in the state would like to be recognized for what they have accomplished in those intervening years, not simply by a dark history. Again, the state and its people deserve better.

In addition, the facts behind the narrative have not been easy to accumulate, much less to analyze and communicate. During the period of the turn of the century (nineteenth to twentieth), newspapers reflected their southern heritage: here, one does not speak of shameful or bad things. That reticence was part of the culture, whether in a family or within a community. Too much of the story has to be gleaned from newspapers outside the state. Thankfully, both *Proquest* and *Chronicling America* have helped make digital searches possible and accumulation of fact accessible. Moreover, even when newspaper accounts were available, especially with the constitutional convention, the state's African American newspapers remain missing for this period, as they are no longer extant. Helpfully, however, other newspapers, including the *Clarion-Ledger* from Jackson, often referred to those papers and quoted from them.

I need to thank the staff of the Mississippi Department of Archives and History, the Library of Congress, and the Law Library of the University of South Carolina. These librarians went out of their way to help find obscure references. I should also thank my colleagues, Wanda Hendricks, who read chapters and kept me on target referencing African American reactions; Don Doyle, who asked probing questions and encouraged me to work toward publication; Matthew Holden, who is actually from Mound Bayou and probably cares more about this research than even I; and Reece Carlton, also a Mississippi native, who graciously edited my sentences. My sisters, Theresa and Pattie, read the manuscript and went to the state archives at times when I could not make it. My husband, Jack Pratt, also read chapters and courageously suggested edits dealing with legal history. He is greatly appreciated, not only for his insight but also for his endless patience. My dean, Mary Ann Fitzpatrick, also provided support that made the work possible. The University Press of Mississippi staff (along with my anonymous outside readers and Robert Burchfield, a superb copy editor) deserve rich thanks for their help and support in bringing this manuscript to light and life. Finally, to all those who kindly asked after the manuscript that took so many years to reach fruition, thank you all. I needed the encouragement, for at times the story was too much to take in.

During the writing of this history, I discovered not only a powerful narrative but also a number of tantalizing (but tangential) subjects. The book is long enough without having sidetracked to trace these tempting avenues of investigation. There are issues within the constitution that ought to be analyzed by practicing attorneys. The levee problems should be examined by someone familiar with water problems and property law. The infighting between the black Republicans in Mississippi ought to be thoroughly scrutinized, especially noting the problems of class. These and other issues I leave to the next generation of historians of the state.

I also have found in the research and writing of this manuscript a strong correlation between nation-building in the nineteenth century and that of the twenty-first. Failed states in the nineteenth have equally compelling association with the twenty-first century. The difference is that the failed state of Mississippi was composed of Americans who shared a common heritage with the rest of the country. They also shared a common national economy and what should have been a common political structure. What they did not share was a common worldview. Their optimism was not unbounded. They believed that growth was limited—their experience confirmed that belief. Those who controlled that growth and benefited from it would hold the power in the state. The subsequent struggle was immense. To a large extent, the story of Mississippi and its constitutional convention of 1890 is a cautionary tale, one to be ignored at our peril.

It is for these reasons that I dedicate this book to my Mississippi parents and grandparents:

Noah Webster Overstreet Jr. and Hester Seale Overstreet

Noah Webster Overstreet Sr. and Mabel Kinnear Overstreet

Dr. Ira Robert Seale and Bertie Pitman Seale

Who taught me to tell the truth always, no matter how difficult

Sowing the Wind

CHAPTER 1

Introduction and Overview

This book examines the Mississippi constitutional convention of 1890, which became the crucible of change for the state that lasted well into the twentieth century. Historians have long debated the reasons behind the disfranchisement juggernaut of the turn of the last century, when states of the old Confederacy began to write constitutions to disfranchise and circumvent the Fifteenth Amendment. What is surprising is that examinations of the disfranchisement movement in the South have only considered the Mississippi convention and its subsequent constitution in conjunction with events in other southern states, for Mississippi was the first to convene a convention to disfranchise African Americans through novel means. Other states watched with interest but then took as much as five or more years to follow with their own conventions. Some states used a few of Mississippi's ideas but also added other provisions, such as a grandfather clause. Unlike the situation in other states, Mississippi's constitution successfully held up against federal inspection for nearly seventy-five years. What happened in Mississippi set the stage for the other states of the old Confederacy and therefore defined the history of the twentieth-century South, its race relations, economic stagnation, and the strictures of Jim Crow.

The deepest analysis of the Mississippi constitutional convention is a book written nearly seventy years ago, Albert Kirwan's *Revolt of the Rednecks*. Kirwan examined the period in which the convention took place rather than focusing on the convention itself. For him, the narrative of the time incorporated the convention, rather than the convention defining the period.[1] Other historians have followed suit, though the more recent examinations have emphasized the disfranchisement process in the state rather than the consequences of it.[2]

This study argues that the decisions made by the delegates at the constitutional convention created a change in social structure that had profound effects on the state. Though race had long been part of the social fabric of the state and of the old South (through the Civil War and beyond), the fundamental organizational structure of the state depended on class. By the 1880s, however, lack of progress and modernization influences had begun to fray the edges of society. In fact, leading up to the convention, white voters were not unanimous in their support for Democrats; instead, they were split over issues of economics, status, and power in the state legislature. This had led to the rise of the Greenback Party, power struggles within the tiny Republican Party, and the emergence of the Agricultural Wheel.[3] Therefore the constitutional convention met to fix not only the race issue and disfranchisement but also to negotiate the power structures (economic, political, and social) within the state.

The elites had long used the issue of race to control the entire social and economic network, particularly of those below them. In the history of this post-Reconstruction period, race played a part as a cohesive factor among white voters. Violence was the order of the day, often, but not exclusively, directed toward African Americans. Although it would be a mistake to downplay the importance of race, to understand the period one also must comprehend the social, economic, and educational strata of the state. Even among African Americans, class distinctions were real and easily identifiable, but as race became the divisive issue at the turn of the twentieth century, class issues were eventually eclipsed. Until the final collapse, the power struggles between the haves and have-nots of the state puzzled elite African Americans and created uncertainty as to where they fit into the system. As streetcars were segregated, elite African Americans fought to keep a first-class car; for many, this was an important issue, because it confirmed status in society.[4] Compromises made at the convention, however, tilted the scale so that power slid away from the elites to a group that had no use for African Americans and did not even want them in the state. This change did not happen all at once, for at first a number of illiterate white voters were also disfranchised—just as the elites had planned. The shift away from the elites, however, concluded quickly, and so the structures of power changed and created a new political system.

Examination of southern class structure is not without precedent, even for Mississippi history. This division among white citizens is often defined as either white counties vs. black counties, paternalists vs. hard-liners, conservative vs. radical racists, or elites vs. dirt farmers (or other nomenclature, such as yeomen farmers).[5] White counties are the ones specified as having a majority of white citizens, and black counties are the ones with a majority of African American citizens. The other words are easier to discern. For the most part, though, these are simply different terms applied to the same groups, albeit with some variation in emphasis. All these names show up in the following chapters and their use reflects the contextual emphasis, such as the use of the terms "white counties" and "black counties" when geography is an important factor. (A map of these counties, based on the census figures of 1890, is included in this book and can be used for reference.)

The terms themselves have real meaning. For instance, white elites in Mississippi were few. They cannot be defined as necessarily having the most money because the economic difficulties of Reconstruction shifted land ownership: some lost land, and a fair number became land poor. For the most part the elites resided in agricultural counties with deep, rich soil and where their African American workers, who were needed to till the soil and harvest the crops, vastly outnumbered them; they inhabited the black counties of the state. The elites were well-educated; they were also racist, though they seldom resorted to violence.[6] They wanted to preserve the social order of the past with them at the top. Not by chance were these leaders often called the Bourbons, who, like the France of old, looked to the past and not to the future. In Mississippi, this terminology fit.

In contrast, dirt farmers lived in the white counties, where the soil was poorer and where many fewer African Americans resided. The dirt farmers wanted more voice in the state, had little use for education, and had even less sympathy for African Americans. Historians have dubbed them the radicals or the hard-line racists.[7] Both groups were bigoted, but, unlike their experience with hard-line racists, African Americans did not face outright violence directly from the paternalists, which did make some difference to African Americans.

Historians have long argued that the planters in the black counties were wealthier than those in the white counties. For this information, they primarily rely on statements made in the papers and in legislative debates, for composite census numbers are misleading. This does not mean that black counties were richer than white ones. Black counties had—by definition—more African American inhabitants than whites, and since African Americans tended to be poorer, their presence skewed the statistics. In reality, the disparity of wealth was simply greater in the black counties, though even the "wealthy" planters struggled to get ahead.[8]

The story of the convention began with familiar history. Antebellum Mississippi had created a sharply defined class structure that ruled the state and expected deference. The disruption of the Civil War and Reconstruction shook the optimism of elites, but in 1874 they reclaimed nearly complete control of the state and promised a return to normalcy and the familiar. It was not to be. By 1890 the state had fallen into near anarchy, struggled with a dismal economy, and could easily be described as a failed state. The 1889 massacre of scores of African Americans in Leflore County scared a number of influential citizens who feared that white youth did not understand the parameters of "wise behavior."[9] Furthermore, a perceived threat by the Lodge Elections Bill galvanized state leaders into calling a convention to create a new constitution that would protect the state from federal oversight, grant some "peace" to the elites, and safeguard their meager fortunes.[10] The old elites, represented by Senator Edward Walthall, Justice L.Q.C. Lamar, and former governor Robert Lowry, opposed calling a convention because they believed it safer to ignore the national spotlight on how the state handled the franchise. In addition, they had promised Congress, when the state was readmitted to the Union, that they would never change the state's Reconstruction constitution's franchise provisions. The forces for change won, indicating the shifting power structure in the state, and the new governor, John Marshall Stone, immediately called a convention.[11]

The purpose of the convention, as widely admitted, was to disfranchise, but the debates at the convention reveal a startling division between the paternalistic elites and the dirt farmers of the state. Both were bigoted, and both were striving for power. Both sought to eke out a little livelihood in a struggling economy. Both shared a view of a limited future, for by that time most people in Mississippi did not share the boundless optimism endemic in other states; rather, they cynically believed that growth of all sorts would be limited. Their experience following the war was one of privation and struggle, and that is the prism through which they viewed the new world order. In order to be sure that they and their families were the ones who benefited in the economy, interest groups clamored to be the ones in control. This meant that the elites of the Delta and the old families of Natchez and Vicksburg were willing to negotiate governmental participation in exchange for economic (and tax) protection. Thus the power struggles of the constitutional convention were set. Though race issues were bluntly discussed, the real struggle in the convention was between the old hierarchy and those who would change it. Both factions were willing to use race as a wedge issue. The elites, however, saw race as a means to an end. Dirt farmers saw the issue of race as an end in itself.

The architect of the convention was neither a member of the elites nor of the dirt farmers; he was not from the rich Delta or the old cities of Vicksburg or Natchez; neither was he from the piney woods. Instead, the senior senator from Mississippi straddled both camps. James Z. George, who had served as a Confederate officer and a justice on the state supreme court before heading to the Senate, was known in Washington, DC, as the Old Commoner. He wore worn clothing and spit tobacco, but he was respected for his intelligence as a lawyer. Even as convention delegates debated the franchise and the tangential issues of woman suffrage, temperance, schooling, and levee control, the real issue of substance—the search for power—was all navigated by a powerful Senator George.[12]

The most puzzling aspect of the convention has long been the acquiescence of Isaiah Montgomery, the lone African American delegate, in the disfranchisement scheme. In fact, he served on the Committee on Franchise, Apportionment and Elections (hereinafter the Franchise Committee) and gave a remarkable speech in support of their efforts. Yet some of his behavior makes sense, if he is understood as the personification of the shift in the state from class to race. Montgomery was an elite and a member of the upper class. At one point he and his family were the richest African Americans in the country. Members of his family were trusted former slaves of the Davis family (Joseph and his younger brother, Jefferson) and often relied upon a network of support from the powerful they knew. He and his family were well-educated. He walked within the halls of power. Though the non-elites at the convention tried to not seat him at the convention, he was seated with the support of the powerful in the state. There he chided the delegates at the convention for their intemperate speech and their rigid racial constructs. Unfortunately, he did not appear to fully understand the seismic shift that was taking place; he believed the paternalists would maintain power and keep their side of the bargain. That faith was misplaced, because the balance of power was tilting to a new portion of the state—the white counties.

The process of creating a new constitution through compromise, which George and others hailed as successful, redefined the political and social structures on race. Not everyone saw the result as positive, however. The most controversial provision was the "Understanding Clause," which was crafted by Senator George to provide a safety net for illiterate whites: the literacy provision required that any potential voter be able to read a section of the constitution; illiterates had the opportunity to have a provision read to them, which they then must interpret. Newspaper editors pointed to the likelihood of fraud in the administration of the clause and thus began to question the integrity of the convention's proceedings; the press then instigated a campaign to ditch the new constitution and close the convention.[13] Fearing a negative vote, the convention delegates simply promulgated the constitution rather than submit it for ratification. The elites believed they knew best and that others would follow their lead—which they did. By the end of the convention, state leaders believed that they had fixed most of the endemic problems in the state (including the franchise problems), but in reality, they had opened Pandora's box. They had begun the tilt to a growing power of the white counties, which included a virulent racism, a paranoia over strong government and higher taxes, and a loathing of northern influence, such as in industrial development.

Once they promulgated the constitution, state Democratic leaders began to close ranks against criticism of its new organic law by outside influences. Like most dysfunctional families, they argued among themselves, but then closed ranks against outsiders. Though there were some opponents within the state, leaders only noticed two types of opposition. The first was an attack through the legislative branch, because the Lodge Elections Bill was still being debated in Washington, DC. African Americans from Mississippi provided copies of the newspaper of record (the *Clarion-Ledger*) as ammunition for the Republicans. Senator George defended the new constitution against attacks by Republicans on the floor of Congress.[14] And in doing so, he was also helpful in defeating the Lodge Elections Bill.[15] The second source of attack was through the courts on the basis of the provisions of the Fourteenth and Fifteenth Amendments. Again, this opposition came through the federal judiciary, but the source of instigation was among African Americans within the state.[16]

Finally, Mississippi Democratic leaders got what they wanted—to be left alone and run the state the way they wanted. The elites envisioned something quite different from what actually happened, for over the next twenty years they lost power; by 1910 the power shift within the state to the non-elites was pretty much completed. Though there were exceptions, the white counties (those with a majority white population) controlled at least the House in the state legislature and usually the governor's mansion.[17] Throughout the early twentieth century, the elites (as well as those who counted their ancestry as belonging to that category) maintained a polite fiction that they were the leaders of the state. In reality, those who straddled the lines between the economic and social groups and who were able to gain support from across the polarized factions in the state were the ones who maintained control. And often that control came through race-baiting and fear-mongering. The mythology of the Lost Cause was just coming to flower in the last decade of the nineteenth century, when the experiences of the Civil War and Reconstruction would be recast to concentrate on the positive aspects of the war's ideology (yet forgetting the negatives like slavery), all the while creating a past that never was. The effect was to make the bitter memories of the past more palatable to the elites, tie the dirt farmers to a common weal, and confirm African Americans as outsiders.

The simple fact that this is not a nice story makes its reading difficult at times. Heroes were few. Mississippi fell further behind in the national rankings of economic development, and the state government was barely functional. And although exceptions emerged, even the educational system of the state was abysmal. At every point when the state appeared to move ahead, the centrifugal forces of decay, violence, race-baiting, and grinding poverty appeared to shatter any hopes of building a future.[18] Mississippi was slowly developing an African American community in which the upper 5 percent began to accumulate a bit of wealth; unfortunately, this improvement appears to have been founded on fragile foundations.[19] Research provides some information for this nascent culture, but regrettably there are no extant black newspapers from the state in this period. One historian, Neill McMillen, has managed to create a narrative of African American social and culture history from Mississippi at this time, but much is missing.[20] For instance, we know almost nothing of one important African American politician of the period, James Hill.[21] It is, however, possible to create a picture of another world in 1890 Mississippi, with its people firmly tied to the past yet believing they were planning for the future.

Overall, the narrative of the convention is a complex one and not simply a juggernaut of racial bigotry. Class issues played an important role in the debates and eventual portions of the constitution. Economic concerns pushed to the fore in a number of the arguments but also simmered underneath a number of other issues. Finally, beneath all of these concerns was a struggle for power in the state: economic, political, and social. By the end of the convention the elites thought they had held on to their control, but they were wrong. State leaders in 1890 were willing to sell their souls to garner a little peace and prosperity, but they never considered the effect of their decisions on the majority of the state (African Americans), nor did they realize the long-term consequences of their actions. They sowed the wind, but reaped the whirlwind.

CHAPTER 2

The Bourbon Elites

When the constitutional convention convened in Jackson on August 12, 1890, delegates gathered in the antebellum capitol.[1] It was hot, typical for a humid Mississippi summer, and it was the traditional time of agricultural break when duties in the fields were not pressing. Delegates assumed naively that the convention would be over before harvest. That was not to be. Before the end of the session, they knew each other well—perhaps too well. By September one member complained that he believed the convention had been called prematurely since little had been accomplished in twenty-two days. By October the convention was meeting in evening sessions as well as on Saturdays in an effort to finish.[2] The session did not end until November 1, long after harvest. Many of the men simply did not answer roll for days at a time, and there were calls in October to halt the convention and resume in January.[3] Not only did the farmers need to attend to their crops, but the professionals, lawyers, and businessmen also had to attend to their businesses. Nevertheless, the delegates took no respite, and the convention pressed on through October.

In the beginning, however, they gathered with the eagerness of great expectations and the solemnity of ritual. Emotions ran high. One tongue-in-cheek editorial from the *Clarion-Ledger* referred to the convention as having a fair representation of the best minds in the state, which was good, for they "are expected to settle the race question . . . revolutionize the judiciary . . . curtail the appointed powers of the Chief Executive . . . cut their deliberations short . . . be economical and spend as little money as possible."[4] The convention members, though, were serious that first day. They read the act calling for a convention from the legislative session in February and had Bishop Charles Galloway give an invocation, calling upon the Lord to bless and guide the gathering. For full measure, they then read the March call by Governor J. M. Stone for delegates to the convention, followed by the subsequent list of delegates. One hundred and thirty-three delegates answered roll, which included nine floaters and a number of at-large delegates (one man died before qualifying).⁵ One hundred and twenty-nine claimed to be Democrats, two Republicans, one Greenbacker, and one Conservative. Fifty-two were lawyers; another four were both lawyers and farmers. Most of the others were farmers as well, with or without another profession, such as physician or merchant. Only one delegate was identified in the paper as a judge, but several claimed this title during the convention. One was president of Mississippi Agricultural and Mechanical College. Sixty-six were born in Mississippi, and most of the others came from the other southern states. One was from New York, and another from Ireland. Methodists made up the largest religious group at thirty-eight, but Presbyterians were well represented. Six noted themselves as "friendly to all" denominations, two had no preference, and one listed himself as a "liberal."⁶

The overwhelming preponderance of those delegates claiming to be farmers was symbolic of the enormous influence of agriculture in the state. Whether elites (plantation owners) or dirt farmers, both claimed a connection to the soil. The same was true of those who had a profession—such as lawyer and planter. For southerners, this agricultural identity also was indicative of place and its importance. That nearly all also claimed to be Protestant was almost as important, since it shaped choices on fundamental issues of reform. Finally, participation in the Civil War also drew many together and created bonds not easily understood by outsiders.

Delegates elected Judge Solomon Saladin Calhoon as president of the convention.⁷ His speech, well-honed beforehand (since he probably expected the honor), bluntly addressed the reasons for the convention—to disfranchise the African American voter. He argued: "There exists here in this State two distinct and opposite types of mankind . . . the question is how it shall be arranged that we may live harmoniously." He further argued, in breathtaking naïveté or cynical manipulation of the truth, that "it is a fact that each race is fond of the other. . . . There is no black man or colored man in the State of Mississippi who does not feel in the business of life the whites are his friends." To emphasize his point further, he stated that when the five races of mankind met, each tried to be "in the ascendancy," which led to conflict and chaos. He posited that when African Americans were in control, as during Reconstruction, it had "always meant economic and moral ruin." White rule, on the other hand, meant "prosperity and happiness to all races." The state therefore needed to deal with the issues of the franchise and the "over-generous" numbers of African American voters.⁸

Judge Calhoon was only advocating what the casual reader could find in the local paper or among the letters to the editor, and in that vein, plain speaking was not unexpected. Typical was a long letter in the *Clarion-Ledger* titled

"How Shall We Disfranchise the Senegambian: The Main Question After All." The writer wrote that he agreed with Senators Walthall and George that literacy was not a test of fitness for voting, because the effect would be to disfranchise old Confederate veterans who had served nobly (an argument that underlined the shifting issues of race and class). He further argued that "if every Negro in Mississippi was a graduate of Harvard and had been elected as class orator . . . he still would not be as well fitted to exercise the right of suffrage as the Anglo-Saxon farm laborer, whose cross X mark . . . means force and intellect and manhood." Just to make certain that the readers understood his thesis, he added, "This is not a question of intellect per se,—it is a question of RACE." To address this goal the letter's author would simply amend the old constitution to allow anyone to vote who could read any portion of the constitution (the passage chosen by lot) and could write a sentence of the constitution as dictated. The variant was that he would allow the governor to pardon the failures of those he deemed fit to vote, therefore allowing them access to voting.[9]

The connection between race and access to voting was the primary issue, but not the only one. Before examining the convention and the circumstances that led to it, it is essential to understand the environment of the time—the political and economic history of the state and the people who dominated the period.[10] Democrats may have been divided between paternalists and hardliners, but the Bourbons were in power. These men were often identified as those who were nonprogressive, antidemocratic, and untrustworthy—in other words, those who lived in the past. Yet the Bourbons did wish to incorporate a New South mentality; they wanted a vibrant economy but only on their own terms.[11] These men were usually from the black counties, were better off financially, were better educated, and often had served as senior officers during the Confederacy. In fact, more than one historian has referred to the period following Restoration as when the Confederates actually won. Therefore the period has also been known as the age of the "Brigadier Generals."[12]

Understanding the viewpoint of the Bourbons is crucial to recognizing the limited options the Democrats in 1890 thought they had. The Bourbons controlled the state in these years, though not without opposition. The story of those who opposed the white elites will be covered in the next chapter, for they are equally important. This chapter focuses primarily on these conservative leaders and why they came to power, for they are important parts of the history of the state, ranging from Restoration to the turn of the century. To a large extent, these men represented a bridge to the past, rather than hope for the future. These leaders may have become the respected voices at the convention, but these elites reflected the very narrow viewpoint that was honed during Reconstruction. Therefore a brief recount of that history is necessary. There are no heroes in this narrative. The state deserved better.

◆ ◆ ◆

The roots of discord, even among the political parties, emerged during Reconstruction. During that first foray of the United States into nation-building, citizens of the state were desperate for some stability. Their world had become bedlam, and they blamed everyone other than themselves for the problems. Many hoped that home rule (Restoration) would provide some certainty. For white Mississippians, the promise of home rule represented a return to some familiar economic and social structures. For that reason the threat of federal intervention was not their primary fear, though that danger was certainly valid; rather, all government became suspect, which inevitably led to the desire to unravel any power structure.

Race turmoil and economic woes were real, and white Mississippians, more out of emotion than logic, made one reality the cause of the other. After all, they reasoned, in antebellum days the state was one of the richest in the country. They believed that a labor pool that could move, ask for more money, and sign contracts with their competitors was disruptive to the smooth flow of the economy. To the mind of old Confederates, the rights of freedmen undermined economic stability.

In their eyes the events of the Reconstruction period appeared to prove their point. Whether Democrat or Republican, whether African American or white, politicians at the end of the war faced a daunting task. The state needed a great deal. Roads and fencing, which by their nature required constant attention, were destroyed. What few schools had existed before were no more. Investments, particularly in the form of bondage, were gone. The labor pool was uncertain and faced a genuine shortage.[13] Much had to be done. Yet questions remained as to who would and should take on that responsibility.

The first elected governor under congressional Reconstruction, James Alcorn, was a longtime political opponent of Jefferson Davis. So great was his antipathy to Davis that he sat out the war at his plantation in the Delta. Aligning with Republicans, Alcorn hoped for a moderate approach that would heal all portions of the state. The state's politics, however, were far too polarized at the time to end hostilities. Fortunately for him, he had an avenue of escape: the opportunity to be elected as senator by the legislature, an opportunity that he took.[14]

In the midst of this upheaval, a new group of citizens came to power. Former Confederates claimed during Reconstruction that either African Americans ran the state (implicitly meaning badly administered) or that African Americans were the dupes of scheming "carpetbaggers." At the height of their "power," African Americans never held more than 25 percent of the seats in the state legislature.[15] They did dominate, however, in pockets in the state, particularly where they outnumbered whites by a large majority. In these black counties African Americans held two-thirds of the offices during the height of Reconstruction.[16] African Americans also made their presence and power known in the jury box, where it became the custom in these counties to divide the jury members equally between the two races. Other offices fell to Republicans, and then to African Americans, in these black counties, and therefore the power to tax shifted hands. None of this set well with the traditionalists in the Delta, but in particular Warren County (and thus Vicksburg) was troubled.[17]

The economy also played a significant part in galvanizing support for Democrats. Many historians who wrote in the decades following the turn of the twentieth century portrayed the Reconstruction legislature in Mississippi as spending wildly. To some extent this is true: by 1871 the cost of the state government had soared to nearly $3 million yearly. Before the war, the state expended little, for the leaders were still arguing over the roles of the state and federal governments: for example, was it the responsibility of the state to invest in roads and bridges? By 1871 the legislature had decided to invest in infrastructure, as well as in universal public schooling for both races and to provide state subsidies for industry and railroads. As a consequence taxes shot up. The mill rate rose from 1 mill in 1869 to 14 mills in 1874.[18] Following the panic of 1873, farmers could not pay their taxes, and some left the state.[19]

Though the impact on individual and governmental pocketbooks drove the eventual revolt, racism was an essential part of opposition to Republicans in the state and in the South.[20] No matter how erudite or educated an African American might be, white leaders argued he was still uncivilized; women did not factor at all. Ironically, the "civilized" often resorted to violence to control the "uncivilized." A number of incidents have been recorded elsewhere, but the riot in Meridian is especially noteworthy.[21] After the war the town of Meridian grew quickly because of its location on the rail lines. With a population mixed in race, social strata, and politics, Republicans held the advantage. Whites, however, resented these changes. Tempers were frayed, and mistrust was rampant on both sides. On one occasion Republicans rallied to the side of an African American who was arrested under questionable charges. In turn, local whites "were incensed." The town went up in flames, though it is not certain who started the fire. At the resulting trial, tempers again flared and guns were fired, killing the presiding judge. The situation continued to escalate, and white men went on a rampage through the town: "Every man that could do so got a gun or pistol and went on the hunt for negroes." The number of African Americans killed is unknown, although the deaths are estimated at around thirty. The writer of this account, published by the historical society, proudly claimed that this incident proved to white Mississippians that "reason" and an appeal "to a sense of the public weal" were a failure and that "a show of force" was the only thing that worked.[22]

Other white farmers turned to violence, first with the Ku Klux Klan and then with other organizations.[23] Locals explained that the Klan was "organized for the protection of the defenseless, the preservation of law and order, and the traditions of the South."[24] Testimony before congressional hearings leave little to the imagination about what these southern traditions were and how they were "enforced." Simply put, conditions were deplorable.[25]

As late as the turn of the century, white southerners remained defensive about the nature of the Klan and their hatred of all those in the Republican Party. One writer explained that "with the enfranchisement of the slaves, and the coming of the venal alien, came hate and fear which manifested itself in the protecting organization of the Ku Klux Klan." This "venal alien" was the "carpetbagger," but "scalawags" were also included: "The native white Southerner, who for self power deserted his race, was ostracized and hated with a holy hatred."[26] Therefore the division between factions of the white population in the state were already in play during Reconstruction.

During this time, when former Confederates claimed "carpetbaggers," "scalawags," and African Americans controlled the state, the Oxford area elected Lucius Quintus Cincinnatus Lamar as its congressman. Well-educated (a professor), erudite, and moderate in the context of the times, L.Q.C. Lamar was elected on his platform of reconciliation. Lamar was certainly moderate compared to those around him, yet he was also typical of his upbringing and his position as a paternalist. Although he had been a Confederate officer, he was willing to speak of reconciliation (while at the same time working to undo the Republicans). He spoke of cooperating with African Americans and respecting their rights, but he acquiesced to intimidation and to those who resorted to violence. Following the death of Senator Charles Sumner of Massachusetts, a Radical Republican, Lamar gave an eloquent encomium—but at the same time he worked to rid the South of the protection that a military presence offered freedmen.[27]

Throughout Lamar's tenure as senator, he labored tirelessly for reconciliation between the North and South, though his true purpose was to reelevate the South as equal partner in the nation's governance. He was also unorthodox, for he did not hold true always to Democratic Party planks. Though he did oppose high tariffs, he was a hard money man (keeping to the gold standard) and voted against the specific instructions by the state senate to support the Bland Allison Silver Bill. Nevertheless, he remained a popular senator for the people of the state.[28]

The Democrats' promise—to rescue the state from corruption—galvanized old Confederates. Years later, locals would still argue they had acted correctly. One said, "Under leadership of George, Walthall, Clark, Lowry, Barksdale, and others, [we] rid the state of Negro and carpetbag officials." The restoration of the old guard did not happen as fast in the Delta. In 1882 the 4,000 male African American potential voters in Bolivar Country vastly outnumbered the 250 white voters of the county. So white voters resorted to "all kinds of trades and so-called frauds" to keep control.[29]

In 1874 white Democratic leaders split on how to address incendiary events in the state. Senator Lamar urged caution and moderation, but James Z. George, the leader of the Democrats, did not.[30] While George publicly counseled restraint, admonishing delegates to elect officers who would represent the whole state, his definition of representation was questionable at the very least, since it denied the right of African Americans to have a voice in that decision.[31] At the same time, he organized an unrelenting campaign to ensure Democratic success by reaching out to the different white factions in the state. Since he belonged to most of the groups, he was successful. George, like Lamar, had been an officer in the Confederacy. A self-made man, he eventually become one of the wealthiest men in the state, known for his sharp and keen understanding of the law. His nickname, the "Commoner," served him well as a politician in a state that was rapidly dividing not only between parties and races but also between the classes and between the white counties and the black counties.[32]

George conducted a ferocious campaign to take control of the state, relying on more than clubs, parades, and military drills. The Democrats used outright intimidation and violence to get their way. Their campaign, remarkably well executed, became known among the other old Confederate states as the Mississippi Plan.[33] Instructions to the Democratic clubs were to register all Democrats, to make a list of all eligible voters in the district, and to call upon them. Some of the orders were sensible and legal: for instance, watch for underage voting, help the old and infirm get to the polls, and organize speeches by important leaders. Yet there was also advice based on intimidation. Democratic clubs were to be organized and armed with experienced military men as leaders. According to the plan, "Every Democrat must feel honor bound to control the vote of at least one negro, by intimidation, purchase, keeping him away or as each individual may determine, how he may best accomplish it." To make the control possible, Democrats were to attend Radical Republican meetings in large numbers and to be armed.[34] Even more disturbing to the modern reader was the injunction not to threaten Republicans, for if they deserved threatening, it was better to kill them. The writer of the plan admonished, "A dead Radical is very harmless."[35]

George played a careful hand in his quest for Democratic power; he purposefully aggravated Governor Adelbert Ames but cautioned locals not to retaliate enough to precipitate national notice. He read the situation correctly, for when Governor Ames requested federal troops to suppress the mobs, President Grant refused to intervene.[36] By this point, Ames had few alternatives. He met with George, and they agreed to a truce on the basis of a mutual promise of no violence at the polls. The Democrats won easily but with allegations of fraud.[37]

A history of Bolivar County colorfully and unapologetically recounted the procedures used: "When the election came off in the fall, the Negroes in the Loyal League marched to the polls in companies with fife and drum. . . . It was to no avail; all the boxes went overwhelmingly Democratic. There were 20 white men registered at Beulah and 400 Negroes. When the 'smoke' of the ballots had blown away, 400 Democrats had voted and only 20 Negroes." The one exception to the sweep of white Democrats into office in Bolivar County was the office of sheriff. Because of dissension within the Democratic Party, a Republican won. Democrats refused the requisite bond, so stalemate ensued. Thereupon Republicans offered the slot of sheriff to any white Democrat who would bolt the party. George Melchior, who later was a delegate to the convention, volunteered.[38] Once again to the minds of the white Democrats, the ends justified the means.

The new state legislature, controlled by the Democrats, had only twenty-one African Americans. The legislature voted to send L.Q.C. Lamar to the US Senate. Governor Ames tried to fight back when the legislature started impeachment proceedings against him and other members of his administration. Through the auspices of his father-in-law, Senator Benjamin Butler, Ames struck a deal in which he resigned and left the state. Charges would subsequently be dropped.[39] The others targeted in the coup were allowed to resign. With Ames's resignation, the purge was complete, though Blanche Bruce continued as US senator until his term ended in 1881 and James Z. George took his place.[40]

White Democrats now had control. One historian of the state referred to this change as "Mississippi for the Mississippians for now on."[41] What he meant was that old Confederates had returned to power; in his mind, African Americans did not count as Mississippians. Another historian also claimed a triumph for the state: "The result was the complete triumph of the Anglo-American, who trampled under foot negro rule, drove corrupt alien and traitorous renegades from power forever in Mississippi, and dispelled the idea of a mongrel South."[42] President pro tempore of the state senate, John M. Stone, took the oath as governor. Almost immediately Stone called for a new constitution, to rid the state of the incubus of a Reconstruction organic law, but the proposal died, for most thought the call for a convention was premature.[43]

Despite the purge, African Americans continued to vote, although in ever-reducing numbers. White Democrats used several methods to control the voting. The first was entirely legal: gerrymandering. The legislature redrew the congressional districts and created a "shoestring" district, a narrow corridor stretching from the Tennessee line down to Natchez and incorporating areas with heavy African American population. This district was assumed to go Republican, but its creation ensured that no other areas would.[44]

The second avenue of control by the white voters was not legal: intimidation and fraud. No one admitted to outsiders that such behavior was common, but these men were not so reticent within the state. Newspapers reported some accounts of coercion, although most outrages were quickly swept into hiding. References to these events were made in the legislature and even within county records, but the editors appeared to assume that no outsiders would pay attention. According to one historian in the period, "The negro vote was repressed by various methods and devices which were not defensible under the law, because they assumed that was their only choice."[45]

Though African American leaders continued to claim fraud, intimidation, and violence, outsiders began to believe these allegations were exaggerated. Attacks came during Republican parades, Republican meetings broke up from cannon fire or "prolonged Democratic 'applause,'" and Republican voters received threats that their jobs would disappear if they continued to vote the Republican ticket.[46] Those pressing for relief provided no proof, because evidence was difficult to get. And, indeed, most northerners did not want to know the reality. They had their own problems and were tired of dealing with southern issues. Yet the allegations were true, even when denied to outsiders by white southerners. Within the fold, perpetrators admitted to the atrocities and even explained their rationale. In an article written in 1902, Mississippi judge Solomon Calhoon admitted that to "rectify" the problems of Reconstruction, white Mississippians had resorted to force and fraud. Manipulation of the ballot box became "chronic," and Judge Calhoon admitted, "fourteen years of fraud excited nausea."[47]

One of the more startling illustrations comes from an account in a history of Bolivar County, which reveals the extent to which "redeemers" resorted to control elections. What the author wrote is astonishing for its candor and lack of apology or regret. The writer further claimed there were many examples of this effort to defraud, but time and space limited their inclusion in his narrative. He wrote that during Reconstruction, Congress had passed a law requiring two federal inspectors at each ballot "box to guarantee a fair election of Congressmen." In one case in Bolivar County, the two African American inspectors "positively refused to leave the room even for supper." One of the white officials, a doctor, prepared some boxes of sardines and crackers, which "he had, with a hypodermic needle, injected croton oil, or some other violent drug, in the two boxes handed" the men. Shortly afterward, the men "were sick and had to leave hurriedly, and the box showed at the count a big majority for the Democrats."

The writer went on to explain that even after Reconstruction, white officials resorted to numerous schemes to secure votes for the white Democrats in Bolivar County. He proudly claimed that "one favorite scheme was to mix bills of lading at the river and ship by mistake a ballot box to St. Louis while a coil of rope bail of cotton was sent to the country site to be counted; or the ballot box might, accidentally, be dropped out of the window of a train; in fact, any trick might be employed that seemed to promise a chance of success."

The writer admitted that some lower-level administrative positions in the county went to African Americans through fusion voting. Though he claimed that "almost every justice of the peace" in the county was African American, he added, "Let it be said to their credit, however, that they never, at any time, showed any prejudice against white men in their administration of justice; and, so far as the writer can remember, they administered justice as justly and fairly as their limited ability permitted."[48]

Because these white Democrats fully believed in their mission of gaining control of the elections, they were more than willing to intimidate, to defraud, and even to risk poisoning of federal officials to obtain their goal. Temporary misbehavior became a chronic mind-set. What is also remarkable is the final paragraph in this description from Bolivar County—the writer's admission of the integrity of the African American officials he deemed unworthy. Nevertheless, African Americans did continue to vote, and some black counties relied upon fusion voting to quell resentment and allow some lower-level county positions to go to the black community.[49]

◆ ◆ ◆

The struggling political landscape at the end of the nineteenth century was not the only problem facing Mississippi, for the state's economic position was dire and infected all other institutions. The problem was exacerbated by the fact that before the Civil War, the state had one of the strongest economies in the nation. Perhaps a bleak economy ought to be expected at the end of a major war, but Mississippians strongly considered their plummeting national position.[50] By the end of Reconstruction many voters wanted stability and economic growth, though how those were to be defined depended upon varying points of view. For the next fifteen years, the state's economic growth was remarkably feeble, even as much of the rest of the nation surged. Conservative elites in the state became convinced that the potential for growth was limited, because they could not see any improvement, no matter how much they worked or how much extra cotton they raised. Just who benefited from even restrained growth was a critical issue, for it defined power. And who was to be in charge—those with old agricultural ties to the state or those who sought new opportunities through industry and the new technology of the late nineteenth century? In a state that sought to deconstruct its government, somehow government became a source of support for transportation infrastructure and industry and therefore a threat to the old order. Though intertwined, politics did not lead the state economy any more than the economy defined politics. The story is far more complex.

These people of Mississippi, white and black, fervently believed in the Jeffersonian ideal of the independent farmer. Consequently, they held strong reservations about industry. They may have wanted railroads, but only on their terms, for in the previous decades they had lost much over bonds issued by the state and the counties. They wanted manufacturing, but not so much that it would endanger agriculture. Limited industry was one of the reasons mills were acceptable, because they provided a market for cotton grown on local farms. They may have wanted education for their children, but since they had little cash, they did not want to pay the taxes to provide the schools. They may have wanted free coinage of silver, but they feared the growth of banks in the state that could provide cash flow. They may have wanted federal help with building levees and levee control, but they feared the federal government, which white citizens insisted had invaded them and black citizens believed had abandoned them. By the late 1880s the state was moving forward, but with an extreme caution about the future.

The traumas of the period gave birth to a rising bigotry. Many people were profoundly affected by their struggles and feared a loss of power and control. Politicians in the state exploited these anxieties and used them for their own ends, but they could not have done so if there had not been a powerful undercurrent of racism and mistrust. Yet in addition to these internal state conflicts (and undermining any fiscal recovery) were nascent issues of class. The conversation on race and the pervasive fears of losing power played into the hands of those who did not want to discuss class because it distracted. Race bound the white men of the state, but class disrupted those bonds.

Concepts of class were central to the elites of the state and at times trumped race. While black counties were accustomed to controlling the state legislature, white counties resented this imbalance of power. Antagonism had started long before the war, when county allocations for representation had been set by early settlers and had not been reapportioned as population shifted over time. After Restoration the hill counties begrudged the political control that black counties retained. They particularly did not think representation should be based on African American population. Moreover, white counties believed that the black counties, most of which were in the Delta, were controlled politically and economically by a few white men who were then able to extend that control through the entire state. For example, in 1890 the Delta and a couple of counties controlled about three-fourths of the seats in the state senate.[51]

Black counties had a fair number of relatively well-off farmers (plantation owners) who needed black labor. For them, it was important to control African American labor, but not to the point of running them away from the state. These plantation owners were also better educated than the white farmers and steeped in the traditions of gentility and good manners. Their speech was genteel and less provocative to outsiders, and for that reason they often became identified as moderates on the race issue. Just as before the war, this perception was true for some. For many, though, it was simply relative, because so many others were extreme.

Understanding black county elites in relation to the concept of class is difficult and complex. Class is an elusive concept, for it cannot always be defined by income; these planters were not yet wealthy, although they were striving to improve their finances and were better off than the dirt farmers. A designation of upper class might also include education; industry; an entrepreneurial inclination; an inculcation of duty, honor, and country; and a realization of the rights, privileges, and responsibilities of the position. This list included an understanding of the responsibilities and duties owed to those below them on the social ladder. Historians have spent decades arguing whether these points were real or illusions. For our purpose here, though, the perception is more important than the reality. As perverse as their self-concept may have been, the southern upper class thought they held to a code of chivalry and were paternalistically responsible for those who needed protection, particularly women and (prewar) slaves.[52]

In addition, the South worked as a vertically organized society, reflective of the old social order based on lineage and its consequential obligations and duties of patronage.[53] Before the war, a slaveholder was responsible not only for his own slaves but also for his own family, including grown men.[54] The top of the social and political structures in the South was narrow; the organizational structure expanded below toward a larger base. Those at the top saw few as their equals, but they were responsible for many under them in the social, political, and economic hierarchy.

Most historians who focus on this period and examine these elites refer to the "master class" with obvious meaning, with strong reference to antebellum culture. Such use is understandable but fails to clarify what happened following the Civil War and emancipation.[55] Surprisingly little work has been done on the rise of new classes in the South following the war and Reconstruction, particularly among African Americans, where most of the research concentrates on the rise of the middle class rather than the elites. Added to the difficulty of defining class is explaining race: few have noted *African American* classes during the period following the war, even in discussions of class.[56] Without exception, all argue that the number of African Americans in the more fortunate class was small.[57]

The class situation became more complex following the war. As explained earlier, people of all races struggled in the South as they tried to rebuild an economy, a government, and a new social structure. Many of the old white elites struggled to re-create their past lives, economically, politically, and culturally. The adjustment took time. While a number failed in their attempts, moved west, or succumbed to a lesser station in life, others made new homes for themselves.[58] Good examples of those who succeeded were L.Q.C. Lamar, James Z. George, and Edward Walthall, all senators from Mississippi during the years after Reconstruction. These men found ways to supplement their plantation income, such as George's law practice or Lamar's position as professor. Jefferson Davis never regained his wealth, although he tried a number of professions. Some elites lost their farms to those in the next level of property ownership; some elites continued to spend as they always had but did not have the income to cover their lifestyle. In addition, they faced new expenditures, not only to repair their lands and holdings but also to pay rising taxes. Some lost everything they had.

Understanding these narrow, vertical structures of society in the black counties (a culture that remained well into the postwar period) helps to explain the behavior of these planters and politicians. The fact that their world was equally narrow, existing within the confines of a county they dominated and a state that fulfilled their ambitions, makes their reluctance to change logical.

The period following Reconstruction is characterized by southerners trying to re-create a world that they knew and in which they were comfortable.

The problem was that by the end of the nineteenth century, those on the social ladder below these planters—African Americans and dirt farmers—appeared to have forgotten "their place." This shift away from acknowledging "one's betters" came with the understanding that the ultimate goals of the groups in the hierarchy were different. Moreover, dirt farmers were beginning to understand how these differences operated in the structures of state politics. For example, the white counties were correct in their assessment of the political stranglehold of a few white men in the Delta. Following Restoration, Democrats controlled everything political in the state, and this control came from party conventions. In turn, delegates to these conventions were allocated according to representation in the statehouse. Since all state officials were nominated by the convention, the black counties could control the entire slate.[59] As the decades passed, dirt farmers began to distrust the efficacy of black county control of the state, especially by the Delta.[60]

◆ ◆ ◆

More heartening to the economy, and yet troubling, was the growth of railroads.[61] Railroad companies required cash and lots of it, not only for the rails, the engines, and the train cars but also for land, stations, pay for labor, and taxes. During Reconstruction the state had noted its shortage of railroads and had begun to push for their construction, offering a bonus of $4,000 a mile to any company that would build and keep in order only twenty-five miles of track.[62] The panic of 1873, however, made bonds hard to float. Eventually, the state ran into problems.

Railroad building flourished under the Bourbons for several reasons. First, the state had passed through the reorganization period after the war. Second, the panic of 1873 was finished. Finally, the state became a stockholder in numerous ventures. The result was more miles of track laid in the 1880s than in all the decades previous.[63] This boom in laying track continued until the end of the century, when mayors noticed that not everyone was eventually going to get on the line. Towns began to feel the push to make certain that the trains did not pass them by.[64]

As essential as access to railroads was for modernization and expansion of the economy, farmers began to feel slighted by the monopoly (which is exactly what railroads were—they held a monopoly on the roadbed and therefore prevented competition). This suspicion on the part of agrarians was not unique to Mississippi, for it formed the basis of some planks in national third party platforms for the rest of the nineteenth century. To entice the railroads, towns and villages offered several incentives, but if a rail company found a better avenue, it could divert the line and bypass towns, even ones that had invested in stock for the building of the line. Farmers also fretted, with good reason, about corruption. State judges received passes to ride the rails and, when pressed on the issue, responded that this practice was usual; farmers, however, viewed the passes as bribing judges to view railroads sympathetically.[65]

Railroads became another source of worry among the elites, for their presence and behavior toward workers spawned unions, both the Brotherhood of Specific Skills (firemen, conductors, and so forth) and the Knights of Labor. Unions in themselves concerned the elites, but in particular the national policy of the Knights rankled, because they allowed all races to join.[66] In fact, they forbade only bankers and lawyers and a couple of other specific subgroups. Because of the frustrations in the economy and in social movement, membership grew and union members became a force.[67]

◆ ◆ ◆

In the fifteen years following Restoration, the two governors of Mississippi fit the mold of the Brigadier Generals fairly well: John Marshall Stone (1876–1882 and 1890–1896) and Robert Lowry (1882–1890). Stone, though from a white county, was a colonel during the war, and as governor he sided with industry, particularly railroads. Stone "reduced taxes, cut state expenditures, encouraged railroad development in the state, and proposed the construction of a southern railroad route to the Pacific." Mississippi Agricultural and Mechanical College (now Mississippi State University) was founded during his tenure. He was a popular governor but was criticized for his hard money ideas and his veto of the Barry Railroad Regulation Bill of 1878 that would have benefited the common person.[68]

Governor Lowry, who really did rise to brigadier general during the war, had been a practicing lawyer.[69] He was a particular friend to the railroads but also pushed for tax exemptions for all new industry (usually for ten years). When Lowry became governor, he found state finances in real trouble yet again and unable to meet payroll for public schools, colleges, and state officials. A number of citizens thought the simple answer was to reduce state expenditures rather than raise taxes. Not meeting payroll to them had a simple answer: get rid of the teachers.[70] Frank Burkitt, leader of the state Grange (Patrons of Husbandry), had another suggestion; he thought that the problem in the government was corruption.[71] Lowry, however, had little alternative except to increase the state debt.[72]

As quickly as the Republican Party disintegrated, fissures erupted among the state Democrats. The 1880 vote for US senator revealed a deep split between the Bourbon leadership and the agrarians. Senator Lamar, though genuinely popular, had offended the state legislature in a number of ways through his independence. In this election, he threw his support to General Edward Walthall, an old line aristocrat.[73] The other wing of the party was represented by Ethelbert Barksdale, a leading news editor in the state.[74] The state senate, acting on exhaustion and probably prudence, decided on a third candidate, state supreme court justice J. Z. George, who had led the hard-line redeemers in 1875. Senator George was not like the other leaders: Governors Stone, Lowry, Lamar, and eventually Walthall—all aristocratic.[75] According to an early historian, "George was a man without polish or the lighter accomplishments of polite society. . . . His dress was exceedingly plain . . . and [he was] somewhat brusque in demeanor." More damning was the accusation that "as a popular orator, George was not a success. His speech was low and often indistinct."[76] On the other hand, his mind was feared, as well as his legal acumen. One of his colleagues described him as a "keen and shrewd" lawyer who "was able, learned, and practiced in the science of legislation." In highest praise, he added that as for Senator George, "no one can be better entitled to have inscribed in the records of his life, 'an honest man.'"[77] That assessment did not always hold, as noted in subsequent chapters.

As senator, George was at first quiet, but as an astute lawyer and former state supreme court justice, he caught on quickly to the Senate rules. His first occasion to speak on the Senate floor indicated his conservative sympathies. Senator Henry Dawes of Massachusetts spoke of a native northerner who had been run out of Mississippi "by political persecution" and had had his factory burned. George leaped to his feet to defend his state, arguing that no such incident had occurred, no factory burned, and no one of that description had lived in Mississippi.[78] Indeed, over the years George was consistent on race. His first speech of note supported the Chinese exclusion bill of 1882.[79]

Walthall eventually became the junior senator from the state when Lamar was appointed to the US Supreme Court. Little has been written on Walthall, other than to acknowledge that he was in the old-line, aristocratic, black county mold of politicians. Walthall did support the Interstate Commerce Act and the Sherman Antitrust Act, as well as unlimited coinage of silver, lower tariffs, and federal aid to education. He was never trusted by the agrarians, for he had been an attorney for the railroads.[80]

◆ ◆ ◆

Once the former Confederates regained control of the state in 1874, they had to be careful to maintain a positive image by keeping national attention focused elsewhere, rather than on the state. Violence may have raged in counties, but the national press took little notice. In addition, the Bourbons had to control events within their own state: this meant preventing African American majorities from the polls—not all voters, only enough to accomplish their mission. It also meant keeping white Democrats together; the task was difficult, for Democrats across the state had different agendas. The only things they agreed upon were keeping African Americans under political, social, and economic control and allowing the economy to grow. The difficulty was that they differed on how to improve the economy.

Though occasionally worried about rising threats in the state, Democrats were still firmly in control of state politics.[81] The problem was to address the local concerns without spending anything or increasing taxes. The overriding concern of the state officials was finances. They fervently believed that the state's finances were in dire trouble and, moreover, that the only way out was to cut the "ruinous" taxes of the past. As one editor stated, "Economy was the watchword."[82] The Bourbons abolished positions in state government and then cut the salaries of the remaining staff to the extent that few could survive on their pay. L.Q.C. Lamar went so far as to suggest selling the state governor's mansion to save money; he thought that the governor could live in a boardinghouse.[83] The state militia, a source of problems from the past, was slashed, and "pay for officers was reduced to five cents a day." Similarly, funding for schools dropped precipitously. But the "redeemers" got their wish: by 1881 the state indebtedness was gone and state warrants sold at ninety cents to the dollar.[84]

In short, during the period following Reconstruction, state leaders debated the very nature of government. In a state that had been a vanguard of states' rights ideology, the citizenry wondered just how little government was necessary: the less government they had, the fewer taxes were needed, and the less government, the less powerful those political institutions. According to the views of the white elites, powerful institutions threatened their familiar social and economic structures. After all, they believed that the state government under Reconstruction had endangered their way of life and had threatened their entire worldview. The answer for these men was to dismantle enough of the state government to reduce its power while keeping a low profile nationally. By 1890, however, leaders had begun to find that a weak state government created anarchy, and anarchy created violence that rose into the view of Washington. At the beginning, white state leaders saw only the need to gain control and re-create the familiar, in which a stability they craved could be reinstated; the problems (at least from their viewpoint) only came later.

CHAPTER 3

Opposition to the Bourbons

Opposition to the Bourbons emerged from two political and economic groups within the state: the Farmers' Alliance and the Republican Party, which was dominated by African Americans. While differences of race divided the groups, there were areas of agreement: both were ignored politically by the white elites, and both suffered economic deprivations. On the face of it, class should have bound them, but race was beginning to overshadow class. Moreover, African Americans had class divisions of their own. The economy, however, was an issue that cut across political and racial lines. Understanding the opposition to Bourbon control of the state necessitates a serious examination of the state's economy as context for their motivations.

◆ ◆ ◆

Mississippi has always been an agricultural state. In spite of attempts to entice manufacturing, farming has been the linchpin of the economy since statehood. To Mississippians, industry included agriculture, an extraordinarily wide definition of industry that reveals the strong appeal of farming to the region.[1] In 1876 the state was overwhelmingly rural, remarkable even in a nation of farmers. While the nation shifted from rural mode to urban during the period from 1870 to 1920, this shift did not occur in Mississippi, where farmers controlled the state and continued to grow crops exactly as they had for generations.[2] Although agriculture continued to expand after Reconstruction, it took a while for new patterns of hiring and stability of ownership to reach an equilibrium. Between 1870 and 1900 the number of Mississippi farms increased. The most telling numbers, though, concern the falling value of property in the state throughout the rest of the nineteenth century. Not until 1910 did the value of lands surpass that of 1860.[3]

Most people reached the simple conclusion that to revive the economy of the state, they needed to revive agriculture. This conclusion may have been self-evident, but the practical application was difficult. The fundamental problem was lack of cash. Cash was in such short supply that planters and workers had to be creative: tenancy and crop lien developed from an innovative push to make a flawed system work.[4] Sprung from necessity, tenancy and crop lien originally reflected vestiges of the past, hope for the future, and a pathetic pragmatism for the present. Mississippi passed a law in 1867 allowing the pledging of future crops against the requirements of supplies in the present; legal authority could be exercised to enforce these pledges.[5] Admittedly, the need for this system was profound: the farmers either had to have cash to purchase, credit to buy, or starve. Cash was not available in 1867 and little more by 1880. Farmers had to have credit, as did even shop owners (they had little or no cash and were relying on credit themselves, often from northern banks or agencies that offered usury interest rates). In fairness, these banks often saw these loans as very risky—and they were. Mississippi banks were few and not well funded, so options were limited.[6]

Sharecropping provided only a short-term solution with long-term effects that caused terrible damage to the state's economy as well as to the South and the nation. When a farmer could not repay the loans or when cotton prices plummeted, the farmer was absolutely trapped. He could roll over his loan, a decision that made making a profit the following year nearly impossible, or he could run away in the night. The notations on the Mississippi tax rolls during Reconstruction continued into the Restoration period with the familiar GTT (Gone to Texas). Landowners, then, no longer totally controlled the sharecropper. This shift led to confused patterns of allegiances, politically and economically, over the right of contract, even if at usurious rates.[7] Landowners themselves ran into difficulties in the 1880s as the number of farm mortgages increased from 4,800 at the start of the decade to 11,250 at the end.[8] For farmers, the numbers were even worse, with the census identifying a jump in tenancy from 27,118 farms in 1880 to 45,894 in 1890.[9]

An economy with little available money made a cash crop necessary. Though farmers had joined the market revolution long before the Civil War, it was the period following Reconstruction that made cotton king. The need to pay for the little luxuries of life, not to mention the ever-present taxes, propelled an ever-growing dependency on cotton in Mississippi.[10] Under the pressures of sharecropping, crop liens, mortgages, and the need for equipment, the search for cash became even more important.[11] Moreover, in the desperate search for cash, emphasis lay on the crop that did pay. Cotton was a crop that grew well in the state; the climate, the soil, and the expertise of the local farmers made it reliable. What made cotton less secure was the perplexing problem of overproduction. The more crops that were produced, the less farmers received for their crops and the less money they had.[12] Adding to these problems were the drops in crop prices during the later nineteenth century, a situation that led to frustration on the part of farmers struggling to work their way out of the imbroglio of agricultural finances. Cotton prices dropped by half between 1894 and 1897.[13] These factors caused farmers to operate at a loss.

The collapse of the cotton market led to a number of disruptions. Less money was available to be used for upkeep on the farms, and as people fled to villages for jobs, absentee farmsteads fell into disrepair.[14] Others migrated to where the soil was richest. The most fertile land was in the Delta, which was being cleared and protected by levees after the war.[15] The state, however, was slow to respond to the unique needs of the Delta. Not until 1898 did the state pass a general statute that authorized bonds for drainage work and allowed counties to pass taxes specifically for this effort.[16] Far more difficult for a state with limited resources and an adherence to individual rights and responsibilities was the problem of river flooding. The state could not afford to maintain the levees, much less build new ones. In 1879 Congress provided for a national commission to investigate and oversee the building, maintenance, and protection of a levee system. The commission's first report verified the practicality, not to mention the economic benefits, of a levee and jetty system. Because the commission tended to prioritize the areas just north of New Orleans, the state eventually had to assume the problems of the Mississippi Delta.[17] After the debacles of the huge floods and levee breaks of the 1870s and 1880s, the state received money for levee construction and improvement.[18]

These problems led to a belief in the Delta that help needed to come from an entity larger than a cooperative of small farmers in a county. This recognition ran counter to the prevailing wisdom of state leaders who tried to keep Washington's eyes away from the state. Negotiating a path to using federal support without inviting federal oversight became a unique problem for the elites in the Delta. These realities of living in the Delta created a division between the black counties near the rivers that flooded and the white counties that had no problem with flooding.

The white counties had their own issues. Not all the land in the state was rich and fertile. Mindful of new demands for beef, some farmers turned to cattle by utilizing public lands in the piney wood region.[19] In consequence, corn for feeding livestock became a valuable crop.[20] Truck farming, the growing and shipping of foodstuffs, made huge advances in this period. For example, Crystal Springs, near a rail line for transport, began growing fruits in 1874, and by the end of the century was well known in the region for its fine tomato production.[21] Canning was another logical development in the shipment of fruits and vegetables; once canning started, its technology extended to the shipment of seafood on the Gulf Coast.[22]

As creative as farmers were in searching for viable crops, a serious problem loomed—a shortage of labor, especially critical in the plantation areas of the state. Moreover, because the soil there was rich, agricultural traditions were strong and the need for labor intense. For this reason, it behooved the white, educated elites to share some power with freedmen in the black counties. In contrast, in the white counties the population ratios were reversed. The soil was rocky and not as given to wealth-producing agriculture.

The dirt farmers of the state did not need labor. They tended to be more racist, less educated, and profoundly suspicious of elites, particularly in the Delta.[23] Over the years historians have sought names for this class of farmers, often using the term "yeomen." That term does not fit the Mississippi group, who were scrambling just to survive. Dirt farmers tended to rely on their own efforts, along with their family. The acknowledged leader of the farmers, Frank Burkitt, was willing to use African Americans when needed, and he could suddenly react in unexpected ways. Born in Tennessee, Burkitt had served in the Confederacy and moved to Mississippi following the war. He lived in Okolona in northeastern Mississippi, where he was owner and editor of the *Chickasaw Messenger* and known for his support of the common man. Always in a fight, whether ideological or physical, Burkitt espoused railroad regulations and wanted lien laws repealed or modified.[24] He also vehemently opposed the convict leasing system. His followers hated the misaligned political power structure in the state, which tilted strongly in favor of the Delta. He also wanted the state to stop spending "unnecessary" funds and to lower expenditures and therefore taxes.[25] Many of these dirt farmers expressed hostility to the African American population in the state, often seeing them as tied to the Delta power structure that threatened the economy of the white counties. Yet there were notable exceptions to the generalization of racism, even though bigotry was fairly widespread. Around the time of the convention, there was a meeting of the state press association; Willis E. Mollison, an African American editor from Vicksburg, attended the banquet, provoking issues of seating arrangements. Both Frank Burkitt and Ethelbert Barksdale, Alliance men, offered to have him at their table and placed his seat between them.[26]

From a practical standpoint, for the state's economy to improve substantially, it needed to expand in other directions. Among many of Mississippi's leaders the common thesis regarding growth was to develop balance between agriculture and manufacturing. For many, the Jeffersonian ideal of the independent farmer was only the beginning of the argument. They firmly believed that the basis of civilization was agricultural life, which would be undermined through too much industry. In addition, the structure of the life they knew meant a classed and raced society, and changing that social structure was "dangerous."[27]

Pockets of economic improvement were based on the state's natural resources or agricultural production. For instance, timber provided the resources for the largest industry in the state, but Mississippi's pine trees became a source of turpentine.[28] In 1860 the state had only one turpentine mill, but by 1900 there were 145, which rivaled North Carolina.[29] Other forms of industry were equally related to natural resources, such as textile mills and cotton gins. Mississippi Cotton Mills, established in 1871, became the largest plant in the country in 1892.[30] By the 1880s the factory in Wesson, Mississippi, had electric lights, was running twenty-four hours a day, and employed 800 people.[31] At first opening, a mill offered the promise of prosperity, drawing workers from surrounding areas to jobs that produced cash. The state legislature, noting these potential benefits and yet feeling rivalry from other states, offered incentives, such as waiving taxes on mills for ten years if they would locate in the state.[32] Eventually reality set in, with workers receiving wages of only twenty-five to seventy-five cents a day for eleven hours of work.[33] Just as with the railroads, workers began to coalesce around nascent unions. For example, in 1886 in Wesson, the Knights of Labor started to organize, much to the horror of the manager, Captain William Oliver. He discharged members of the Knights and broke the union.[34]

Though the quality of life improved for some people in Mississippi after Reconstruction, the reality was that times were tough. While some of the problems were the consequence of war, some were the direct results of people's choices (such as a stubborn adherence to agriculture). Many struggles, though, derived from circumstances beyond people's control. For instance, adding insult to injury was the national contraction of currency, which meant that the price of crops fell just as the cost to borrow increased, even assuming that a farmer had access to capital.[35] Nationally, the tariff loomed as a problem, for shipping goods out of the country became difficult when other countries retaliated for higher tariffs; purchasing needed goods was also problematic as tariffs pushed prices higher. Trusts appeared to be grasping control of the national market with no regard for the plight of farmers. Railroad pools determined prices to ship goods, often charging less for larger freight than small shipments. Farmers began to create a fatalistic view that all the gods were against them—and indeed they were.[36]

◆ ◆ ◆

The first reaction to these problems came early after the war with the Grange (Patrons of Husbandry). The Grange was not a political entity but rather a club, usually with secret ritual, that formed to educate and support farmers and their families. Mississippi alone had 30,000 members by 1875, but many other states also had a significant membership. Though the Grange was known in the South to have Bourbons among its principals, Mississippi was more egalitarian, with people like Frank Burkitt as a county leader.[37] Nationally, a number of frustrated men broke from the Grange to form more political sects that could speak for the "voiceless" farmer; these organizations included the Farmers' Union and the Agricultural Wheel, which started in neighboring Arkansas. The Wheel championed cooperatives where the farmers could pool their interests, resources, and influence. In Mississippi, a similar organization was called the Great Agricultural Relief.[38]

The group that produced the most viable political, social, and economic movement was the Farmers' Alliance. It started in Texas but quickly expanded, for farm prices hit a nadir in the 1880s.[39] Similar to the other movements, it pushed for farmer independence from the money pools. By 1886 the Alliance combined the platforms of the Greenback Party, the Grange, the Wheel, and even the Knights of Labor.[40] An invigorated Alliance pressed for cash wages, unlimited coinage of silver and gold, fair taxes for railroads, an interstate commerce commission, and the prohibition of an agricultural futures market, among other demands. In order to inform farmers, using the old Grange concept, it sent out lecturers to the different states in the South and in the West.[41]

The Alliance came to Mississippi in 1887 and by 1889 already had 80,000 members and eventually claimed in the state over half of those eligible to join.[42] The biggest successes tended to be in areas settled since the Civil War, which included the hill country in Mississippi. The regions with old-time settlers were more conservative. The Alliance itself was comprised of landowners, but not the planters. It was also not the voice of the tenants or sharecroppers, who often did not have the cash to join.[43]

For years, historians have questioned how radical the Alliance was. Answers vary, depending on the locality and the time. For Mississippi, the organization was not particularly radical, but it did threaten the dominance of the Bourbons. The Alliance was more unusual than cooperatives of the past, for it allowed women as members, a decision that proved both a strength and a weakness. Women could take part in the rituals, know the passwords, vote on issues, and hold office. A few of the men, however, took exception, for they believed that women did not know their place.[44] Membership by African Americans, however, was not allowed. Since the goals of the Alliance were suitable for all farmers, African Americans created their own competing organization that resulted in friction within the communities.[45] The Alliance was strong in Mississippi until the provisions of the 1890 constitution took effect. What had begun as a promising organization, with leadership notable among the states of the South and West, faltered and nearly disappeared. Unlike in Georgia and North Carolina, Mississippi's disfranchisement did not take place to corral the influences of the Alliance. Disfranchisement, however, proved nearly fatal to the organization.

In the 1880s Mississippi politicians, whether state or national, represented both major wings of the Democratic Party—aristocratic and agrarian. Yet few of the political leaders and certainly neither governor paid much attention to the hill county farmers regarding the issues that meant the most to them. Even with great effort, only small advances emerged. For instance, similar to those in other states in the South and the West, dirt farmers reacted negatively to the strangling control of the railroads and to the favors granted by the state government. Rates were ruinous, as far as they were concerned. The difficulty was that shipping prices were not consistent, and often transporting goods over small distances cost more than shipping long distance. The issue became a major one in the 1880s, and agrarian newspapers and also the Grange spoke strongly in favor of doing something. Strong demands resulted in the creation of the State Railroad Commission in 1884, predating the Interstate Commerce Commission by two years. Unfortunately, it had no authority for enforcement and ran into similar problems experienced by other states regarding regulation of interstate commerce.[46]

This division between the elites and the dirt farmers was profound and could therefore be manipulated politically by both sides resorting to race-baiting. During the 1880s a number of issues in the state, mostly economic, led to a growth in the Greenback Party, and the Republicans also made a concerted effort to revive their political presence in Mississippi.[47] According to one historian, the Greenbackers controlled a number of counties following the 1879 election and managed to send a number of legislators to Jackson.[48] The Greenbackers even offered a fusion gubernatorial candidate in 1881. Benjamin King made a strong run, although given the fraud of the period, no one knows whether he could have been elected. Certainly he was a colorful candidate, often appearing shirtless in public. The ticket, though, was real: King ran as an independent, and he gathered the support of Republicans, Greenbackers, and agrarian Democrats.[49] Savvy as a politician, King focused on the agrarian issues of the time, particularly the controversial rewrite of the Mississippi codes (Campbell's Codes) that further entrenched crop-lien and sharecropping protections for the landowners.[50] King, as an Independent, was able to collect nearly 40 percent of the votes cast in November, but the

Greenbackers and Republicans argued that he had won a much higher number; they pointed to fraud, intimidation, and ballot stuffing. None of these objections was proven, but the election left members bitter.[51]

The 1881 election created not only bitterness but also violence as both sides returned to old policies to control voting, whether by African Americans or by dirt farmers. In riots that erupted in Marion and Meridian and in Sharkey and Panola Counties, African Americans lost their lives. The numbers are hard to verify, but newspapers blamed tensions heightened by the threat of the Greenback Party.[52] One state leader later justified reactions by white citizens: "Confronted with this large negro majority, that stood as a constant menace to good government, and consequently as a menace to all of the great moral and material interests of the State, to its very civilization in fact, it is not surprising that in the presence of these apprehensions the white men stood solidly together, nor is it surprising that repression, intimidation, and other irregular or illegal devices were used to overcome the negro majority." He admitted that "those methods were deprecated by the best class of citizens in the State, but argument and expostulation were alike ineffectual for their prevention, as long as the negroes held so large a vote in the electoral body in the State."[53] The Republicans were not finished, either. In the 1882 congressional election, Republicans in the Delta, with its majority black population, nominated Elza Jeffords, a respected white planter who had served in the Union army. The Democrats nominated no one, and Jeffords served as congressman.[54]

This new threat to the Democratic Party and its foundation of white supremacy created venomous reactions in the state. Those who threw in their lot with the agrarians faced ostracism by elite white society. A good example was James Chalmers, who had lost to Republican John Roy Lynch in the 1880 elections. To be certain that Lynch no longer had a power base, the legislature had redrawn the district boundaries. Acknowledging his ties to Holly Springs and to Panola County, Chalmers ran for Congress in the new northern district as a Greenbacker with fusion to the Republicans.[55] A number of locals, particularly black voters, viewed Chalmers with suspicion, since he had run against Lynch a couple of years earlier; so to a certain extent it is surprising he did as well as he did. As Lynch had done, Chalmers protested to Congress when he lost. Inevitably, Chalmers claimed fraud, pointing to a "clerical error" that gave a number of votes to a "J. R. Chambless" rather than to Chalmers. To his opponents, the issue was not fraud, but a question of whether Chalmers could be the representative since he now lived in Memphis, not Mississippi. Chalmers won his petition and was seated by Congress in June 1884.[56]

Chalmers's success, though, was short-lived. Some patronage granted by the national Republicans to Chalmers's supporters offended James Hill, not to mention John Roy Lynch and Blanche Bruce, who saw themselves in control of the party in Mississippi.[57] The Lamar-George wing of the white Democrats in Mississippi had long recognized that if the national Republicans provided patronage to the African Americans in control of the state Republicans, then the African Americans would keep control of the party but would ultimately fail in the general election.[58] To have Chalmers threaten this source of power and money (from patronage) was not to be endured. Hill set out to undermine Chalmers and succeeded, because Chalmers did not carry the district the next time.[59]

The 1883 election continued the split between elites and agrarians, with third party candidates creating fusion confusion. Some counties, like Panola, fused Republican and Democrat, while others fused Greenback and Republican. In Copiah County, the Democrats created a vigilante group to intimidate voters, particularly African Americans. The reports of bullying surfaced beyond Mississippi's borders and received notice in northern papers, particularly when white Independent candidates were murdered. One candidate (Print Matthews, Independent sheriff nominee) was shot only feet from the ballot box where he was to vote for himself. With the failure of the agrarians in the 1883 election, one newspaper expressed relief that the threat of African American votes and election no longer existed, in spite of the fact that the real danger came from agrarians. Independents and Greenbackers made a respectable showing in places like Rankin County, but their victories were short-lived. By 1885 most of their gains were gone, and when, in 1886, three Republicans ran for Congress (Judge Horatio Simrall, Chalmers, and Lynch), all three lost. Jackson, which had remained a Republican stronghold, went Democratic as African Americans pulled out of the race because of intimidation; consequently, in the 1888 race no black votes were cast in the capital. Increasing African American control of the Republican Party was solidified, and where fusion existed, some elected positions were still theirs.[60] The Republican Party, though, rested on patronage from Washington. As long as jobs came their way, the party could survive.

◆ ◆ ◆

During the fifteen years following the restoration of the former Confederates in 1874, intimidation and reprisals suffered by African Americans did not cease. And since they were building their livelihoods from scratch, they had further to go to reach economic stability. Yet to the surprise of historians who have examined the issue, the number of African Americans moving into property ownership rose during the very period when so many struggled.

In spite of all their problems, African Americans had slowly built a modest amount of wealth. In 1870 in Warren County, only 80 out of 2,500 African American heads of household had any personal property. By 1900 African Americans owned 33,212 acres of land in the county, just under 20 percent of all the available farmland. Out of the African American farmers in the county, a third owned their property. Though their numbers were small, other African Americans in the state moved up the economic ladder; but like their white compatriots, it took creativity, hard work, and some luck. John Roy Lynch and Bruce Blanche, political leaders in the state, grew wealthy through purchasing plantations, Lynch in the Natchez area and Blanche in Bolivar County, where he had served as sheriff.[61]

A small number of African Americans succeeded very well, but the documentation of this group is sparse, partly because of little evidence beyond the census but also because theirs is not the predominant story of the period. Their numbers were few, but of course correlate with the very definition of a "better class" or especially an "upper class." It is from this better class, however, where leaders emerged in politics, religion, education, and business. The few historians who have looked at these groups have spotted key characteristics shared by those who were successful: they tended to have been free people of color or house servants before the war, they were usually of mixed race, they were educated, they lived in urban areas, and they were either professional or artisan or had strong entrepreneurial inclinations.[62]

Mississippi had a number of African American politicians who served the state. For example, during Reconstruction the state had one lieutenant governor, one secretary of state, and one superintendent of education who were black. These political leaders were of mixed-race ancestry. Hiram Revels, a US senator, was a native of North Carolina and, as often described, a quadroon, or one-quarter African American. He moved north to seek educational opportunities denied to him in his home state, studied theology, and was ordained in the African Methodist Episcopal (AME) Church. During the war he became a recruiter for African American soldiers, and following the war, his church sent him to Natchez. After briefly serving as a state senator, he was appointed US senator in 1870, taking the unexpired seat of Jefferson Davis.[63] He only finished the term, which was brief, before returning to his adopted state to take the presidency of Alcorn University.[64] From there he continued to have some influence within the state.

One of the more notable African American politicians was Blanche Bruce.[65] Bruce served as the only full-term African American senator during the Reconstruction period. As he took office in 1875, the political landscape of Mississippi was changing; the Democrats had taken charge, and so he more or less served a state that failed to acknowledge him. Like Revels, Bruce had a passion for education—acquiring it and teaching.[66] He immigrated to the state after the war and settled in Bolivar County, which was quickly being cleared and settled as one of the last of the frontiers in the region, and he rapidly amassed a small fortune from planting and as a tax assessor.[67] He became involved in politics and served as sheriff in Bolivar County, where he had few critics, even from the most racist whites.[68] He played the political game well, and some white Democrats of the region backed him in his run for senator, for "Bruce was tactful and very deferential to the old slave-holding class and courteous to all white men."[69]

Elected as senator by the state legislature, Bruce headed to Washington, to the consternation of a number of representatives, some from northern states.[70] As senator, Bruce was silent, although supposedly he moved behind the scenes. Bruce did address Congress concerning the 1875 Mississippi election, which surprisingly gave the white minority in the state a large majority. He cited Yazoo City as an example of the scheme, where the local paper had declared that the Democrats would win, whether by fraud or force, including threats of lynching. Bruce questioned whether state officials could keep the peace and protect the state's citizens.[71]

Surprisingly, Congress listened to Bruce's speech questioning the 1875 election and appointed the Boutwell Committee to investigate the elections in Mississippi. The committee documented the atrocities to which Bruce referred and claimed the time to be "one of the darkest chapters in American history." The Senate, however, had no real interest to interfere and allowed those "elected" to take their seats.[72] Like Revels, though, Bruce was a conciliator most of the time. For instance, he voted against his party and for the seating of L.Q.C. Lamar. He did object, however, to the removal of troops from Mississippi in 1877.[73] As a landholder in the Delta, he was aware of the problems of flooding, and he shares in the credit for the creation of the Mississippi River Commission in 1879 near the end of his term. After leaving office in 1881, Bruce was appointed to a number of responsible governmental positions in DC under Republican presidents.[74]

Understandably, given the tenor of the times, Bruce never really returned to Mississippi from Washington, DC. His rivals during the period, James Hill, John Lynch, and Hiram Revels, also made money in Mississippi—a lot of it. Except for Hill, they were born outside the state, were of mixed race, had been house servants, were better educated than most, and were heavily connected with politics and governmental appointments of the period.[75] Though he remained in DC, Bruce remained the acknowledged leader of the black Republicans in the state during and after Reconstruction.

While Bruce may have been the recognized and influential head of the Republican Party in the state, the real power belonged to John Roy Lynch, who also lived in Washington, DC, and, like Blanche Bruce, enjoyed federal patronage jobs. Lynch served the Mississippi "Shoestring" district as a US congressman, but had been born in Louisiana, a child of a slave and her master. Following the war, he ran a photography studio and attended night school in Natchez. Still young, Lynch served in local and state politics and was elected Speaker of the House in Mississippi in 1871 when he was only twenty-four. Two years later he was elected to the US House of Representatives at the age of twenty-six. He was the only Republican congressman in the state who won in 1874.[76] In spite of his rising fame, in 1874 Congressman Lynch was thrown off a railroad car because the car was "reserved for whites." Although he left without incident, he spoke of the event on the floor of Congress with "frankness and candor."[77] He used that same candor to attack Grant's refusal to supply troops to Mississippi in 1875.[78]

As noted earlier, much to the embarrassment of state officials, Lynch not only continued to run for office but also was willing to appeal to Congress for investigations of the election process. Though Lynch approved publicly the fusion agreements in the Delta as being the best alternative in a difficult situation, he firmly stated that he and other leaders did not accept Democratic control of the state. He was reelected in 1875, from the old Shoestring district, which was the only section not in the Democratic sweep in the state. His seat was contested in 1877, and he was not seated. He ran again in 1880 against Democrat and former Confederate general James R. Chalmers.[79] Not surprisingly, according to the state election officials, Chalmers won, but Lynch appealed to Congress for a review on the grounds of intimidation and fraud, which were violations of federal election law. In a letter to Chalmers, Lynch notified him of the reasons for the appeal, including "named frauds and violations of the law of the land and of the purity of elections ... by our Democratic friends and supporters with your connivance."[80] After an investigation of over a year, Lynch finally was seated in 1882 and thus had little time to prepare for the next election to be held in November, which he lost. Lynch remained the ostensible head of the Mississippi Republicans until the 1890s, sharing control with James Hill, who really did live in the state, and Blanche Bruce, who, like Lynch, resided in Washington. Their power was based on Republican Party patronage, an arrangement that gave access to federal positions like postmaster.[81] This visibility of a meaningful African American presence in the state displeased white citizens, resulting in intimidation and violence.

The continued leadership of Bruce and Lynch, even when they were living in DC and returning infrequently to the state, is perplexing. To some extent this is understandable when their economic status is considered. At a time when few succeeded economically, their success created pride in the community. At a time when African American voices were ignored in the state and nationally, theirs were heard and at least acknowledged. But African Americans endured much in the confines of the state during Reconstruction and the period following the restoration of the Democrats. Intimidation directed toward those who demanded participation in the decisions of the state and who expected respect created an atmosphere of fear. Just how much African American leaders who remained in DC understood this new normal is not clear.

African Americans in the state were not silent, nor did they cower. They sometimes fought back. On July 4, 1875, a riot erupted in Vicksburg, where white tempers were still frayed not only by Reconstruction policies but also by the presence of black militias.[82] For example, on September 4 the little town of Clinton endured a resurgence of brutality.[83] Both political parties had called for a joint debate at a local barbeque, but neither side really wanted to hear the other. At the peaceful Clinton parade, Oliver Cromwell, a local African American leader, donned a stove-pipe hat with a plume, carried a saber, and rode a horse as he led a column of African American militia. Whites reacted, for they viewed his display of power as arrogance and a threat; following the picnic, they attacked African Americans.[84] Accounts differ as to who started the fight and gunfire, but white militia were poised nearby to swoop into town. White men from surrounding counties and even the state of Alabama poured into the area to "support" their colleagues. No one knows the number killed in the ensuing days, although estimates are that twenty to thirty African Americans died.[85] Not surprisingly, another riot erupted at Friar's Point a couple of weeks later.[86] Other flare-ups included Dry Grove in Hinds County, Yazoo City, and the capital, Jackson, where black militias were armed with needle guns.[87]

◆ ◆ ◆

Most enlightening as to what it took to succeed in the state, whether black or white, was the success of Isaiah Montgomery. His story is unique, for it does not fit the categories listed in the previous paragraph; yet he not only succeeded, but his biography is reflective of the complexities of race and class in the state. Moreover, he is a conundrum. Isaiah Montgomery was the sole African American delegate seated at the convention, but he actually voted for the constitution and in fact was on the committee that wrote the disfranchisement provisions. In one sense, Montgomery filled the same spot that

Senator George did among white delegates. Both had feet in a number of camps. Senator George was a self-made man, a commoner. But having gotten an education, having succeeded in the legal profession, George was able to communicate and gain the trust of both the white elites and the dirt farmers of the Alliance. So, too, did Isaiah Montgomery straddle positions of class, but in the modern world, we classify him by race. Montgomery was more, for he identified himself by both class and race, and understanding this precarious position can help to explain his behavior.

Members of the Montgomery family, each one unusual, were former slaves of Joseph Davis, brother to the president of the Confederacy. Members of this African American family saw themselves as different, as gifted, and therefore with responsibilities to others placed on the cultural ladder below them. The Montgomery family was not alone in securing economic and social success. Others also prospered, but too many are unstudied and remain invisible to history.

What is known of the Montgomerys' story began in 1837, when Joseph (Joe) Davis traveled from his plantation, Hurricane, on Davis Bend, Mississippi, into Natchez to purchase new slaves. There he found a likely candidate when a slave startled him with a handwritten note requesting that he and his wife be purchased together. Intrigued, Joseph bought both—Benjamin (Ben) Montgomery and his wife, Mary—and thus began one of the most interesting collaborations in the antebellum period.[88]

Historian Janet Sharp Hermann has written extensively about this relationship, certainly giving credit to Joseph Davis for his "enlightened" views, which were influenced heavily by an early conversation with Robert Owens, the utopian reformer and founder of the New Harmony community in Indiana.[89] Davis fit the stereotype of the paternalistic slave master who believed he was in charge not only of his slaves—physically, mentally, and spiritually—but also of his own family, which included his younger brother, Jefferson. At Davis Bend, Joseph set up a unique structure for dealing with slaves—a "legal system" in which his slaves essentially wrote their own codes of behavior and pseudo laws. Most Sunday mornings Davis presided as judge over trials on the plantation; slaves brought their own charges and complaints before a jury of their peers (though under the firm hand of "Judge" Davis). Writing many years later, even Isaiah Montgomery (Ben Montgomery's son) acknowledged that Joseph Davis "was a man of superior judgment in the selection and management of slaves."[90] Arguably the more interesting part of the collaboration between Ben Montgomery and Joe Davis was the negotiated relationship between the two men. Years later Isaiah Montgomery revealed that his father and Davis "reached a mutual understanding and established a mutual confidence which time only served to strengthen throughout their long and eventful connection."[91]

In these years before the war, Ben Montgomery became the most trusted slave at Davis Bend, a confidence that began with evidence of his education, although we do not know the origins of his skills. He had a knowledge of reading and writing that was encouraged by Davis. He read extensively and became a noteworthy mechanic, civil engineer, and businessman. As a slave, he ran his own store, planted his own cotton, kept his own profits, and oversaw the civil engineering needs of a plantation that required a lot of help to control the frequent flooding.

Ben and Mary Montgomery produced four surviving children, including Isaiah, all of whom continued in the ambitious vein of their parents. Their offspring were educated and learned to read and write at an early age. The Davises provided instruction on Sunday mornings by one of the slaves for a number of the children on the plantation, but the Montgomery children had their lessons supplemented by their father, who proved to be a tough taskmaster. At the age of ten, Isaiah Montgomery was trained for household work, though his father feared that this training would interrupt Isaiah's schooling.[92] Davis promised that the young man would have free access to the extensive library at Hurricane, and indeed, he did. Young Montgomery's responsibilities in the house quickly became the position of "private secretary and office attendant," except when Jefferson Davis came home from Washington, DC, when the child's duties shifted to the younger brother.[93] In short, Isaiah Montgomery was educated, mainly by having access to one of the finest libraries in the country, to which he availed himself, and he continued to value education for the rest of his life. He used that education to create a solid economic foundation that survived his lifetime, in spite of the vagaries of national panics and local difficulties.

The Civil War was a particularly difficult time for Davis Bend. Joseph Davis kept a watchful eye on events, but so too did the slaves. After the Confederate losses in the spring of 1862, Davis took his family and most of his slaves to his land near Bolton, Mississippi, leaving behind the Montgomerys to help manage the plantations.[94] When Admiral David Porter reached Davis Bend in the Union gunboats, he found the Montgomery family, who profoundly impressed him. Porter sent the family to Cincinnati but kept young Isaiah with him as an aide until discharged because of illness. Isaiah Montgomery joined his family in Cincinnati, where he studied carpentry and accounting.[95]

The years following the war presented new challenges and opportunities for this ambitious, newly freed family, and the further changes in their position and demeanor were astonishing. One of the characteristics of upper-class families is that they worked to ensure generational continuity of their values. These values not only encompassed education but also social behavior expected of the elites and defined by the etiquette of the period, which included manners and dress code.[96] Following the war, the diaries of Mary Virginia Montgomery, Isaiah's sister, reveal a family with ambitions. Mary Virginia and her sister, Rebecca, were required to spend time daily in their studies; eventually both studied at Oberlin College.[97] Both played the piano, sewed a fine seam, and could discourse on a number of topics. Isaiah Montgomery was known for the rest of his life for his dapper appearance and dignified demeanor.[98]

The transition of the Montgomery family from slaves to upper-class planters could not have happened without money to back their ambitions and to secure a place for the next generation. For a while the Montgomery family appeared to have a golden touch. Following the war, after purchasing the Davis plantation, the Montgomerys were the richest African Americans in the South. This accumulation of wealth happened quickly. In 1865 Isaiah's older brother, Thornton, returned to the old plantation and set up a store, underwritten by his father with the family's savings. During the war, when the Union gained control of Davis Bend, the Freedman's Bureau had tried to run the plantation as a showplace but ran into difficulties. Most of the freedmen there were not the former Davis slaves, but those who had gravitated there in the disruptions following the shifting fortunes of war.[99] The former Davis slaves who were living on the plantation were worried about the administration of "their land," as were the Montgomerys, so the move back to Mississippi made sense to the Montgomery family. In 1866 the rest of the Montgomery family returned to Davis Bend, purchased first their old home from Joe Davis, and then in 1867 acquired the entire Davis estate of some 4,000 acres. Based on a reasonable down payment of cash that his family needed, Joe Davis had extended a mortgage on lenient terms to Ben Montgomery to purchase the Hurricane and Brierfield plantations in 1866: he was to pay 6 percent interest a year, or $18,000, and the principal of $300,000 was due to Davis in 1876 as a balloon payment. The original sale had to be kept quiet because of the restrictive nature of the Black Codes, but the following year the sale was legalized.[100]

The story of the Montgomery family in the next twenty years parallels the history of the rest of Mississippi in general. The Montgomery family owned the land, but they hired many of the former slaves from the Davis plantation to work for them. In a surprising number of ways, the plantation became an eerie replay of conditions under the Davis ownership, although no one was enslaved. Ben Montgomery certainly viewed himself as the father figure responsible for the well-being of the entire concern, economically, politically, and socially. Agricultural development was erratic, but the plantations Hurricane and Brierfield, and eventually Ursino, produced mostly bumper crops of superb cotton.[101] Records indicate that they yielded between 2,000 and 3,000 bales every year until they abandoned the cotton business just before Ben Montgomery died in 1878.[102]

In spite of the fact that Isaiah Montgomery was doing better at farming than most of his neighbors, he failed to meet the payments a number of years. Most of this difficulty was the result of factors beyond the family's control. The price of cotton fell for nearly every year of the next thirty, so that even bumper crops did not produce the return they needed; their store tended to keep the family business afloat. Moreover, the Mississippi River treacherously began to shift from its banks, and when it subsequently did, the entire area flooded. Levees, much needed, depended on the ability of the Montgomery family and their neighbors to produce the requisite cash, not to mention cooperation. Most of the attempts failed, and the levees were never repaired adequately.[103]

Though difficulties were enormous, the Montgomery family succeeded whereas others did not. In 1873 a financial reporter estimated the firm of Montgomery & Sons as having a net worth of $230,000, which, when compared to other African Americans in the period, made the Montgomerys (Ben, Isaiah, and his brother, Thornton) the richest in the country. The same year, the family paid taxes of $2,447.09, one of the largest assessments in the state.[104] Compared to other citizens of Mississippi, he ranked in the top 2 percent.[105] That evaluation assumes a definition of class based on income, a controversial classification and by no means complete.[106]

The warm relationship between Joe Davis and Montgomery continued until Davis's death in 1870.[107] His will instructed that the executors extend liberal terms to the Montgomerys. To some extent the executors followed the will, but they required that the Montgomerys turn over the title to the Ursino plantation, which they had purchased some years earlier, to secure the mortgages on Brierfield and Hurricane. In 1874 Jefferson Davis, who had expressed reservations about the Montgomerys because they were African American, sued, arguing that his older brother had given him Brierfield and that therefore that plantation could not have been sold legally to the Montgomerys. As evidence, Jefferson Davis pointed to his years as de facto head of the plantation, even though there was no bill of sale or other indication of title. The trial court ruled against Davis.[108] Because Davis had served as an executor, he had also agreed with the will's terms, which identified the Montgomerys as owners of the plantation property. Davis appealed, but by this time the political tides had shifted and the superior courts therefore ruled in favor of Davis.

In addition, the flooding on the plantation became extremely treacherous in springs of the early 1870s, and so when Ben Montgomery died shortly after the appeal loss, his son Isaiah decided it would be better to abandon the plantations. They were sold at auction to the Davis family.[109]

After he lost the old Davis plantations of Brierfield and Hurricane in 1877, Montgomery set up a new store in Vicksburg. The business did not thrive as well as he had hoped, in part because the economy and the political climate of the period made any such endeavor difficult.[110] Hoping for a better opportunity, Isaiah's brother, Thornton, left Mississippi, headed west, and did well, owning and operating a grain elevator and farming 700 to 1,000 acres. Isaiah Montgomery, who had not given up on his home state, heard about land openings near a new railroad line in the Delta. With the help of his cousin, Benjamin T. Green, he bought a large parcel of land. Clearly Montgomery and his cousin had something few others in the state had—money to purchase land. Cash was hard to come by, for tenancy numbers were on the rise all over the nation, particularly in the state of Mississippi. On this new land, the cousins founded an African American community called Mound Bayou; technically, though, the cousins never forbade a diverse racial mix for the district.[111]

The philosophy of this settlement was different from their experience at Davis Bend. This time the community allowed the residents to purchase their own plots of land and run their own businesses, which quickly succeeded. In 1890 Montgomery reported that the African Americans in the "vicinity of Mound Bayou already owned about 5,000 acres" and were "increasing their holdings rapidly."[112] Only three years later the settlement included over 20,000 acres. Personally, Montgomery benefited financially: he held many of the mortgages, "grossed a profit of eight thousand dollars per year on lumber" alone, and was "reputed to be the only Negro in the United States who could put his hands on fifty thousand dollars 'cash money' on an hour's notice."[113] Although the settlement eventually struggled to survive, at the end of the nineteenth century the promise of the community was startling and offered a prime example of the fallacy of the racial bigotry of the period. The rising tide of racism nevertheless affected the Montgomerys as much as any African American family.[114]

Throughout these years the Montgomerys were known for their private virtue. The notes recorded by the Dun Reports, which evaluated credit-worthiness, observed that the Montgomerys were "negroes, but negroes of unusual intelligence." Notations from subsequent years included reference to the family as "they stand high as negroes . . . most reliable negroes." Even when the written entry doubted the Montgomerys could possibly repay their debt, the notes supposed that the "inability to pay will embarrass them considerably" and that the family stands "high in Vicksburg" and is "considered reliable and safe at present."[115] In a different section, referencing the general store rather than the plantation, another recorder acknowledged that "they are a family of remarkable negroes, who seem to be flourishing."[116]

To a large degree the Davises had trusted the Montgomerys with their lives and fortunes, and the Montgomerys maintained contact with the Davises and sent food when they were in need. The other former slaves in the area acknowledged Ben Montgomery and his sons as leaders and protectors. This acknowledgment mirrored a shift to public virtue, when those at the top of the social structure in a society were expected to serve the greater good.[117] The older concepts from the nascent republic persisted longer in the South than in the economically vibrant and socially fluid North. Even in the North, men who succeeded economically in industry and banking during the Gilded Age, the Robber Barons, were often not completely accepted into better society until they contributed to the general good. Thus Andrew Carnegie became a hero when he began to give away his fortune, and John D. Rockefeller and Leland Stanford resuscitated their public image when they endowed colleges.

Ben Montgomery resisted this hallmark of the upper class, but his son did not. For the most part, the Montgomerys avoided confrontation by not participating in controversial arenas, including politics. He went so far as to press his workers on the Davis Bend plantations to avoid election to political positions, though he always voted and encouraged his family and workers to do so. In 1868, under pressure of the state military commander, E. O. Ord, Ben Montgomery served as justice of the peace, but assured his white neighbors that this was a job he did not really want and that he would not hear cases involving his white neighbors.[118] Isaiah Montgomery, however, moved cautiously into the political field. Shortly after moving to Bolivar County he served on a Republican committee and represented the county in Washington, DC, to lobby for control of the flooding of the Mississippi River.[119]

In a real shift in philosophy, Isaiah Montgomery, according to his own notes, realized that other African American families needed to purchase their own land in order to secure their future, but that release of control only went so far. For example, Mound Bayou was never a plantation, but instead a planned town with surrounding agricultural fields.[120] Each of Montgomery's positions at Mound Bayou—leader of the community, developer, levee lobbyist, and politician—reconfirmed his position at the apex of the local network. Isaiah Montgomery controlled the town to such a degree that he shaped behavioral norms: those who were living together without marrying were pushed away, while those who did not work were "called upon," and everyone attended church. He also owned or held interest in most of the businesses of the town, including the gin, the warehouse, the lumberyard, and the general store.[121] As the leader and protector of his people, he argued he was building a "place of safety and refuge."[122]

Mound Bayou may have been a place of safety and refuge, but it was surrounded by a wilderness of troubles. The eruption of violence, based on race and class, triggered the calls for a constitutional convention in 1889 and 1890. As a political entity, Mississippi no longer had an effective government. Corruption and mismanagement were rampant. The already dismal economy was worsening. Violence threatened the well-being of its citizens. And few had faith in the future.

CHAPTER 4

Calling the Convention

By 1890 Mississippi was a failed state. Government had ceased to work effectively or democratically. Corruption was rampant as leaders were willing to sell the state's soul to entice a bit of railroad expansion or new manufacturing. Even among the white men of the state, fissures developed along economic lines as factions vied for control of an ineffective legislature. The Greenback Party and the Alliance wanted changes, but were constantly foiled at the ballot box. This, then, was the context of the convention.

Yet something pushed state leaders into considering changes in their organic law. Oddly, they did not act from a recognized need for "reform," though some did use the word. Rather, they feared a disruption of the status quo and their stability, and, even more important to some, they feared a replay of Reconstruction. These were among the issues that underlay the call for a constitutional convention in 1890.

Between Restoration in 1875 and the convention in 1890, several attempts had been made to call a constitutional convention. During the 1880s newspapers and some politicians had been suggesting such a convention to address economic issues, but these proposals had failed. The ostensible purpose of these efforts was to rewrite the Reconstruction constitution, often portrayed as having been "thrust" upon the state.[1] While other southern states had successfully rewritten their Reconstruction constitutions, Mississippians remained convinced that such a move would tempt fate and that calling attention to the state would not be prudent. They had what they wanted (reduction of the African American vote, and therefore a return of power to the old conservatives). Eventually events beyond the state, in Washington, DC, provided the final push to the calling of a convention.

• • •

Two events that finally resonated with the white population and stoked their fears precipitated the convention. The first was the threat of an elections bill, first introduced in the Senate in early 1890. Eventually the bill, which would have taken control of federal elections by Congress, was debated concurrently with the meeting of the Mississippi convention and in the months thereafter.[2] The state perceived the bill as a growing federal threat, and, as a result, it struck fear into the hearts of Mississippi white voters who remembered Reconstruction. The other impetus for the convention was the rise of the Colored Farmers' Alliance in the state, which at one point resulted in the arming of black farmers in Kosciusko. These changes created a sense of urgency, and state leaders at last called a convention to remake their organic law and thereby gain some protection from federal oversight.

When Benjamin Harrison was elected president in 1888, the Republicans in Congress turned their attention to electoral problems in the South. Accusations of power grabbing and issues of government control reemerged. The election of Grover Cleveland in 1884 had shaken the Republican Party to its core, and the Republicans admitted they wanted to make certain they stayed in power.[3] The South's problems and the illegal disfranchisement of African Americans had been ongoing for years, and yet it was a Democratic win at the federal level that caused the Republican Party to turn its attention back to the South.

Harrison and his advisers were certainly correct that if elections had been fairly administered in the old Confederate states, then the outcome would have been different in 1884. Yet accusing the Republicans of simply being manipulative, or "political," would be missing the point. Harrison, as well as other Republicans, was committed to a fair deal for African Americans in the South. The party, however, was not unanimous in its support of the renewal of commitment, for there were a number who worried about the economy, particularly the tariff and the money supply, which they thought were far more important issues for the new administration.[4]

Even before Harrison took office, he made a speech before a meeting of the Grand Army of the Republic (GAR) in Indianapolis regarding the issue of disfranchisement, and he was blunt about his concerns. Indeed, he returned to this theme in his inaugural address when he warned the South not to let old race prejudices get in the way of economic development.[5] Although this was a play on the concepts of Henry Grady's New South ideology, southerners had no trouble distinguishing his real meaning. That meaning was even more transparent when the elderly William Tecumseh Sherman added his comment that the war itself would not really be over until African Americans had secured the rights that the US Constitution gave them.[6]

Almost immediately after Harrison took office, he faced a concrete example of election fraud. Since the Civil War, Congress had had to investigate a growing number of contested elections.⁷ In 1888 the new attorney general pointed to Florida as an egregious example, where a federal witness and a deputy marshal had been murdered. In the following months reports of murders of political candidates in other states began to emerge. John M. Clayton, a Republican congressional candidate from Arkansas, was "shot while investigating the disappearance of a ballot box whose theft had cost him the election." In the recent election in Virginia, Indiana congressman Joseph Cheadle came to help former governor William Mahoney run for governor. Cheadle declared, "It takes courage to be a republican here." He wrote Harrison, "The National Government undertakes to guarantee a republican form of Government to every state. . . . There is not even a semblance of such a Government in Virginia." Little wonder that these reports galvanized Harrison into action.⁸

Harrison's plan to produce a bill appeared to be sensible from a political standpoint. The Republicans were in real power for the first time in fifteen years, and therefore the president should have found support within his own party. Circumstances were changing, however, as were the political ambitions of the party; the country itself was undergoing a radical transformation.

A good example of this change was the response to Senator Henry Blair's bill for federal support of education, which he had introduced biannually for some years. The purpose of Senator Blair's bill to support education was to raise literacy rates, particularly in the South, even though he was from New Hampshire.⁹ This time, Blair found opposition within his own party. The crux of the opposing argument by some Republicans was not the fundamental importance of literacy, but rather the role of the federal government in it. Foreshadowing the coming debate on elections, however, was his use of an argument to be utilized on both sides: literacy was imperative to good government.¹⁰ Senator George pressed him on the issue and asked if a literacy requirement could be imposed on the franchise. In response, and setting the stage for future argument, Republican senator Frisbie Hoar thought that a literacy test, as required in Massachusetts, his home state, and which was "fairly" applied, would be acceptable.¹¹

In reality, the tide was turning in the North against special consideration for freedmen. Many considered it to be a violation of the principles of social Darwinism. By the end of the century, the philosophy became entrenched in universities and inculcated into the average voter. If the natural order meant an evolution for both biology and cultures, then there were logical consequences for not allowing nature to take its course. The most extreme view questioned whether an institution extending a helping hand to a group in distress violated the natural order. Was not nature demanding crises to weed out those who should not survive? If a group interfered, such as with the Salvation Army, then would the country itself eventually suffer by not creating a strong culture and vibrant people?[12]

Such ideas made a number of voters question the efficacy of identifying freed people as worthy of special help by the federal government. Certainly southerners were pushing the race question as a particular problem in the South, but it was a question that received much attention in the North as well. Even perennially stalwart Republican journals and newspapers, such as the *Tribune* and *Harper's*, began to question whether the "help" given to African Americans, particularly those in the South, was simply making them lazy or unable to fend for themselves. Consequently, support for help for African Americans in the South was weak.[13]

In this case, help also meant patronage jobs, which went to Republicans under a Republican administration: in the South often this meant jobs given to African Americans. These appointments produced a rising backlash as Democrats became bolder. While Democrats had wanted government jobs under Grover Cleveland, they saw the push for Republican jobs as corrupt.[14] One newspaper claimed that in the South, President Harrison had been appointing African Americans to the types of jobs that northerners would not have approved or supported. If the North thought these men should have these jobs, then African Americans should be appointed to the positions in the North.[15] The mounting backlash against African American appointments in Mississippi gave rise to violence and murder, though convictions were hard to produce. In one instance, whites in McCool, Mississippi, fired on F. G. Blevins, an African American post office clerk. Prosecutors could get a conviction in this case only because one defendant confessed, though witnesses endured local intimidation.[16]

When Congress convened in December 1889, Harrison requested a law to help "secure to all our people a free exercise of the right of suffrage." To buttress an argument that he fully believed should have been self-evident, Harrison reminded the nation of African Americans' participation in the Civil War and therefore the nation's debt to them.[17] But African Americans were not the only Republican voters in the South. With some reservations about how the party was to be defined, white voters mostly realized that if the issue of the franchise were not stable, they might as well close down the Republican Party in the South.[18]

Several bills to govern elections also were introduced in both the House and the Senate.[19] Senators at that time were elected by state legislators, and the Constitution gave oversight to Congress only over federal elections. Thus congressional elections were the ones at issue.[20] Although several southern politicians moved quickly to oppose the bills coming to the floor, they were not successful, and the bills were remanded to committee. Henry Cabot Lodge, a new congressman from Massachusetts and a descendent of an abolitionist family, assumed the chair of the elections committee in the House. He believed that the House, rather than the Senate, should be the source of an elections bill. Lodge quickly realized that the bill should not be too broad, for that would give more power than Congress wanted over elections, and also it would be too expensive. Therefore Lodge and his committee determined that if 500 constituents in a congressional district asked for help, they could get it. The result was the Lodge Elections Bill (HR 11045), which combined a few of the proposals and was reported from the committee on June 14, 1890.[21] Democrats began to refer to the bill as a "Force Bill," rather than the Elections Bill, and the two terms were used throughout the period. Each name appealed to the respective political bases of the two parties.

The heart of the bill was the shift from allowing southerners to certify congressional elections to put that power into the hands of federal supervisors or federal judges.[22] In the contested presidential election of 1876, the reasoning behind the allocation of votes to Rutherford B. Hayes, rather than Samuel Tilden and the Democrats, was that the committee refused to "go behind the ballot box."[23] In other words, committee members would only determine who could certify, rather than determine what had happened. When a certification was complete, it did not matter to them what had happened within the state, either leading up to the election or at the casting of the ballots or in the counting thereof. This principle had held for many years, benefiting the Republicans in 1876, but in 1890 it was a principle that Democrats wanted to retain.[24]

Once the bill made it to the floor, the debates began in earnest in both houses. They were blunt and racially charged. Among the allegations from the floor managers was specific reference to Mississippi and its recent fraudulent elections. Republicans alleged that their party had to withdraw candidates in the most recent elections in the state because of violence and intimidation. Senator John Ingalls, Republican from Kansas, stated that the Mississippi Republican gubernatorial candidate had to withdraw because of "nameless killing on creek and bayou, on highway and byway. . . . We dare no longer carry our battered and blood-stained Republican flag."[25]

Charges of unconstitutionality by the Democrats brought Lodge to his feet in the House, where he reminded everyone that Article I, Sections 4 and 5, provided the directive for such action. He not only pointed to the Federalist Papers for support but also to recent Supreme Court decisions, such as *Ex parte Yarbrough*.[26] Had Lodge simply quit at this point, history would have seen him as principled in the face of real trouble. He continued his argument, however, pointing to a resulting malapportionment of representatives resulting from denying African Americans the vote. The consequence, he argued, using statistical charts, was that representatives from New England, for instance, represented far more voting constituents than those in the South.[27] Of course, the problem with this argument was that women were not voting at all, in spite of the fact that they were counted for use in congressional district apportionment. In addition, the number of those voting in the North was also dropping, though not because of intimidation or structural efforts of disfranchisement.

Because he was not consistent in his argument, Lodge left himself open to charges of attempting to protect the dominance of the party rather than proceeding on principle. Certainly there were those who would never believe that principle could ever be involved in protecting African Americans, but there were others who were not sure about the appropriateness of the vote and the intent behind it. The origins of the bill, of course, lay in the reaction of the national Republican Party to the problem of declining southern votes, particularly black Republican votes, which had created a win for Cleveland in 1884. The fact that they were so open about their concern over the practical effects of the lack of votes in the South for their party did not help convince those who were uncertain.

There were some Republicans, however, who were convinced of the righteousness of their cause. John Sherman had said, "Before the South can complain of injustice and wrong, they ought to do what is right and just."[28] Republicans pointed out that rather than saying African Americans had not gone far enough, it was more honest to point out how far they had come in such a short time and against impossible odds. Even more important, according to Henry Morey of Ohio, was that "the preservation of the rights of the strong and powerful can be permanently maintained only by a jealous protection of the rights of the ignorant and weak." He added, "There can be no safety for the republic and republican institutions when the rights of the people can be disregarded and trampled upon under a plea of race inferiority."[29]

One congressman, Nils P. Haugen of Wisconsin, spotted a problem previously unnoticed. He believed that white elites were using the cry of white supremacy to hold down white voters, "simply as a means to further the oppression of the lower classes." David Kerr of Iowa agreed with this class-based analysis, pointing out that "selfishness combined for oppression, as to retain class supremacy, has been a great foe of human freedom and human progress in all ages." Beyond the issues of race and class, David Henderson returned to a more fundamental element by asserting, "Fair play is the foundation stone of our citizenship." Violation of the ballot box was so egregious that Charles Hill of Illinois referred to it as "treason." Fraud was so serious that Hill argued, "wink at it, apologize for it, tolerate it, let it spread, and sooner or later this great republic will totter to its fall."[30] Newspapers reported that the House Committee on the Election of President and Vice-President heard testimony concerning the fraud perpetrated in the South. John R. Lynch was one of those who testified. The *Washington Post* noted that Lynch reminded the House that, although the state of Mississippi had 20,000 to 30,000 more African American voters than white ones, the state could always "be relied on to return a Democratic majority. He then related the different methods by which he asserted these results were accomplished." The paper did not include further information concerning Mississippi problems.[31]

Moving the Elections Bill through the House was surprisingly quick. The *House Journal* does not print the actual debates, but efforts to register opposition were noted in newspapers. What the *Journal* does report was the repeated delaying tactics. John Randolph Tucker of Virginia asked to amend the bill, but his amendment was then strengthened by yet another amendment by Jonathan H. Rowell of Illinois. Democrats also tried to have the bill returned to the Committee on the Election of President, Vice President and Representatives of Congress. That scheme, too, was voted down. They even tried to table the bill, a futile proposal. Congressman William M. Springer of Illinois (Democrat) had the engrossed bill read on a point of order.[32]

However polarizing the debate, and in spite of a few renegade Republicans bolting the party to vote against the bill, the Lodge Elections Bill passed the House on July 2, 1890, by a vote of 155 to 149. The Senate sent the bill to Hoar's committee, where he began to work on it to make it more palatable to western Republicans, thereby ensuring support. One of the offending portions contained an enforcement provision. Hoar believed that by getting rid of enforcement "by bayonet," which he did not feel was needed, he would avoid accusations of a return to the extreme measure of Reconstruction.[33] Hoar convinced Lodge of the efficacy of removing the provision, but in doing so, he lost some support from those who insisted on the need for enforcement. The *Chicago Tribune*, certainly a Republican organ, weighed in, arguing that if the bill were not passed and "fraud prevails, the country is not to be ruled by the people." The paper went on to emphasize that failure to pass the bill would ensure that power did not lie with the people, but rather with the criminal classes.[34] Democrats thought otherwise. As early as May, when they realized the bill might get to the Senate, they made plans to filibuster.[35]

Discounting Southern white reaction as overblown and a political ploy would have been easy to do, yet the Democratic interpretation of the "threat" by the Elections Bill was real. The issue had always concerned who would control the state. The passage of the bill would be a blow to the thin veil of legitimacy covering a pattern of intimidation and violence to keep control of the elections and therefore the social and economic structures of the state. In an interview with Frank Carpenter, a well-respected reporter of the period, Supreme Court justice L.Q.C. Lamar, who was former senator from Mississippi and perceived to be a racial moderate, made gloomy assessments. According to Carpenter, Lamar "thought Mississippi would eventually be a negro State and the whites forced to emigrate." Lamar further argued, "The influence of the present administration is in favor of the blacks at the expense of the whites, and the whites will not permit black rule. The outlook of the South seems as dark as can be, and what will be the future God only knows."[36]

◆ ◆ ◆

The events in Washington, DC, however, were not the only factors galvanizing white Democrats back in Mississippi. They feared that their control was slipping. African American Republicans suddenly realized they were not forgotten: President Harrison had said so. They took him at his word, for it provided the very opening they needed. In the summer of 1889 black Republicans met in Jackson, Mississippi. At first, delegates from forty counties requested that the Democratic Party in the state agree to a set of fusion tickets that would guarantee that some African Americans would be represented in the state and local government. Democrats thought that fusion had "proved unsatisfactory to both parties, and was abandoned as impracticable."[37] When the Republicans received no answer to their request, John Roy Lynch called a Republican convention for the state.

The convention, which included not only men from the state but also representatives from around the country, produced a long petition to be delivered by an appointed committee to President Harrison. Their petition claimed that there was little antipathy between the races but that "certain selfish and designing persons have endeavored to create a different impression upon the public mind, and we regret to say not without some success." They also claimed the perpetration of fraud at the last elections as a "criminal suppression of free suffrage." The petition then asked for federal supervision of elections—a federal law to allow federal judges to create juries fairly (even in states that restricted jury duty), to enact the Blair Bill, and to reimburse the depositors who lost money at the failure of the Freedman's Bank. They also referred to the new laws requiring segregation on rail cars as "odious."[38]

Finally, shifting from detail to principle and reminding Republicans of their heritage, the petitioners claimed, "Between right and wrong, justice and injustice, there can be no compromise. The Republican Party is known to be the party of liberty, justice, and equal rights—the party of free speech, a free press and honest elections—the party that believes in protection not only to American industries, but also to every American citizen at home and abroad, without regard to his race, color, nationality or religion. The Republican party cannot afford to abandon any one of these great principles." The signatures affixed included John R. Lynch, Blanche Bruce, James Hill, and other prominent African Americans in the state.[39] Though the petition still reads as eloquent over a hundred years later, the *Clarion-Ledger* did not think it so. In the same edition of the paper in which the petition appeared, the editors included an article on the amount spent by the state on African American education, which they thought was excessive. They pointed to this Republican petition as an "envenomous attack" on the state that showed how misspent such appropriations were.[40]

For the first time since Redemption, state Republicans produced a complete ticket.[41] Little evidence of this party convention remains, though the meeting was large and frightened many white leaders in the Democratic Party who thought African American voters had been firmly subdued.[42] The *Atlanta Constitution* recorded some of the events of the convention, although in racist terms, and noted that the black delegates outnumbered their white brethren by six to one.[43]

General James Ronald Chalmers, former Confederate general who by now had thrown his lot in with the Republicans, received nomination for governor.[44] Willis E Mollison, a noted African American lawyer, was their nominee for secretary of state. Mollison was a good choice.[45] He had been educated at Fisk and had been a lawyer, an editor, and a banker in the state. He had been appointed as the superintendent of public education by the Democratic Board of Education in 1881. Two years later he was elected as clerk of the chancery court in a predominantly African American town in Issaquena County and served two terms.[46]

Response from the Democratic Party, which relied on intimidation, was effective, and the Republicans withdrew their ticket.[47] Though Chalmers had long been a fixture in Mississippi politics, he had moved to Memphis, where he was practicing law. A campaign started to have him removed from the ballot because of his residency in Tennessee, rather than in Mississippi.[48] The *Clarion-Ledger* noted in October that General Chalmers resigned his nomination, ostensibly due to his poor health.[49] There is no verification of his health status in 1889, and Chalmers eventually died in 1898. Whether the attribution to illness was true or whether it was caution is undetermined.[50]

The color line was firm in Mississippi that summer of 1888. In Jasper County, near the little town of Paulding, a race riot took place in September, though little remains of the story other than in the *Clarion-Ledger*. According to this account, in early September a group of masked men went to an African American church and violated its sanctuary by holding a mock meeting and firing into the pulpit area. The men then moved to an African American school, where they repeated their actions. The men then called on two African American families at their homes and attacked the men, women, and children and finished by burning down their homes. They also called on one white family but did not hurt them or violate their premises other than through intimidation. What is astonishing in the news account is that the sheriff arrested a group of African American men for these actions and placed them in jail. The paper claimed that a number of them confessed, saying the conflicts developed because of a split in "union" activities. Local African American leaders, though, stated emphatically that the "union" was for political purposes only. White families in town armed themselves with 500 Winchesters. Subsequent events remain unrecorded.[51]

Far more disturbing to the white community was the effective leadership in the Mississippi Delta of a new organizer for the Colored Farmers' Alliance. This Alliance started in Texas in 1886, when the Farmers' Alliance took a white supremacist stance and did not allow African American members.[52] Within four years black membership spread across the South, with Mississippi claiming 90,000 members, and only Alabama with a larger number.[53] Organized to emphasize self-help and new and efficient farming methods, it quickly moved to boycotts, demanding higher wages and espousing some types of legal and social reform. Not surprisingly, this new assertive attitude irritated white planters, who feared a "militant" black population. Therefore, to create a vibrant and growing membership, the organization resorted to clandestine organizers, many of whom where local ministers.[54] The Colored Farmers' Alliance, like the Farmers' Alliance and many other fraternal and social organizations of the time, relied upon ritual to bind the members, including the use of secret passwords. Secrecy—popular at the time—served other purposes, including safety for its members, who struggled in a hostile environment. Ironically, although secrecy was important, it did not truly exist because newspapers published the names of members.

The Colored Farmers' Alliance sent delegates to the white Farmers' Alliance in Meridian in 1888 to determine what areas of mutual concern could be a combined effort. Though the delegates from both groups believed that mutual concerns regarding railroads and monopolies made it possible for them to join together, they made little headway in the effort. Too many issues divided the group because of differences on the socioeconomic scale. For instance, members of the Farmers' Alliance were the employers of the Colored Farmers' Alliance members.[55] Other states had marginally more successful efforts at mutual efforts.

Membership in the Colored Farmers' Alliance, though, continued to grow through the efforts of its organizers. Little is known of one of these men, including the organizer who carried the startling name of Oliver Cromwell.[56] Cromwell traveled from farm to farm in the state drumming up support for the Colored Farmers' Alliance; membership grew in Mississippi, as it did nationally. By 1891 the national membership reached over a million, but by then circumstances had changed and the Mississippi membership had plummeted. In the late 1880s, though, Cromwell was effective. Known as a notoriously "bad negro," he spoke openly about the plight of African American farmers.[57] And he had a practical side, for he encouraged local farmers in Leflore County to boycott local general stores and shop at an Alliance store, a shop that sold both to Farmers' Alliance and Colored Farmers' Alliance members in Durant about thirty miles away. Local store owners did not like this development. It not only affected their profits, but it also meant less control over African Americans, who were often stuck in a mire of loans owed to local merchants.[58]

By August 1889, the same summer that Republicans put forth their first complete ticket since Reconstruction, local whites began spreading rumors about the duplicity of Cromwell, who, they said, was making himself rich off local African American farmers. Someone even sent Cromwell a threatening letter, complete with an image of a skull and crossbones. Cromwell, neither a coward nor a fool, took the letter to an Alliance meeting. In addition to expressing their support to Cromwell that night, around seventy-five African American farmers marched into town military-style and gave a letter to sheriff, signed "Three Thousand Armed Men."[59] White citizens sent their wives and children to safety in Greenwood. The sheriff, who claimed he feared a race war, telegraphed Governor Lowry for state militia troops, which he sent. When they arrived, supposedly they were told by the sheriff that they were no longer needed because a local posse had located the troublemakers and arrested them.[60]

Newspaper accounts of race problems in Mississippi were censored by local editors, a tradition that continued for a nearly a century after this. Therefore there are few references to the Leflore County massacre in 1889, but a handful of national papers (particularly, but not entirely, African American ones) reported on a disturbance in the Delta.[61] No one is entirely sure of the numbers involved of either race, but historians increasingly have come to accept the fact that something nefarious happened that late, hot summer of 1889 in Leflore County.[62]

The story is confusing. The number of victims reported ranged from 20 to 100, all African American. Sheriff L. T. Baskett of Leflore directed a posse of 200 men, but whether they were the culprits or whether they were members of the militia, some of whom remained behind, is unknown. National newspapers reported that returning members of the Capital Light Guard spoke little of what they had seen. One reported seeing six dead people, while others said they saw none; what actually happened is unclear. A New York textile agent, J. C. Engle, was in Greenwood during the time of the massacre. The following week in New Orleans he told reporters that African Americans were "shot down like dogs," including women and children. His account included the accusation that one sixteen-year-old guardsman beat a child to death while his older brother held the parents at bay with a gun. No one was ever charged with this crime. Reports included accounts of killing of "ring-leaders" of the Colored Farmers' Alliance and hanging of prisoners when the militia left. The Detroit *Plaindealer* reported the incident, but the paper feared that the true numbers would never be revealed because of a reign of fear gripping the African American community after the massacre.[63]

Once violence by white vigilantes within the community began, both races feared the worst. Apparently few African Americans were armed, in spite of the letter from 3,000 armed men. There were reports of desperate attempts to secure arms by local blacks. Two African American men were captured while attempting to run guns to the Colored Farmers' Alliance in Leflore. They had "rifle cartridges, buckshot and gunpowder."[64] Certainly the lack of reporting of a single white death confirms the apparent lack of ammunition, if not rifles themselves. One oral history varies the narrative. According to a descendent of Cromwell, he did not escape, but after five days of running he was caught by the posse. He was armed and "took out" five of his opponents before he died.[65]

Following the massacre, a number of white citizens of the county met and adopted a resolution in which they claimed the Colored Farmers' Alliance was "corrupting" African Americans. They "ordered" the Durant Commercial Company to cease selling to the Colored Farmers' Alliance members and that the Colored Farmers' Alliance Advocate (Carroll County) no longer campaign locally, lest they face the "wrath of a united and outraged community."[66] Mississippi, at least in the Delta, was returning to the intimidations of the past, if the past had ever passed.

According to a state historian writing shortly after the convention, the leaders in the state recognized that continuing to rely upon the machinations of the Mississippi Plan used at the end of Reconstruction was hurting the ethics and sensibilities of the newly emerging white voters of the state.[67] Though the behavior of the previous decade had gained the state notoriety, many white citizens had begun to take such behavior as normal and to be expected. Most leaders realized that with the decline in African American voting, the "need" for such tactics was no longer necessary, although a few expressed resentment that their well-intentioned actions of the previous two decades were questioned. In fact, pointing out that the actions taken then were necessary only served to emphasize the change that had taken place in the state. White citizens were no longer worried and subsequently did not want to take the risk of creating a new constitution.[68] Senator Walthall and Justice Lamar typified this group, who worried "that an effort to limit negro suffrage would bring evils upon the state in the way of adverse congressional legislation and Federal administrative proceedings."[69] Thus the push for a convention in 1886 was defeated within the legislature on these grounds.[70] Walthall continued to oppose a convention until it actually met. He also expressed reservations about how difficult disfranchisement might be, for he believed it imperiled the position of poor white voters.[71]

At the beginning of the 1888 legislative session, state senator Joel P. Walker of Lauderdale County introduced a bill in the legislature that did not call for a convention, but rather required an election for qualified electors who would decide whether one was needed. If affirmed, a convention would be called.[72] The bill moved quickly through committee and the legislature, and was sent to Governor Lowry in record time, on January 20. The governor vetoed the bill. His official response to the legislature indicated he did not find the provisions of the constitution so odious as to need replacement. Seeing dangers in calling a convention, he pointed out that there was no consensus among the people as to remedies for problems and that the suffrage issue was dangerous to contemplate. Finally, the cost of a convention would be prohibitive.[73] After extensive debate among the legislators, not to mention unfavorable editorial comments in state papers, the veto could not be overridden.

The following year, 1889, was election year in Mississippi. Frank Burkitt, editor of the Okolona *Chickasaw Messenger* and acknowledged local leader of the Farmers' Alliance, made the expected reference to a Reconstruction constitution foisted upon the state; he then moved to a new territory. Certainly within the line of the leaders of the Farmers' Alliance, he argued that the opponents of a convention knew that a new constitution would "limit the terms of certain State and county officers and thus protect the public from bossism, defalcation and corruption.... The era of the one-man power vanishes, and henceforth no man will be permitted to exercise authority over citizens who have no voice in his selections." Burkitt did not stop there, but went on to pinpoint other political problems within the state. Mississippians hoped that "the inefficient judicial system shall be exchanged for one more economic and better qualified to meet the demands of justice." Mississippians insisted "that the elections laws ... secure the rule of honesty and intelligence and that ballot-stuffing and bull-dozing will be made impossible in the future." Finally, Burkitt argued, they "favor a just and equitable free school system which distributes the money to rich and poor alike." In short, Burkitt and his followers were asking for the unseating of the conservative Bourbons of the state.[74] In 1888 the legislators had already indicated their stance on both the calling of the convention and regarding the governor himself. When Lowry vetoed the bill to explore a convention, the Senate passed a proposed constitutional amendment that would limit the term of office of any governor to one term and also dictate the election of judges.[75] The proposal failed, for it failed to receive the required votes in the House. The point, however, was made.

Perception of a growing corruption that was contaminating the entire voting process spread far beyond the Farmers' Alliance. According to an early twentieth-century writer who had been a party to the convention struggles, reform of the system became paramount to a number of the leaders, so long as that system legitimately reinforced white supremacy: "In the decade of 1880 to 1890 it became apparent that the 'Mississippi plan' of dealing with black majorities would, unless checked, pollute the very sources of representative government. Symptoms of the diseased political condition grew so acute that the demand for suffrage restriction to effect an electorate under which there could be white supremacy through honest elections became quite apparent."[76] One of the leaders of the period, writing a decade later, argued similarly that "the white men in the State had given unlimited negro suffrage a fair trial, and found it to be a failure. They had reached the point where the two races stood solidly and hopelessly arrayed against each other politically, with no indication or possibility of a break in either line." He further argued that "to give the law its full and proper course, was to surrender ultimately the control of the State to the negroes. This had been demonstrated during the six years of Republican rule. To prevent this catastrophe, unlimited negro suffrage had made the white men in many parts of the State intimidators or contrivers in elections." Just to be sure everyone understood the stark realities, he reminded readers that the "State [had] a solid negro majority of over 40,000 in the electoral body. The thinking men of the State realized the magnitude, the perplexities, and the complexities involved in the treatment of a situation in which two races, so dissimilar in all respects, were clothed by the Federal organic law with equal political rights and privileges."[77]

Thwarted in the legislature, a grassroots movement grew on the county level. In March 1888 the Copiah County Democratic convention called for new state constitution, for it dubbed the Reconstruction constitution a fraud. According to the delegates, it was written by "aliens, strangers, Negroes, carpetbaggers, [and] ignoramouses [sic]."[78] Though pockets of opposition still worried about the pitfalls inherent in any rewrite, the mood of the state was changing.[79] By 1889 the movement toward a convention was outstanding the newspaper editors of the state. Though a number of editors opposed a new constitution, others took up the cause. In June the *Meridian News*, not being shy about its racism, called for a convention that would "perpetually inhibit the negro race from holding office."[80] Others were not as blunt and openly questioned the behavior of the white supremacists in the state. The *Greenville Times* said that white "supremacy must be made to consist with the law, statute and moral [sic]. There must be devised some legal, defensible substitute for the abhorrent and evil methods on which white supremacy relies."[81]

Former governor Stone, who was running for a new term of office, acknowledged this groundswell of support and hedged his position so as not to offend either side. He declared that if the legislature wanted to call a convention, he would not interfere, for he believed that such a decision was appropriately within the purview of the legislature. State leaders got the message. Once the popular former governor had been elected to a new term, the legislature moved quickly.[82]

Unlike Senator Walthall, Senator George supported a constitutional convention. In October 1889, in a speech in Greenville, Mississippi, George acknowledged the need for election methods to be lawful and "elections fair and legal . . . if the public morals of the people are to be preserved and the civilization of the State maintained."[83] He emphasized the new threats to Mississippi's control of African American voting. He also played upon the fears of the white population in a speech delivered shortly afterward in Jackson in which he predicted that the census of 1900 would show the African American population in the state outnumbering whites by two to one. For that reason, he wanted to ensure a "home government, under the control of the white people of the State," through a new constitution. With a nod to the Burkitt group, known as the "wool hat boys," he further argued that a new constitution would also provide new regulations for corporations as well as forbid local legislation, both of which had led to corruption in the state.[84]

In response, later that month Senator Walthall spoke to the Mississippi House of Representatives. He opposed the calling of a convention on the grounds of being "unnecessary, expensive, and a dangerous experiment." Rather than remedy the "problem" of African American suffrage, he argued that a convention would serve to aggravate the issue and draw attention nationally to the state. He also warned that property and literacy qualifications for voters would necessarily affect white men as well. Notably, he suggested that gaining education and acquiring property were two pathways that would benefit African Americans and provide them a way out of their lowly position.[85]

The November elections in the state were simply pro forma. The Democrats won, for the Republicans had removed their ticket. In a ringing assault, the Republican State Executive Committee met in Jackson and wrote a polemic explaining the party's withdrawal. Republicans claimed they knew "our votes would be stolen and our voters driven from the polls, but we hoped in the larger towns and cities . . . the semblance of free speech might still remain to us, but our candidates are not safely allowed to discuss or protest." Since Reconstruction they had endured not only the deaths of their well-known leaders but also the "faithful flowers known only in the cabins of the lowly." In one of the few references to the massacres, they referred to the slaughters at various places and also to "the nameless killing by creek and bayou, on highway and byway." These affronts they laid at the door of the Democrats and asked for national help.[86] The following week the editors of the *Clarion-Ledger* rejoined the attack, for they were appalled that John Lynch took the request directly to Washington. Here was a threat of consequence. Mississippi had tried to avoid national notice, and Lynch, who had a network of supporters, was bringing material directly to their notice. The first attack was to call the allegations a falsehood. Lynch declared that "absolute anarchy prevails. There is no state government. The slaughters at Kemper and Copiah, Clinton and Carrollton, Wahalak, Vicksburg, Yazoo City and Leflore have been a foretaste of what we might expect." Lynch further claimed that their gubernatorial nominee, General Chalmers, was surrounded by threats from a mob of armed men in Columbus. In West Point, Chalmers was threatened with a riot if he tried to speak; the sheriff had left town that morning. The scene was similar in other places, and so Chalmers, unable to canvass the franchise, withdrew.[87]

By this point a number of state leaders believed it was time to act to forestall national interference. In January, at the start of the new legislative session, T. V. Noland, a House member from Woodville and a practicing attorney, introduced a bill once again calling for a constitutional convention. The bill moved quickly through committee, the House, and the Senate and passed by substantial margins within eleven days of its introduction. Governor Stone, who had campaigned on the promise he would not veto such a bill, simply noted the passage.

The vote within the House produced counterintuitive results. Everyone understood that the constitution would limit the franchise of African Americans, yet the representatives from black counties in the state, primarily stretching from the Delta down to Natchez, mostly voted against a convention. An unpublished master's thesis from the 1940s argues that this surprising vote occurred because the representatives feared a reapportionment that would be unfavorable to representation in these counties. The fear of unfavorable reapportionment eventually proved accurate, but whether this threat was sufficient motive to object to a convention remains uncertain, because proposals on reapportionment were not widely disseminated in January 1890. Similarly, the predominantly white counties in the northeastern portion of the state also opposed the convention; supposedly they feared a literacy qualification that would affect their constituencies. This argument, like the one on reapportionment, assumes a debate that did not take place until after the vote in the legislature.[88]

Within the next months, before the convening of the convention in August, debates flourished over the proposed provisions. Every man in public life wanted his say, and the newspapers reflected this interest. Those without political ambition wrote under a pseudonym, while those with ambition ran for office. In March Governor Stone called for convention delegates to be elected on July 29. Each county and district represented in the statehouse was eligible for a representative, and there were fourteen delegates for the state at large.[89]

In late June African Americans in the state met in Jackson, where they were urged to canvass the state for delegates to the convention who would protect their rights. Though their meeting created some stir in the state, most editors thought that nothing much would come of it, since the mood of the white people was toward franchise restriction. Republicans fielded only a few candidates, mostly in the black counties. One African American Republican, F.M.B. (Marsh) Cook of Jasper County, campaigned actively in the heat of the summer and was hot and intemperate in speech, for he daily chastised the white community for their behavior. His body was discovered riddled with bullets, and his assassins were never found. While the Jackson *Clarion-Ledger* expressed reservations over the assassination, it acknowledged that the "people of Jasper County are to be congratulated that they will not be further annoyed by Marsh Cook."[90] Ultimately, the elections in August showed as few voters in Jasper County as ever before.[91] The turnout was sparse, but in the end, voters entrusted their future to the new delegates.

Ideas on the provisions of the constitution were as equally heated, as the election had been to choose the delegates, and no clear proposal won the backing of the voters. Proposals were creative and ranged from the cautiously conservative, like the position of Walthall, to the ingenious. Many of the conservative positions could have been accomplished by amendment: the Australian ballot, the poll tax, and even a grandfather clause.[92] At every turn, the editorials and letters to the editor revealed a belief that these ideas were needed to reform the franchise. They all agreed that the problem was the African American vote, but how to control it "morally" was at issue. Violence and intimidation had to stop; they wanted to proceed "legally," even though they wanted to circumvent both the Fourteenth and Fifteenth Amendments. One letter to the editor baldly stated the white southern perspective: those two amendments were passed in 1865 and 1867 simply because the returning Confederate states "had" to ratify them, which was not "fair."[93] Moreover some were well aware that restricting access to the ballot for African Americans could trigger the enforcement provisions of the Fourteenth Amendment (Section 2), which would reduce the state's representation. Some were willing to take that penalty.[94]

A few of the proposals were more creative. The first of these was Judge J.A.P. Campbell's idea of plural voting as documented on the front page of the *Clarion-Ledger* in April. He proposed allowing citizens with real property and larger tracts of land to cast additional votes. Property qualifications had been part of the Mississippi Constitution of 1817, so at least that part was not new.[95] What was original was the conjoining of the ideas of property and universal suffrage. In explaining his idea, Campbell argued, "Our claim is that the intelligence and wealth of the South are chiefly with the whites; and, therefore, they should govern in the interests of all classes." He contended that this deprived no one of a vote, but put "power in the hands of the intelligent." Campbell believed in every county whites controlled the land.[96] Further clarification appeared in the following week's paper, in which the plan was correctly dubbed "novel."[97]

The plan provoked a number of responses, particularly from those who called the idea "undemocratic." Although Campbell had carefully crafted his proposal to avoid disfranchising, while simultaneously using enfranchisement to dilute votes, he did not foresee some of the reactions. Only half-reading the proposal, but still understanding the real results, one writer asked how the state could resort to either education or property qualifications without affecting the redshirts (the unlettered white Democrats) who had fought beside them in Reconstruction. He thought it would be "treason."[98]

In response, Campbell wrote an open letter to the *Clarion-Ledger* in which he reminded readers that the "evil is a large negro majority. The remedy is to increase the white vote." In that regard, his proposal to allocate more ballots to property owners was an appropriate remedy. In addition, both as explanation and as warning, he added, "The right to vote is political, not natural—a privilege rather than a right."[99] Such an argument, however, did not sit well with H. L. Long, who wrote that favoring large landowners was undemocratic. He added that the use of the scare tactic of "negro supremacy" had long ago ended.[100]

The following week the editors of the *Clarion-Ledger* discussed several plans that were before the public, including the poll tax, a residency requirement, property qualification, and educational qualifications. They saw problems with all the ideas, including the potential of disfranchising illiterate white voters, and they pointed out that African Americans could, and were, learning to read and write. The advantage they saw in Campbell's plan was exactly what he argued, that it did not disfranchise anyone, but the increase in white voters would destroy the majority held by African Americans in the state.[101] Later in the month, the paper, still backing the plan, reported that support was growing across the state. Referring to the Lodge Elections Bill, the editors added urgently and ominously, "Let us take warning from the republicans [sic] who are entrenching in power, in the hope of permanent control of the Federal government."[102]

Reactions were not long in appearing from across the state. At times there was legitimate opposition based on principle, but other times opponents had their own proposal. The *Newton County Progressive*, a white county paper and a voice of the small farmer, opposed the plan, which it argued would be worse than what the state then faced. Judge S. S. Calhoon, shortly to be elected president of the convention, and Judge W. P. Harris, shortly to be chair of the Judiciary Committee, opposed property qualifications.[103] Calhoon had his own idea, which was gerrymandering, and Harris wanted an educational qualification. Calhoon worried especially that property qualifications might divide the state between rich and poor farmers rather than race.[104] Judge Calhoon suggested a more integrated approach, including the Australian ballot, residential requirements, and a poll tax.[105] Campbell, in a letter to the editor of the *Memphis Commercial*, responded that race was stronger than class. He added, "In the late war non-slaveholders fought valiantly to maintain slavery."[106]

Watching the debates in Mississippi were many northern newspapers. The *Great South Newspaper* in New York City noted that at least Campbell was honest about his intentions of disfranchising African American voters. The paper acknowledged that other states were likely to follow suit, but it warned Mississippi to be certain that any remedy applied was not based on color.[107]

Campbell replied that every other avenue did exactly that: effect a change based on race.[108]

As the debate continued to swirl in the weeks before the start of the convention, I. W. Storis suggested that Campbell's idea be expanded to descendants of landowners. He worried about the number of former landowners who had been pressed into tenancy, a rising problem across the South and one not relegated to African Americans.[109] The issues of race and class continued to be intermixed, although some leaders continued to try to tease them apart. Acknowledging this problem was a column in the *Clarion-Ledger* that argued that a property qualification, and possibly an educational one, would divide the classes in the state and lead to the inevitable collapse of the Democratic Party.[110] Eventually, but not unexpectedly, the question arose as to whether plural voting itself was constitutional. The editors of the *Clarion-Ledger* believed it was but then suggested that the plan deserved contemplation though not necessarily adoption.[111] Support continued for the plan throughout the summer and into the convention, but there were too many reservations among the leaders, who also had plans of their own.

Chief among the others with an agenda was Senator George, who also proposed a carefully crafted but novel approach. He offered his ideas to colleagues before leaving Washington, DC, as remembered by Senator David Turpie of Indiana.[112] George was using Judge Calhoon's plan of apportionment and electors for the state government, but went further. According to George, since they agreed African Americans were not capable of government, then the counties with more of them should have less power; essentially the state should return to the constitution of 1832, which allocated power according to white ascendancy. Within the Senate, if each county could have but one senator, white control could be assured: "The certainty of one co-ordinate branch of the Government being always under white control would tend to prevent the negroes of the State being led by bad advisers and adventurers, as no hopes would be presented of absolute control of the State and the taxing power." He added that whites must remain united: "The negro is not aggressive except when badly led and is most easily controlled by white men when in dense masses." Finally, George suggested that the legislature, not the people, elect the governor, thus ensuring white control.[113]

Just to be sure that he reached the largest number of voters in the northern part of the state, George also wrote C. E. Wright, the editor of the Memphis *Commercial Herald*. George argued that the ideological underpinning for the rewriting of the Mississippi Constitution was white supremacy, but he specifically acknowledged "that the civil and political rights of the colored race, as guaranteed by the constitution of the United States, are not to be denied or abridged, but protected. Their incapacity must be acknowledged and guarded against to the end that their rights and the rights of the other race may be protected." To protect the establishment of a government based on integrity, he suggested that the legislature appoint state officials, perhaps including the governor (yet to be decided). Then he added:

> Every man who has held an office or registered as a voter in Mississippi since 1868, has taken an oath to support the constitution of the United States. We must obey this constitution or violate our oaths already taken. That the constitution in any part of it may be wrong does not relieve us from that obligation. That any particular provision in it was placed there by force or fraud does not relieve us so long as it remains a part of the constitution. We cannot, as some Northern men did before the late civil war, announce our obedience to a higher law than the constitution itself and obey it in good faith.[114]

The rest of the letter betrayed the high-minded approach. He added that although African Americans were part of this agreement, as citizens they must be taught to revere the state and look to it for protection. Whatever Mississippians might think about the ability of the two races to live in the same polity, "we must make a fair trial to accomplish it." He further argued that African Americans must be able to vote but that the state could resort to reapportionment, and he pointed to New Jersey as an example of manipulation. Keep it simple and straightforward, he stated, as he referred to the distrust created by "extra-legal" manipulations of the franchise.[115] Senator George's comment should not be interpreted as his being a moderate in race relations. Few politicians were, for polarization on this issue was profound. Statements by George in the fall, as the convention progressed, were illuminating. He referred to African Americans as "that race which had no other conception of government than a blind and slavish obedience to a barbaric chieftain, who by any means, whether of force or conjuration or voodooism might have acquired supremacy in a tribe—that race as endowed with the great and important trust of suffrage."[116]

Despite extensive and vigorous debate printed in the newspapers, when the voting for delegates was completed, no clear plan had emerged. Deliberation may be good for politics, but the *Natchez Democrat* found this controversy troubling, both for the lack of consensus and the apparent split within the white Democratic Party. The editors feared no good could emerge when two giants of age, Campbell and George, were fighting over ideas. The convention, the editors said, should make as few changes in the organic law as possible. In a startling departure from the nascent Lost Cause ideology then gripping the state, they added, "We urge that the delegates sent thither avoid the quixotism which sees giants in the windmills of Federal elections bills and the **ghosts** [their emphasis] which arise from the graveyards of carpetbaggism—and follow steadily the undeviating hue of Democracy as we know it and have it." The delegates who came to Jackson that August believed they were looking to the future, but they were inexorably tied to the past.[117]

CHAPTER 5

The Convention Debates the Franchise

Though a number of separate issues helped move Mississippi toward a new constitution, disfranchisement was the raison d'être for the convention. The unseen question, hovering below the surface, was whether disfranchisement was merely a question of race or whether it included class.[1] Ostensibly, delegates realized that the way around the restrictions of the Fifteenth Amendment was to create qualifiers, rather than disqualifiers, for voters that would apply equally to white and black citizens. The rationale was that the specifications could be crafted to apply principally to African American voters, but everyone understood that some white voters would be disfranchised in the process. The result of these conflicting ideas was a notable split in the conventions between white and black counties and produced some of the sharpest arguments when the debates began.[2]

Another illuminating split revealed in the debates emerged in the Democratic Party between paternalists and hard-liners. There is a tendency among historians to discount this difference, for both groups were racist. From a practical standpoint, however, it is not possible to do. Paternalists, who certainly believed the white race was superior, were willing to work with African Americans, especially those who were educated and pliant. Paternalists wanted to control, but not to banish, their workers. In contrast, hard-liners were willing to send them away to rid themselves of the presence of the black race. Paternalists believed they had an open mind, for they tended to be the more educated of the group.[3] Radical racists, who often represented the white counties, were candid and left little room for misunderstanding about their motives. Though there were exceptions to this general rule, for the most part alignment of delegate views and the type of county represented was consistent. This split was not unusual for the South in general, for it represented two competing visions about the future of the region, both based on misunderstandings about the past.

These delegates, both paternalist and hard-liner, were products of their time and place, and most were counted in the language of the period as "good people." They were churchgoers, advocates of temperance, supporters of law and order, and spokesmen for the underprivileged—yet unreservedly racist. On the opening day, they called on the Almighty, through the ministrations of Methodist bishop Charles Betts Galloway, to bless their proceedings and guide them with wisdom through their efforts.[4] These delegates viewed themselves as responsible reformers, ones who would tackle the enormous issues of the state and rectify its problems.

First among these issues—and covered in this chapter—was the franchise. The delegates recognized that the abuses of the past, which included intimidation and violence, could not continue. The evident disrespect for law and order was undermining the integrity of the young men of the state, which of course meant white youth. To their minds, if the body politic should be formulated into a character of intelligence, responsibility, and ability to govern effectively, the state, by protecting that identity, would ensure a productive future for all its citizens. As surprising an assumption as this argument appeared to be, it was held to an axiom that each delegate should hold dear and from which they should not deviate. Though delegates differed on such matters as taxation, apportionment, and election of judges, reform of the ballot was paramount. Delegates viewed this reform as not only rectifying problems with the actual ticket but also access to the franchise.

These debates reveal an undercurrent often ignored in examination of the Jim Crow South, for race was such a dominant feature. Yet class appeared solidly in the debates. Far more than race, it underlay issues between the white and black counties. It provided the foundation for the debates over tax rolls and assessments. It lurked beneath the issues over railroads and corporations. It was the structure of the perceived differences between racial paternalists and hard-liners and motivated the decision to seat the one African American delegate to the convention. It even affected Isaiah Montgomery's perception of what was really happening at the convention and where he should cast his support.

❖ ❖ ❖

The issue of race was close to the surface at the convention, but it erupted in an unexpected quarter the opening afternoon. Since the state split into white and black counties, there was a power play as to who would control the politics and economy of the state.[5] Immediately following President Calhoon's opening speech, the question of the legitimacy of seating certain delegates arose. M. Farish from Issaquena County in the Delta moved that a committee of five be established to investigate the contested elections of Bolivar County, also in the Delta.[6] Both counties were overwhelmingly African American and fell into the black county camp. The only two Republicans elected to the convention were from Bolivar, which had a long history of fusion voting between the parties and races. Indeed, one of the two delegates was Isaiah Montgomery, the only African American delegate.[7] Because of his financial success, Montgomery represented an affront to the other delegates based on both race and class. The other Republican, George P. Melchior, was white and a member of a prominent family in Bolivar. His inclusion was problematic but not nearly so much as Montgomery's. The fact that the convention moved so quickly to cast the issue to committee is therefore not at all surprising.[8]

A more subtle issue related to race also emerged. The newly created Pearl River County petitioned to have its representative seated. Should it be included in the roll of counties with delegates? This issue seemed appropriate for a committee on delegates to handle, but there was more to the matter. The first controversy was straightforward: since the county was created after the call for the convention, its representation was uncertain. The other reason the county was controversial was the fact that it had relatively few African Americans and therefore fell on the white county side. In the coming power struggles, debating issues relating to both Bolivar and Pearl River County representatives provided some room for negotiation and compromise. As is typical of any convention, the matters were referred to committee.[9]

On the seventh day of the convention, the committee brought in the report on the Bolivar delegates. The majority report argued that many of the ballots had been illegally cast and counted since they did not conform to state law; the names on the tickets were too far apart, and the length of the ticket was different. Concluding that Melchior had received only nine legal votes and Montgomery none, they resolved that both Melchior and Montgomery should be unseated.[10] In contrast, the minority report, written by the former attorney general and which was startlingly clearer and more coherent, argued that the size of the tickets was not a violation of code since they were only a fifth of an inch different in length. After a brief debate, which went unrecorded, the report was remanded to the next day for vote.[11]

The elites of the state took notice, for the following day (August 20) the minutes report that the hall was crowded with so many viewers that extra chairs had to be brought into the hall. The chair, Judge Calhoon, asked that the governor and the supreme court justices, who were not members of the convention but attended that day, be allowed to sit on the floor. At no other day do the minutes refer to the worthy in attendance en masse. This question of the legitimacy of the Republicans from Bolivar was important, for it hit at the heart of the very reason for calling the convention. Apparently state leaders supported the seating of both Melchior and Montgomery, and their attendance helped to keep unruly observers under control. Delegate W. S. Farish from Issaquena, a black county in the Delta, moved that the majority report be accepted on the Bolivar County delegates. Delegate T. S. Ford, representing the state at large, offered a substitution to the motion, so that both Melchior and Montgomery could be seated.[12] The minority won by a vote of 79 to 28, which allowed the seating of both Melchior and Montgomery, but the motion was forced into reconsideration and shifted to the next day. Neither the minutes nor the local paper reported any such debate.[13] Instead, the proceedings shifted to the franchise problem itself.[14]

Some historians have argued that Isaac Montgomery was part of a compromise in that he exchanged his seating for support of disfranchisement. A few have even suggested collusion between Calhoon and Montgomery. Certainly the fact that the issue of seating seemed to have disappeared quite suddenly is suggestive, and even more dubious is the fact that Montgomery was appointed to the Franchise Committee. There is, however, no firm evidence of collusion. The Bolivar County controversy exposed a split between paternalistic and outright bigoted leanings within the white delegation. Both groups questioned the abilities of African Americans, but their differences were a question of degree, which mattered not only to the state, but especially to African Americans. The elites, who showed up to support the seating of Melchior and Montgomery, tried to stem the tide of hatred, but their efforts were not successful in the long term—in the convention and in the coming decades.

Race as a central issue was so bluntly discussed that everyone, in and out of the state, knew it to be the reason for calling the convention. Certainly African Americans also were cognizant of its purpose, but reaction among African Americans in the state is harder to gauge because few newspapers of the era remain, and none among the African American community in Mississippi. The *Clarion-Ledger*, however, did refer to one reaction. During this time the state Farmers' Alliance was meeting in Starkville, and the Colored Farmers' Alliance convened in Meridian, where an interested reporter slipped in the back door, hoping to be unnoticed so that he could observe the proceedings. Dr. L.W.W. Manoway, an agent of *Fair Play*, a newspaper for African Americans, spoke to a gathering concerned about what the convention was doing in Jackson and how it would affect them. Manoway argued that the convention would really do nothing, and even if it did, African Americans in Mississippi had nothing to fear since they still held the majority in the state. If the convention succeeded in disfranchising "ten whites to get at 80,000 negroes," they still held a majority. In addition, if the convention gave women the vote, African American women also had education and property, and so there would be no real gain by the white population in the franchise. At this point the white reporter admitted his presence was noticed and the room cleared of outsiders. The editors at the *Clarion-Ledger* agreed with Dr. Manoway, saying that he made sense. There was nothing for African Americans to fear, they argued, an opinion that surely contradicted everything they had been arguing on their editorial pages.[15]

Fundamental to the purpose of the convention was whether options for disfranchisement were constitutional and whether they conflicted with the Fourteenth Amendment (citizenship) and the Fifteenth Amendment (voting rights to freedmen). Early in the convention Mayre Dabney of Warren County worried specifically about the problems of the Fifteenth Amendment and suggested appealing to Congress to repeal its "pesky" provisions.[16] In addition to constitutional issues, a fundamental problem was the Readmission Act of 1870, to which Mississippi submitted to rejoin the Union.[17] Under this act, Congress limited "the right of the State of Mississippi to impose certain restrictions upon the right of franchise and otherwise prohibit[ed] the State from changing the Constitution of the State of Mississippi."[18] In fact, the Readmission Act specified that "the constitution of Mississippi shall never be so amended or changed as to deprive any citizens or class of citizens of the United States of the right to vote who are entitled to vote by the constitution herein recognized."[19] Without doubt, this was exactly what the state proposed to do in 1890.

On the tenth day of the convention came the report of the Judiciary Committee, which had been charged with investigating the possible conflict between disfranchisement and the constitutional amendments. The report acknowledged that a state could not specify African Americans for disfranchisement, but rather any restriction must apply to both races; this interpretation did not mean there could be no restrictions at all. The committee quoted *Cruikshank*: "The right to vote comes from the State, but the right of exception from the prohibition discrimination comes from the United States."[20] According to Wiley P. Harris of Hinds County, who chaired the committee, "The elective franchise was never conferred by the Federal Constitution, but was granted by the States," and remains so "except so far as it is limited or abridged by the Fourteenth Amendment." As to the Fifteenth Amendment, Harris added, it "did not confer the elective franchise on any voter, but provided that the right of suffrage could not be denied to any citizen by a State on account of race, color or previous condition of servitude." Thus suffrage could be restricted, as long as it was not based on race.[21]

The committee further examined provisions in Article IV, Section 4, of the US Constitution, which guarantees "a republican form of government."[22] Sanctions in the Constitution allowed Congress to reduce a state's representation in Congress because of violations of this principle.[23] Clearly, the convention wanted to avoid this problem, but delegates noted that, by having a penalty specified, Congress intended that states have a choice in the matter.[24] Another approach to the problem then debated was whether Mississippi, once readmitted to the Union, could define its laws the way it wanted. This was not an unknown argument, for Illinois had argued this very issue in proposing to allow slavery in the early years of statehood, a clear violation of the Northwest Ordinance.[25] According to a number of Illinois state legislators, once a state was admitted and was no longer under congressional control of a territory, did it not have the right to determine its own laws?[26] The conclusion of the committee was that "Congress cannot confer suffrage, cannot make a voter." That is a right of the state. Since the Fifteenth Amendment declared that a state, in defining voters, cannot "discriminate against the colored man because of race or previous condition of servitude," any restriction must be applicable to all.[27]

This discussion of the relationship between the federal and state governments disquieted a number of delegates, who were loath to relinquish state sovereignty, even in the limited form of compliance with federal amendments to the Constitution of the United States. J. Jamison of Noxubee County proposed a statement for the convention to confirm that "Mississippi is a free and independent state subject only to the Constitution of the United States . . . nor will the State ever assent to any amendment or changes of the Constitution of the United States which may in anywise impair the right of local self-government belonging to the people of this State."[28] Of course, this opinion was not only what John C. Calhoun had argued during the nullification crisis of 1832, but it also went further by claiming new amendments would not necessarily apply to the state when it did not approve. Clearly some ideas had staying power beyond the calamitous results of the Civil War.[29]

A special committee on the franchise and the Fifteenth Amendment reported on September 30 on the proposals remanded to the committee. In a startling development, but perhaps not so illogical given the earlier tenor of debate at the convention, the members of the committee proposed that the representatives from the state ask for a repeal of the Fifteenth Amendment. The language was formal. Within the language of the proposal the report noted that the state of Mississippi, and some other states, had nearly equal numbers of the two races. The writers of the report further postulated that "these two races, though friendly and homogeneous for all business and industrial purposes, are widely separated by race instincts and prejudices in all political and social matters." For this reason, in spite of the fact that there were areas, such as the economy and levee construction, that were of "common interest to them," the writers believed that the two races would be forever "divided in all political contest in the main, on race lines" and were "without any well founded hope of a change." They argued that "one race or the other must have charge and control the government" or there would forever be conflict between the two; thus "such condition of insecurity is not only a great political or social evil, but greatly impedes all industrial development." At this point they reached their fundamental understanding of the issue: "the white people only are capable of conducting and maintaining the governments," for "the negro race, even if its people were educated, being wholly unequal to such great responsibility, if they should come into control of such government." They resolved that the only "true and efficient remedy . . . lies in the repeal of the XV Amendment of the Constitution of the United States."[30]

To further underscore the beliefs revealed in this special committee report, when the delegates presented a Bill of Rights to the floor, Section 1 argued that the political power rests with the people of the state, and Section 2 stated in bald terms that "the people of this State shall have the inherent, sole, and exclusive right to regulate the internal government . . . provided such change be not repugnant to the Constitution of the United States."[31] Just in case anyone wondered about the first two sections, the third section tempered the language by stating that the right of secession would never be exercised again.[32] As a further nod to the Thirteenth Amendment, Section 12 provided that "there shall be neither slavery nor involuntary servitude in this state, otherwise than in the punishment of a crime, whereof the party shall have been duly convicted."[33]

◆ ◆ ◆

Having dismissed possible constitutional conflicts, the delegates turned to the practical question of how to gain control over the polity. As discussed in chapter 4, a number of ideas had been proposed by state leaders through circuit speeches or articles in local newspapers. A few of the proposals rested on historical provisions, such as property qualifications; others were entirely new, such as woman suffrage. All of them, however, had original concepts that made them unusual and even slippery to grasp by the opposition.

The first of these was Judge J.A.P. Campbell's idea of plural voting, as documented on the front page of the *Clarion-Ledger* in April 1890. He proposed allowing those citizens with real property and larger tracts of land to cast additional votes. Property qualifications had been part of the Mississippi Constitution of 1817, so at least this part was not new.[34] What was original was the co-joining of the ideas of property and universal suffrage. In explaining his idea, Campbell argued, "Our claim is that the intelligence and wealth of the South are chiefly with the whites; and, therefore, they should govern in the interests of all classes." He argued that plural voting deprived no one of the franchise, but put "power in the hands of the intelligent." Campbell believed that in every county whites controlled the land.[35] The following week's paper gave further clarification, in "Dual Voting Plan," in which the plan was correctly labeled "novel."[36] Support for the proposal waxed and waned over the summer, but eventually collapsed. Though well known and respected in the state, Campbell was not elected to the convention, probably an indication of the bedrock opposition to his plan.[37]

Campbell's was not the only novel concept under consideration. Two other proposals to control or dilute African American votes began to take on a life of their own: gerrymandering and woman suffrage. Both of these are more fully covered in chapter 7, but because they began as ideas to control the franchise, they deserve some consideration here. Judge Calhoon and Senator George suggested the use of some sort of reapportionment, relying heavily on gerrymandering, that would ensure white control. Because of the underlying power struggles between black and white counties, this issue moved beyond a race matter and shifted into uncharted class matters. The other controversial subject that began under questions of disfranchisement was woman suffrage. The original concept was closely connected with the problem of creating a voting mass that ensured white supremacy.[38] In pondering the disfranchisement dilemma, John W. Fewell (who represented the state at large and lived in Meridian) supposed that if prosperous white women could vote, then they would add a sufficient number of voters to outnumber African American males. Fewell's original proposal specified that the women should be over twenty-one and have resided in the state for six months, and that she or her husband should own property worth $300 or more. More startling to the modern reader, but certainly understandable to the gender conventions of the Victorian period, was the stipulation that her husband should cast her vote on her behalf.[39] Frank Burkitt, who also represented the state at large and was a firm supporter of the Farmers' Alliance, asked that the petition be moved to the Franchise Committee, for he thought it belonged there, where it would be considered in secret rather than be debated on the floor. R. A. Dean of Lafayette County thought that sending it to committee would imply that there was an implicit instruction from the convention that the proposal deserved priority, which no one could actually say at that time, since the idea had not been debated.⁴⁰ The proposal was remanded to the committee, but it continued to reappear throughout the subsequent two months.

A more mainstream approach than woman suffrage surfaced a few days later, when the proposal emerged that all elections should be by ballot and that official ballots were to be printed by the state. No person should remove the ballots before the end of the day, blind people were to be given help, and a voter could not mark more than one X in a slot. This regulation would create in Mississippi the use of the "Australian ballot," sometimes called the Dortch law (the name it was given in Tennessee), an innovation that was becoming increasingly more popular at the end of the nineteenth century in the country and around the world.⁴¹ Up until this point, Mississippi, like most states, relied on the parties to print their own ballots, which were called tickets. Voters literally cast a party ticket. These ballots were regulated according to size and type of paper, for there had been a number of fraudulent ballots printed and cast in Mississippi and in other states.⁴² Such regulation, however, also lent itself to abuse, as indicated by the controversy over the seating of the delegates from Bolivar County, in which, although the ballots were off only a fifth of an inch, the Democrats were willing to use that difference to cast out the ballots.

The use of the state-printed ballots served to legitimize the idea of reform: the ballots themselves were not as subject to fraud if the state printed them. In addition, the voter would have a choice between candidates of the parties. If voters wanted to "split" a ticket, they literally had to split or cut apart tickets from opposing parties and pin them together to vote, leading to complications in counting and questions of legitimacy. A few groups printed a formal fusion ticket, but that effort required more organization than most were willing to create. The most controversial outcome of the use of the Australian ballot was secrecy. For many, the idea of voting in secret was somehow shameful. Citizens should, according to them, be confident enough to declare preferences and allegiances. To shift to a tradition of secrecy of voting required a change of attitude as to the nature of voting. In addition, to the minds of some, the parades and parties connected to the male voting ritual were essential to the dominant culture.⁴³

The proposal to shift to a secret ballot, however, made sense to a group attempting to circumvent the Fifteenth Amendment's prohibition against curtailing the right of suffrage for African Americans. As the Judiciary Committee had noted earlier, no restriction on voting could be based openly on race. Therefore, if the demand for a secret ballot, based on reform ideals that were resonating across the country, would restrict the number of persons voting, the result would be "good." A printed ballot required literacy, and most delegates assumed that few African Americans could read. Although Mississippi, as with other slave states, had forbidden the teaching of reading to slaves, a number of them acquired the skill one way or another, while others benefited from the efforts of northern missionary women during Reconstruction. Literacy was not universal among African Americans by any means, but the same was true among white farmers, who often had not had the means or opportunity to learn to read. Indeed, the secret ballot had the potential to be the proverbial two-edged sword and therefore did not appear to delegates to be sufficient for their purposes.

The other innovation to control access to the vote was the poll tax.[44] This tax had been used in the United States since colonial times, but for different purposes. Early on, the proposal in the convention was for a poll tax of $2.00, although some counties would have the option to raise it to $3.00, if the money were needed for education.[45] The tax was in addition to the usual regulations of males, over twenty-one, who were "not insane or Indians non-taxed," not felons, and had been resided in the state two years and one year in the county. Old ideas on the franchise had not assumed universal access, but rather limited voters to those with property. By the time of Jacksonian Democracy, universal white, manhood suffrage had become the norm and had certainly been embedded in Mississippi's constitution of 1832. The Reconstruction constitution of 1869 further widened the electorate to universal manhood suffrage.[46] For some delegates, then, an attempt in 1890 to restrict the franchise on the basis of money and standing in society made historical sense. For others, it did not. The poll tax would have consequences for both races, for the money, though small, loomed large to those who had little real income. The fact that the tax would have to be paid ahead of time, perhaps over several years, added to the frustrations. Further complicating the issue was that the provisions imposed no penalty for nonpayment, since the purpose was to reduce the franchise.[47]

The provisions also included a uniform poll tax of $2.00 for males between the ages of twenty-one and sixty, "except for persons who are deaf, dumb, or blind, or who are maimed by loss of hand or foot." This money was to go to schools, but, as noted earlier, there was no penalty for failure to pay. Registration, exactly like the poll tax, was to be limited to males, "not idiots or insane, not Indians not taxed."[48] They were to be citizens of the United States, twenty-one years old, two years in residence in the state and one in the area (although ministers "of the gospel" were allowed to vote after only six months' residence).[49] In addition, men who wanted to register must take an oath of allegiance and also swear that they had not been guilty of "bribery, burglary, theft, arson, obtaining money or goods under false pretenses, perjury, forgery, embezzlement, or bigamy, and who has paid all taxes . . . legally required of him."[50]

The fear of universal consequences to a poll tax propelled the Farmers' Alliance, then meeting in Starkville that August, to petition that the convention not resort to property or educational qualifications to "reform" the state constitution. Alliance members pointed out that such a restriction would affect white men who were economically disadvantaged. Frank Burkitt, the at-large representative who championed the farmers' cause, continued to press this demand throughout the convention, and he also attacked corporations with the same vigor. In contrast, R. H. Taylor of Panola County proposed to restrict voters to those who could read and write and had a demonstrable amount of property.

◆ ◆ ◆

During the first month of the convention the actual debates took place in the Franchise Committee itself.[51] The committee did not keep minutes, at least not ones that have survived. Why they did not is open to conjecture. Certainly there is no evidence of the arguments presented on either side, and that may be exactly what members wanted. Delegates knew they were being watched and did not want to create grounds for opposition. Members of the convention, however, appeared have been more candid about their intentions than prudence allowed. Such debates included the secret ballot. The ballot was to be printed as state official ballots and the expense of printing the ballots borne by the county registries or municipalities.[52] To appease the members who favored fusion options, including the Farmers' Alliance and the old Greenback Party, the proposal included an option for a blank space to be included under the title of each office so that a write-in option was available.[53] A Department of Election Commissioners and the local sheriffs were to oversee the elections and ensure their fairness.[54]

These requirements for access to the franchise were not particularly unusual compared to those of other states in the Union that restricted voting to males over twenty-one. There were provisions that were tweaked, however, to produce a result that would help narrow the franchise base further. For instance, most states forbade voting by persons convicted of a felony, but a careful examination of the list of crimes reveals offences perceived at the time to be mainly African American problems, particularly bigamy. The exemption for ministers is especially interesting, because it is unusual. The proposals also included a provision for helping people who were blind vote, obviously a problem with a secret ballot. Others had to cast their ballots quickly (stipulated to be no more than ten minutes). Section 17 of the proposals demanded that voters had to take care that their ballots not be seen or marked for later identification.[55] In any election, if a group relied on fraud to stuff ballot boxes or exchange the boxes themselves, a voter who marked his ballot might be able to prove fraud. This sort of evidence was not something the delegates wanted. Removed to ordinances in support of the constitutional provisions were sections on official ballots and regulations on the security of the ballot that granted supervision to the local sheriffs. Specifically, provisions stated that if a ballot was unclear as to its intent, it could not be counted. Ballots were to be secret and not shared with anyone.

Particularly unique, however, was the provision requiring that after January 1896 any voter should be able to read any section of the constitution "or explain when read to him or give a reasonable interpretation thereof."[56] Earlier in the session an education requirement had been proposed and then opposed, because of the likelihood of its disfranchising whites along with African Americans. It is not clear who made the first suggestion of an Understanding Clause, but it came to be the avenue chosen to circumvent the effect on whites.[57]

The reporting by the press concerning these novel ideas caught the interest of the nation, and the local *Clarion-Ledger* often reported the reactions, not to mention suggestions, from other papers. These included comments from African American papers and institutions, although the accounts were full of pejorative comments. A good many of the other papers quoted in the *Clarion-Ledger* commented on the proposal for woman suffrage. There was more, however. An editorial by the *New Orleans States* opposed reading as a prerequisite, since illiterate whites were better for the polity than African Americans who could read.[58] A letter from a Mississippian summering in Virginia emphasized that the people in Virginia were watching the convention, for the Old Dominion had similar problems and wanted to see what Mississippi chose to do.[59]

As the weeks passed, interest in the proceedings grew, and citizens of the state faithfully followed the newspaper reports. Because they found it difficult to take down verbatim the invigorating speeches delivered on the floor of the convention, the *Clarion-Ledger* reporters suggested that if the members would give them a copy of the speeches, the paper would publish them the following week. A number of members took advantage of this offer, so that the size of the editions increased.[60] Judge J. B. Chrisman of Lincoln County was one of the first to have his speech printed in a complete form. He continued his argument predating the convention itself for a property qualification, which he set at $250. He admitted that this number meant that most whites would qualify and also a number of African Americans, but the convention needed to remember all restrictions had to apply to all males. He went further in presenting the foundation of his argument in which he baldly stated that no man could be in favor of Mississippi methods of controlling elections since 1875 without being a "moral idiot." The state, he argued, needed a bedrock of integrity for the ballot and for the good of the people. While this convention offered a $2.00 poll tax, the Australian ballot, and apportionment, he stated that none would work well. According to Chrisman, the Understanding Clause did not "look honest, straightforward and manly." He called the Australian ballot a "farce," since it was really an educational qualification under another name and not nearly as effective.[61] Apportionment was founded on the mistaken belief that whites would always vote together. He therefore argued that a property qualification was the only viable alternative, for it "builds the bridges." His "passionate" speech was followed by applause.[62] Agreeing with Chrisman, the *Vicksburg Post* opposed the Understanding Clause as being too subject to corruption by state officials, not to mention allowing the "ignorant" to vote.[63]

In contrast, W. A. Boyd of Tippah County responded in his speech that Chrisman was right at times but wrong at others. Boyd agreed that he also wanted reform, "if possible by honest efforts." Chrisman's reference to the illiterate white voters as "ignoramouses," [sic] however, Boyd declared as a slur on white farmers, thus indicating the state's profound class divisions.[64] Tempers were heated in a number of disagreements. For example, Colonel Fewell and Senator George argued over the franchise. Fewell was still supporting and arguing vociferously for his woman suffrage amendment; George was satisfied with the proposals from the committee. Once again Fewell stated his concern as to whether the proposed provisions by the Franchise Committee would withstand congressional scrutiny. In that vein he asked Senator George what would be his defense on the floor of the Senate. At first George evaded the question, but when pushed, he replied: "I deny here, as I would deny in the Senate, that the educational test was intended to exclude Negroes from voting.... Its sole purpose was to exclude those ... [who had a] want of intelligence." After all, he pointed out, both Massachusetts and Connecticut had an educational qualification.[65] No one, at least in the record, pointed out the obvious conflict between George's statement and Judge Calhoon's opening address to the convention regarding its purpose.

On September 20 the convention devolved into the Committee of the Whole to evaluate the proposals from the Elective Franchise Committee. The advantage to this maneuver was that it could be done without minutes, but since at times the reporters stayed, some record of the debates remains.

The *Clarion-Ledger* reported much of the debates. Chrisman made an "earnest and forcible speech" asking for a property qualification. J. L. Morris of Wayne County rebutted Chrisman's arguments, referring to an old history of the state of Mississippi by Patrick Claiborne, which reported that some early state legislators could not write their own names but were well informed.[66]

The following day the Committee of the Whole resumed further discussion of the franchise issue. Former chief justice Horatio Fleming Simrall of the Mississippi Supreme Court, at times identified as a Republican and at others an Independent, spoke to support the Dortch law, a longer residence requirement, and payment of the poll tax. He reminded members that, when thinking about "the whole issue of the elective franchise," they must protect the "negro in all his rights ... and our young men from the debasing and corrupting practices that have been inaugurated" to control the ballot box and its elections. T. P. Bell of Kemper County agreed, thinking that the Dortch law would have the greatest effect. Revealing strong racial and class divisions, he argued the law would place Mississippi "in control of the white race—the only race fit to govern this country."[67] Boyd objected to any restriction that would destroy the right of suffrage for white men. He believed white male suffrage was a "human right." If the convention resorted to a property or educational qualification, he stated, the result would be the establishment of an aristocracy.

Watching the rising tempers, W. G. Yerger of Washington County rose to speak and to "spread oil upon the waters" of dissension. He admitted that Chrisman was correct in his ethical concerns, for "we cannot continue methods that are as destructive of the youth of this country as fire is to the magnificent forest. We are here to bring order to Chaos. Concessions must be made." As Blair pointed out, the question of what those concessions might be remained the principal issue. He drew attention to the practical problems of Chrisman's proposal, but heeding Yerger's injunction to be civil, he did so in an amusing manner that set the members to laughter.[68] W. F. Love of Amite County, however, supported Chrisman's solution as the only viable alternative that was both honorable and simple. Suffrage, he argued, was not inalienable or natural; rather, privilege is "based on intelligence, honesty, and interest," so they should make the restrictions honorable. He cautioned not to give a right in one sentence and take it away in another. Specifically, he pointed to the Understanding Clause as leading to fraud.[69]

In returning to the debate the next day, members reviewed their options: the Franchise Committee proposal (residence requirements, no conviction of certain felonies, the Dortch law, and the poll tax); extension of voting rights to women who were educated and owned property (Fewell's proposal); plural voting (Judge Campbell's proposal in which those who owned property over a specified amount would be able to vote more than one ballot); and creation of a system of electors, in which a gerrymandering of counties would provide white governors and legislators (Judge Calhoon's proposal). Judge Calhoon's idea seemed to have the least backing, probably because the practical application would be the most tenuous. In contrast, the other two proposals were more straightforward. While agreeing that the Judiciary Committee members believed that the readmission provisions in the 1870 act were no longer applicable, Fewell argued that congressional leaders reviewing the new state constitution were not friendly toward the state and would look for problems. The only way to avoid them was to enfranchise women. He objected to plural voting on principle and thought the poll tax would end up hurting poor whites. He also objected in principle to the secrecy exhibited by the Franchise Committee.[70]

Edward Mayes, a member of the Franchise Committee and representative at large, said the committee's secret meetings were not only understandable but also "wise and justifiable," for its "avowed purpose was an alteration of the whole basis of franchise and necessarily in the shape of restriction."[71] He reasonably pointed out that the report was on trial here, not the committee, and that members should remember that "we are all Mississippians; we are all brothers." When he came to the convention, he had believed that the 1870 act was a problem, but he conceded that the Judiciary Committee could make a better understanding of the issues than he—with a wise, considered, and moderate proposal. It would produce the results they wanted: ensuring control by the white race. After all, he pointed out, the purpose was not to make a Democratic constitution, but rather to help white people.[72]

The Mayes plea for support for the report and civility in the debates went unheeded by many of the delegates. W. S. Eskridge of Tallahatchie County said he could not support the report of the Franchise Committee. He thought the situation was dire, for he counted 70,000 African American voters above the number of whites voting, numbers that indicated freedmen could "overthrow the present civil government." He argued that a two-year residency requirement was not sufficient. While Judge Simrall indicated that young African American males "changed their homes and precincts every year," his own experience in Tallahatchie County indicated these males stayed put, although they did change plantations. The $2.00 poll tax, he added, was too small to give security. Felony restrictions affected only a small number. He added that those convicted, when released, fled to the Delta, changed their names, and started new lives: "White people do not know them and their own race will not betray them." As for the Dortch law, it would be effective to start, since the rate of illiteracy in the state among African Americans was high (which he put at 76 percent based on the 1880 census). The problem was that it would disfranchise illiterate whites as well (which he put at 11 percent); he reflected "that they cannot read is a misfortune, not perhaps a fault." Eskridge did not want to disfranchise them, for white illiterates are "good and honest men" who have "sound judgment [and] good morals."[73] Instead, he declared himself in support of the Campbell plan, which would set up voting blocs through primaries and electoral votes. In addition, he wanted to give more votes to those having property exceeding a value of $250. Eskridge did not think this provision undemocratic because all states originally had either property or educational restrictions. For good measure, he also supported woman suffrage, which he argued was "a matter of right."[74]

J. B. Boothe of Panola, who also served on the Franchise Committee, answered another set of objections, although his concerns have gone unrecorded. From what the modern reader can discern, Judge Chrisman was the leader of the group that objected to the hearings having been held in secret. Boothe reminded people that he served in the Mississippi Senate, where at times committee meetings were held in secret because of the controversial nature of issues. He referred specifically to Fewell's objection to disfranchising any white man and also to the apportionment controversy, but he reminded members that, for the "good" of the state, compromises had been necessary. The report had moved wisely in this direction, but if the members objected, Boothe would simply return home and say that the convention was a failure. That he threatened to leave indicates there was more to this argument than remains in the written records. What the problems were remains a mystery.

Other members disagreed with a property qualification. Irvin Miller of Leake County said that he had come to the state thirty-five years ago from Kentucky, when Mississippi was a poor state with few educational opportunities. Some of these original citizens were still in the state, had fought in the war, had produced large families, and had struggled to survive. These were the people he believed would be opposed to property qualifications. The state Farmers' Alliance had already voiced opposition. While he was not a member of the group, he understood its misgivings; it was not so much the amount of property, but the principle itself the Farmers' Alliance opposed.[75]

The following day the convention moved yet again to the Committee of the Whole. Presiding officer Calhoon spoke to the delegates and reminded everyone that this ought to be a harmonious debate. The committee had been chosen to represent fairly all facets of the interest groups of the state. He supported all the options within the report, with the exception of apportionment, preferring to place control of the state under white counties while differing on details. In particular, he thought it unfair that in the proposed scheme Hinds County would have to give up one of its representatives. Finally, he reminded everyone that the purpose of the convention was to give control back to the white voters of the state through legal means. He made the unusual argument that the "black race" was second only to the white race to run the government, but government could not have both. While he admitted, regarding African Americans, that "we want them here," he asserted, "It was a law of Divine ordination that the white race cannot tolerate divided sovereignty."[76]

By that afternoon, on the twenty-seventh day of the convention, the debate centered on educational and property qualifications. Though delegates expressed misgivings as to how this would affect white voters, none mentioned a concern about African Americans. With an impulsive pull to tangential issues, Gore of Webster County thought that the franchise report itself gave too much credence to Alexander Hamilton's idea of federal supremacy; why the state should have to bend to the Fifteenth Amendment was puzzling to him. Continuing this theme, two delegates argued that they would not "take away from any citizen rights that he now enjoyed."[77]

Efficacy was another issue, beyond the principled objections. Would the proposed provisions accomplish their intentions? A number of delegates opposed the Dortch law as an educational restriction, just under another rubric; one even referred to the Australian ballot as a subterfuge, with the implication that it would be ineffective. William Witherspoon of Lauderdale County argued that the committee did not go far enough. He pointed out that the options included repealing the Fifteenth Amendment, lodging power in certain individuals, having an educational or property qualification, or placing power in certain localities. Auxiliaries to these options would be residency requirements, the poll tax, and woman suffrage. His choice would be not to choose one, but all of these. J. W. Odom of DeSoto County agreed that the report needed additional provisions, for African Americans were accumulating wealth and getting an education and, through natural increase, would remain in the majority. He would take all the other proposals on the table (the Calhoon plan, the Campbell plan, or woman suffrage) to reach the desired end of putting the government firmly and permanently in the hands of white voters.[78]

Which white voters, of course, became the issue, revealing the turbulent class issues of the state. Property qualifications would adversely affect white voters, much as educational ones would. Judge Campbell rose to reintroduce his own proposal of plural voting, which he argued would allow everyone to vote, including African Americans; therefore his plan would not adversely affect the congressional view of Mississippi's proposal. By allowing extra votes for propertied electors, his scheme was simple and cost free, and would solve the issue for many years. Specifically, the plan allowed an additional vote for those with an assessed property value of $250 and two votes for values over $1,500. Alternatively, members might substitute taxes paid of $15 for one additional vote and $30 for two. There were those delegates, however, who were still uncomfortable with any property qualification, whether it added voters or took some away. Frustrated with the debate and pushing the limits of the choices, J. H. McGehee of Franklin County asked if someone was willing to risk his life for a country, why not give up a vote to save it?[79] To that question, no one had an answer.

CHAPTER 6

The Convention Adopts the Understanding Clause

Though the delegates continued to debate the Franchise Committee's proposals for the rest of the 1890 Mississippi convention, none engendered more violent opposition, within the Capitol and without, than the Understanding Clause. This one issue revealed both the open concern and the undercurrent issues of race, class, and power. The fact that the provision passed, in spite of virulent opposition, exposed the power structure in the state and its fragile foundation. Because of its significance, the controversial passage of this clause requires full examination before turning to the other issues before the convention, which are covered in subsequent chapters.

Given the mood of the debate, the editors of the *Clarion-Ledger* suggested that opposition to the Franchise Committee report was growing. They related that the previous Friday night, a caucus of the opposition had met and forty delegates attended.[1] The problem was that these delegates did not agree on a suitable set of proposals. For example, the same editorial page noted the *Vicksburg Post* had called for straightforward educational qualifications, which, according to the *Post*, should result in a white majority of 40,000 voters and so fulfill the charge for the convention. The Understanding Clause would therefore not be needed.[2] The editors of the *Clarion-Ledger* announced they were in support of plural voting; they feared that apportionment based only on race would violate the US Constitution and invite federal intervention. Surprisingly, they concluded that gerrymandering was not honest and that the Australian ballot was too prone to manipulation to be useful.[3] The editors did agree that voting was not an inalienable right, but rather a privilege conferred; therefore, the goal of disfranchisement was acceptable to them. What they could not agree upon was the mechanism, and the Understanding Clause became the flashpoint of opposition.

The one person everyone expected to oppose the disfranchisement proposals, and especially the Understanding Clause, was the sole African American delegate, Isaiah Montgomery. In simplest terms, Montgomery did not act as expected. Rather, he served not only on the Franchise Committee but also voted for the constitution—including the disfranchisement components. While historians have questioned Montgomery's motive, which remains an enigma, his actions reveal far more about the class structure in the state in 1890 than the divisions of race, which became more important in subsequent years.

The question, of course, is why he supported the disfranchisement provisions, for Montgomery was not unaware, uneducated, or poor. Instead he was a leader, wealthy by anyone's terms, and well-educated. To grant him a partial pardon, some historians have explained that Montgomery was a realist who saw the troubles of the time and recognized he could not oppose the destructive politics of the period.[4] Certainly Montgomery argued that a pragmatic approach was part of his reasoning, for he acknowledged the difficulties of the period, calling it a "needless conflict." He went further and stated that the acquiescence to disfranchisement was a "sacrifice" that had "been made to restore confidence, the great missing link between the two races, to restore honesty and purity to the ballot box."[5] Yet even accepting the theory of pragmatism does not address how Montgomery perceived the realities. In addition, there is a difference between accepting reality and colluding with the problems: Isaiah Montgomery served on the very committee that deliberately reduced access to the franchise.[6]

The crisis point came with the publication of Montgomery's speech in the *New York World* on September 27 but unrecorded in the *Proceedings*.[7] Days earlier, the *Clarion-Ledger* noted that Montgomery had made a speech before the convention in support of the Franchise Committee report. The editors acknowledged that "his language was chaste, elegant and grammatical." According to the paper, "Whilst deprecating the disfranchisement of one hundred and twenty-three thousands of his race, he admitted it was a sacrifice for the good of the State." The speech, noted in the editorial space, is not quoted verbatim, although the editors had promised to publish in toto any speech, typed or written, given to them from the delegates. Whether the *Clarion-Ledger* received a copy of Montgomery's speech and refused to publish it, because Montgomery was African American, or whether Montgomery did not provide them with a copy, is unknown.[8]

In the speech Montgomery argued explicitly that "the work of this Convention, in order to be successful must restrict the franchise by prescribing such qualifications for voters as would reduce the Negro vote considerably below the white vote of the State."[9] Montgomery did not stop at this assertion, but went further. He was blunt about reasons for disfranchisement: it offered a way to stop the disintegration of society and stability in the state. To the surprise of many, he argued that "our race has not yet attained the high plane of moral, intellectual and political excellence common to yours."

His speech, however, was nuanced. Forgotten in the turmoil that followed was the request that African Americans be allowed to "press onward and upward." He continued that during the race conflict, "the conditions of the State have languished, while the energies of the best citizens have been wasted in a needless conflict." Permanent settlement of the conflict was impossible, since neither side trusted the other. Montgomery viewed himself as a guide to a bridge over the chasm of misunderstanding until tempers settled. Speaking directly to "my people," he added, "We have not taken away your high privilege, but only lifted it to a higher plane and exalted the station of the great American birthright."[10]

At the same time, he argued that his particular role was to "bridge a chasm that has been widening and deepening for a generation." He then proceeded to remind his listeners, the white members of the convention, of the debt they owed to the slaves who cleared the fields and made the state blossom economically. Following the Civil War, he continued, white citizens had reacted negatively to racial equality and restricted the limits of progress by the black race. For that reason, Montgomery argued, "we still lack confidence in your professions of good will." To restore confidence on both sides, Montgomery believed that the restoration of "purity of the ballot box" would go a long way toward healing the wounds. He pointed out that previously Mississippi suffered from the reality of the suppression of voting by "every form of demoralization—blood-shed, bribery, ballot stuffing. Corruption and perjury stalk[ed] unblushingly through the land." In contrast, the new constitution would provide an improvement over the past and should ensure to the state a "safe and intelligent voting population, capable of comprehending the intricate responsibilities."[11]

Arguably Montgomery had a point: people who are educated and can read make more informed choices. Yet to have failed to understand or believe that the regulations would not be equally enforced is bewildering to the modern observer. What could he have been thinking? Montgomery gave his own explanation of the convention and his subsequent support in the article in the

New York World that included his speech. There he stated that he knew the convention would result in disfranchisement, but as long as the provisions were "fairly applied," he would have no objection. He acknowledged that the provisions would affect "the colored vote to a greater extent, because of their inferior development in the line of civilization."[12]

News organizations quickly picked up the entire speech, which startled both the state and the nation with Montgomery's explanation of his support of the franchise provisions. When the *New York World* published the address in its entirety, many national African American leaders reacted vehemently, claiming that Montgomery was a Judas to his race.[13] Montgomery spent the rest of his life trying to justify his actions and public remarks.[14] Little has changed in the last 120 years, for historians are nearly unanimous in their condemnation.[15] Some have gone so far as to place the entire blame of the Jim Crow era at his feet, arguing that Montgomery was brought up to "serve his white masters"; consequently, "all public acts and utterances marked him a believer in the inferiority of his race."[16] The question in many minds, however, was whether the speech itself, which was a defense of his behavior, or the action behind it was more egregious.[17]

In contrast, others have argued that Montgomery was a victim of the time and had little choice in the matter.[18] Certainly the climate of the convention, as chronicled in the previous chapter, along with the violence preceding the convention and concurrent delegate election, makes this explanation all the more feasible. There are problems with this interpretation, however, for in many ways Montgomery does not fit the pattern of someone caught inextricably in a vortex of turbulence of the period. He had options.

No one would argue that he had an easy time or that wealth came effortlessly to him; yet he was insulated to some extent by his money and connections. While building his fortune, for the most part, Montgomery had eschewed politics, but in 1890 he agreed to run for the position of delegate to the convention for Bolivar County. Once in Jackson, he did not have to serve on the Franchise Committee, much less speak for it publicly in Mississippi and before the nation, but he did.

Some of Montgomery's "people" did not agree with his arguments. The opposition came most often from those outside the state and from those who represented the state but who lived away from it. Montgomery claimed he had warned his own constituents in Bolivar County what he would do if they voted him as a delegate.[19] To fully understand the negative reaction, though, remember that 1890 was five years *before* Booker T. Washington made his famous Atlanta Exposition speech, often cited as an example of accommodation toward the growing racist views of the period. Certainly Washington was moving in that direction before 1895, but the Exposition was a defining moment. Following his Atlanta speech emerged the famous split within the African American community, manifested by the personalities of Booker T. Washington and W.E.B. Du Bois. Yet Montgomery's address preceded this better-known ideological conflict.

The answer to the query about his motivation lies in the life of Isaiah Montgomery and in an understanding that his was a life of privilege, despite his having been born in slavery. Ignoring the issue of race in the South was impossible, for it was central. There were, however, exceptions, and class, in addition to gender, was one area. In anyone's definition of class, the Montgomery family fit the profile of upper class, not middle or the generic term "better." The difficulty in making this argument is that of defining upper class for all races. While race, gender, and class are acknowledged as tools to examine the social and cultural changes in history, class is often ignored or mentioned in passing. This state of affairs may not be surprising when one considers the baggage that the term "class" carries with it as a hallmark of Marxist philosophy.

As historians have moved away from Marxist analysis, the very notion of class has been disputed. Although a number of historians still use class, most analysis is restricted to those in the underclasses or as an effort to understand the movement between classes, whether real or perceived. Others have questioned the concept of whether class, with all its accompanying baggage, is really a useful concept, or whether stratification of society is a better descriptor since the euphemism does not provoke the same reactions.[20]

Throughout the literature, however, a number of recurrent themes define the upper class of a social order: an intergenerational family of power, money sufficient to keep status, education beyond what others have (because that changes over time and place), and, in nineteenth-century terms, a life of public virtue, with obligations to the community (particularly those lower in the social hierarchy).[21] Often these attributes were ones of perception rather than reality, although the illusion of being a member of the upper class could be as important as actually fitting it.

The problem becomes more difficult when examining the nineteenth-century South, which must include the institution of slavery. The Mississippi constitutional convention took place twenty-five years after the passage of the Thirteenth Amendment, but the social order of previous decades and centuries was not forgotten. Indeed, anthropologists argue that in periods of stress following disruption of social norms, social hierarchies, and the resulting obligations, people struggle to reorder the new reality in formats similar to old ways.[22] Attributing these mind-sets and cultural norms to the elites of the states is easy, but that is not the complete story.

Isaiah Montgomery also revealed these attributes, in addition to possessing real wealth. Montgomery's speech included references that meaningfully revealed a mind-set of paternalism. He clearly viewed his responsibility to the people in his community who relied on him as a priority. He thought they deserved his protection, as shown by the sole entry in the *Proceeding*'s index pointing to his comments on the levees. Flooding was a looming disaster, one he knew and understood from his days at Davis Bend, and it now was a problem in the Delta. He had already given testimony in Washington about this issue, and it was important to him and to his people.[23]

Though Montgomery did not ignore racial connections, he simply did not identify with the bulk of his fellow African Americans. He viewed himself as different, and he was. In so many ways, he was a man very much alone, in the convention, among his race, and with his fellow plantation owners. His references to other African Americans as not being educated enough and not as well evolved are also telling. He saw himself as the equal of any man in the room but was extraordinarily careful about not pushing the issue. That was not the same way he perceived the fellow members of his own race. Note, however, that he argued for upward mobility through education to move into a more elevated plane (not unlike Booker T. Washington's position on social uplift).[24] Until that time came he did not want the options closed off for moving forward, and he believed himself responsible for clarifying this opinion.

Why, then, did he believe that the constitution would be administered fairly? He had lived through one of the most corrupt periods in the political and social history of the state. Certainly he acknowledged that reality in his speech, but he goes on to say that the provisions of this constitution were at least better than the intimidation and violence practiced in the past. His call for peace and tranquility between the races is also understandable: how could his town of Mound Bayou move ahead without being left alone to create success? He also asked for honesty and integrity in administering the franchise provisions, but the very fact that he asked for it indicates that he knew there was potential for misadministration.[25] Montgomery's experience had shown him that the better classes of whites would intervene when asked properly; that was what he knew from Joe Davis and a young Jefferson Davis. Moreover, in spite of difficulties with Jefferson Davis after his father's death, Isaiah Montgomery continued to correspond with Varina Howell Davis, Jefferson's widow, until her demise.[26] Even at the convention, when some questioned Montgomery's attendance, others pointed out that he was of a different class altogether, partly because of his close association with the Davis family, and that he was essentially under the protection of that family. Isaiah Montgomery believed therefore that the best classes would ensure that the state would act with integrity.[27] What he did not understand was that the old rules were fast disappearing. Class and social position, although important, were giving way to racial solidarity. It came faster to white Mississippians than to African Americans.[28]

◆ ◆ ◆

The Understanding Clause cut to the heart of issues of class and race. Institutionalizing franchise provisions that would affect the poor white farmer could no longer be accepted without some nod to alleviation of the problem disfranchising some white Democrats. Alignments were shifting. Isaiah Montgomery was a vestige of the past, while Frank Burkitt was a harbinger of the future. The dirt farmer, particularly those in the white counties, had to be assuaged. The problem was that continuing fraud and violence had exhausted citizens of the state, who truly wanted reform. How to manage those conflicting goals engendered debate, and was reflected in a number of issues.

The debates on the floor were not the only discussions taking place in the state. Because of the heated exchanges on the floor of the convention, not to mention the newspaper accounts, the general public wanted to contribute to the options. And since the earlier debates of the committee had been held in secret, this was the first time that the public could make their ideas known. On the twenty-ninth day of the debate on the franchise provisions, a number of delegates read letters from constituents. Irvin Miller of Leake County read a passionate letter opposing any property qualification for voting, as did three other delegates. Chrisman read a letter that agreed to anything but gerrymandering, and Fewell read one letter suggesting that disqualifying some white voters would be all right if best for the state. He did not state whether this correspondent would be one of the people who would be disfranchised.

The debate continued throughout the afternoon, some delegates wanting small changes and others advocating large shifts in the proposals. D. T. Guyton of Attala, a member of the committee, while giving reluctant approval to the report, said that an educational qualification would not work permanently because African Americans were getting an education and were acquiring property. This acknowledgment of realities of the present and the future appeared to have been considered by few of the delegates. Why disfranchise if all they needed was education and property?[29]

Finally, Senator George arose to chastise the members for not being realistic. First he wanted delegates to stop calling the present election system a "fraud," a term that surely would be picked up by northern papers and Congress. He would not call the events of 1877 fraudulent or violent–but rather necessary. Second, he wanted to remind delegates that reference to the founding ideas was fine, but that circumstances changed with the war and subsequent loss. Slaves had become citizens. George reminded the convention that, as a senator, he had taken an oath to defend the US Constitution, and thus he would not infringe on the rights of African Americans. The state could curtail those rights, however. After all, males over twenty-one were always in the minority. "We want," he added, "to make a government of the correct political majority."[30]

In contrast, T. S. Ford, who represented the state at large, was uncomfortable with the way the debates were proceeding. He reminded the delegates that the Fourteenth and Fifteenth Amendments were realities, that northern men had fought and died for their beliefs just as southern men had died for theirs, and that these ideas were held equally dear. Delegates must recognize reality, he argued, and not "shut our eyes" to truth. He was also unhappy with the Australian ballot proposals, which he knew would disfranchise too many, white and black.[31]

Equally worried was George Melchior of Bolivar County, who (along with Isaiah Montgomery) had been threatened earlier with not being seated at the convention. Exasperated, he pointed out the fallacy of claiming a goal of integrity at the ballot box, and submitted certain provisions for the disfranchisement of parties on conviction of election frauds. These were read and then submitted to the Franchise Committee: "Whereas it is the manifest intention of this Convention to secure to the State of Mississippi white supremacy, Whereas, it is desirable that a free and untrammeled expression of the right of franchise be exercised and the honesty and sanctity of the ballot be maintained; therefore be it resolved that the following clauses be engrafted into the State Constitution." He then listed two items for consideration: "Hereinafter no one shall be allowed to vote or hold public office in this State who shall commit any fraud at any election or willfully and intentionally violate any laws of the State in relation thereto." Obviously providing a penalty for ballot fraud was not sufficient to stop such activity unless it could be detected and caught. So Melchior further suggested that the state needed a challenger at the polls "who shall watch the whole proceedings of voting and counting of the ballots and be present immediately with the officers of election at the opening of the polls to the final termination of the count thereof."[32] These proposals from Melchior disappeared in the abyss of the Franchise Committee.

Extant copies of the *Clarion-Ledger* skip from the week of September 25 to the month of October. During that period the debates had continued and were becoming ever more rancorous over racial issues. According to one writer to the *Clarion-Ledger*, African Americans, whom he blamed for all of the problems of the South, should be sent to Africa. In a sudden surge of "compassion," he suggested that the government would pay their way and subsidize the colony for a number of years. Those over fifty years of age could stay in Mississippi, he added in another magnanimous moment, for they would eventually die out and cause no future problems.[33]

By this time the Understanding Clause was causing a vigorous reaction among Mississippi newspapers. The *Clarion-Ledger* quoted the *Memphis Appeal* in joining the chorus for its repeal. The Memphis paper said: "With the very best intentions, and realizing that every power should be placed in the hands of the dominant party and race, the section was adopted, and had the support of such thinkers as Senator George and a majority of the Franchise Committee." The paper admitted that "there was little opposition to it from the press or public at first, because it was considered necessary and expedient.... A change came in public sentiment—a change led by the *Clarion-Ledger*, and other papers of the State, who saw in it something dangerous that would be constant menace to white supremacy." Why the provision was dangerous appeared obvious to the editors: "In the first place it is not honest ... this is not good government ... if a few men unfaithful to the white race should get in power, there is no telling how much damage would result."[34] The Memphis editors were not alone. The *Raymond Gazette* called the clause a "disgraceful absurdity."[35] Although the *Greenwood Democrat* defended George's position, the *Vicksburg Post* saw the inherent problems in George's logic: "men in the Convention ... have determined that no illiterate white shall be deprived of his vote ... not withstanding their apparent contradictions. No white illiterate is to be deprived of his vote."[36]

At this point the convention was in a difficult position. The delegates were seeking a way to navigate the tricky waters of federal laws and constitutional requirements and yet disfranchise a group that these laws required the state not to disfranchise. To bypass this conundrum, the delegates thought they could suit everyone (among the white race) by creating a loophole. A literacy requirement would, of course, disfranchise illiterate African Americans and Caucasians. By allowing an Understanding Clause, Senator George thought he had created the very way to keep everyone happy. The problem was that they had argued from the beginning that one of the overriding reasons for calling a convention was to remove fraud and intimidation from elections and thereby protect the moral development of the young men of the state who were beginning to show signs of questioning the legitimacy of law.[37]

Once the argument for electoral reform began, it resonated with the Democratic constituents. These men were immersed in the ideology of white supremacy, nursed on stories of the "nightmares" of Reconstruction, and schooled to fear a loss of power to people for whom they held contempt.[38] From these nascent ideas, the men moved toward legitimizing their concept of government and defined it as "good." Many of the delegates, convinced of the righteousness of their cause, continued to return to the concept of reform. When the ideas were firmly on the floor, however, the debates began to move in several different directions. Some delegates, supported by the press in the state, viewed the Understanding Clause (called Section Five) as a violation of ethics and morality. While they were not concerned with cheating African Americans out of their votes, they did not like the mechanism that would create an atmosphere conducive to the very fraud they were trying to reform. Others saw the move to an ever more open debate on race and white supremacy as an opening for a more virulent type of racism.

A letter to the editor of the *Clarion-Ledger*, titled "The Everlasting Negro," offers a prime example of the eruption of hatred. The writer argues that if not for African Americans in the South, there would not have been a Civil War, no devastation in the South, no terrible loss of the young men of the nation, no national debt of nearly $3 billion to pay off, no expenditures for pensions, no "necessity for that political revolution in 1875 and 1876." The writer went on to argue that without the presence and "problem" of African Americans, the South would be densely populated and there would have been no Reconstruction, no military rule in the South, and no "Force Bill" pending in Congress. The writer resented good pay for African Americans in federal positions in Washington and in Mississippi, where they served as postmasters and railway agents. He suggested resettling African Americans in Africa.[39]

The conflict over Section Five did not disappear. The following week, the *Clarion-Ledger* included a column that took the clause to task and claimed backing from other newspapers. The editor pointed directly to the uneducated portions of eastern Mississippi, "who have no education at all, but have some claims upon the county." The difficulty with the clause, according to the editor, was the very idea that illiterates should be able then to explain a portion of the constitution when read to them. All constitutions, said the editors, have disagreements, so how could anyone explain something that was unclear and that, in fact, no one really understood. The editors quoted the *Memphis Appeal* regarding the clause: "It is regarded by many of the very best men of the Convention as a manifest sham and a down-right misrepresentation of the courage and intelligence of Mississippians." They believed that the clause was too Machiavellian and would result in disuniting white people. In addition, if the clause were misapplied, there was no remedy.[40] Others delegates were not quite as forceful in their opposition. L. P. Reynolds from Alcorn County wrote to the *Corinth Herald* that he was uncomfortable with the provisions, but he would "take it."⁴¹

The *News of the World*, which had a correspondent in Jackson at the time, quoted Colonel H. L. Muldrow, a delegate from the state at large who had given notice he intended to push for repeal of the Understanding Clause. He found the clause "objectionable in an extreme degree because it establishes no certain test, and leaves it to the fairness and discretion of election officers to determine a most immediate matter. Such a clause could be easily used for the disfranchisement of all illiterate negroes and no illiterate white men." He added that disfranchisement of illiterates should be equally applied to both races, as so eloquently argued by Isaiah Montgomery, who represented to him the "patriotic and self-sacrificing spirit of the colored race."⁴²

By October the last provisions of the constitution regarding the franchise had been negotiated. The Franchise Committee reported on October 10 (day fifty-three) to the convention regarding the Understanding Clause, then numbered Section Three. This wording was more precise and would have disfranchised more whites, for it simply stated, "Persons who cannot read any section of the Constitution of this state, but who are nevertheless qualified electors, shall not be registered."⁴³ This proposal was in direct contrast to a provision proposed by William Witherspoon the previous day, in which he suggested, "Every qualified elector shall be able to read any section of the Constitution of this state; Provided [sic] that the Legislature at its next session may confer the right of suffrage upon any citizen of approved intelligence who has not met the qualification test above mentioned and who is not otherwise disqualified."⁴⁴ Clearly there was comment and discussion around the forthcoming report, and there were still delegates who feared the requirement and what its consequences might be.

When the complete draft of the constitution was read to the assembled delegates on October 10, dispute over the Understanding Clause erupted yet again. By then the section was listed as fifth rather than third. Debate on the clause turned on whether Mississippi should be bound by a US constitutional amendment that violated its sovereign rights, stating that "Mississippi is a free and independent state." Clearly the problem of coordinating their constitutional provisions under the Fifteenth Amendment still rankled the delegates. The debate finally came to a point of order on whether an amendment could be introduced. A 59 to 36 vote allowed it. The proposed amendment, remarkably little changed, read, "He shall be able to understand the same when read to him, or give a reasonable interpretation thereof."⁴⁵ Notably, the convention's proposed amendment did not pass.⁴⁶ Other suggestions for changes to the

Understanding Clause, not specified but supported by twenty-seven signatures, were tabled.⁴⁷ The delegates were near mutiny.

Nor was the *Clarion-Ledger* finished with the Understanding Clause. On the front page in small fillers the editors quoted several other papers that expressed opposition, if not outrage. The *Port Gibson Reveille* voiced disapproval on the simple grounds that it gave room for fraud. Every state, the *Reveille* acknowledged, has some problems with fraud, but no other state actually set up its constitution to shield the deception. The *Vicksburg Post* argued that the convention delegates should strike out the Understanding Clause and simply let the education section stand, although the provision should be placed into effect at once. The *Post* continued that the press, both within and without the state, were firmly opposed. The *Lexington Advisor* said Section Five would "incur the contempt of the honesty and intelligence of the Union.... Such a wicked and silly scheme can be seen through by any man of sense, and is indefensible, morally and politically." The *Monticello Press* agreed, calling it a fraud "more gigantic perpetrated upon the American people."⁴⁸

The *Clarion-Ledger* continued these attacks on the second page of that day's issue, in which the editors called the clause "odious." They again argued that "the Convention was called to put an end to Fraudulent Practices and not to originate swindling devices." They continued by quoting other Mississippi newspapers but then concluded by pointing out that the finished constitution would be difficult to defend in Congress and elsewhere, and thus would jeopardize the entire effort.⁴⁹ Other papers spoke for themselves in nearby columns. The *Vicksburg Post* argued forcefully that the people of Mississippi deserved better, for the clause "rests upon no defensible principle, and stands as a self-confessed sham.... Surely the virtue of the people must be worthy of candor and courage at the very least in whatever may be done in this Convention."⁵⁰

Other editors were equally frank. The *Natchez Banner* said the clause actually set up the temptation to practice fraud, but the *Brandon Republican* went further, arguing that the clause specifically gave judges of elections power to commit fraud, a state of affairs that would be a "lasting disgrace to the state." The *Yazoo Herald* agreed and called it a badly tainted section that "savor[ed] of corruption." Both the *Aberdeen Examiner* and the *Brookhaven Leader* believed it was not too late to change this section and that the convention delegates should move in that direction.⁵¹ In fairness, the paper pointed out that the *Houston Free South* defended Senator George's position, but then went on to refer to other papers that were appalled.⁵²

In addition, the editors argued that the Australian ballot proposal would not work because the literacy rate among African Americans was rising.

Inexplicably the editors then advocated a "true" education clause with proof of schooling. They did not explain why this would work when the Australian ballot, which rested on the concept of literacy, would not.[53] They did point out that Senator George, whom they said had written the clause, had the power to get it changed.[54] Their final plea was that the paper truly wanted the convention to succeed, so that expunging Section Five was imperative.

The following week brought new responses to the convention on franchise issues. A letter to the editor by "Falstaff" pointed out that there had been four possible solutions to the franchise issue: "property qualification, plural voting, educational qualification, and women suffrage." Any of these, according to Falstaff, would have worked. What the convention had done, however, would not suffice, and all that remained to the state were the bills for the convention.[55]

A number of state papers agreed with Falstaff, particularly concerning the Understanding Clause. The *Neshoba Democrat* and the *Magnolia Gazette* printed editorials supporting the stance of the *Clarion-Ledger*. The *Aberdeen Examiner* called the clause a clumsy trap, and the *Natchez Democrat* claimed it was sowing seeds of sectionalism across the state. Both the *Lexington Advisory* and the *Greenwood Enterprise*, which represented different sections of the state, also opposed the clause.[56]

As in the preceding week, page 2 of the *Clarion-Ledger* included extensive references to other state newspapers that objected to Section Five. The *Fayette Chronicle* did not like the subterfuge of the clause and asked who was to judge: "We don't like such subterfuges; we prefer a straight educational qualification." The *Brookhaven Leader* asked that Section Five "be expunged and the honor and fair name of Mississippi and her people preserved." The *Natchez Democrat*, increasing its opposition to the clause, referred to it as an "abomination."[57]

The delegates read these papers, just as had their constituents. Movement began in the hall to rescind Section Five, but there were equally vigorous moves to counter proposals for revision. Almost no personal notes remain from the delegates, but the debates and the shifts of support can be discerned from the newspaper accounts. Muldrow's warning that he was to put forth an amendment was not the only volley to attack the provisions. In response to this deluge of opposition, delegate H. M. Street, a member of the Franchise Committee, offered a resolution to strike Section Five. He agreed that the assumption that registrars would "honestly perform their duty" was "rubbish." At the same time, while not trusting the registrars, he asserted that "the people of Mississippi are honest and honorable. They believe in fair play, the moral sense of the whole people was actually shocked at the passage of this section." He agreed with the claim that the result of the clause would be to create dissension among the white population.⁵⁸ On the fifty-fourth day of the convention, C. K. Regan moved that a supplemental report of the Franchise Committee would be available the following week. This delay did not suit J. H. McGehee of Franklin County, who proposed an immediate abolition of Section Five, but the proposal was voted to lie on the table subject to recall. Under the Rule of Order, if a proposition from a member appeared at the "wrong" time, it could be placed "on the table" and brought up for recall when the subject appeared in an orderly fashion. Such a vote required the proposal to be available when called, rather than ruled out of order.⁵⁹

The *Clarion-Ledger*, though, did not give up its crusade in opposition to Section Five and continued to refer to other editorials in state newspapers. According to the *Clarion-Ledger*, the *Corinth Herald* opposed Section Five, which it regarded as "an open door to fraud and unfairness." The *Carrollton Conservative*, the hometown of Senator George, was pessimistic. The *Conservative*'s view of the convention was that "they failed." To buttress its argument, the paper listed the failures: the elective franchise, county courts, "disfranchisement of the negro" without affecting white voters, the Campbell plan, the Calhoon suggestions. "Failure seems to hover about the capitol and flap its hideous wings over every radical measure brought up for the consideration of the Convention."⁶⁰ From outside the state, even the Baton Rouge *Advocate* elbowed its way in to object, but thought the general will of the people, which opposed an Understanding Clause, would be respected and the provision rescinded.⁶¹

With support from other newspapers, the *Clarion-Ledger* asked why not rescind the clause, especially since the convention would likely not adjourn before the first of November. The paper warned that the Force Bill supporters were watching the state convention and that continued reference to and the passionate debates concerning "fraud, ballot-stuffing, bulldozing and perjury" did nothing but hurt the state in the eyes of the rest of the country.⁶²

In spite of the push by the *Clarion-Ledger* for the convention to at least debate Section Five, the leaders appeared recalcitrant. Judge Chrisman, who held the respect of the delegates, set off a powerful reaction with his blunt and honest speech about the electoral situation in Mississippi for the preceding years: "Everybody in Mississippi who is not an actual idiot understands the meaning of the polite phraseology of 'our present methods.' And the man is a fool who does not know what has been going on in the State for fifteen years. Our nerves are very sensitive to plain, blunt-speaking, and such terms as 'frauds in elections' and ballot box 'stuffing' offend a delicate and refined taste, and grate upon the nervous system." The *Clarion-Ledger* editors pointed out that everyone in the state had been saying the same thing since 1889, including Senator George and most of the newspapers in the state. It asked, "If Judge Chrisman did not tell the truth, what did the Convention come to Jackson for any how [sic]? If everything is pure and sweet why disturb a condition of serenity and repose?"[63]

Exactly how the people of the state interpreted the actions of the convention is confusing at best. About the reaction of African Americans, we know little, for as noted above, no copies of state newspapers for African Americans remain. The *Clarion-Ledger*, however, did reproduce some material from these publications. As regarding the franchise, the editors quoted the *Fair Play* of Meridian, saying: "Let every colored prayer-meeting be turned into a night school and every colored teacher and preacher enter upon the work of teaching our men and women to read. Do away with the midnight dance and the cheap excursion, stop taking Saturday evening vacations and let every negro who can stammer over the alphabet, consider himself appointed by the Lord to teach one another of his race so much as he knows."[64] In contrast, a letter to the editor titled "Southern Candor" expressed the more extreme white view. The writer was concerned that northern newspapers interpreted the convention franchise provisions as eventually allowing African Americans to vote once they gained an education. In a paraphrase of an earlier letter to the editor, the writer stated, "If every colored man in Mississippi were a graduate of Yale, the two races should remain just as widely separated as they are now in all political and social matters."[65] Even more disturbing was the letter from a "Grenada Correspondent," who suggested that the Fifteenth Amendment protected only African Americans; those of mixed-race parentage belonged to neither race, so in those cases the protections did not apply.[66]

State newspapers, however, largely continued to side with the *Clarion-Ledger* in opposing the Understanding Clause. Editors of the papers were not open to wide enfranchisement of African Americans, for they were just as convinced as their fellow white citizens that this would be a catastrophic move. They were, however, unalterably opposed to the Understanding Clause because it was fraudulent and not honest. The modern reader would question conflating integrity and disfranchisement, but the white citizens of the South, especially Mississippi, did not question the need for such a move—in spite of the fact that they appeared to want provisions to be clear and open and not rely on circumvention and extralegal concepts.

The *Clarion-Ledger*, which had taken on the mantle of crusader, gathered together a number of other papers to show the delegates the opposition within the state. This crusade became a desperate attempt to repeal the provision before adjournment, which was looming nearer. While the delegates themselves had started to hit back, calling such editorials "obstructionist," such tactics served only to raise the hackles of the local papers.[67] The front page quoted the *Vicksburg Post* in opposing Section Five; one of the largest papers in the state, the *Post* still held some sway among readers in the Delta counties. The paper added a new twist in arguing that the delegates must themselves be unconvinced of the efficacy of the suffrage sections, for they had extended the terms of office of state officers until new elections could take place two years hence. The *Post* wondered why this delay was necessary if the delegates thought the suffrage provisions adequate.[68]

The *Clarion* quoted the *Brandon Republican*, which called "upon the members of the Constitutional Convention to wipe out, strike out, blot out, kick out that outrageous, unjust, iniquitous, miserable and disgraceful clause in the franchise law, known as the 'Understanding Clause.' Everybody knows that it was put there for the purpose of swindling men out of their votes under the cover of law, and that it is a disgrace to the State."[69] Both the *Crystal Springs Meteor*, south of Jackson, and the *Oxford Eagle*, far to the north, denounced Section Five.

In light of these references, the *Clarion-Ledger* asked the delegates, "Has section five been forgotten? The 'Understanding Clause' needs to go." If the other newspapers were not enough, the Baptists had recently met in both Franklin and Lincoln Counties and had fervently expressed their opposition to Section Five as being simply a provision for fraud. The *Baptist Record* argued that the state was more moral than that, while the *Brookhaven Leader* argued that only two state newspapers, out of hundreds, supported Section Five.[70]

By the next week, the end of October, near the end of the convention itself, the newspaper editors were becoming more desperate in their attacks on the Understanding Clause. The *Aberdeen Examiner* editor wrote that if he had a line item veto, he would vote against the Understanding Clause, but he would also oppose the apportionment scheme, the doubling of the poll tax, the advance of the exemption for the poll tax to sixty years of age, and the Australian ballot; he would then vote for everything else. (One wonders what he had left to support.) The editor of the *Yazoo Sentinel* said he would oppose those provisions and the educational scheme, although he was not clear about what he meant by that phrase.[71] Nearing the end of the convention, the *Clarion-Ledger* realized that changing Section Five was getting more difficult to do. The *Clarion-Ledger*'s editorial titled "The Fraud Stands" pushed yet again for debating the Understanding Clause, but the tone of the editorial suggested a rising frustration. The editors referred to the clause as a "disgrace to the State, a foul blot that should be wiped out. It is indefensible, a monstrous, glaring fraud."[72]

Emotions were running high. A letter to the editor from a "Plain Farmer" was the most revealing, when the writer complained, "the Convention has outlived its usefulness. Let them return to the bosoms of their families."[73] In a belated response to the uproar, Muldrow, having had his provision tabled, asked that there be a reconsideration of the Understanding Clause because of the "universal protest from the press and from the people."[74] Fewell was also concerned. Rather than have the issue debated again, he suggested that the whole franchise debate be handed to the legislature. This was too much for most of the delegates who had worked diligently on the franchise section, and Fewell's proposal was voted down 59 to 39.[75] The convention eventually faced the tabled bills regarding reintroduction of the Understanding Clause. The proposal to reconsider it was voted down 67 to 34. In disgust, the *Clarion-Ledger* referred to the vote with the title "The Clause Denounced by the Press and the People as a Glaring Fraud Becomes Part of the Organic Law of the State."[76] Delegates who opposed the clause were not finished even at this point. Frank Burkitt introduced an amendment to prohibit any property or educational qualifications for the franchise. This, of course, would have changed the entire franchise provisions. Dabney moved that the amendment be sent back to the Franchise Committee, but was reminded on point of order that it would take sixty-eight votes to change any of the franchise provisions.

On the sixty-ninth day of the convention, at the last moment, Muldrow's amendment was called. Each side was allocated twenty minutes to debate the issue. Muldrow argued that the Understanding Clause would lead to more fraud, rather than less. In addition, he pointed out that the press was solidly opposed, and that public opinion also opposed Section Five. As an example, he listed the resolutions by several assemblies, including religious ones that indicated disapproval. Judge Harris spoke in support of Section Five. He denied that the press represented public opinion, and he pointed out that all the provisions on the franchise were interrelated. If the delegates voted to change one section, all other sections would be affected. The Understanding Clause passed with support of sixty-seven votes, only one vote shy of rescinding the provision. The Understanding Clause then stayed in the constitution.[77]

The final draft of the constitution was read to the assembly and passed. Section 240 set up the ballot, and Section 241 limited voting to males age twenty-one and over and those not insane or Indians not taxed; required citizenship and residency in the state for two years and in the district or municipality for one; and required that voters not have been convicted of the crimes listed in the original proposal. Also remaining was an oath of allegiance, the exemption of ministers from the residency requirement beyond six months.

A poll tax of $2.00 was required for someone to vote; the money went to education, but failure to pay the tax did not receive a penalty.[78]

Most significant was the final argument among delegates regarding enfranchisement. As the end of the deliberations neared, the delegates turned to some of the specifics of what they deemed a traditional constitution; arguably there should have been more agreement and less controversy. Yet even here they found dissension in their proposed Bill of Rights. Having completed their charge of disfranchisement, as well as addressing other issues (covered in chapter 7), conflict erupted over the nature of the relationship between the state and the federal government. Even minor word choices suddenly disturbed a number of delegates, such as whether a right derived "from" the people or "with" the people, or whether Mississippi laws had to be subject to the US Constitution or simply not repugnant to the federal provisions. In particular, George Dillard introduced an amendment regarding secession. Since their reentry into the bosom of the Union under new constitutions during Reconstruction, the old Confederate states had to admit, under the contract of reentry, that they would never seek secession again. The choice of words became a delicate game. Dillard suggested "that the State of Mississippi is co-equal member of an indissoluble Federal Union of indestructible States." When this opinion was tabled, Street offered a revision that read, "That the right to withdraw from the Federal Union shall never be assumed by this State." Again this suggestion was tabled. The following morning Senator George, who apparently feared the direction this debate was taking, suggested an amendment to the Bill of Rights that affirmed the superiority of the US Constitution; when this was also tabled, George withdrew it, his point having been made. The strange conclusion by the delegates was that to mention the subject would be rude, since the subject was no longer at issue.[79] The issue of the relationship to the federal government was not finished, however, nor was this debate to be the end of the matter.

Governor Robert Lowry. Courtesy of the Archives and Records Services Division, Mississippi Department of Archives and History.

Governor John Marshall Stone. Courtesy of the Archives and Records Services Division, Mississippi Department of Archives and History.

Governor James K. Vardaman. Courtesy of the Archives and Records Services Division, Mississippi Department of Archives and History.

Senator Edward C. Walthall. Courtesy of the Archives and Records Services Division, Mississippi Department of Archives and History.

Senator J. Z. George. Courtesy of the Archives and Records Services Division, Mississippi Department of Archives and History.

Justice L.Q.C. Lamar. Courtesy of the Archives and Records Services Division, Mississippi Department of Archives and History.

Senator Blanche Bruce. Courtesy of the Archives and Records Services Division, Mississippi Department of Archives and History.

Senator Hiram Revels. Courtesy of the Archives and Records Services Division, Mississippi Department of Archives and History.

Congressman John Roy Lynch. Courtesy of the Archives and Records Services Division, Mississippi Department of Archives and History.

Isaiah Montgomery. Courtesy of the Archives and Records Services Division, Mississippi Department of Archives and History.

Map of Mississippi, based on the Census of 1890. Created by William Pitts.

CHAPTER 7

The Convention Considers Reform Agendas

As covered in the last two chapters, when the Franchise Committee first met, it had several options for disfranchising African Americans. The committee, and subsequently the convention, chose some of these, but two became more complicated, for they involved tangential agendas that quickly took on a life of their own. The first of these was the enfranchisement of women, which at least to modern eyes was more progressive in its foundation compared to the other options. This proposal moved out of the confines of the convention and into a state and then national debate. Though the Franchise Committee eventually rejected the proposal, the convention continued to debate it until the end of the session.[1] The second proposal, reapportionment, was eventually adopted by the convention and is covered in the next chapter. The difficulty was that it placed the white and black counties into conflict over representation and became a battleground, albeit mostly below the surface, over who was to be in control of the state.

What ties these issues together is not race, but rather class. The source of these issues was power: who was to be in charge? As noted earlier, these delegates did not have the same worldview as many other Americans. They truly believed that progress was limited; there was only so much money to go around. Each group wanted to be the beneficiary of whatever money there was, and they wanted to be sure that when they had it, they were not to be taxed by the other groups. This resistance to taxation was as important for the planters in the Delta as it was for the poor white farmers of the piney woods.

Other issues also emerged, foreshadowing the populist movement with conflicts over the obligations of the state to its people and whether protection of the weak against the incursions of the strong (as with corporations, especially the railroads) was an appropriate role for the government. The delegates of the convention split on these lines, much akin to similar divisions revealed around the country: those who championed economic progress and uplift by manufacturing conflicted with those who feared the rise of outside, moneyed influence. The fiscal conservatism of the delegates, who did not want to spend a nickel if they could help it, often encouraged debaters to resort to a charge of higher taxes to help settle any dispute. That ancient red herring of wasteful spending was powerful enough to allow the combative opponents to settle matters.

To fully to understand the fiscal issues of the remaining portions of the constitution itself, remember that race, like taxes, was a strong weapon in any debate, whether education or the structure of penitentiaries. The one issue that appeared to lie outside these pulls was woman suffrage, though it, too, had its roots in racial animosity. Woman suffrage resurrected into a second life when it appeared to have some monetary savings attached to it. Its attraction to some delegates, though, was through the thorny issue of class.

♦ ♦ ♦

Colonel John W. Fewell, who lived in the up-and-coming town of Meridian but represented the state at large, startled the convention when he proposed that women should be granted the right to vote. Although the movement was gaining ground in the West and some states allowed women to vote in school elections, the proposal was shocking to many. Fewell had a very conservative take on the issue. His idea was that if the Fifteenth Amendment prohibited the convention from disfranchising African Americans as a group, then the way around this blockade was to increase the number of white voters in the state. Since, unlike the rest of the country in this period, Mississippi had few immigrants to use as a counterweight, the obvious avenue was to enfranchise women. He did not, however, want to enfranchise all women, particularly not African Americans. What he wanted was to allow woman suffrage if she or her husband owned real estate valued over $300. Her vote was to be cast by a male elector on her written authority. It was a strange proposal based on fear of African American power and on trust in the propriety of the white elites.

Fewell did not originate this idea. According to historian Marjorie Spruill, the credit, oddly enough, goes to Henry Blackwell, a former abolitionist.[2] In 1867, during the confused times following the Civil War, Blackwell wrote to the legislatures of the South suggesting that women be granted the vote to counterbalance enfranchisement of newly freed men. Blackwell continued to argue this point vigorously for the next forty years, but over time he became a bit more precise in his arguments and shifted to advocating that the franchise should include educated women. Blackwell concluded that "unqualified enfranchisement of women would actually compound 'the negro program' in states with high percentages of blacks like Mississippi, Louisiana, and South Carolina, and in the black belts of other states." He believed that enfranchising educated women could offset the "negro problem" and would "insure white supremacy without taking the vote away from those already enfranchised and raising the consequences of violating the Fifteenth Amendment." Blackwell maneuvered an introduction to the Mississippi congressional delegation, received their attention, and then at their request flooded them and the newly inducted delegates with literature.[3] No record exists of a direct connection between Blackwell and Fewell, but the parallels of the proposal and his ideas are too closely aligned to be ignored.[4]

The response to Fewell's proposal for woman suffrage was immediate. Frank Burkitt, delegate from the state at large, rose to request the proposal be sent to the Franchise Committee. Fewell, who did not want the proposal buried, answered that since the convention was the master of the committee, why relegate it to the committee? A few members rose to support Fewell, such as Odom of DeSoto County and R. A. Dean of Lafayette County. Though Odom supported the idea, he suggested that the proposal properly belonged with the committee.[5] A letter to the editor of the *Clarion-Ledger* also approved of the proposal. The author, signed "Wide Awake," suggested that the fear that women would be contaminated by the rowdiness of elections was untrue; in fact, women did not even have to use a male elector to cast their ballot. Rather, they could arrive by carriage with much the same safety issues as simply going shopping. According to "Wide Awake," women were more worthy electors than the "sons of Ham," who had not participated wisely in elections. For support, the author pointed to Wyoming, Kansas, and Massachusetts, which by 1890 allowed some limited voting by women.[6]

At first the *Clarion-Ledger* thought the proposal clever and pointed out that it would solve many residual issues regarding disfranchisement and African American voters. The idea of enfranchising, rather than relying upon controversial disfranchisement, appeared nearly too good to be true.[7] Even the *Commercial Herald* noted that enfranchising women opened no constitutional objections, but that was before the reactions set into play.[8] On the twelfth day of the convention, several absences were noted for the first time. Irvin Miller, ever a quick wit, thought that the delegates had returned home to visit wives and babies. Another delegate countered that it was really to get instruction on female suffrage.[9] When a proposal becomes a joke to some, then laboring for support becomes more difficult. The *Daily Commercial Herald* printed a letter from "Senex," who wrote he first assumed woman suffrage a "light hearted proposal," but had realized some people were serious.

He did not think woman wanted to be taken down from their "present exalted state." Moreover, if such a proposal passed, would not women want to be considered for public office, an idea he found ridiculous.[10]

By the first of September the *Clarion-Ledger* could print a number of responses. The *Winona Advance* suggested that women themselves should oppose such an outrageous proposal, while the *Memphis Appeal* claimed that the chair of the committee, R. C. Patty, was right to oppose woman suffrage.[11] Other newspapers in the state also voiced their opposition, including the *Neshoba Democrat*, *Tupelo Journal*, and *Democrat Star*. The *Journal* explained its opposition with the old argument that the "sanctity of the home is the true mission of women." The *Star*, blunter, argued that women "already have rights enough and we are opposed to giving them any more."[12] The *Clarion-Ledger* had not yet fully changed its position. Its editorial page provided a lengthy article about which states allowed some sort of woman suffrage. Wyoming was alone in allowing full suffrage; seventeen others allowed woman voting on school-related issues. Only three of the states were southern (Tennessee, Kentucky, and Louisiana).[13]

What bothered the *Clarion-Ledger* were three points: reactions of other newspapers, reactions by outsiders, and effectiveness of the proposal. Within the state the *Clarion-Ledger* identified only the *Biloxi Herald* as supporting female suffrage. On the same page, it asked whether the proposal was making Mississippi the laughing stock of the nation and worried whether it was manly to hide behind petticoats. Even the *Memphis Appeal* suggested that Mississippi not "conscript" women to solve an issue among men; the *Appeal* wondered what the "scheme of female suffrage" would do in the "Delta with ten negro women to one white lady." This new concept was startling to several delegates, since the issue of disfranchisement had always centered on how to disfranchise one race without affecting the other. The assumption had been that enfranchising women and having a property qualification would suffice to create a white pool large enough to outnumber African Americans. Then they started looking at numbers, just as Blackwell had done.[14]

African American ownership of property had grown with time, but there were still people who were blind to the new realities and assumed that all African Americans had nothing. Some had noticed the changes, as seen in a letter to the editor entitled "Female Suffrage"; "Swamper" from Hollendale pointed out that African Americans also owned property and that the subsequent numbers could have African American women "swamping" the vote of white women.[15]

Despite vigorous opposition, Colonel Fewell continued to conduct the effort to enfranchise women like a military campaign. Unfortunately, he began to take personally the attacks on his idea. Fewell read telegrams on the floor of the convention backing the proposal but was countered by an equal number on the other side. Convinced that his cause was right and more ethical than disfranchisement shenanigans, Fewell shifted from a Machiavellian approach to the franchise to a simple moral claim that women "were entitled to it."[16] From this vantage he attacked Senator George, the author of the franchise sections. Fewell did not believe that a new constitution written as George wanted could be defended on the floor of the US Senate. When pressed, George initially evaded the question until he finally exploded: "I deny here, as I would deny in the Senate, that the educational test was intended to exclude Negroes from voting.... Its sole purpose was to exclude those [with a] want of intelligence." After all, he pointed out, Massachusetts and Connecticut had educational qualifications, which would give Mississippi shelter from accusations.[17]

Notwithstanding opposition from numerous state newspapers, Fewell picked up some impressive support, including that of General S. D. Lee of Oktibbeha County, who believed that women could solidify white supremacy; the general pointed out that women were just as patriotic as men and would be willing to do their duty. Lee deplored the present lawlessness used to preserve white control of the state.[18] In a passionate speech Fewell admitted he thought that the readmission requirements to which the state had acquiesced in 1870 were no longer applicable, but the state would have to defend the new constitution in Washington before unfriendly political groups. Objecting to the alternatives of plural voting as undemocratic, he believed the use of the poll tax would end up hurting whites in addition to African Americans (as in Virginia), so therefore the most reasonable alternative was woman suffrage.[19] The following day W. S. Eskridge, delegate from Tallahatchie County, agreed with Fewell on moral grounds. He saw it as "a matter of right" since women were "intellectually our equal," especially if they owned property and paid taxes. Further, he viewed the opposition to woman suffrage as "sentiment and assertion, not reason." Reliance on the old assertions of domesticity was peculiar, for it made the women of Mississippi "weak and feeble." Granting them the franchise would only extend the "sphere and field of her virtues."[20]

Several delegates rose to express opposition to the proposal. J. H. Jones, from the state at large, agreed that his opposition was based on sentiment, but sentiment could be good. He acknowledged that women were intellectual equals and virtuous but that there was a set limit on their abilities. As an example, he claimed, that if she voted, she must also bear arms. He concluded on a high note that never in history had there "been a grander or nobler civilization than the South."[21] As the convention delegates began to bicker about the franchise proposals, D. S. Johnson of Chickasaw County rose to bring the convention back to the central issue. He asked why should delegates argue, for "negro dominance" might result if the convention failed in its duties. Others agreed. E. O. Sykes of Monroe County reminded the convention that hope lay in unity and pleaded for unity.[22] Odom said he thought any of the proposals might be helpful, for what had already been suggested was of limited value. African Americans were accumulating wealth and getting an education, and they were also gaining population through natural increase. Therefore to be more effective it behooved the convention to consider additional qualifications, such as the Calhoon plan, the Campbell plan, or woman suffrage.[23] Taylor of Panola County went a step further and suggested expanding suffrage to males and females eighteen and older. Others, though, continued to object, including one delegate who referred with loathing to Susan B. Anthony and "other strong-minded women of the North."[24] Fewell, frustrated with the continued attacks, asked that those supporting the proposal gather that evening in the Senate chamber.[25]

As the debate progressed in the following days, delegates moved to include (within the constitution) language that would emancipate married women forever "from disability on account of coverture." Delegates noted that Mississippi had been "among the first of the political bodies of the world, to brush away the technical subtleties which surrounded the common law rights (or rather wrongs) of married women; so that today a married woman is as good as a married man in Mississippi."[26] The convention continued to reword and strengthen the emancipation clause until, at the last minute, by motion of Taylor, the clause was removed.[27]

Exactly why both proposals (woman emancipation and suffrage) disappeared is open to conjecture. Certainly the support was there from some influential people.[28] Eventually the state would move in that direction, but not in 1890. What appears to be the case is that the white counties, representing lower-class white men, won this debate. Proposing voting rights for women, when men—white and black—were losing the franchise was more than many delegates could handle.

◆ ◆ ◆

Other issues before the convention also took on the cloak of reform. Like the issues of the franchise and the urge for white supremacy in the state, reform did not always work out for the best. Temperance was a reform almost entirely run by women through the churches, but regulation or prohibition of liquor threatened taxes that supported levee building or repair. In education, for example, the results were mixed, and left some long-lasting problems. In penal reform, circumstances were bettered for convicts, but much was left undone.

Most of these reform issues derived from morality taught by churches in the nineteenth century. Religion was important to the culture of the state, and whether or not individuals were true believers, the culture demanded acquiescence to its strictures. Denominations also demanded strict allegiance. Church attendance was expected to the extent that normal inquiry among newly introduced people was what church someone attended. Baptist men did not date Methodist women, and vice versa. Even if they could barely read, people knew the differences among denominations. But not only did they know and discuss theological differences, they also perpetuated earlier splits between northern and southern sections of denominations.[29] Presbyterians might still use the same catechism, but northern and southern congregations did not reunite following the war. A few, like Catholics and Episcopalians with allegiance to authorities outside the United States, had not divided over theological or political controversy.[30]

Denominational decisions among African Americans were more complicated. Most elected not to remain in the balconies of white churches but rather formed their own congregations. Whether they remained under the authority of the older white churches depended greatly on the organizational structure of a denomination. For instance, among Presbyterians, African Americans eventually formed a synod of their own, the Presbytery of Ethel, but they were members of the larger Southern Presbyterians. Others moved in similar directions. Black Methodists had several options, and churches in the state reorganized themselves a number of times during the latter part of the century. By 1890 the largest African American church membership in the state could be found in the varying options of Methodists, with the Baptists following some distance behind, and the Presbyterians at a distant third.[31]

With the strong influence of church membership came not only affiliation with a particular community and its support system but also to a wider belief in the cleansing influence of Christianity within a larger context. Reform was an obvious next step. Women formed missionary societies focused on local and foreign needs. The largest single area of reform through the churches involved temperance.[32] Before the war, temperance had been a strong movement, but it took on new vigor following the war, galvanized by the realization that many young men had taken to drink during the war and the upheavals thereafter. In consequence, temperance supporters radicalized to prohibition, usually with the hope that such action would curb violence and lawlessness, and reformers shifted from state control to a county option. The first of the counties to go dry was Lawrence in 1880, followed by others. Sale of intoxicating beverages was prohibited on Election Day.[33] Though some people blamed intoxicated African Americans for the rise in crime and lawlessness and thought that prohibition might solve the problem, many African Americans worked tirelessly for temperance. Isaiah Montgomery, noted by one author as the "leading Negro of the state," reportedly pushed "fully to the dry side and caused practically every Negro vote in the county [Bolivar] to be for local option."[34]

These efforts attracted the notice of the Woman's Christian Temperance Union (WCTU). Francis Willard, the founder and president of the group, came to Mississippi in 1882 and spoke across the state, including to the state legislature. Subsequently membership grew, as did interest. The standard joke was that the work she performed should grow, for it was literally sown under water: it rained the entire time she was in the state.[35] By 1886 the state had passed legislation allowing counties to vote themselves dry rather than wait upon the legislature to ban alcohol sales.[36]

Although eventually men were involved, women led the temperance movement. It was perceived as a woman's issue, for it affected their lives in an immediate and personal fashion. In some minds, however, the connection between prohibition and woman suffrage was all too apparent and therefore should be avoided.[37] One writer of the time referred with pride to his wife's involvement, which also entailed his tagging along to the union meetings and his subsequent election as an honorary life member. His involvement was so controversial, however, that an unsuccessful attempt was made on his life in 1883.[38] Indeed, violence over the issue spread and even took on racial overtones. In 1886 both sides accused each other of using African American voters to buttress their votes; in particular in Hinds County, the accusation was that the wets were plying African Americans with drink to vote their way. A leader of the dries, Dr. G. W. Luster, was ambushed and stabbed when returning home from a rally, but in retaliation he shot and killed two of the attackers. Another prohibitionist accused a wet promoter, Jones Hamilton, of having defrauded the state over convict leasing to the tune of $80,000. Hamilton killed his accuser, admitted to it, but then the jury acquitted him. In Winona, a set of editors took sides over the Hamilton trial and subsequent acquittal and ended up shooting at each other. Similarly, two editors in Jackson argued over the same Hamilton trial and shot and killed each other.[39]

As early as 1874 the state legislature agreed to consider petitions from female reformers, long before they considered enfranchising women.[40] Following Restoration only two years later, legislators changed their minds about women's participation, though it is not clear what precipitated the change. There were efforts from the antiprohibition leagues to attempt to make such petitions and votes difficult to manage. As the state slowly went dry, county by county, the die was cast, and by 1907 only seven counties remained wet.[41] In the 1880s, however, the end was not yet in sight. A growing number of prohibitionists began to fear the increasing influence of the remaining African American voters who could tip the election either way. Though a number of African American leaders pressed for a dry vote, white voters firmly believed that African Americans were malleable and open to bribery. To make the state safe, they believed, voting needed to be regulated.[42]

Levee support from saloons was not the only concern conflicting with temperance values, which were gaining support in the state. Early in the convention, a group of women from various temperance groups petitioned the convention to prohibit state licensing of saloons, houses of prostitution, lotteries, and gambling houses. Support appeared strong, for among the seventy-five counties in the state, forty were already dry. Backing, though, was not universal. In a satirical letter to the *Daily Commercial Herald*, one man warned that "a Prohibition oaf has quietly gotten into the meal tub" of the convention on the pretext of saving Mississippi from the "menaced domination of ignorance" and is "seeking to wipe out the dram shops of the State. Ye innocents abroad, look out for squalls."[43] One member argued, however, that the remaining counties were wet because of the African American vote.[44]

Although the issue continued to emerge, the committee charged with evaluating a state position on prohibition returned the report with the explanation, "the subject is not of sufficient importance to engage the attention of the Convention."[45] Specifically, the committee members argued that the real issue before the convention was white supremacy and that temperance was merely a diversion. The minority report, written by Chrisman, strongly objected. He argued for a compromise, stating that white people "understood" the problems of liquor but did not want state prohibition. Therefore he proposed that saloons be declared a "public nuisance" and may be "suppressed." The editors of the *Daily Commercial Herald* believed the proposal to be dangerous, for it would give the state no revenue, create a black market for drink, and solve nothing other than to create a tyranny by the state.[46]

The debate continued the next day. Chrisman suggested that saloons were "un-American" and were brought here by foreigners.[47] Others thought that county option was sufficient: if a county wanted to be dry, then they voted to prohibit alcohol. As former governor Alcorn pointed out, saloons existed because people wanted them. When called for a vote, the minority vote failed, 72 to 17. Yet the *Daily Commercial Herald* correspondent stated, "The convention is believed to be largely in favor of prohibition, and the minority report was lost, because it was deemed inexpedient for the convention to take action proposed therein."[48] The convention delegates did not vote the state dry because they believed white supremacy was more important.

A recurring theme, though, was whether some of these reform issues rightly belonged in a constitution or whether they were correctly to be given to the legislature to decide. The issue of temperance was certainly questioned as to its appropriate inclusion in the constitution. In particular, this was the argument of Fewell, Martin, and Dillard. Senator George pointed out that it was not a subject included in the conversation in calling a convention; therefore it should not be added to the constitution.[49]

◆ ◆ ◆

The issue of education was not so easy to ignore, though eventually delegates also began to question the appropriate nature of its inclusion within the document. Moreover, the issue exposed the rifts between the elites and the dirt farmers as well as between the races. For many, state-funded education was a new development, and citizens of the state divided over its efficacy. Only during Reconstruction had the state created a public school system for both races. A state board would appoint county officials responsible for administering their programs. According to state law, each school district had at least 3,000 in population and was to educate students between the ages of five and twenty-one for at least four months a year. For both races, only about a third of eligible students actually attended, since there was no attendance policy until nearly the First World War.[50]

Of interest to people and politicians was the problem of funding education, especially since it cost money, and a lot of it. Funds came from liquor licensing and tax levies. Salaries depended on the level of teacher qualification, but were grievously low; yet in 1873 they were set even lower because of complaints from taxpayers. In particular there were those who complained about funding African American schools, for too few African Americans could pay taxes.[51] In addition, state requirements for standard textbooks seemed outlandish and arbitrary to dirt farmers who were not even sure schooling was necessary and not a bizarre experiment.[52] It took some time for people to adjust to the need for public schools, but by the late 1880s a push began to improve quality. For example, teacher examinations became a requirement, although 70 percent failed in the first attempt. Improvement came. Salaries also increased with passage of qualifying exams by teachers. Normal schools increased in size, and the quality of instruction also improved. By 1885 the State Teacher's Association began annual meetings.[53]

Recovery of higher education took a while. The University of Mississippi (Ole Miss) reopened following the war with only five professors.[54] Fearing a push for integration, the state set up Alcorn University for African Americans in 1871 under auspices of the Morrell Act. Hiram Revels, the state and the nation's first African American United States senator, became the first president.[55] Also created under the act as a land-grant institution, as well as through the efforts of the Grange, was Mississippi Agricultural and Mechanical (Mississippi State), which was chartered in 1878 and opened two years later. The trustees of the college were Grange members.[56] Women also received their own public college in 1885 in Columbus. The state had promised but had not funded a woman's college in the years earlier; by the 1880s the state had a growing realization of the need for teacher education, which was rapidly growing into the concern of women.[57]

Private education, whether lower or higher, had been present since the founding of the state in 1817, but it also struggled in these years. Many of the colleges were supported by religious denominations and, given the economic difficulties of the later nineteenth century, struggled to survive. Mississippi College, which was founded before the war and stayed open during the conflict, continued to struggle.[58] The Methodists opened Millsaps College in Jackson in 1888 through the beneficence of a local banker, Major R. W. Millsaps.[59] A number of smaller institutions survived, such as Blue Mountain Female College, which, though family owned, eventually made formal connection to the Baptist Church.[60] The financial support for African American colleges was equally precarious, if not more so. Tougaloo, founded in 1869 by the American Missionary Association, managed to stay open by being named a state normal school for African American teachers, so the state gave some money for support. Shaw College in Holly Springs eventually became Rust College in 1890, also a normal school.[61]

Despite the parallel growth of these private schools, for the most part the state concluded that public education was desirable. In addition to a committee report on education, the convention relied on the advice of the president of the University of Mississippi (Mayes) and the president of Mississippi A&M (Lee). The majority report produced by the convention's Education Committee emphasized that the "stability of a republican form of government depended mainly upon the intelligence and virtue of the people."[62] The report, by President Lee of the agricultural college, advocated keeping a number of the specific details of the previous years: keeping state and county superintendents (though their term of office lengthened), relying on a poll tax to create the base school fund (though adding money from the state general fund), and allowing counties to add more funds. The counties would divide the money based on the number of school-age children within the district. A minimum of four months of education would be required. In addition, schools had to be segregated.[63]

President Lee admitted that the committee was not unanimous and in fact held sharply differing views. One of the most important differences was the question on whom the burden of education rested: the state or the county. As noted earlier, county funding differed dramatically across the state; black counties argued that the white ones simply were not supporting their own schools. White counties responded that they did not have the means to fund schools as in the Delta. The majority report wanted to pass the burden to the counties as in the past; but the minority report, espoused by Jamison, argued that education was a state issue and ought to be run by the state to ensure equalization of money to each county.[64] The issue did not die and was eventually picked up by Burkitt, who reduced the argument to the pressing need for educating white children in white counties.[65]

How much education the state should fund, for whom, for how long, and what should be taught became the issues. In 1890 most of the education in the state was conducted in one-room schoolhouses, and it was all most of the delegates knew.[66] A high birthrate in the South, coupled with its poverty, put a strain on the region unmatched in the North.[67] A letter from Holly Springs started much of the debate. The writer suggested that the state get rid of higher education, for common schools were good enough for manual labor. After all, what more did men need in an agricultural state? Underlying his argument was a fiscal conservativism that would not loosen itself for education.[68]

Most of the debate recorded in the minutes or the local newspaper had to do with the lower schools. Debates within the committee were not recorded, or, as with others, if they were, have not survived. The question focused on which age groups the state should target. Should it be seven to twenty-one, younger or older? The appropriate ages continued to be debated until the last day of the convention. At first this age span was guaranteed only elementary education, available at least four months every year, and restricted to reading and writing, arithmetic, and English grammar, "and no others."[69] As the debate continued, however, not only did the age group shrink and expand, so also did the subject areas to include reading, history, grammar, arithmetic, and writing. At one point the delegates questioned whether children could learn to read earlier than age seven, making education available for an earlier age group moot. Miller objected, saying that his four children learned to read early and that all children should have the opportunity to do so. But Mayes objected, arguing few would learn earlier than age seven, and the function of a school, he added, was to offer an education, not to be a nursery. On reflection, he admitted that since many children started work at age ten or twelve, why not let them start school early.[70] Surprisingly, the delegates then referred to eventual plans for high schools.[71]

Fiscal conservatism regarding schools paled in comparison with racial matters. There was always someone who wanted to know how much a particular idea would cost the state, but the race issue shifted the question to how much the state was obliged to pay to support the education of African American students. No one questioned the need for segregated schools, for that provision slipped in without debate, but some went a step further to the support of African American schools.[72] Given the racial animosity and the pinched wallets, the question (though repugnant today) was not illogical. The minority report argued that tax monies from the state should be divided by race: white taxes should go to white schools and black taxes to black schools. The logic behind the minority report was disturbing: "Under present conditions, with a large majority of the educable children belonging to a race which differs from that which pays the cost, a race which contribute but a small part of the moneys called for, and which seems to grow yearly more alienated from our own; it is not to be expected that our people shall fail to look with a jealous eye on the creation and distribution of a fund so enormous and so partial in its results."[73]

The proposal was referred to committee to evaluate its practicality, not to mention its potential constitutionality, and even though the committee reported back in opposition to reducing support for African American schools, some members continued to press the idea on the convention floor. S. W. Robinson of Rankin, a white county, offered one proposal: "That the legislature shall have power to so separate the school fund that the white schools shall be supported by funds collected exclusively from the white race, and the colored schools shall be supported by funds collected exclusively from the colored race." That afternoon, R. F. Abbay of Tunica County, fearing yet another bitter division between black and white counties, proposed a compromise: "The money thus collected shall be retained in each county for the education of the race from which collected, to be apportioned as the Board of Supervisors of each county may direct."[74] This issue did not go away, for it cut along lines of race and class. Witherspoon, that same day, pointed out that African Americans were pushing ahead; literacy requirements soon would be undercut by education. At the same time, poor whites would be denied the franchise.[75] No one missed the point that the future of disfranchisement depended upon an illiterate African American population.

One of the problems that some of the delegates identified was a long-term trend among African Americans to get an education. Odom of Desoto County saw the strengthening of education as a two-edged sword.[76] D. T. Guyton of Attala, a member of the Franchise Committee, agreed. If education could be restricted, long-term control could be ensured. White students would get an education and African Americans would not.[77] W. F. Love of Amite County said the ages of seven to twenty would be suitable, since those still in classrooms after age twenty were African Americans, and Muldrow, on hearing this comment, reminded delegates that African Americans might use the state's largesse to "move ahead."[78] In fact, Muldrow argued, that opportunity was exactly what was needed so that African Americans might be prepared for citizenship. Additionally, Muldrow wondered if separating tax monies by race would violate of the Fourteenth Amendment, and Judge J. J. Chrisman agreed such division was problematic. James Henry Jones, a delegate from the state at large, said that he could not "endorse the doctrine that education made a man a worse citizen." General Lee cautioned delegates to remember the Force Bill, for if the state did not educate African Americans, the federal government would. At this point former governor Alcorn called for sanity and conscience, while H. J. McLaurin of Sharkey County bravely said that he believed the convention had gone far enough against African Americans and should call a halt.[79]

This rallying of the paternalists among the delegates did not sit well among some citizens in the state. One writer to the local paper argued that "if this [threat of education] were really the case, the blacks could afford to accept the proposed restrictions and go to work to qualify themselves accordingly, thereby removing all cause of discrimination against their race. But the fact is that the whites have no such feeling upon the subject. They do not object to negroes voting on account of ignorance, but on account of color."[80] Paternalists were not ready to admit to this bigotry. And, in fact, the measure to allocate money equally among the races passed and was applauded by the Vicksburg paper. The editors noted that while African Americans did not pay as much in taxes as the laboring class, they created the "product that produced the taxes"; therefore they "should reap the benefits."[81]

◆ ◆ ◆

In addition to education and temperance, another area of concern by the churches was convict leasing, a system that ostensibly had existed for thirty-three years before abolition, but in reality had endured for longer. During the military occupation immediately after the war, when labor was unstable and money short, military officers resorted to leasing convicts. In 1872, already recognizing the problems inherent in the system, the state legislature tried to limit its use to public works, but the promise of quick wealth through little effort lured too many planters. The legislators simply argued that this system cost the state nothing and so was reasonable, although they did limit length of contracts to expire no later than 1880. Following Restoration, with the heavy push to save money under any circumstance, the legislature developed the idea of leasing convicts to industry or agriculture. Instead of draining money from the treasury, convicts would be making money, albeit a small amount. The contracts themselves, though, were profitable. There were whispers of concern, but according to one politician of the time, the complaints were "stifled" and failed to reach the "legislative ear."[82]

Despite the lack of a full public protest there were small adjustments to the system, but those came at the expense of the convict, and there was no "champion" for the convicts themselves. The state merely asked that the lessees treat the convicts humanely, but no effort was made to check on conditions. In fact, in 1880 rather than viewing convict leasing as a remedy for state outlay, the state realized money could be made from the convicts. Legislators wanted a share of the profits for the state, a situation resented by many of the lessees. The legislature created a Board of Public Works, but again this creation was only to benefit the state coffers and the old system continued. The state did require a payment by the lessees of $50 in addition to convict support, and so casually looked at some of the conditions of these leases. Yet, according to investigators, "these perfunctory efforts were of little practical good, for the evils of the leasing system were a part of the system itself and its entire destruction alone could correct them. These feeble and mistaken efforts to better the conditions showed, however, an evolution in the public mind which boded no good to the system."[83]

The matter came to a head in the 1880s. At the start of the legislative session of 1884, the *House Journal* included a reference to the unsatisfactory convict leasing system, but gave no further explanation.[84] Later that year, eighteen convicts were shipped from the Delta through Vicksburg to the prison hospital in Jackson. Local citizens were horrified at the condition of the convicts, who were waif thin and showed scars, as well as broken fingers and toes. Investigation by the legislature revealed abuses that needed a remedy, and several contracts were canceled immediately.[85]

What the state should do about convict leasing became a source of controversy and discussion over several years, even among politicians who were always seeking a cheap remedy. Immediately after the Vicksburg reaction, its state representative, Marshall Miller, moved for an investigation, which was approved by the House. The subsequent report was not published by the *House Journal*, and although a few newspapers did publish it, the report itself has been lost. The report listed the abuses the committee found: "cruel and brutal punishment, bad and insufficient food, open houses, affording no shelter, quarters crowded and filthy, scanty clothing, heartless neglect of the sick, overwork, cruel exposure to the cold and wet weather, and as a corollary, an appalling death rate, the evidence taken showed that some of the convicts had died under the terrible punishments inflicted."[86]

The citizens of Mississippi were outraged, but nothing was done, for "the leasing system was strongly entrenched, with a powerful lobby to work for it." The fact that the state itself was culpable added to the problem, for it benefited from the system. What was needed was a set of powerful advocates for reform, and so Frank Johnston and J. H. Jones began their own lobbying efforts. Johnston had reached the position of captain during his service to the Confederacy. Afterward he practiced law, until he served as state attorney general between 1893 and 1896. Jones, who also had served in the Confederacy, was a state legislator and eventually senator. He would later serve at the 1890 constitutional convention as an at-large delegate and then as lieutenant governor from 1896 to 1900. Even before Jones joined him, Johnston began a one-man publicity campaign to keep the issue before the public by writing columns and editorials for several papers in the state.[87]

The campaign was effective, for in 1886 the state legislature decided to investigate. Legislators immediately found they had a problem of their own making. The state penitentiary was not sufficient to house the number of convicts (estimated by Jones as 800 to 1,000 men) that would be returned to the state's care. The large number of convicts was a direct result of a misguided state legislature, which had passed a law stating theft of a domestic animal, even if valued under the usual threshold of $25, would be considered a felony, and thus required a prison sentence. The result was not deterrence, but rather a swelling of the number of convictions in the state. Nevertheless, the state decided to modify the system rather than to create something new. In 1888, having dawdled, the legislature sent out its board of control to investigate. This newly resuscitated board was composed of the railroad commissioners, who were deemed to be the best men in the state. Because the lessees knew when the board was arriving, they threatened the convicts so they would not talk. Yet the members of the board discovered enough to disquiet them, and their report made particular reference to cruel guards who were themselves underpaid.[88]

Despite a death rate of over 15 percent, the commission was willing to excuse the owners of the Gulf and Ship Island Railroad, concluding that they were trying and were "gentlemen."[89] According to the commission, the system was the problem, or at least ill-paid guards, but not the gentlemen who ran it. Their report began with the following paragraph:

We submit that the leasing system, under any form, is wrong in principle and vicious. Experience teaches us that where human labor is farmed out for a consideration, uncontrolled by any interest the contractor may have in the welfare of the laborer, the laborer is very apt to be worked with a view to the highest possible gain to the employer; and where the power of the employer is absolute, as in the employment of convicts, it is almost certain to be abused in that direction. So natural is their thirst for gain, even at the price of humanity, that the owners of slaves were not always deterred from exactions, and sometimes cruelties, which jeopardized the lives of their valuable chattel. The system of leasing convicts to individuals or corporations, to be worked by them for profit, *simply restores a state of servitude worse than slavery,* in this that it is without any of the safeguards resulting from ownership of the slaves. The good treatment of the convict must depend entirely upon the humanity of the person who immediately controls him, and we regret to say that the evidence taken by us shows that this sometimes affords but slight protection to convict labor in the hands of contractors.[90]

Other members of the committee noted similar but varying issues. Frank Johnston remarked on the number of young boys in the system, some as young as thirteen. All of the committee members worried about the lack of sanitation. They pointed out that the guards were only paid $12 a month, which did not ensure the best candidates. T. L. Thomas saw evidence of whipping, working on Sundays, bare feet (swollen and cold), inadequate clothing, filthy conditions, and the allocation of only one light blanket per person. According to Thomas, the men were worked from 4:30 in the morning to dark. He believed that the lessees should have made it their business to know what was going on, but the other committee members believed that the Gulf and Ship Island convicts were better treated than under earlier lessees. In a more startling vein, these men who worried about the conditions of the camps were paradoxically also willing to admit that physical punishment might be appropriate, since these people were actual prisoners who had broken the law and were not particularly suited to following directions or working in a group. Therefore, given their conservative nature, these committee members believed that the tales of abuse were exaggerated; but then they saw the death rates that could not be easily explained away.[91]

This leasing system was common to all the southern states after the war, except for Kentucky. Mississippi was among the first to address it, albeit imperfectly. According to Jones, "It is difficult to understand how a system so barbarous could have been tolerated in any Christian community. It is evidently the product of human rapacity grafted upon the conditions that a defunct slavery had left behind it. It could only have flourished in an ex-slave State where ex-slaves made up the majority of its convicts." Writing in 1902, Jones added, "Let us rejoice that it is no more."[92]

When debated at the convention, a few voices rose to support convict leasing, the most surprising of which was former governor Alcorn, a Republican (who now claimed to be an Independent). Miller was the first to broach the subject and quoted from the 1884 report. Jones, who was there, argued the circumstances were now very different, but Miller disagreed, pointing out that the wrongs had continued and the death rate among the convicts was shocking. McLaurin asked for an alternative to convict leasing, if it were prohibited. He thought that the problem was not in the system itself (which he would continue), but in its administration. He stipulated that the death rate was not so awful among the convicts if the comparison was to all of those incarcerated and not to just the leased ones. He did not see the problem with his analogue. Alcorn thought convicts were necessary to use for the protection of the levees. In fact, he believed that convicts needed to be punished for their behavior; the scale had now fallen too far to the other side, and convicts now enjoyed "comforts, privileges, and luxuries that but few of us enjoy." He never produced any data to back up this assertion. Fewell reduced the discussion to the foundation of the issue: he saw the proposal as a return to convict leasing, and he "denied the right of the state to make money out of crime."[93]

There were moves among the delegates, however, in a more traditionally progressive vein. Early in the convention, J. H. Jones, representing the state at large, broached the subject of convict leasing.[94] He called it a "dark blot on the State."[95] Originally the state had fallen into this pattern for dealing with prisoners because of little access to cash. Prison systems cost money, and often a great deal. Sending prisoners to work for private entities (such as farms or railroads) made upkeep cheap for the state. Yet because there was little oversight, abuse flourished. As these stories were exposed, a reaction set in.[96]

With the proposal to abolish convict leasing, the question quickly became what would take its place and how much reform would cost. General W. S. Featherston of Marshall County, who held great sway in the convention, opposed convict labor, stating simply that abolishing the system was the right thing to do. Morris, a delegate from Wayne County, agreed. He believed that convict leasing was similar to slavery, often worse. African Americans had monetary value during slavery, but since prisoners had none, abuse was frequent. Astoundingly, former governor R. H. Alcorn vociferously supported convict leasing, but his rationale stemmed from his experience in the Delta with the dangers of flooding threatening his and his neighbors' land. He expressed surprise that the opponents of the system stipulated that even the levee boards did not want to use convicts because of security issues, for the levee board at that moment was using many prisoners.[97]

A compromise proposal for the convict issue appeared in an editorial in the main Vicksburg paper: after January 1895 convicts would not be for any private entity but "work for the State.... by the State and for the State alone."[98] What the convention delegates eventually did was to rid themselves of convict leasing to private entities after December 31, 1894, to void all contracts after that time, but to allow convict leasing by the state or in emergencies—just as the Vicksburg paper proposed.[99]

The debate then shifted to what would take the place of leasing. The proposal to establish a farm had the most support, which would mean getting rid of the prison in Jackson, then within sight of the capitol, from which men were leased. A new farm would be segregated by race and gender, and juveniles were to be kept away from "hardened criminals." Convicts were to be used, however, for levee repair if an emergency existed. By this time, as the details became more complex, McLaurin of Rankin County rose to protest on the basis that the constitution was to be organic law and therefore should not contain so much detail. The details should instead rest with the legislature to determine.[100] In an editorial, the *Clarion-Ledger* mused that the convention delegates, on the issue of convicts, had "marched up the hill and then down again," only to return to the place they started. The result, however, was to get rid of leasing.[101]

Other issues of note before the convention included the need for a new capitol and the issue of capital punishment, but the fiscal problems of the state influenced discussion. General Lee brought to the floor a committee report that advocated keeping the old capitol and simply adding to it. The money saved would be substantial, the committee argued.[102] The delegates decided this proposal really did not belong in the constitution. Monroe McClurg of Carroll County wanted to abolish capital punishment and substitute jail for life, but in the short debate the proposal did not get far. Given the debates over convict leasing, the shortage of money to fund reforms of any sort, and the fact that far more convicts of all levels were African Americans, the result was not surprising; it was remarkable, however, that the issue came to the floor of the convention at all.

What did gain the support of the delegates, despite a need for funding, was public health, for the state moved to set up a public health administration within the confines of the new constitution. For many of the delegates, this was clearly a responsibility of state government, for too many had experienced the ravages of epidemics in the previous two decades. In consequence, the health of citizens of the state became a subject of legislative inquiry. In the days before air-conditioning, the climate in Mississippi brought mosquitoes and subsequent virulent disease. In 1877 the state caught up with its neighbors by creating a state board of public health, and the move was just in time: a smallpox epidemic hit the state in 1878, followed by a huge yellow fever epidemic.[103] Holly Springs, in the northern part of the state, was hardest hit. Though knowledge that the disease is spread through infected mosquito bites was yet to come, early records claimed that refugees from the town of Grenada brought the disease with them. In turn, many people fled Holly Springs. Of the 1,500 who remained, all but 100 became ill; of those, over 350 died. Throughout the state, the epidemic killed 3,000.[104]

The proposal for public health administration was surprisingly uncontentious, given the caution with which most the delegates approached any sort of government regulation and institutions to enforce them. Other reforms, though, were far more problematic, for they revealed the latent (and often hidden) class issues lurking below the surface. Arguably a fairer apportionment within the legislature could be viewed as a reform. Certainly changes within the jury system and for the selection of judges would be a reform. These issues, and the question of reestablishing a militia, were contentious because of the class issues they provoked. Yet in most places, there is more to the story, and in Mississippi there surely was in the convention that fall of 1890.

CHAPTER 8

The Convention Exposes Class Divisions

As the convention moved away from the contentious debates over both the franchise and reform, the delegates turned to an even more prickly and polemical set of issues: reapportionment and ratification. The disputes over apportionment revealed hard set lines of battle between the white and black counties of the state, with neither trusting the other. Tax revenue, and how it was to be spent, was so contentious that Farmers' Alliance members nearly left the convention. Distrust between the two groups also emerged in the debates over the judiciary, over industrial and railroad support, and as to whether the state needed a militia. The final great argument at the convention—promulgation—came close to shutting down the entire effort. "Promulgation" was the term used to refer to simply announcing the constitution as passed and operational, rather than submitting it for ratification by the people. As most newspaper editors pointed out, the delegates were well aware that a vote for ratification would never pass; therefore simply to promulgate the new constitution was arrogant, a grab for power, and—at the same time—cowardly.

What lay behind these issues was caution based on class. The black counties, with a sparse number of white inhabitants and yet more than their share of elites, had long dominated the state and did not like to relinquish power. As noted in earlier chapters, citizens of the white counties in turn had long resented the stranglehold black counties had not only on the legislature but also upon the party conferences. Party nominations were determined by delegations based on representation in the legislature. As long as everyone was eligible to vote, though, representation based on population made sense. When African Americans began to be underrepresented at the polls and their franchise reduced, the black counties were dominated by just a few white planters, who in turn then controlled the state legislature and the governor's office by dent of their controversial control of the Democratic Party.

Making this all the more difficult was a truism: people vote their wallets, though how they perceive threats depends on where they fit within the community. If the economy is good, stable, and promises improvement, voters support the incumbent party. The reverse is also true. If people are cynical, if they predict a declining economy and see conspiracies that hold them back, they will vote the incumbents out. Senator George feared this reaction in the white counties where the Farmers' Alliance was strong. Members of the Alliance, nationally and locally, had identified a number of threats to their well-being, which included monopolies, railroad conspiracies, and inequitable taxes. To keep them happy, the senator moved to meet some of their demands. To some extent he was the obvious person to attempt this negotiation, for he came from the center of the state, he was a self-made man, and he was known as the "great Commoner." In the end he succeeded, but at the cost of support within the state.

◆ ◆ ◆

The other proposal on the table to control the franchise, that of reapportionment, was supported and eventually included in the constitution; nevertheless, it released an entirely new set of objections and revealed a split between the black and white counties of the state, between the haves and the have-nots. The eventual trajectory of state politics was unforeseen by the delegates, but well documented by Albert Kirwan in his book *Revolt of the Rednecks*.[1]

As noted in earlier chapters, Senator George proposed reapportioning representation within the legislature to ensure white voters were in charge of the state.[2] This was not a new idea, since he had proposed reapportionment in July, before the convention even met. He considered it a safer alternative, for "nothing in the Constitution of the United States ... prevents a State in adjusting the political forces in its borders."[3] How he would accomplish this goal remained unclear, but the Franchise Committee made specific proposals for compromise—to make the House chamber controlled by the white counties and the Senate chamber controlled by the black counties.[4] Since the white counties (those poorer counties with small farms, a smaller African American population, and a large number of illiterate white males) would be penalized by the application of the Australian ballot and a reading requirement, the committee offered more representatives in the legislature, ostensibly beyond their relative numbers.[5] Of course, if African American voters were disfranchised, the resultant count of available voters would have made a reallocation of representatives logical, though not fair.

From the vantage of the white counties, there was already a problem in the state, which would only be exacerbated by the franchise restrictions in the new constitution. If the provisions worked to exclude African American voters, the results would be further control of the state by a select few from the Delta. According Kirwan, the white population in the black counties was only 44,500 eligible voters, and in the white counties there were 71,000. "Yet the black counties sent sixty-eight representatives to the lower house ... while the white counties sent only fifty-two." The party nominating convention also reflected this "imbalance" and resulted in the black counties controlling the nominations for governor and other elected state officers. The question, then, for the delegates was whether the legislature represented all the citizens of the state (including women) or only eligible voters. White counties thought they knew the answer, and they pushed for change that they would view as equitable.[6]

Opposition to the plan was based on two issues: race and taxes. The *Clarion-Ledger* was not certain the plan would help at all and suspected that in fact the proposal would actually allow African American voters to hold the balance of power.[7] In one of those unbelievable and incomprehensible moments, the *Winona Times* admonished African Americans to take note of George's plan, for it indicated that there was no evil intent.[8]

Chairman Patty of the Franchise Committee read his report on September 2. While the provisions for the franchise consumed much of the debate in the convention, a lesser portion of the proposal entered the discussion as well. Committee members had not been sure that the disfranchisement methods would work, and they remained fearful of federal oversight. Therefore they added yet another provision that triggered debate and nearly fractured the convention: reapportionment of the state legislature.[9] Wisely, the committee did not propose to take away seats from counties, but rather to add seats to the white counties, increasing the total lower house seats by thirteen. In addition, the committee proposed an electoral college scheme to elect the executive branch. Much to the frustration of the white counties, however, the executive was to appoint the judiciary, rather than have an elective set of judges.[10]

Several proposals for reapportionment had come before the committee for consideration. One member from the Delta proposed simply reducing the number of legislators in the House from 120 to 100, thereby requiring all the sections to lose some representation. In the Senate, the numbers would be reduced from 40 to 33. Since this proposal assumed representation would be based on all the population, including African Americans, it would not accomplish a shift in the power base. The Delta, of course, did not want a power shift, so the proposal was understandable. Because it accomplished nothing, the proposal was shelved.[11]

In contrast, Dillard, who opposed Delta power, proposed substantially reducing Delta representation (seventeen to thirteen in the House and by one in the Senate) and increasing the representation of the eastern counties. Unlike the black county representatives, Dillard and those from the white counties thought that representation should be based on white population. Interestingly, as much as the delegates were willing to fiddle with reapportionment, they held to their belief that representation had to relate to population on some theoretical level. In fact, a compromise measure struggled to make that connection. R. H. Thompson, a floater delegate, proposed dividing the state into twelve political sections with ten representatives for each in the House and two in the Senate. Black counties were to comprise only three of the districts, so the other nine would ensure white control of the legislature.[12]

The eventual report was a true compromise from ideas proposed by Edward Mayes, who suggested basing the House representatives on territory and the Senate on "qualified electors." At first this did not please the committee, and so President Calhoon suggested simply letting the legislators figure it out for themselves rather than include it in the constitution.[13] By the time the report was given, Muldrow, from a black county, suggested that the committee itself was not pleased with the proposals. He pointed to the secrecy of the committee as the source of the problem, which had led to a stagnation of ideas.[14]

Neither side (white or black counties) viewed the original proposal with much favor, for both groups mistrusted officials in the opposing counties; therefore the report produced heated debate. W. A. Boyd of Tippah County fired the first shot when he stated that he would only support proposals that did not disfranchise a single white voter. Moreover, he questioned whether the convention delegates even had a right to consider such ideas, since by doing so they would create a "wedge" between the black and white counties of the state, which threatened to destroy the unity of the Democratic Party.[15] The *Daily Democrat* of Natchez agreed with him, arguing that the "reapportionment scheme is undemocratic and rather than lead to unity, will lead to a rise in sectionalism, just at a time when white people need to stick together."[16] J. B. Boothe (Panola County) countered with the assertion that these proposals only benefited the white counties at the expense of the black ones. In response, J. H. McGehee (Franklin County) asked everyone to be willing to compromise for the greater good.[17] To him, compromise meant that someone had to lose, and as far as he was concerned, that was the black county coalition.

None of the delegates, or the population in general, could envision exactly where the franchise provisions as a group would take the state, but the vagueness of these proposals made them uneasy. Would the disfranchisement sections be enough, or would the state need to rely upon apportionment changes? To attack these proposals on a level that was easier to understand, the counties turned to the reliable area of taxation. The black counties, primarily those in the Delta or directly on the Mississippi River, complained that the effect of representative changes in the legislature would put them at the mercy of the poorer counties, which would overtax them. As an example, the *Clarion-Ledger* pointed out that the twenty-nine black counties paid a full two-thirds of state taxes. In addition, their population was greater than the other counties, and therefore they should have the larger number of representatives.[18] Delegates assumed the taxes from the county derived from the small number of white farmers rather than from African Americans. Judge Calhoon, president of the convention, was so worried about this proposal that he requested a substitute for his chair so that he could speak to the convention as a delegate. In that role he argued forcefully that the committee had done a good job with its charge, that the debaters needed to maintain their equanimity, and that he would accept all the provisions for disfranchisement—except for apportionment. As a resident of a black county (Hinds), he realized that the apportionment section would reduce the county's representation in the legislature, a situation that he deemed prejudicial. Putting the state under the leadership of the white counties was "unfair," he thought. He suggested alternatives to the proposal, such as "voting in spots," though he never explained what he meant.[19]

Some delegates combined their unease with both Section Five and the reapportionment provisions. Others, however, were more specific in their response to apportionment. F. K. Winchester (Adams County) thought too much power would be given to the white counties at the expense of his area. While W. G. Yerger (Washington County in the Delta) startled everyone by claiming that he thought the delegates from the white counties would rise to the occasion and be good stewards of the trust imposed on them, Judge Chrisman believed otherwise. He claimed reapportionment would result in an enormous battle over control of the state.[20] Bringing the debate back to the main points, Thomas P. Bell (Kemper County) reminded delegates that white supremacy was at issue, and if that meant that some counties lost some power in the effort to secure the primacy of white voting, so be it.[21] That is, in fact, what happened. A compromise based on all of the proposals gave wider representation to the white counties, with county boundaries providing the basis and allocation of representatives based upon population. The Senate, however, relied on geographic districts.

The debates on apportionment continued sporadically throughout the convention. The *Clarion-Ledger* was loath to let it go, even when approved by the delegates.²² It referred to both the *Tunica Independent* and the *Greenville Democrat* as "red-hot" over apportionment and the reduced representation in the legislature for their areas.²³ The *Vicksburg Post*, also a voice for one of the black counties, was even more outspoken. Its editors hit at Senator George, whom they blamed for the apportionment compromise, which they called gerrymandering. According to the editors, "Never before in the history of a civilized people was such a miserable juggery placed in the organic law of a state." They added that even if "all the 60,000 negro majority is voted [sic] and honestly counted (and Senator George's purpose in advocating a convention was the purification of the ballot box), then the Legislature will still have a white majority."²⁴

The black counties were willing to compromise over apportionment because of their concern over taxation. They managed to negotiate some relief regarding taxation by assuring that at least levee taxes would be based on the value of land rather than on a statewide tax on amount of land.²⁵ Yet near the close of the convention, contention was still evident in the debate over the wording of the tax restrictions.²⁶ At the end of October a group of citizens from Greenville petitioned the convention to address a number of matters that concerned them; in addition to the controversial Section Five, they asked for redress for the taxation issue. They viewed the apportionment compromise as harmful to their Delta town and asked that the convention provide protection against "unjust and unequal taxation, whether accomplished through special or arbitrary assessment or otherwise," either by limiting legislative power or by the requiring of a majority vote to pass revenue acts. Failure to do so, they argued, "would subject us to taxation without representation and leave us without the power of self-defense."²⁷

An editorial by the *Daily Democrat* argued persuasively that "the convention must stop the stuffing of ballot boxes, stop committing perjury, stop carrying the elections by fraud and violence, cease educating the rising generation that subterfuge and methods are permissible." The editors admitted this was true, as well as that the "morals and honor of the young men of Mississippi must be protected from such contaminating and damaging influences." The problem was that "every plan which has been proposed in the convention ... has been deeply dyed with the taint of expediency, trickery or subterfuge." They continued, "The convention is seeking to do the same thing ... under cover of law, a transfer of trickery from the polling places to the floor of the convention." They had hoped that the Australian ballot, residency, and the poll tax would suffice, but resorting to reapportionment was wrong at every level.²⁸ At the very end of the convention, the *Natchez Democrat* refused to support the new constitution and then listed the sections to which it objected, including reapportionment.[29] The result was a compromise that required a three-fifths majority vote for revenue, but the issue still rankled and had long-term consequences for the state.[30] In spite of all the controversy and the fact that most citizens were unaware of the provisions, one state historian claimed years later that apportionment was the "legal basis and bulwark of the design of white supremacy."[31]

◆ ◆ ◆

Taxes were not the only monetary issue facing the state. A number of matters close to the heart of the populist movement emerged during this period and were vigorously espoused by the Farmers' Alliance. Certainly the call to prohibit both an educational and a property qualification was at the center of the emerging reactionary pull to protect farmers and their emerging plight in an industrialized society. Farmers saw their position in society plummeting and their status, politically and economically, in peril. Mississippi was not unique in this problem. Yet the situation in the state was more complicated than in, for example, Kansas or Oregon. Once again it was complicated by both race and class.

As noted in previous chapters, in the past plantation owners and farmers had aligned themselves as representing the Jeffersonian tradition of the independent farmer, the backbone of the Republic. As an indication of the shift in alliances, the *Clarion-Ledger* printed a list of delegates to the convention with their professions. Most of the plantation owners claimed to be both owners and part of another profession, such as lawyer, editor, or doctor. This was the educated class. The others, those who were not listed as town-dwellers with a profession, were a small number when they declared themselves as simply farmers. Self-identification was changing, though the pull to the land was still strong.

By 1890 the Farmers' Alliance was making headway into the eastern portions of the state, with a larger membership among the traditional white counties. These were also the counties with the fewest towns and the largest number of small, struggling farms. The Alliance met in Starkville that August, just as the convention was under way in Jackson. The president of Mississippi Agricultural and Mechanical College, Stephen Lee, was both a member of the Alliance and a delegate to the convention. Although some feared where this new, vocal group was headed, the *Clarion-Ledger* tried to allay "groundless" fears by reminding people that "the Alliance is composed of Democrats, and the best Democrats in the State."[32]

Although some delegates, like Frank Burkitt, were also members of the Alliance, others were not but at least were sympathetic to the Alliance. For example, Irvin Miller of Leake County spoke in support of the concerns of the Alliance members. Miller said he was a native of Kentucky and had migrated to Mississippi thirty-five years previous. When he arrived, it was a poor state with citizens who had little access to formal education. These same citizens, he argued, were still in the state.[33] They had fought nobly in the war, returned to set up homes, produced a bumper crop of children, and struggled to survive. These were good people who did not deserve to be disfranchised with an educational or property qualification. While he admitted that the numbers suggested for property holdings were relatively small, he could not vote for the franchise restrictions as then proposed. It involved principle rather than absolute numbers. Miller was not alone in this feeling, but he was the one who connected it most vociferously with the Alliance.[34]

One of the Alliance committees submitted a report to the convention that opposed both property and educational qualifications for voting, although members specifically added this demand was not to be construed as opposition to the Australian ballot.[35] Since the Australian ballot required literacy on the part of voters, this exception was interesting; apparently the assumption on the part of many people was that the Australian ballot was truly a reform and that a simple requirement of literacy was therefore manipulation. Other proposals included an elective judiciary; election of a railroad commissioner; a short term for the executive branch positions with no opportunity for reelection; legislation providing for public education for those between the ages of six and twenty-one and for not less than four months; a prohibition of lotteries; and a board that should be the only issuer of pardons. Alliance supporters specifically voiced their opposition to trusts and combines and to taxation that was not uniform and equal. They wanted to ensure that the credit of the state and the counties would not "be pledges to corporations or individuals," and they wanted to ensure that the legislature would be "prohibited from encumbering our statute books with local legislation."[36]

◆ ◆ ◆

Among the issues so important to the farming community, an elective judiciary is the most difficult to understand. An appointive judiciary had become the cause célèbre for the average voter, who instead perceived an elective judiciary as one representing democracy. The farmers wanted people to control the judiciary. In contrast, those who backed an appointive judiciary viewed election as dangerous because it might result in unqualified, uneducated judges who would be inclined toward the general populace rather than behaving as independent jurists. As early as the first days of the convention,

Judge L. A. Byne of Arkansas, who was present and watching the Mississippi proceedings, expressed his concern that Mississippi might be leaning toward an elective judiciary. He feared such a change would result in corruption when judges had to make the popular rather than the appropriate ruling.[37]

The minutes of the convention and the reports of the *Clarion-Ledger* omit a number of the debates, and they do not include the details of the compromises within the committees themselves. What is interesting, however, is that the earlier proposals on the judiciary refer to an elective judiciary, but just before the end of the convention, they shift to an appointive one.[38] Furthermore, they set up the supreme court, as well as the separate levels of judiciary, based on the three geographical divisions of the state: north, central, and southern.[39] The Vicksburg *Daily Commercial Herald* suggested that if the new franchise provisions worked as hoped, it would remove uneducated voters, for such voters could not be trusted to elect good judges. Therefore appointment of judges would be safer. If the uneducated were removed, the state could return to an elective judiciary. On the same page, a letter to the editor from an Alliance supporter reported his friends to be "blue" that an elective judiciary was not part of the new constitution: after all, he said, lawyers were the ones who did not want a convention or a new constitution, but they appear to have won this argument.[40]

Tweaking the judiciary system by the delegates revealed much of the convention's mind-set. The salary for the supreme court was set within the constitution itself and was relatively generous compared to other positions, especially in light of the parsimonious attitude of the convention. The issue of juries and people who could serve on them was also debated. In his position with the Farmers' Alliance, Burkitt continued his efforts to prohibit educational and property restrictions for the franchise but then argued that jury members should reflect whatever restrictions were placed on electors.[41] As for votes within the jury, no one, at least on record, advocated anything less than a unanimous decision for criminal courts, but that was not so for civil courts. Judge Calhoon suggested that a nine-person vote on a civil court case should be sufficient, although he strongly advocated that an educational qualification for jury members was essential to the well-being of the jury system.[42]

◆ ◆ ◆

The more usual and familiar issue of the Farmers' Alliance concerned corporations, whether the railroads or the dreaded "trusts and combines." Given the economic and ethical problems faced by Mississippi in the previous decades, the inclusion of restrictions on railroads was not surprising. Mistrust was certainly evident, but there was also the realization of the economic importance and necessity of the railroad. Proximity of the rail lines meant cash for locals, who not only worked on the rails but also sold their eggs, meat, and produce.[43] The convention discussed requiring any railroad built within three miles of a town to build a depot within the town (just as sixty years later, when the interstate highway system was being constructed, there was a realization that bypassing a town meant either lack of growth or death). Although they wanted and needed the railroads, their rapid expansion in the period had meant a conflict between farmers and the right-of-way claimed by the railroads. Early in the convention William McGaughan of Gulfport petitioned the convention to require railroads to fence their lines so that cattle would not be killed by locomotives. According to McGaughan, fencing was already such a problem that land prices were affected by proximity to rail lines.[44]

At the same time, the debates reveal a caution about the power of the railroads, a mind-set typical of a number of states in this period. The convention debated the need for a railroad commissioner, who would have the authority of the state behind him to balance the power of the corporation.[45] Frank Burkitt, the usual spokesman for the Farmers' Alliance, wanted to be certain that the railroads would be responsible for an employee's injury or death caused through negligence of the corporation.[46] Even if the railroads were out of state, the Alliance men wanted to have the ability to sue, an issue then before the US Supreme Court.[47] In particular, they wanted to regulate the railroads to curb excesses, which would include unequal rates, a sore point among Alliance members throughout the southern and western states. Railroads were prohibited from giving passes or free tickets or even reduced rates unless "applicable to all alike." The delegates did exempt reductions, though, for "orphans, disabled, destitute or homeless persons" or "excursion rates . . . or reduced rates for ministers or to their own employees."[48]

Given the problems of the past, the convention also wanted to be certain that the state would not repeat earlier problems regarding issuance of railroad bonds. The easiest solution, the delegates thought, was to gain some oversight by declaring railroads as common carriers.[49] They also forbade the state or any county to donate lands to the railroads or, for that matter, to any corporation or individual. To forestall potential conflicts of interest, county officials could not be stockholders on land credit to companies, nor could railroads give stock to municipal officials.[50]

This fear of corporations extended beyond the railroads. While Mississippi was a strong agricultural state and did not have the manufacturing presence of other states, delegates read their newspapers. They knew of strikes, strike breaking, watered stock, and tax break frauds. In an attempt to control access to the state by outside corporations, they forbade monopolies in the state.⁵¹ In addition, they attempted to preclude the creation of holding companies by restricting access to company boards; members of competing companies could not be represented on both boards.⁵²

Senator George attempted to calm these efforts, for he represented a number of corporations in the state. Attempting to calm discourse, early in the debates he offered a resolution for a state charter for corporations, wherein the state could alter the process of incorporation, except when a charter had been granted previously and a business was still running. All charters were to be given for only ninety-nine years. If a business failed, the state could rescind the charter.⁵³ Banks were to be included in these regulations, but at issue was whether local or national banks had the most to offer the state regarding growth and capital. After lengthy debate the stipulation remained that state banks were to be taxed at the same rate as national ones to entice national money.⁵⁴

Money remained at the heart of the issues before the convention. The state wanted growth and the ability to compete with its neighboring states, but it did not want to become a manufacturing state. The delegates wanted the state to remain agricultural, but they also did not want to be left behind in the national economic growth. The problem was balance. How did they regulate corporations without hindering advancement? How did they encourage growth without unleashing the forces of the Industrial Revolution? Their answer was tax revenue. The state and local governments needed tax money, but they had to be willing to forgo some revenue in order to entice the "right" kind of corporation. Thus a Meridian businessman petitioned the convention to exempt from taxation any new industries for a number of years. He called it a practical measure to allow the nascent businesses to get on their feet.⁵⁵

The convention meant to be sure, though, that the power to tax corporations "shall never be surrendered or abridged"; but at the same time the delegates wanted to allow the legislature temporarily to allow the suspension of taxation for a period of five years.⁵⁶ S. E. Packwood (Pike County) was more specific in his proposal that the legislature could not surrender the power to tax corporations.⁵⁷ Weeks of debate over the issue followed. In particular, the delegates wanted to allow textile mills to be exempt from taxation for seven years, for, as they pointed out, similar deals had been offered successfully in neighboring states.⁵⁸ The Vicksburg paper was particularly forceful in its support of making capital work for the state. Do not tax capital, it argued, but invite it into Mississippi rather than fear the state's invasion by greedy corporations.⁵⁹

Other economic topics briefly appeared. One delegate proposed that the state could not pass legislation to lure immigrants to the state, a reflection of the issues emerging in the Delta over the enticement of both Mexican and Chinese workers for building levees. In response, W. S. Eskridge of Tallahatchie County proposed a Bureau of Immigration and Agriculture.[60] In a nod to changing times, the proposal came to make telegraph and telephone companies "common carriers." The concept behind this designation was that common carriers were in business but functioned for the public good and therefore could be regulated by a governmental body or agency. Designating telephone and telegraph companies was a more progressive approach to technology regulations than might be expected, given the tenor of the rest of the debate.[61]

All of these economic matters before the convention indicated an interest in and a fear of manufacturing or new technology; this caution, however, was typical of other areas of the country in this period.[62] Senator George, in his national role, certainly had been exposed to a number of debates on the issue of money, including what it actually was and how more could get into the hands of people in different parts of the country. Was money firmly fixed on the gold standard? Could silver suffice? How much money needed to be in circulation to allow all sections of the country to be able to get cash? Modern readers are often startled to find that at times even people who had money in a bank might not be able to withdraw cash, for there was none. Paper money, in the guise of greenbacks, had been largely withdrawn from circulation by the federal government, and so states and banks had moved into the resulting vacuum and issued script, just as they had done before the Civil War. Unfortunately, once having had currency that was backed in some way by the federal government, most people found the new state or bank scripts suspect. They wanted something different.

George had taken part in these debates in Congress, but it is clear he had a confused concept of the function of currency. So, too, was his understanding of corporate stocks and stock manipulation. He wanted to protect the state from "watered stock," which was corporate shares with an inflated value. The problem was how to value stock, which most states put on par value, often founded on property values. The two did not correlate. The unfortunate result was a series of defaults, wherein a company had claimed more value in stock than was warranted and therefore hurt stockholders. George believed he could protect the state by requiring that capital stock of a company should not "exceed the amount of money actually paid in for such stock ... unless the legislature determines profits make it worth more."[63] How the legislature would make this determination was unclear.

❖ ❖ ❖

Maintaining Mississippi as an agricultural state required some collective protection for farms near the rivers that bordered or flowed within the state. The Mississippi, Yazoo, and Pearl had frequently overflowed their banks and the levees, and inundated property, destroyed homes and crops, and taken lives. The levee system, begun decades earlier, served as a symbol of the struggle between local control and federal control, for, however much they might wish it different, the planters discovered that federal coordination and federal money were critical. Early levees were built by contract with private cooperatives using slaves from nearby plantations. Following the war, with labor in short supply, locals hired a group of Irish contractors, but according to locals, the men got drunk on the weekend when paid and "fought and howled like Bedlam turned loose." These early constructions relied upon wheelbarrows to move dirt; barrow pits where dirt was taken created low areas that pooled water.[64] By no means were these levees constructed with engineering principles in mind, and money that should have been used for upkeep was diverted to building anew. Certainly flooding was cyclical, but lack of upkeep was a growing problem that added to budget concerns. In 1882 levees broke because crawfish had undermined them.[65] Another Delta flood in 1897 was so bad that hundreds of people were evacuated following prearranged signals from church bells. To stem the flow, two levee contractors, one of whom was the son of Nathan Bedford Forrest, worked feverishly with their staff to fill sandbags and stack them upon the levee. The state also provided help from convicts. In spite of these efforts, water rushed in and killed nine people quickly, including children. People on rooftops awaited rescue from local volunteers manning boats. In a limited fashion, the federal government stepped in to help stabilize the levees, but to little avail. The floods continued, culminating in the great Mississippi flood of 1927, which covered 1,800 square miles and killed 147 people in Bolivar County alone.[66]

John Barry's *Rising Tide* provides a brief background to the development of the Mississippi River levees, but a more immediate example of the issues involved was Isaiah Montgomery and his family's loss of Brierfield and Hurricane plantations.[67] When Montgomery was seated at the convention, he bore the burden of not only representing his race but also serving as a speaker for the plight of troubled farmers in the Delta who faced loss of property and life from the nearly annual floods. It is within this context that it is important to understand how contentious the levee repair was. Those living on the floodplains knew the constant danger lurking every spring, while those living beyond the Delta resented the idea that they should contribute to the relief of the plantation owners or to building the levees. After all, why should they, already struggling, help to relieve the "wealthy" planters of the Delta?[68]

Apportionment may have hurt the Delta, but the leaders of the river counties were not going to give up levee support without a fight. Early in the convention members petitioned for a standing committee on levees because of the ever-present danger.⁶⁹ Some delegates used other means. Isaiah Montgomery was among those listed as absent from the convention in early October. Rather, returning home for the harvest, he was giving testimony before the River Commission, then meeting in New York. He testified that taxes were heavy and that, although the people had done all they could to protect themselves, they were still in jeopardy. Shortly after his return, Montgomery entered into the minutes of the convention a petition from E. H. Moore, the Bolivar County levee commissioner. In the petition Moore pointed out that the flooding of the Mississippi River means "it is necessary for the people of the Delta to use every endeavor to raise funds to build up and strengthen our levees; that the life and property of the people of this section depends [sic] on the strength and security of the levees." "Private citizens," he continued, "pay not only a heavy ad valorem tax, but a burdensome cotton tax for levee purposes." As an alternative to unrelenting tax increases, he suggested that the railroads should be a target, for presently they were "exempt from payment of all taxes, save a per mile tax for levee purposes." In consequence, he argued, "We do not think that the levee tax now levied on said railroads is commensurate with the profits derived from such railroads from leveed protection." Moore wanted "fair and just" taxes on railroads, "as these lives would be valueless without levee protection."⁷⁰

In an effort to compromise the need for money with the continued avoidance of tax increases of any sort—not to mention the conflict between local control and federal support—the delegates faced some difficult choices. The majority report by the Committee on Corporations and Internal Improvements suggested that the levees remain under local control but with the right of eminent domain by the state; also money for levee maintenance should be raised (as it had in the past) through taxes paid to the local sheriff by saloons. The minority report expressed outrage. Not only did the report oppose saloons of any sort in the state, but it also preferred a tax on assessed value of land. Just as with the issue of tax control between white and black counties, those in the minority feared a uniform tax would be unwise. Some land, they pointed out, was simply more valuable than others. They therefore requested a board to represent everyone and the taxes to be apportioned according to assessed value.⁷¹

Questions of trust between the sections of the state and allocation of tax revenue also emerged in the debate over the militia. This issue also took on a racial overtone, although not necessarily in the way one might expect. Certainly the state had expressed concern during Reconstruction over the arming of freedmen, and it should come as no surprise that the delegates dithered over how to restrict the militia to white men. The federal government had allocated money to be spent on equipping a guard unit as long as a state had at least a 900-man militia; Mississippi did not. Essentially, the delegates argued that the state annually was leaving thousands of dollars unused by not having a militia. The question was whether the state needed one, for many still feared a militia as used during Reconstruction.

The real issues, though, were not reported in the *Proceedings* or in the *Clarion-Ledger*. The debates are only reported in the *Daily Commercial Herald*, which revealed a division between the black and white counties. Moreover, the statements by the delegates are blunt, which is probably why the other presses did not pick up the information; the Leflore County massacre remained a sensitive issue to the white population. What is interesting is that the Vicksburg reporter appeared to jump into the middle of an argument, ignoring previous references to lynching, rather than report what led to exchanges on the floor on the evening of September 6.

A few delegates wanted a militia as a provision in the constitution. Both Fewell of Meridian and Ward of Madison believed that a militia would "secure peace and be money well spent." McLaurin of Rankin County (a white county) opposed the idea of a "standing army" and indicated that "we only have the newspaper reports about the Greenwood affair cited by gentlemen."[72] The "Greenwood affair" was not explained, although given later comments, readers may assume that the reference was to the Leflore County riots of the previous year. General Lee would not let the issue go; he replied that the state really did need a trained militia to secure the well-being of the state. In particular he pointed to a disregard of a rule of law in the region: "An unsavory odor was attached to our State on account of frequent lynchings." He went further, picking up the relevant issue of funding to assert that it was "better to spend thousands of dollars than to have one man lynched."[73] The people, he argued, wanted assurance of law and order; the state should not expect young men to give their time and require them to pay their own way. McLaurin of Sharkey County pointed out that the legislature previously had refused to allocate funds for a militia and suggested that the legislature would not do so, even if directed by the convention.[74] Typical of the time, Gore of Webster County said he opposed any expenditure on a militia and asserted that no one had shown a real need for it. According to the reporter from the *Clarion-Ledger*, Taylor then "made a great speech in support of the appropriation" in which he argued there were two great forces in government, the "ballot and the sword."[75] The state needed both. Although a number of delegates questioned this need, the report was eventually approved.

The next day Senator George arose to claim authorship of the militia proposal and to explain why he believed it was necessary. He said that "in his own experience he had known the necessity of suppressing racial disturbances." Though he stated he hated to bring up the subject, he pointed to two riots in Leflore County, one recently and the other many years earlier. In both cases "unorganized bodies of men from other counties, without warrant of law, had slain black men under the idea that they were rendering assistance to their white brethren." In another case, as long as the militia was present, law and order prevailed, but "as soon as it was withdrawn, the lawless proceedings were renewed. He did not know how many were slain, but it was enough to make it a horror." As far as he was concerned, these examples proved that a well-organized militia was "necessary for the protection of both races." Even more startling was the following sentence in the paper: "In answer to questions propounded by members he said that he favored a general provision because one discriminating between white and black counties would subject that state to severe criticism."[76]

The split in this instance between black and white counties had roots in the traditions of fiscal economy. Neither side wanted to foot the bill for the needs of the other. So even when confronted with the reality described by Senator George, delegates begrudgingly gave support, though always with reference to money issues. Miller, a representative from a white county, said he would back the militia provision even though he advocated economy. Martin from Adams County, a black county, pointedly said that the convention had been working to take power away from black counties and give it to white ones. This provision would make that trend even stronger, and he compared the situation to rotten boroughs in Britain. Black counties were the ones that had to pay for the militia.[77] McLaurin of Rankin County thought that the board of supervisors for the militia was actually the sticking point for a number of delegates; he advocated handing the power to the counties rather than to state appointees. Love thought the legislature already had the power to handle these police power issues, but George argued that the legislature was not exercising the power it already had. Former governor Alcorn thought a national guard was not really needed; as an example, he claimed that his own county had a large mob that was dispersed by a group of seventy from the county. Alcorn also pointed out two other problems: the state had no money for a militia (returning to the recurring theme of funding and taxes), and, as long as the white and black counties did not trust each other, there would be no funding for a standing army. In this and in other issues before the convention, Alcorn revealed the strong pull of the wallet upon his politics. Though he had served as a Republican governor and senator, Alcorn was consistently supportive of the black county issues that would have benefited his Delta plantation, even when it conflicted with Republican values. From the other side of the state and political values, Frank Burkitt pointed out that he was from a white county, but there were some counties that definitely should not have control of a militia; they could not be trusted.[78]

◆ ◆ ◆

The final controversial provision for the convention concerned the manner of ratification. Unlike what had occurred with the US Constitution and most state constitutions by this point, the convention decided not to send the constitution to the legislature or to the people for ratification. Ostensibly the delegates were worried that the franchise provisions would result in wholesale disfranchisement of African Americans, not to mention many white males. Why would anyone assume that people would vote to disfranchise themselves? Senator George proposed that the Judiciary Committee review this issue and report back to the convention. Its report, written by Judge Wiley Harris, stated there was no reason to present the constitution to the people of the state for ratification. The only previous constitution, committee members pointed out, that had been submitted was the one of 1867. That constitution was not an adequate demonstration of democratic probity, for they claimed it was "forced" on Mississippians by bayonet. Indeed, secession itself had not been tendered to the people. According to the committee, ratification had "no support on any principle of Constitutional law, and is mere political theory."[79] The debate reemerged in the convention weeks later, when C. K. Holland of Calhoun County proposed that the constitution be submitted to the people.[80] The state Farmers' Alliance agreed.[81]

Local newspaper editors objected vociferously to promulgation. The *Clarion-Ledger* noted that the power to write the constitution had been given the convention but not the power also to ratify.[82] The following month another editorial by the *Clarion-Ledger* questioned whether the delegates were the masters or servants of the people. If the constitution was good, it would be adopted. If bad, then it would be rejected. Since only eighty-four members of the last legislature had called for the convention, the editors argued this low number hardly qualified as sufficient to represent statewide approval. The constitution therefore should be submitted to the people of the state.[83]

Other newspapers from both black and white counties joined the fray. The *Tupelo Ledger* and the *Oxford Eagle*, both in the northern part of the state and both speaking for white counties, called for ratification. The *Brandon Republican* and the *Yazoo Sentinel*, from the central part of the state and a black county, also called for ratification.[84] The Vicksburg *Commercial-Herald*, though, did not support ratification, arguing it was unnecessary.[85] The Grenada *Sentinel* agreed, since the people had voted for the delegates, whom they should be able to trust. The *Sentinel* did quote the Aberdeen *Examiner*, home to a number of Alliance men. Those editors accused the convention of purposefully disfranchising poor white men under the guise of dealing with African Americans. The editors logically then moved to the assumption that if submitted for ratification, the constitution would never pass.[86]

These objections remained largely unsupported by the delegates other than through Frank Burkitt, again speaking for the Farmers' Alliance. Burkitt went so far as to offer a date for ratification, the first Tuesday after the first Monday in November 1891. George Dillard from Noxubee County, certainly one of the most conservative of the delegates who often opposed Burkitt, asked that the motion be tabled. It was.[87] Burkitt's motion came in the waning days of the convention, an indication of some remaining objections to the constitution in general and to the issue of ratification specifically. The *Natchez Democrat* is a perfect example of a paper that was uncomfortable with the whole convention; the paper admitted it had not wanted to call the convention, and did not like Section Five, reapportionment, or the lack of ratification.[88]

The convention ended the evening of November 1 at a previously agreed upon set time. Typical of the period, the members presented gifts to the leaders in commemoration of their efforts, including a clock to Judge Calhoon, the president of the convention. After the constitution was officially read, Calhoon called a vote. Seven men voted against the document and four refused to sign it, all of whom represented white counties with constituents who risked being disfranchised.[89]

Judge Solomon S. Calhoon made a lengthy and flowery speech before adjournment in which he complimented the convention on its work. He reiterated the reasons for the convention and based its existence solely on the race question. According to him, African Americans did not have a history of civilization: "The race up to this time has shown no science, no literature, no art, no enterprise, no progress, no invention." He added, certainly with no actual knowledge of the history of Africa, that African American rule had always meant "stagnation, the enslavement of women, the brutalization of man, animal savagery, universal ruin." Just to make sure that everyone, including those watching from outside the state, understood the stakes (as he saw them), he argued: "In my judgment the material interest and moral advancement of the people of both races here depend on the predominance in government of that virtue and intelligence which, for the present at least, can come only from that race which in the past has shown a capacity for the successful administration of free institutions." He went on to argue "that race alone can now safely exercise the functions of ruling with moderation and justice and accomplish the great purpose for which governments are established." Although he added reference to the necessary control of corporations and evil cartels, his emphasis for the entire speech was on race matters, and so firmly shifted the controversial issues of the convention from class to race.[90]

This message alone, with its shift to race, was enough to quiet a few editors. The *Clarion-Ledger*, ever watchful of the state's pennies, complained that the convention cost the state around $700 a day. It did acknowledge, though, that the work had been completed. Though previously the editors had objected to a number of sections, they believed that now was the time to read the constitution, to understand it, and to quit dwelling on the problems. If changes were needed, the editors should push to have them made. Some of the efforts of the delegates were good and some bad, but not because of a lack of effort, for they had worked diligently for weeks.[91]

The question remained, though, for the state to determine how this new constitution would work. Would it fulfill its purpose? Would African Americans be effectively disfranchised and white voters largely unaffected? These were the questions posed to former governor Alcorn, who had voted for the constitution, when interviewed in late November. He believed that the purpose of the convention was "honest" and had been dealt with in a forthright manner; the delegates tried to do the best they could for the state. He admitted there were problems in the constitution as written, particularly Section Five, which was open to fraud. Surprisingly for a former Republican, he argued that the leaders had to do something, for the old system "was demoralizing the young men of our State by breeding in them a contempt for the law. The Southern man thought that for the negro to vote was a pollution of the election franchise." He added that under the new system, "there will be no chance to buy votes, either."[92]

The effect of the new constitution was not what the delegates expected, but that problem was for the future. On the surface, ostensibly the purpose for calling the convention may well have been reform and a return to integrity and rule of law, but the various debates revealed far more sinister purposes. Reports of the convention had come to the attention of the nation, and some in the North were asking questions. Now the first item of business was to defend it against the accusations and attacks of the northern press and Republican senators. Whether Mississippi's senators could justify the new constitution without circumlocution, much less outright lying, remained to be seen.

CHAPTER 9

Defending the New Constitution in Congress

Promulgation of the constitution was not the end of the story. Not surprisingly, struggles over the constitution moved from the confines of the state to a much wider arena and provoked national debate. The opposition to Mississippi's new organic law had two options for redress: appeal to the US Congress or to the US Supreme Court. The first opportunity for some sort of remedy came through the provisions of the Force Bill (also known as the Lodge Elections Bill), then before the Senate.[1] Both those defending and opposing the new constitution recognized the applicability of the bill's provisions specifically to the Mississippi document.

Having created the new constitution during the hiatus between the passage of the Elections Bill by the House in July 1890 and its eventual movement to and debate in the Senate, Senators George and Walthall returned to Washington in November, just in time to defend the state's document on the floor of the Senate. To the floor came two dominant and controversial issues about the constitution: a lack of ratification by the citizens of the state and the potential fraud seemingly inherent in the Understanding Clause.

The Republicans viewed the new Mississippi Constitution as the very embodiment of all the wrongs in the South that needed redress through the Elections Bill. Although vigorous debate over Mississippi's new constitution began under the rubric of the Elections Bill, Republicans soon shifted ground to defend their interest in a state constitution by arguing specifically that Mississippi was in violation of the readmission provisions of 1870, and that gave Congress the authority to review the new constitution. The new Mississippi Constitution became the flashpoint for the debates.

Senator George's angry response in defending his state was typical not only of the Mississippi delegation but also of the South in general, for the fear of a return to Reconstruction remained a strong undercurrent in southern politics. George argued that once Mississippi had been readmitted as a state, it had all the rights and privileges of any other state, which included rewriting its constitution as it wished, as long as the result was still a republican form of government. George went on to point out that other states previously had or still held literacy or property qualifications for voting. Mississippi, in that regard, was not unique.

In one measure, at least, Mississippi was unique in 1890. It alone among the old Confederacy proposed a new organic law that would circumvent the intent of the Fifteenth Amendment. As northern senators voiced opposition to the constitution, fellow southern senators rose to help defend Mississippi. This support was expected. If the state could protect the provisions of its new constitution (including the Understanding Clause) against the pressure and oversight of Congress, other southern states had a chance to make similar provisions. In fact, they eventually did. The first hurdle was the Elections Bill. If the southern states could forestall this sort of legislation and keep the federal government out of their affairs, Democrats would have a free hand at crafting the sort of government and society that they envisioned.

With hindsight, the timing of the Elections Bill's arrival in the Senate was unfortunate. The country faced other problems that some believed were more pressing. Before the Senate lay both Sherman's Silver Purchase Act and the McKinley Tariff. With the backing of President Harrison, though, the Elections Bill was first on the agenda. What was remarkable about the subsequent debates in the Senate was not the cohesion of southern senators and their Democratic colleagues, but rather the growing divide among Republican senators. Republicans had differed after the war, splitting into Stalwarts, who wanted to maintain their backing of freedmen in the South, and Half-Breeds, who wanted to be a party of the future by concentrating on reform and business interests. Over the years historians have settled on defining the cause of the split as patronage—with the Half-Breeds being the ones who wanted civil service reform. The issues were not that simple, however, especially when they touched the freedmen of the South. And, of course, there was another region that thought itself ignored—the West. Western senators most often fell into espousing business interests, particularly the issue of gold and silver as the basis for monetary policy, to the exclusion of southern issues. In addition, they had their own problems with race, particularly Chinese immigrants. The evolving debates over the Elections Bill fully exposed the cleavage within the party.[2]

As soon as the bill arrived from the House that late summer of 1890, Democrats prepared for a fight. Sensing not only danger but also a weakness in the Republican Party, southern senators started a filibuster, which created a stalemate for all business before the Senate, including these urgent financial bills. In desperation, Senator Nelson Aldrich (R-Rhode Island), then the floor manager, investigated the use of cloture to close debate, but since this effort would involve a change of Senate rules, it failed to go anywhere.[3] A compromise to push consideration of the Elections Bill until later and turn instead to the tariff showed more promise for passage.[4] This plan suited Aldrich just fine, for he believed that the bill was doomed to failure, given the filibuster. Senators who were firmly in support of the Elections Bill, however, were appalled, fearing that such a decision would wreck the bill. Both sides were hearing from their constituents, and both thought themselves pushed toward differing priorities. In particular, African Americans were unhappy, because their party was ignoring their needs.[5] As a result, the party held a stormy caucus on August 14. As a compromise, the leaders agreed that the bill would be "shelved" for the moment but renewed for debate as the first order of business when Congress reconvened after the November elections.[6] November, of course, was also the month in which the new Mississippi Constitution was promulgated and so neatly provided the Senate with a ready-made example of southern perfidy.

Not everyone was happy with the shelving of the bill. Vexed with Congress, President Harrison pointed to the party platform that promised action on an elections bill. The Afro-American News Company, an association of black correspondents, expressed concern as well.[7] Frustrated but a pragmatist nonetheless, Frederick Douglass watched from the sidelines.[8]

The Senate passed the tariff bill, and historians have questioned whether there was a compromise between some silver Republicans and southern Democrats to swap votes; that is, some Democrats would support the Sherman Silver Act and some Republicans would vote against the Elections Bill. No real proof exists.[9] In reality there were shifts in voting patterns that appear suspicious, but the disputes were more complex. Issues in the Senate became far more complicated following the November elections in 1890, when the Republicans suffered dramatic losses at the polls. Some viewed the results then, as now, as a loss because of the Republican support of the tariff and the Elections Bill. Others believed it was because of a *lack* of support.[10]

Never one to give up, Harrison called for consideration of the Lodge Elections Bill when Congress reconvened on December 1. A lame-duck Congress, it still had a commanding Republican majority. Not surprisingly, a few senators pointed out the theoretical problem of proceeding with a "partisan Republican bill."[11] The new Congress coming in January would not likely pass the bill, but by the terms of the Constitution, the old Congress and its Republican majority were still seated and in control and could continue to work. They had agreed to take up the Lodge Elections Bill on return, as Harrison admonished them. Harrison also reminded Congress that the Supreme Court had indicated such a law would be constitutional and that present laws were simply ineffectual. Although the president received vocal and written support for his stand, Lodge feared that the Senate debate would be a "dress parade."[12]

Democrats were preparing a thorough filibuster with heavy references to race. What is surprising is that, while the debates in Mississippi had centered on race and class, class was ignored in the national debate. What is further surprising about the Democratic response is the blunt and open debate about race that displayed a remarkable and unrepentant bigotry. Several Deep South senators were honest about their philosophies and intentions, as exemplified in a speech given by Alfred H. Colquitt (D-Georgia). He pointed out that, demographically, African Americans were such a small percentage of the population in the North that their suffrage was not really an issue, unlike in most southern states.[13] Of course, the assumption, if not the implicit argument, behind the statement was that African American preponderance at the polls was a threat. More direct yet were the long speeches delivered by the Mississippi senators Walthall and George.

Republicans were not unanimous in their support of African Americans. Clearly some were influenced by the dominant philosophies of the period of social Darwinism and race evolution. The most surprising of the silver Republicans to oppose the Elections Bill was Senator William Stewart of Nevada, who, after helping to write and pass the Fifteenth Amendment, now claimed it was unworkable.[14] Enough of the old-line Republicans remained, however, to eloquently defend the Elections Bill. Although the Democrats began with the delaying tactic of reading aloud both the old bill sent up from the House as well as the newly amended bill from the committee, the political game was under way.[15] The Republicans were ready. But first came the Democratic response.

Using familiar tactics from the past to stall, one Democratic senator expressed his surprise that the Senate managers would even bring the bill to the floor for debate because of the sound defeat of the Republicans at the November polls.[16] Tactics for delay continued, for the new Congress, which would be Democratically controlled, would be installed at the first of the year. In response to a motion on December 11 to have evening debates and therefore speed progress, Senator John Reagan from Texas objected. He argued there should in fact be more lengthy discussion: "We are acting in a great deal of haste to propose at this time repressive measures for the passage of a repressive and coercive force bill for the people."[17] Another senator argued forcefully that the economic problems of the country were far more important than the consideration of this bill, which he called simply partisan.[18]

The most expansive speech on the bill came when Senator George took the floor on December 10. In the tradition of filibusters and in an effort to stall for time, he padded his speech with numerable references to outdated material, but the research was thorough and prodigious. How he managed to have time to produce this speech without a modern-size staff to help is puzzling. He began with the Constitutional Convention of 1787, made reference to the original Pinckney plan, and then proceeded to a tenuous and lengthy argument on who has the right to control elections and what constitutes a republican form of government. He concluded that James Madison did not believe Congress had the power to make that determination, for doing so would have meant a violation of states' rights.[19] George then shifted to a lengthy examination of the ratification of the Constitution by each state, and he made the rather startling argument that North Carolina narrowly ratified the Constitution because of the fear of losing control over elections.[20] By the time that George had reached Reconstruction, he had hit his stride. He claimed that the enfranchisement of freedmen had been "in direct violation of the pledges of leaders of the party.... It had added to the electoral body of the Union more than a million of ignorant barbarians, noncitizens and incapable of being made citizens but by a change of the Constitution, upon whose ignorance, whose superstition, whose servility it could rely on."[21] In concluding his presentation, George reminded the senators that since African Americans voted "blindly" for the Republicans, this bill was for that party's benefit and therefore partisan.[22]

In response to George's lengthy and candid speech, Senator Blair was equally blunt about his stand on the bill. He thought the South was under a despotic government and was controlled by an aristocratic tyranny. He added: "The South was never a republic, it was never a free country, and it is not a free country today. It has always been an aristocracy."[23] Senator George Vest (D-Missouri) was opposed to the bill because he thought that passage might make things worse in the South for African Americans. In support of his assertion, he referred to Isaiah Montgomery, who had made a well-reasoned testimony on levees before Vest's committee last session. Vest said that Montgomery was opposed to the Elections Bill and thought its passage would be "calamitous." To further verify Montgomery's standing, Vest asserted that he was "the most intelligent negro whom I have met in years, a gentleman who owns a plantation in Mississippi, who is the owner of a large amount of personal property." In a startling aside, Blair asked Vest whether Montgomery was a "full-blooded negro"; Vest not only affirmed, but he described him as "black as the Senator's coat."[24]

A couple of days later the official referral of the Elections Bill from the House appeared. Senator Colquitt from Georgia began an extensive lecture on the bill, in which his speech unexpectedly revealed the mind-set of the southern Democratic caucus. Although he began with references to the dangers of sectionalism, which he believed this bill would aggravate, race was the "problem." These issues did not touch the North directly, but they were "the very heart of the South." He explained his position by stating in social Darwinist terms that the African American came from a continent where "he has never emerged from savagery to civilization and in his native condition is as rude in his behavior to-day as he was in the beginning." While other races had made progress, those of African descent had not. Caucasians and Africans represented, according to Colquitt, the two extremes of civilization. He admitted that the conditions under slavery did not elevate the race, so according to his logic, the attempts under Reconstruction to grant the franchise were a blunder. Reconstruction was "made up of punitive legislation and arbitrary force bills, in the reversion of natural laws and the displacement of natural elements from their proper places."[25] It would behoove the nation to learn from the mistakes of the past and avoid the previous blunders.[26]

Suffrage, according to Senator Colquitt, was the real issue, for it granted power. He referred to the inequity of granting suffrage to African American men, when women were not enfranchised and yet were brighter. Woman suffrage made more sense, he argued, for empowering African Americans was a mistake. He referenced the spectrum of "negro domination" and the resulting misrule during Reconstruction.[27] According to Colquitt, southerners "understood" African Americans and had sympathy for them, and so northerners could leave the race to the care of southerners. Northerners, though, needed to be careful about sectionalism, which he argued had more to do with their support of the bill rather than the other way around. Sectionalism was a "deadly foe to our welfare and to the successful continuance of our free institutions." He revealed his real fears when he added that "it imperils home, soil, property, family, society, civilization itself. It is that detestable thing, the culmination of all things frightful, a result for all apprehensions, tyranny unspeakable, a government by an inferior race at home backed by a hostile and dominant race abroad."[28] To finalize his argument, he forcefully said the Elections Bill was little more than a scheme by northern states to "take possession" of the South and its "whole election machinery, to canvass districts, to whoop up reluctant voters, to form an election force and to march it through the Union with a judicial cap on its head."[29]

Senator Ephraim Wilson (D-Maryland) reiterated the by now familiar argument of the border states: passage of the Elections Bill would only serve to further antagonize the races. He pointed to Reconstruction and claimed that the policy, though kindly meant, powerfully aroused "the hatred distrust, and a blind passion for the mastery in the one race and in the other a deadly fear lest property, social order and civilization itself should perish in a wild moral and material chaos."[30]

On December 16, to further delay consideration, Senator Randall Gibson of Louisiana proposed that the Senate put aside the Elections Bill and turn to the issue of an eight-hour workday, which he claimed was more important. Although the motion was tabled, the idea of pressing the urgency of other bills simmered among the southern Democratic caucus. In the meantime, Senator Joseph Dolph (R-Oregon) brought the Elections Bill back for discussion and gave the floor to Senator John Morgan (D-Alabama), who began a long speech based on social Darwinism. Morgan then apparently surprised nearly everyone with his claim that the Fourteenth Amendment applied only to African Americans and not to Native Americans or to the Chinese. When pressed by Senators Dolph and George Edmunds, Morgan said that the issue had been clarified by both the Supreme Court and the Senate Judiciary Committee, an explanation that both senators found inadequate. Senator Frisbie Hoar (R-Massachusetts) interrupted Morgan to remind the senators that the Fifteenth Amendment did not grant voting rights, but instead stipulated that the franchise could not be denied on the basis of race or previous condition of servitude. As long as a state restricted the access to the polls in a manner not based on race, then it would be permissible. Morgan was not pleased with the insinuation that naturalization of a citizen could define suffrage, so he and Hoar continued the argument concerning "Chinamen" at some length. Morgan pointed out in turn that since women were excluded from the franchise, why could not a state do the same for other groups?[31]

That afternoon Democrats returned to another of the old arguments: Republicans had benefited enormously from the Reconstruction bills and stood to benefit from the Force Bill as well. To buttress this position, they turned to the "mishandling" of government during the years following the war, when "men were driven ... from their homes."[32] The cause of this dislocation was the "horde of slaves ... placed in mastery of the things they knew not of. Ignorance and violence held sway."[33] One Democrat claimed that the real reason the Republicans wanted this bill was that it was a "cunning contrivance to place in the hands of a minority the control of the institutions of this great people, with a bayonet for every ballot to perpetuate their ruin."[34]

At last the Republican leadership was able to rebut the arguments presented by the Democrats when Senator Dolph rose to speak on the afternoon of December 16. He positioned himself quickly into the old Abolitionist and

Radical Republican wing by referring to the "slave power" and to the Sumner-Brooks affair of 1856. He then reminded the senators that it was not disputable that African Americans had been freed, granted citizenship, and given voting rights but in some southern states had been denied voting. This bill should remedy that situation, for "the ballot is the foundation of free institutions, the medium through which the sovereign people ... control and give direction to the Government." Although he admitted that the South did have some unique problems, "it does not follow that the solution must not be in accordance with law and justice."[35]

At this point Dolph turned to answer the charges in Senator George's speech that George had questioned the authority of Congress to enact such a bill. Dolph complimented George's legal abilities, for "his positions are always stated with a clearness and terseness." That said, Dolph asserted bluntly that George was wrong in his argument, for the Constitution granted Congress that power in Article I, Section 2.

Dolph then turned to the newly written and promulgated Mississippi Constitution and moved directly to the Understanding Clause, which had caused so much discussion at the convention and among Mississippi news editors. Dolph argued that the clause itself was the "cunningly devised scheme" rather than the Elections Bill. As to why the Elections Bill was necessary, Dolph looked first at present conditions of violence directed at African Americans to intimidate them and keep them away from the polls. This system of intimidation had become so ingrained that "no artiface [sic], no expedient, no fraud, no violence, no disregard of public opinion in the North or of the moral sentiment of the world, is going to deter the solid south from maintaining its supremacy by a suppression of the colored vote." Only federal authority exercised by Congress could deter it.[36]

The next morning Dolph returned to the floor to extend his argument. He began by reading excerpts from the *Clarion-Ledger* of Mississippi in which the editors, speaking of the Elections Bill, threatened federal election supervisors: "They are likely to find the job unhealthy." How he (or any of the other Republican senators) managed to get a copy of the *Clarion-Ledger* is unrecorded, but he did. He continued by reading excerpts from news accounts in the South about mistreatment and abuse of African Americans. Dolph chastised the Democrats for their provocative speech, for talk of a race war was nonsense. Furthermore, he resented the suggestion from Democrats that Republicans were merely cynical and manipulative and that they did not have "motives of patriotism of a desire to promote justice."[37]

When Senator James Eustis of Louisiana interrupted Dolph and tried to shift the issue to Chinese immigrants and voters, Dolph replied that the question was simply a diversion. The Chinese, he argued, did not come to stay. More important, Oregon, unlike Eustis's state, would never fight against its own country.[38] To Dolph, the rebellion by the Confederacy served as a distinct separation between the behavior of the other states in question.

For the rest of the day, southern Democrats delivered more speeches on the horrors of Reconstruction, social Darwinist interpretations of African American abilities, and suggestions that African Americans had no history and no creation of a civilized society. One of the more interesting exchanges took place between Senator Matthew Butler of South Carolina and Senator Hoar. Butler, having finished his claim that Reconstruction produced a "carnival of debauchery, corruption, and crime, never before equaled in the history of civilized government," referred to a particular "carpetbagger." Hoar knew of him and pointed out that the man had immigrated to South Carolina before the war, not after. Butler had to back down.

The next day Senator Richard Coke from Texas expressed surprise that such a partisan bill was able to come to the floor of the Senate. From the House, he could understand, but the Senate had committees to bar this sort of partisan bill.[39] Senator Shelby Moore Cullom (R-Illinois), a member of the committee, took offense. He argued that the bill was constitutional despite what Senator George claimed and that the cry of "Negro equality" was like the "tar baby"; a race war was highly unlikely. He pointed to John Brown, who could not start one even during the height of slavery. Rather than dangers presented by African Americans to society, white men were the problem. Good men refused to act wisely and stop those who were running amok and creating a need for the bill to become law.[40]

The Senate continued to debate with vigor but with less planning and fewer delay tactics, although one asked what the hurry was: if the bill was important, why not slow down the debate? Senator Stewart (R- Nevada), representing the western wing of the party, expressed his concern that the South had no intention of following the provisions of the bill. African Americans were not in a position, "unaided by the military, uneducated, poor and weak," to withstand the onslaught of the "united military force of the late Confederate States." He had been in the vanguard following the war to pass the Reconstruction amendments, which still stood and could not be changed. There were remedies in the Constitution already, which included suspension of habeas corpus when a locality was in rebellion or reduction of representation in Congress if that body determined one of these solutions was appropriate.[41]

Senator Hoar objected. He read portions of the old Force Bill from 1875, which gave the president the right to suspend habeas corpus in Mississippi, Louisiana, Arkansas, and Alabama if those states interfered with free elections; but that bill was never used in spite of evidence of interference. During that period congressional Republicans were of two minds and split between Stalwarts and anti-Stalwarts. Because of this stalemate, the plight of African Americans was ignored.[42]

The following day, December 20, Senator John Spooner chastised the Democratic side for claiming they spoke for the Anglo-Saxon race, which, he pointed out, also comprised the Republican side. Fraud, he claimed, happened at polls in even the best-run states, in the North and in the South. That pervasiveness did not mean, however, that officials should not try to stop the schemes. According to Spooner, "No election can be too fair ... too honest."[43]

Spooner then turned specifically to the Mississippi Constitution. He discounted the idea that the Understanding Clause was included to expand the franchise. If the state had only determined that it did not want to be governed by ignorance and had left the restriction to a literacy requirement administered to both races alike, "that would have been honest." Instead, the state chose a connivance that was too vague and too open-ended, so that white men who could not read could get the vote while black men who could read could be denied. Echoing the editors of the *Clarion-Ledger*, he asked, "Who in the name of Heaven is to decide what is reasonable or not?"[44]

Just as the southern Democratic senators returned to a sympathetic narrative of Reconstruction, so, too, did the northern senators. Spooner referred to Judge W. W. Chisholm of Mississippi who was killed by a mob as Reconstruction was drawing to a close. With great color, Spooner retold the story of Chisholm and his family besieged in jail. Both his fourteen-year-old son and "lovely" daughter, Cornelia, tried to save him but died in the process. This story, he claimed, was his moment of realization that what was happening in the South was wrong: "I am here to say that there is wrong in this suppression of the votes in the South by force and violence and constitutions, a wrong of many phrases of which we have a right to complain ... it is not simply a local question." He pointed to the recent example of South Carolina when, in a difficult election, African Americans were warned to stay away, for it was "none of their business." Senator Butler retorted that it was good advice, to which Spooner agreed, since Prentice Matthews, a local, had been warned to stay away but came to vote and was shot down. Senator Spooner declared, "I do not approve." Southerners, he said, had no more right to deprive African Americans of the vote than to deprive them of trial by jury or freedom of religion. The guarantees of the Constitution were for everyone.[45]

Senator George rose to answer allegations from Senator Spooner regarding the Mississippi Constitution. He apologized for his recent absence and said that family duties lately had kept him away from the Senate, but he was now present to answer questions. Going directly to the heart of the matter, George affirmed that if someone could vote in Massachusetts or Connecticut, he could vote in Mississippi. When asked specifically regarding the Understanding Clause, George said the provision was similar to that in the Idaho constitution, as well as Vermont's and Connecticut's. Hoar objected and stated that George was incorrect; Hoar was well acquainted with the Vermont constitution.[46]

Senator John James Ingalls (R-Kansas) took the floor to rebut the Mississippi senator's arguments. He stated he supported reconciliation, but not in this circumstance, for clearly the Mississippi Constitution was created with the sole purpose to disfranchise and did so in direct violation of constitutional amendments. Ingalls then read from the *Clarion-Ledger* of September 18, in which H. S. Eskridge wrote that, although the constitutional convention was assembled to create a permanent white majority, he (Eskridge) objected to the Understanding Clause and called it a fraud. Ingalls asked George directly if the *Clarion-Ledger* was a reputable paper, and George affirmed it was. Ingalls then returned to articles from the paper stating that, although the new constitution reapportioned more power to white counties, the black counties had the wealth. Senator Edmunds (R-Vermont) asked what the problem was with African Americans if they had more wealth. Ingalls responded the problem was that they voted Republican.[47] Senator Ingalls then read from the October 2 issue of the *Clarion-Ledger*, which reported a growing sentiment for repeal of the Understanding Clause. Ingalls referred to the frankness of the papers of the state that implied the clause was "not good government" and that referred to gerrymandering reapportionment as a fraudulent effort to produce white control, and to the failure to submit the constitution to the people as astonishing. And just to be sure that everyone in the Senate understood the fundamental problem, he quoted the October 9 issue of the *Clarion-Ledger* that referred to Senator George as behind the Understanding Clause.[48]

Senator Anthony Higgins (R-Delaware) rose on December 22 to support the bill as a measure that would help rather than hurt; prevent fraud rather than encourage it; and facilitate supervision rather than the stealing of elections. The purpose was simple, and he was astounded that the South opposed the bill, for the conditions in the South were a violation of Christian morals. In a moment of perception that appeared to elude others, Higgins pointed out that the underlying axiom of the Democrats was that granting suffrage to African Americans had been a bad idea, and the logic of their argument built on that point. The issue, however, was moot, since the franchise had been granted.[49]

Some other points emerged from the subsequent debates that afternoon. Senator Wilkinson Call (D-Florida) argued that this bill was one of the most important in years because it would deprive the people of their power; he went so far as to say that if the Supreme Court upheld this law (if the bill were passed), then the ruling itself should be null and void.[50] Taking Call's point a bit further, Senator John McPherson (D-New Jersey) opposed the bill because he thought it mistrusted the people. In any event, he mistrusted the Republican Party, claiming it "in the spirit of fanaticism was born, and in the same spirit it exists today. In the space of two short years it has done all that [a] party could do to bankrupt the people, and it now seeks to pervert our form of government."[51]

The Senate finally broke for Christmas but returned just afterward. On December 29 Senator Frank Hiscock (R-New York) spoke. He was puzzled how the Democrats could argue they were protecting the ballot when they were the ones behind the terror and fraud at the election box. These evidences of fraud were so far reaching, he argued, that they affected the public will, just as similar problems in the cities affected the public will there.[52] He was willing to "grant the superiority of the Anglo-Saxon race," but at the same time he argued that they were "just people, generous to the weak and ever ready to extend them a helping hand.... Political rights and equalities are essential to protect the black man from being degraded, brutalized, and relegated practically to slavery."[53]

On December 30 Senator Hoar rose to support the bill before the Senate, arguing emphatically that the Lodge Elections Bill was the "last of the great measurers" to protect the Fifteenth Amendment.[54] He pointed out that this bill would not create political equality, for its reach was limited to congressional elections. In fact, during Reconstruction no more than a total of seven or eight freedmen had ever served in Congress. As an example of the lack of real threat from African Americans voting, he pointed to Bolivar County, to which Senator Walthall had alluded. That county had an overwhelming majority of black voters, yet not all the officeholders were black. Where, then, was the harm to civilization? The harm, he argued, as perceived by Democrats, was that African Americans tended to vote Republican.[55] Hoar reminded the senators that this bill would apply to federal elections, which really meant congressional, and was not to affect local elections. In making his point, Hoar was defending the Republican position against Democratic accusations that the bill would affect a state's right to regulate elections (a veiled reference to the problems in other states regarding immigrants). Southern states might want to clean up their local elections, though, for in the "present case, the crime, the blame, the barbarism, have been on the side of the superior race." He went on to argue that the assumptions of the southern Democrats, who put race above "love of country ... the principle of equality ... Christianity ... and justice," were wrong.[56]

Hoar warmed to his subject and gave specific examples. In particular he turned to Mississippi. George interrupted him to claim that the state legislature could pass a law that would enable those stricken from the rolls to be reinstated or to be removed from the rolls if incorrectly placed there. Hoar replied that the constitution contained one subterfuge after another and covered fraud by the Democrats. He then quoted Judge Calhoon, chair of the Mississippi convention, who said that the reason the convention gathered was to limit African American voting rights. Moreover, Calhoon claimed that if the convention failed in its purpose, there would be political riots that would result in African American deaths. Hoar quoted from Mississippi newspapers regarding violent containment of African American voting as "bulldozing." A murder of an African American voter in the capital city of Jackson resulted in others staying away from the polls. The former mayor of Jackson, a Republican, was interviewed for a St. Paul, Minneapolis, paper, which reported that his administration was not corrupt and was peaceful. At the end, however, intimidation became so rampant that fearful African Americans refused to go to the polls, although they constituted half of the population. The former mayor referred to a "red circular" that threatened any black man who would run for office; Hoar indicated the threats came from the White League.[57]

Upon questioning from Senator George Gray (D-Delaware), Hoar admitted that the Mississippi Constitution did not ostensibly violate the Fifteenth Amendment, but that it did depend upon trickery, fraud, and artifice. Gray then pressed to know why Hoar would trust federal oversight more than those democratically appointed within the state. Hoar pointed yet again to the trickery involved in the constitutional provisions, indicating that these people were not to be trusted. Gray attempted to draw a parallel with corruption of balloting in Philadelphia, but Hoar quickly rejoined that those problems were under Democratic Party bosses.[58]

The most damning portion of Hoar's presentation, however, related to the underlying issue of racism founded on social Darwinism. The "thousands of outrages" on African American Mississippians lay at the feet of barbarism but were perpetrated by the "superior" race. None of these atrocities had been punished, Hoar added. As examples, he pointed to the murder of Print Matthews in Mississippi, who died while trying to cast a ballot, and to the shooting of a Republican postmaster in Carrollton, Mississippi, the home of Senator George. The postmaster, an African American, was only twenty-one.[59]

Senator Joseph Dolph of Oregon was even more eloquent following a lecture given by Senator Randall Gibson, a Louisiana Democrat and graduate of Yale. Gibson had argued that democracy was founded on intelligence, education, virtue, and property. Dolph angrily declared that the United States was not elitist:

> The theory of republican government is that those admitted by the constitution and laws to have a voice in the control of the government are equal, and that the vote of the college president and the unlettered man, of the millionaire and the day laborer, of the moral and immoral (if not disfranchised for a crime) are equal in their effect, and that the will of the majority legally expressed controls. In a republic, so far as political rights are concerned, there is no aristocracy of learning, of wealth, or even of virtue.... Whenever one class of citizens can say to another class of citizens entitled in a republican government to the elective franchise; "I am intelligent and you are ignorant; I am wealthy and you are poor;" or "I am holier than thou and I will do your voting for you, and you shall not vote," that government is no longer, in fact, a republican government.[60]

Senator George rose to speak to the assembled senators on December 3, propelled not just by the allegations and arguments by the Republican speakers but also by direct references to the new Mississippi Constitution. The previous day Senator Hoar had challenged it, in particular for its Understanding Clause. Senator Dolph had referenced the new constitution back in the debates on December 17, when he referred to the clause as a "cunningly devised scheme." As far as Dolph was concerned, the Mississippi Constitution was only one example of a long problem in the South of violence directed at African Americans. According to Dolph, "No artifice, no expedient, no fraud, no violence, nor disregard of public opinion in the North or the moral sentiment of the world ... would deter the solid south from ... suppression of the colored vote."

George said that the new constitution of Mississippi was irrelevant to the debates under way. According to George, when the Senate was threatened with cloture and with night sessions under way, going off on a tangent was unproductive. Senator Spooner interrupted to note that the subject was not irrelevant, for the push to suppress the "negro" vote in the South was not right. George then proceeded to give an extensive response, which clearly he had been preparing for some time. Underlying his arguments was the assertion in his early remarks that many years had passed since the war and that the Mississippi Constitution had nothing to do with the perceived problems. The defensiveness with which he quickly diverted attention away from issues surrounding the Confederacy and Reconstruction revealed that the old wounds of war still festered.

George was an astute lawyer, having practiced for many years. He also served on the Mississippi Supreme Court and was noted for his erudite opinions. It would be wrong to assume that his lengthy speech was not effective or that it was completely off-base theoretically since he relied on racism. Instead, much of his speech in December and then another in January were well considered and reasoned even if repugnant on matters of race.

George began by asserting the very assumptions of the Republican Party, reminding them that "Mississippi is a state in the Union" and stands on an "equal footing with any other State in the American Union." He went further to assert that the state "has the same rights, the same faculties, the same powers of local self-government that any other State has," even with the franchise as long as it did not violate the Fifteenth Amendment.[61]

In his aggressive but defensive posture, George turned to the hypocrisy of northern states and argued that they also had a history of property qualifications as well as literacy qualifications, pointing in particular to Connecticut. Despite an irritated Senator Joseph Hawley's response (R-Connecticut), George forcibly contended that he had researched Connecticut when he was planning to work on the Mississippi Constitution. George then turned to restrictions placed on African American citizens of Massachusetts and Rhode Island. Until recently, Massachusetts had not allowed service on juries or in the militia, even after emancipation. Rhode Island's right to the franchise was extended only through the Fifteenth Amendment, and the state did not allow intermarriage or licensing for taverns.[62]

George continued his listing of negligent practices of northern states and African Americans. When speaking of Vermont, he was again interrupted by Hawley, who had sent out for confirming information. According to Hawley, the offending statutory language had been removed in 1876. Why then, asked Hawley, was George listing old, antiquated rules and laws long since gone? Hawley emphasized that what was happening at that moment was more important and asked why Mississippi was out of step from the rest of the country. In response, George continued his roll call of northern states and their regulations regarding the public life of African Americans in their states, but, as Hawley pointed out, most of these situations referred to a century earlier.[63] George continued to return to Connecticut as an example, and Hawley always jumped up to defend his state. Eventually, George pointed out that Hawley's response was understandable, for no one liked to sit and listen to his state being attacked on the floor of the Senate by outsiders.[64]

The list continued for another hour, as he slowly headed west, producing heated responses from the senators of those states. George concluded his catalog by saying that other states were equally as concerned about the status of African Americans within their midst and regulated their access to the polity and other civic duties. Michigan, for example, allowed foreigners to vote, but not African Americans until the passage of the Fifteenth Amendment. George returned to his belief that the divisions on both sides of the Civil War were as inflamed as in the past and that the North still wanted retribution. As a case in point, he observed that Michigan's case revealed that "when their minds were not distorted by sectional prejudices," they also regarded with caution the "fitness of African American citizens for civic responsibilities."[65]

Arguing that Reconstruction was simply a way of punishing the South for the war, rather than acknowledging higher motives, George pointed out that by 1876, "there came an end to all this corruption and misrule." Mississippi, he noted, had a large majority of African Americans, whom he described as "unlettered, ignorant, more than 100,000 of the voters being, as I am informed, unable to read, unused, unpracticed, uninformed." He thought that Mississippi, in its "wisdom," saw it "proper to call a convention to correct the evil, not of negro suffrage, but of ignorance and debased suffrage." Because there was nothing in the Fifteenth Amendment that forbids discrimination based on education and literacy, and since Mississippi wished to have an educated and responsible voter base, the state sought relief through a new state constitution.[66]

Hawley, however, was as equally as adept as George. Hawley found the references to the *Clarion-Ledger*'s attacks on the Understanding Clause, which the paper called "cowardly and evasive" and "ridiculous and odious." He said this attack by the state's own press was what should be explained rather than Connecticut's ancient history.[67] George simply replied that he had no intention of defending the press, for it had a freedom to speak for itself. Rather, he would defend his state's constitution on "legal and just grounds in accordance with the precedents set." At this point it was clear that George had read his extensive list of northern abuses of African American rights not as examples of hypocrisy but as precedent from a legal standpoint.[68]

When Hawley asked George the simple question—why not allow the majority (by 72,000) to rule—George replied that Connecticut also did not allow majority rule. In fact, certain Republican townships in Connecticut held a stranglehold over Democrats because of the boundary lines and the way in which they were drawn. As George pointed out, Connecticut, which had a majority of registered Democrats and had voted Democrat for president, "never gets a Democratic governor and never gets a Democratic representative in the Senate of the United States."[69]

The question arose then from the senator from Vermont as to the promulgation of the constitution rather than submitting it to the people of the state for ratification. George said that Mississippi had had only one constitution submitted for ratification (the one under Reconstruction, which he implied was not a good example), and that Vermont had never submitted its constitution to the people. The senator from Vermont countered that their present constitution was written in the eighteenth century.[70]

George was trying to indicate that the "problem" in the South was recognized as one nationally, that all states shared these reservations, but that the South was the most at risk of "negro domination." This threat was based on the greater numbers of African Americans in the state and the perceived injustices of the Reconstruction era, which he attributed to the newly freed slaves. Despite his long-windedness and use of out-of-date material, his arguments resonated with some Republican senators, who feared immigrant and particularly Chinese voters. The South was not the only region with an identified racial animosity, for the West erupted with sporadic riots aimed at Chinese immigrants. During the 1880s violence targeted at Chinese communities exploded in San Francisco; Denver; Rock Springs, Wyoming; and Hell's Canyon, Oregon.[71] The Chinese Exclusion Act, passed in 1882, was the first such law to restrict a type of immigration and was supposed to assuage the growing unhappiness of the nativists in the region. Both the immediate and long-term effects remain debatable, but the act does reveal a distinct racial animosity toward this ethnic group in the West—hence the resonance of white southern concerns with ones in the West. If the South could address its "problem," then could not the western states do the same?

Eloquence was not enough to bring northern Republicans back into line. Business and economics were rapidly becoming the major issues of the party. Senator Edward Wolcott (R-Colorado) bluntly declared that the franchise was important, but that the economy was far more important than the question of the franchise for African Americans. In fact, he added, if the economy would improve in the South, better race relations would follow. He also expressed concern that passing the bill would bring too much interference by the federal government into the states, saying: "Such interference is contrary to the spirit of our institutions and an obstacle to the right enjoyment of our liberties."[72]

Although President Harrison continued to press for a vote, the tide had turned. Stewart moved that the Elections Bill be shelved in order to consider the Sherman Free Coinage of Silver Act, and the Democrats happily agreed. The Senate passed the motion 34 to 29, moved to the Sherman bill, and passed it only nine days later. To bring the Elections Bill back to the floor, however, Vice President Levi Morton had to vote to break a tie.[73]

When the debate began again in January, Senator George returned to the floor for further "edification" of his colleagues on the new state constitution. With a nod to the issues under debate, George continued his extensive list of northern states in violation of the principles of the Elections Bill itself. Having endured suggestions that his state used purposefully vague phrasing regarding voter registration, he pointed in particular to similar language in these northern constitutions. After proceeding down his list a bit, he asked, "Can any man cast a stone at the constitution of Mississippi as containing a loose and indeterminate standard for the registration of voters" compared to Vermont and Connecticut?[74] Answering his own question, he asserted that Mississippi's provision is "less indeterminate, less lax, less liable to abuse than the constitution of any one of the states to which I have called to the attention of the Senate."[75]

After returning briefly to his list of abuses in other states, George returned to his thesis. Because he could not understand anyone who would acknowledge equality of the races, he believed that the motive behind the Reconstruction acts was simply "bitterness and hatred and as a punishment" for the South: "The statesmen of that day, [were] maddened with passion, embittered by a long and bloody war . . . filled with bitterness." So, George concluded, they "adopted negro suffrage under the temper expressed in these extracts." He then referred to an assertion of James Garfield, who had said, "It was the right of the victorious government to indict, try, and convict and hang every rebel traitor in the south for the bloody conspiracy against the Republic, and that they had forfeited every right of citizenship by becoming traitors and public enemies."[76]

To further buttress his argument that spite and bitterness, or, as he put it, "wormwood and gall," were the motives behind congressional Reconstruction, George continued to quote from damning sources. According to George, Senator Frank Brandagee of Connecticut had said that the rebellion still seethed in the South: "It has made loyalty odious and treason respectable by forcing traitors into the gubernatorial chairs. . . . It has armed treason with the sword of the law. . . . It hisses out curses against the Union from the sibilant tongues of its women." Pointing to Thaddeus Stephens, who had certainly been open about his motives, George quoted him as saying, "'I believe in my conscience that on the ascendancy of that party depends the safety of this great nation." Stephens advocated African American suffrage to counterbalance the power of the rebels, but "if it be a punishment to traitors, they deserve it."[77]

George continued his theme of evil and selfish intent on the part of the Radical Republicans of the Reconstruction period by quoting Roscoe Conklin (former senator, Radical Republican, and a leader of the Stalwarts), who admitted this viewpoint by party leaders: "by appealing to the passions, the enmities, and the bitterness which had grown out of the war, by threatening the Northern people with an immigration of negroes into their borders, was the American Congress led ... to the imposition of the concededly unfit suffrage of negroes."[78]

But George had not yet ceased castigating northern states. At this point George was less concerned with the past than he was with the present prejudices regarding immigrants in the North and West (particularly the Chinese in the West), where he suspected he had the most likelihood of support. George argued that these immigrant groups, whether African American, Chinese, or southern European, did not have the history or traditions of a high civilization. Clearly the Ming Dynasty and the Ashanti Kingdom were unknown to him, but apparently so, too, were the Greek and Roman civilizations. In contrast, he thought that white southerners, who remained undiluted by immigrant populations, held to an Anglo-Saxon culture, with its traditions of duty, honor, and love of home. Because of these traditions, inherent to the good running of democratic governance, a white man did not have to have formal education or be able to read. He pointed to men in his state who had made fortunes through hard work even though illiterate.[79]

Senator Hawley interrupted George to ask his colleague, Senator Walthall, about counties in Mississippi that had a majority of black voters. There followed an interesting and revealing exchange. According to Walthall, they were doing well, but George interrupted to add, only if they took advice from white men. When Hawley pressed the issue, having understood that some counties were controlled by African Americans, Walthall rose to respond. He admitted that in no county were African Americans holding the tax power. According to him, in some counties they held two out of the five board of supervisor positions, emphasizing that "the negroes in those counties hold every office consistent with the safety of the public and private interest." And when further inquiries came from Hawley, Walthall added that the African Americans in those counties voted for congressmen and did so "peaceably." The counties to which he was referring were those with fusion traditions, which were shortly to disappear. Hawley admitted that free voting was all that the Senate asked, and Walthall retorted, "There is no necessity for a force bill." At this point Walthall had walked into a trap, for Hawley responded that he did not believe that African Americans could vote freely in the South, since George argued about the "utter impossibility of permitting it."[80] If nothing else, this difference between the two Mississippi senators revealed the paternalistic leanings by Walthall and the white county philosophical tilt by George.

George appeared oblivious to the logical difficulty of arguing that the allegations were untrue, that there was no corruption and no violation of the Fifteenth Amendment, and that southern prejudices were true and noble and based on science. George asserted that the northern states were hypocritical. For example, he pointed to Lincoln's advocacy for African colonies for resettlement of African Americans; now even Massachusetts did not want a migration of African Americans to its borders. Mississippi, he reiterated, did not want a return to the "horrible" days of Reconstruction, which he referred to as a "dark period" overrun by an "ignorant and besotted and incapable race." Then African Americans were "held under the influence of foreigners and strangers' high carnival of crime, or corruption, and incompetency in our halls of legislation and in our courts of justice."[81]

Senator William Fry (R-Maine) interrupted to ask whether there had been more state "treasurers who have been defaulters since the carpetbag rule departed than there were while it existed in the South." George responded he did not know. There had been one such man in Mississippi, but he was not in prison. Fry pressed and asked if there were not six in the South? George said his only concern was Mississippi, but he noted that the bad influences of misbehavior had continued after Reconstruction![82]

George continued to argue that Mississippi had been readmitted and was now on the same standing as any other state in the Union. So long as it did not violate the US Constitution or its amendments, it had a right to create a polity the way it defined it. Mississippi, he asserted, had no choice but to look for ways to ensure a literate and educated set of voters, and to do so, it had passed restrictions akin to those already established by other states. The only novel avenue was an effort to expand the voting population by offering an Understanding Clause to ensure that people who had never had the opportunity to learn to read nevertheless could prove that they were as able as those who were literate.[83]

When the Senate reconvened on January 20, George returned to the Understanding Clause and said that the negative reaction to it appeared to be based on the looseness of its construction. He reminded his colleagues that in his previous speeches, he had addressed the problem of loose construction in other states. He then claimed that the only reason that there were doubts was that Mississippi was a southern state. Laying down the gauntlet, he said that such protestations were objectionable: "Mississippi is an American State or she is not. She belongs to the American Union or she is a province of the United States.... There is no such thing as a union of unequal States."[84]

In answering newspaper objections to the interpretation of the clause indicating that there was no appeal of the decision of the registrar, George said the papers were misinformed; the word "registrar" was used as a verb, not a noun.[85] At this point Hawley objected, pointing out that the people of Mississippi were not blind; they knew what was going on. As an example, he read from the convention's opening statement by Judge Calhoon, which was brutally clear about the primacy of race. George, though, argued that the constitution was about far more than race, and he pointed to several areas in the document that dealt with important, progressive ideas, such as women's rights. George was right and wrong about the complexity of the constitution, a typical position for him, and one that certainly engendered some ethical questions. Despite Calhoon's opening statement, the constitution was about more than race, but race was strongly present. Those other issues were not always as benign as his fellow senators might have one believe.[86]

Senator Stewart continued his conservative move away from his earlier stance of support for freedmen. Although he nodded to the problems in the South by arguing that passage of the bill would result in renewed violence directed at African Americans and further sectional discord, he also contended that the bill made federal powers much stronger, and thus would endanger the nation: "Such interference is contrary to the spirit of our institutions and an obstacle to the right enjoyment of our liberties."[87] He further argued that local government might well be wrong, but the purview of democracy was to allow wrong decisions (for who was to decide what was right or wrong but the people themselves?).

The motion to shelve the bill carried 35 to 34, and the Lodge Elections Bill was dead. Stewart thought this move saved the country.[88] President Harrison, though, responded that one saying that one section needed to be left alone meant the majority did not rule. Hoar privately blamed businessmen who put their selfish interests above party and the country.[89] Newspapers, even Republican ones, were expressing concern. The *Philadelphia Inquirer*, which polled Republicans, hoped for defeat of the bill, and the *St. Louis Globe-Democrat*, which was a Republican organ in spite of its name, believed it better to "tolerate the evil" of disfranchisement rather than to see "Federal interference in local affairs."[90] The result, according to Hoar, was that more people left the Republican Party over the Lodge Elections Bill than joined: "A strongly partisan Republican Congress had made its final surrender in obedience to the clearly expressed sentiment of the nation. The last threat to what Southerners cherished most—control of their domestic affairs—was permanently destroyed."[91]

By 1892 the issue of the Elections Bill had become so polarizing that Democratic strategists played on the fears of the entire country, often ignoring the tariff, which was more problematic for each political party. Democratic pamphlets in New York hammered at the threat the Force Bill posed, for if Congress could pass this bill, the federal government could take over most state legislatures.[92] Charles Dana of the *New York Sun* pointed directly to the corruption issues of "black" administrations at the end of Reconstruction as a prime example of the dangers of "negro domination" that would emerge from passage of the Elections Bill. Although there were expressions of continued support for an elections bill, even some Republican candidates came out forcefully against a bill that had already died, clear evidence of the opposition they found back home. Given the context of the time, however, threats of a corruption of government, and inevitably the capitalist system, were palpable. The Populists were a rising threat in the West and in the South. Their source of power sprang from the frustrations of farmers in both regions. Yet agriculture was not the only area of concern, for 1892 was the same year in which the strike under way at Homestead, Pennsylvania, became violent and added to the nation's fears about the rising of the underclasses. Also unwelcome was an Elections Bill provision that would empower African Americans, whom many in the North and the South had come to distrust and fear as unreliable. Moreover, reenfranchisement might well tip the balance toward political philosophies that were both innovative and untried and therefore a violation of the perceived natural order.[93]

The defeat of the Elections Bill was not the end of the matter, at least so far as the Democrats were concerned, for they feared a return to the restrictions imposed during Reconstruction. More urgent to them, at least nationally, was the continuation on the books (and therefore a threat) of the federal elections laws from the period following the Civil War. The time to expunge forever these laws from the books came to the Democrats in 1893 with the election of Cleveland and the subsequent sweep of Congress. When Cleveland called a special session of Congress to deal with the emergency of the economic panic, the members of his own party had other plans.[94]

The idea of repealing these laws had been tempting for some time. Without question southern Democrats wanted them gone, and they argued vociferously that these laws were unconstitutional, because citizenship itself derived from the states. This argument was not without legal basis, for that is exactly what Chief Justice Roger Taney had argued in *Dred Scott*.[95] The difficulty for their position was the intervening constitutional amendments—Thirteen, Fourteen, and Fifteen—which recognized not only citizenship for African Americans but also the right not to be denied the franchise on the basis of race or previous condition of servitude. While modern readers might well interpret the Fifteenth Amendment as awarding the right to vote, white southerners did not see it that way; nor did many northerners. All states had some restrictions on voting—for instance, restricting the franchise of women or not allowing it at all. As far as Democrats were concerned, states had the right to decide for themselves, just as long as they did not specifically target

African Americans. The fact that they were targeted appeared not to matter if discrimination was not stated openly in the law or constitution itself.

As explained in the previous chapter, this idea of not openly denying the franchise to African Americans because of race or previous condition of servitude was the foundation of southern manipulation of the franchise. Mississippi's experiment appeared to be holding. Other states were watching, for they were as concerned about fraud and violence at the polls as Mississippi had been.[96] They thought that they would have to follow Mississippi's example or would have to continue to secure the ballots. Since the end of Reconstruction, they had been able to use violence to intimidate and to control the polls. Why, then, did southern Democrats of the old Confederacy become concerned and worried about a perceived threat? The simple answer was political, starting with the Elections Bill itself.

Though the Elections Bill failed, it might have succeeded had not the 1892 elections intervened. With these elections, the Democrats regained control. When Cleveland won the election in 1884, Republicans had taken stock of their position and determined that the reason they had lost was that the South no longer allowed free elections. In short, the old Confederate states were in violation of the Reconstruction amendments. Republicans believed that if they could correct the problem in the South, they would be in control again. A cynic might point to this position and think that the Republicans only wanted power. Yet there is every indication that a moral certainty underlay the Republican position: this was simply the right thing to do. When they returned to power, the Republicans then introduced the Elections Bill, but they did not have the full support of their own party. When in turn the Democrats returned to power, they pushed to defeat the Force Bill—and did. Although still in control of the House, Democrats, who certainly viewed the issue more cynically, decided that the Republicans would again try to retaliate when they returned to control (as cyclically, they would). Therefore it behooved the Democrats to expunge any laws that might interfere with the right of a state to determine its own franchise and to run elections the way it saw fit. In addition, Democrats from all over the country had never liked the Reconstruction laws, which they viewed as granting too much authority to the federal government. The chance to undo them was tempting.[97]

By 1893 a Democratic-controlled Congress was ready specifically to allow states to order their own elections, and so they repealed the last of the Reconstruction legislation. President Cleveland had called Congress into session to deal with the panic of 1893 by repealing the Sherman Silver Purchase Act, the very act that Republicans had been willing to jettison the Elections Bill to enact. The Democratic Congress not only revoked the Sherman Silver

Purchase Act but also dismantled the remaining Reconstruction laws that provided for federal oversight of congressional elections.

When the House met to discuss repeal of the Sherman Silver Purchase Act, Congressman Henry St. George Tucker of Virginia introduced a bill to repeal over forty sections of the Reconstruction laws regarding federal elections. These sections provided for election supervisors, in addition to enumerating penalties for violation of election laws. According to Democratic congressmen, the original laws were unconstitutional since they interfered with a state's right to create, interpret, and enforce its own laws on the franchise. Debate erupted, but the fireworks were over quickly. The discussion centered on what the federal government legitimately could do. According to Republicans, Congress not only could intervene, but must. They pointed to Article I, Section 4, of the Constitution, which gives to Congress the right to regulate "times, places and manner" of elections; Congress also might alter regulations, which they stipulated would often mean state laws. Given their belief in the righteousness of their position, Republicans used everything they had to make an effective argument. They quoted from the Federalist Papers, particularly the ones written by Alexander Hamilton on elections.[98] They pointed to decisions by the Supreme Court that had upheld the constitutionality of the Reconstruction laws, particularly *Ex parte Siebold* and *Ex parte Yarbrough*. Finally, Senator George Hoar argued in decisive tones that the real issue was one of fraud or virtue, which he implied only the Republicans could fix ethically.[99]

Republicans revealed that they had not let go of the past any more than had the Democrats. Senator William Chandler hit at the fraudulent and violent practices in the southern states and said, "Year after year, unscrupulous oligarchies perpetuate their absolute political control of the States."[100] A solid number of Republicans before and after the Civil War had assumed that a slave oligarchy was in control of the southern states and did not allow the common man to have a voice in the democracy. Of course, the difficulty with this argument is the logical progression: when the oligarchy has been disrupted from its political, social, and economic domination, then the common man will bring the South back into alignment with the thinking in the North. The reality was quite different.

In short order the House passed the bill to repeal the Reconstruction acts on elections. After the start of the regular session, the Senate passed the bill in only two months, and President Cleveland quickly signed it into law. Under the guise of reconciliation, the Democrats returned control of federal elections to the states. Therefore this avenue for potential redress of the problems inherent in the Mississippi Constitution firmly closed. It only remained for the federal courts to voice their support or opposition.

CHAPTER 10

Defending the New Constitution in the Federal Courts

The ipse dixit promulgation of the Mississippi Constitution did not stop a backlash to it, although options for opposition began to dwindle. Nevertheless, white voters tended to close ranks and claim that the constitutional provisions for disfranchisement would be the salvation of the state. By the end of the decade white citizens were just beginning to realize what had happened. Voting dropped precipitously among white men and reached its nadir in 1892 and another low point in 1904.[1] According to a study in the *Nation* in 1892, only 1,037 whites and 1,085 African Americans utilized the Understanding Clause to vote: "Under the provisions of the new constitution of Mississippi 68,127 of the 110,100 male whites over 21 were registered along with 8,615 of the 147,205 male Negroes over 21." This effort at disfranchisement left a markedly reduced voting population, roughly one in seventeen among African Americans and two out of three whites.[2] In the years following, as state leaders defended their constitution against national attacks, within the state even the former Democratic and Farmers' Alliance opponents of the constitution rallied around the document.[3] That did not mean, however, that factions no longer existed. They did.

Underneath the kudzu-like thicket of politics in the state were issues created by the new constitutional provisions; power struggles to control the future of the state emerged from the reduced voting population. The need for control connected strongly to perceptions of inflicted wrongs, of aspirations for the future, and of the confines of a meager budget. Beyond a reduction in the number of citizens exercising their franchise, other effects of the constitution were less apparent. Historians have argued for years as to who won the black-white county divides within this and other southern constitutional conventions. For example, Albert Kirwan's argument concerning Mississippi in his book *Revolt of the Rednecks* was that the long-term effect was to empower the white counties at the expense of the old elites. According to Kirwan, the result was that Mississippi got James K. Vardaman and Theodore G. Bilbo as governor and senator. While he does not convincingly prove this difficult argument, to some extent he may have been right. From a positive aspect, undermining the power of the old elites may have enabled the state to protect itself (environmentally and progressively) against the worst incursions of industry and urban development. It may have protected the voice of lower-class white men, and it may have kept taxes low. But doing so came at a dire cost, particularly to the treatment of African Americans. Within the decade following the convention, former delegates in at least two major incidents tried to forestall erupting violence from whitecappers from the eastern part of the state. Reprieve was brief. By this point, under tremendous pressure, action became nearly impossible. Empowering white counties unleashed a whirlwind of violence, bigotry, and intimidation that held the state back for over a hundred years.

Among African Americans, however, there was a growing awareness of a need to react. Leaders earlier counseled that the convention could not entirely disfranchise and therefore it was prudent to bide time; but this advice proved to be a faulty assumption, even as accommodationists continued to hold sway in many southern states for several years. Those heavily under the influence of Booker T. Washington had reached similar conclusions earlier, probably because of a realistic appraisal of the overwhelming and dangerous odds they were facing.[4] Others looked in vain for help from outside the South. Hope for remedy from the federal government began to fade after the failure of the Force Bill, especially when the remaining provisions still on the books from the Reconstruction era were repealed.[5] The lone possible opportunity for relief came from the courts (state and especially federal), the final hope for redress. But there, too, their hopes withered. The final blow came in late 1897 when the US Supreme Court agreed to hear a case on the controversial provisions of the state's constitution. The decision in *Williams v. Mississippi* validated stipulations that established disfranchisement.[6] The *Williams* case is often overshadowed by the decision the previous year of *Plessy v. Ferguson*, but southern states were just as interested in the Mississippi case as they looked for signals about their ability to move forward without federal interference.

This was, after all, the period in which the US Supreme Court decided the *Civil Rights Cases* (narrow construction of the Civil War Amendments, striking down much of the Civil Rights Act of 1875, 109 U.S. 3 [1883] and *Plessy v. Ferguson*, 163 U.S. 537 [1896], in which the Court approved the principle of "separate but equal"). Indeed, in the year after *Plessy* the Court declined to strike down the constitutional provisions that established disfranchisement.

Mixed among the federal court decisions were a group of Mississippi court decisions, all of which rejected challenges to the constitution. Nonetheless, the multiplicity of court decisions reflect further light on the thicket of state politics.

◆ ◆ ◆

All the court decisions rode the national tides of political fortunes that shifted in the 1890s. In particular, many Republicans did not understand that their traditional platforms had given way to new realities. At first, because of the rise of Populism in the South, some Republicans saw a new movement providing some optimism.[7] The People's Party began on July 4, 1892, in Omaha, Nebraska, when delegates met to nominate a national ticket. The old Farmers' Alliance of the South began to gravitate to this new party, and, in an effort to break the bonds holding the Democratic Party together, they looked to the time-tested concept of fusion to create a new political voice. Throughout the South, Democrats viewed this new party as a threat to the control of the region, and they sought to undermine it. In fact, their fears were justified in many southern states, particularly North Carolina. For Democrats, the prospects of fusion between Populists and African Americans, between the advocates for the common man and the race they feared, was enough to galvanize many to expunge the remaining Reconstruction laws from federal statutes.[8]

Mississippi, however, was an exception to the national trends, although Populism remained attractive to men in the state. The elections in 1891 looked promising for the Farmers' Alliance, and several organizers flocked to the state in an attempt to unseat the state's two senators, including Senator George. The resulting fight was bitter.[9] According to one historian, "The regular Democrats controlled county election managers, stole registration books, and burned Frank Burkitt's newspaper offices."[10] The election of 1891, though, revealed just how thorough the voting restrictions were in Mississippi. Another historian asserted that "the seven congressional districts of Mississippi posted an aggregate vote that was less than the total in a single district in New York."[11] As noted earlier, both white and black voting numbers plummeted, so that in the 1892 election, which included Republicans, Democrats, and Populists, the total of votes cast was only 52,809 out of a potential electorate of 257,305.[12] Burkitt, who had been a delegate at the convention and voted against the constitution, shifted from the Farmers' Alliance to the Populists, although he agonized over the decision for some time. His decision was based on his sympathies with the common man and a revulsion against the moneyed interests. To him, "the Democratic [P]arty has ceased to hear them cry for relief and I cannot follow it further."[13] Emotions rose so high that during this period Burkitt was once knocked out while speaking during a political rally.[14] Despite this resistance, he created a formidable force that frightened some of the conservative planters in the Delta. If the Populists could gain control, then the Delta planters might well have much more in taxes to pay. Within the state, however, the "wool hat boys," as Burkitt's followers were known, created more of a threat that needed to be addressed.

Many of the issues crossed racial lines, for African American voters also were seeking a voice for the embattled farmer. James H. Powell, a Mississippi Colored Farmers' Alliance official, expressed his frustration with all political parties. He argued that rather than support old politics, "it is the aim of every colored farmer of Mississippi to send men to our national legislature who will represent the farmer." Dependence on the present lot, he concluded, was a delusion.[15] Still frustrated in 1899, the Colored Farmers' Alliance, at its national meeting in Cincinnati, proposed merging both alliances and creating a third party. Mississippi's Colored Farmers' Alliance was more cautious, for the state organization needed to be careful, given the atmosphere of the time. It did, however, toy with nominating its own men. Nothing came of it.[16]

Money was the source of the difficulty, whether for the individual, the farmer, or the state. Between the end of the old constitution and the advent of the new, when persons holding office were to stay until the new order took effect, the state ran into difficulties with money: in short, it could not pay its bills. This shortfall in the budget had been a problem for decades, but it came to a crisis in 1894. Corruption, as in many areas of the country in the Gilded Age, was also a problem. In 1890 State Treasurer William L. Hemingway was convicted of having embezzled $315,612 of the state's money, for which he received a sentence of five years. In June 1894 Governor Stone pardoned Hemingway, who had served three of his five years.[17] Perhaps Stone was sympathetic, for he, too, faced a rising problem in meeting the state budget. To "tide over the treasury emergency," Governor Stone decided that the state should issue special warrants. He contacted the St. Louis Bank Note Company to provide imprints of good five-, ten- and twenty-dollar denominations, which he instructed should look good because they would need to be in circulation for a few years. The local national bank wrote to the Department of Treasury in Washington, DC, to inquire whether these warrants required the 10 percent tax imposed on paper currency not issued by state banks. In a polite but firm note, Hazen, chief of the Secret Service, responded that there was no need for the tax, for states had a right to print special warrants, but that, unfortunately, the designs were entirely too close to that of federal currency and were therefore in violation of federal counterfeit law.[18] In a panic, the governor wrote to Senator George: "I regard the action of Mr. Hazen as unwarranted and presumptuous in the extreme.... The idea that a penal Statute, made to apply to criminal cases, where forgery and counterfeiting is [sic] sought to be prevented and punished, should be made applicable to the execution of a statute of a state is revolting to me."[19] Making matters worse, Stone ordered the state auditor not to comply with the directions of Hazen and the Secret Service, but instead to continue issuing the warrants.[20]

Stone had good reason to be worried. On September 10, 1894, he, along with State Auditor W. W. Stone and State Treasurer Evans, were arrested by agents of the Secret Service. The charge was that they had "unlawfully and feloniously caused to be printed, photographed and made and aided in printing, photographing, and making certain print and impressions in the likeness of the notes of the national currency." In other words, they were charged with counterfeiting. Former justice Campbell said, "This is a scandalous proceeding. It is making a mountain of out of a molehill. The Governor and other officials are treated as felons simply for executing the law of the United States, providing for a special creation of warrants."[21]

Senator George immediately went into action to intervene on behalf of the state. He telegrammed Governor Stone to withdraw promptly the plates from St. Louis, so that any inquiry or trial would have to take place in Mississippi rather than in St. Louis. George then wrote John G. Carlisle, secretary of the treasury. In an undated letter that clearly follows the early investigations, George points out that "after weeks given for investigation and reflection ... it is a matter of doubt, whether there has been any violation of the statute of the United States." Moreover, since there clearly was no criminal intent on the part of the state, to require a hearing in another state would be prejudicial. To show "decent regard" for the fiscal system of a state that would be discredited by any hearing, every attempt should be made to simplify the process. George's importuning worked, and the matter resulted in little harm to the state. The problem with the warrants, however, revealed a state with little understanding of what it needed to be doing by creating these warrants, much less how to ensure their proper distribution. All the efforts exerted to lowering the tax burden of the state had produced immediate and long-term difficulties.[22]

◆ ◆ ◆

The most pervasive of the unexpected attacks on the constitution related to the state's finances, especially those involving education. The constitution had, after all, stated that the poll tax would be for the exclusive use of supporting education. The proviso quickly became entangled in the struggles of politicians to deal with the near insolvency of the state. In addition, there was the conundrum that more money for education required more payers of the poll tax; yet at least in some counties, more payers meant more African American voters, possibly a majority of voters. Although the actual discussion by a court was more than a little arcane, the importance of the issue was reflected in the significance of the attorneys on each side in *W. T. Ratliff v. Ambus Beale*, discussed below.

The state's financial difficulties and tax structure shortcomings meant that the officials of the state struggled to find any alternative they could in creating tax revenue. And they were not alone. At first African American leaders and the few remaining white Republicans were uncertain about what to do. With deep division in leadership, Republicans relied on the guidance of John Roy Lynch, the former Mississippi congressman who had left the state many years earlier and mostly lived in Washington, DC.[23] While he still held land and influence in the state, he vied for control of state politics from afar. His primary opponent for control of the party was James Hill, who was backed by Isaiah Montgomery.[24] Lynch was decidedly unhappy with the disfranchisement provisions of the constitution, but the area that really galled him was the race-based allocation of the poll tax to schools (taxes paid by whites would go to white schools, and taxes paid by African Americans should support theirs).[25] Lynch quickly figured that restricting provisions for African American children would forever condemn them to a life of illiteracy and therefore no franchise. If schools had no money, the children would never have the necessary schools, teachers, or books, much less equipment, for profitable instruction. Lynch's idea was that the poll tax should be required rather than be voluntary; that way, African American children would have more money for their schools than white children, because there were more African Americans in the state.

James Hill, who really did live and work in the state, pushed back.[26] Apparently he feared that Lynch's idea would result in a backlash by white citizens of the state. Several institutions, as well as ministers, pressed for Lynch to back away. He did not. Democrats were overjoyed with this sort of infighting. Lynch realized at this point that he no longer had a political presence in the state. Because he had lost his political base, his leadership failed, but his plan concerning the poll tax did not die. Several black ministers met in Jackson to consider the proposal, since by that time they were getting desperate for money and support for their schools. The state legislature took a good look at the idea as well and then failed to pass it.

Lynch was not alone in supporting this concept of making the poll tax a requirement, whether a man registered to vote or not. The new state attorney general, Wiley Nash, already concerned about the finances in the state, agreed that this plan had possibilities; but the men who had drawn the constitution were firmly opposed.[27] Senator George, Solomon Calhoon, and Frank Johnston feared that requiring the poll tax would produce an increase in African American registration. To their minds, this had the potential to undo the work of the convention. Nash disagreed. The tax, he believed, could be paid before males were eligible to apply to vote, and at that point they would have to prove either literacy or cognizance.

In fact, Nash thought he had an answer through the courts.[28] What if the poll tax was not optional? The money from the tax could be allocated for support of the public schools. He quickly calculated that if the tax was required, it would make a huge difference to the schools. After consultation, he worked with W. T. Ratliff, the Hinds County sheriff, to find a poor African American man whose meager belongings would be confiscated and sold at auction to pay delinquent poll taxes as a test case. Ambus Beale was an adult male resident of Jackson from the Fifth District of Hinds County who owed the poll tax for 1895. He was a laborer who supported his family "by daily labor and owns no property except his clothing, a bed stead, bed clothing . . . a small wash stand and some other small articles of household furniture of a plain and cheap quality, consisting simply of the absolute necessities of life." Court documents explain that under Mississippi law, these items were not normally taxable and had a value of around $20 to $30.[29] Sheriff Ratliff took the bedstead and planned to auction it in lieu of poll tax payments.

The case began in the Hinds County Chancery Court and eventually made it to the Mississippi Supreme Court.[30] Because the issues were profound, Beale was represented by Frank Johnston, Solomon Calhoon (former president of the convention), and former governor Robert Lowry. On the other side were J.A.P. Campbell and Wiley Nash. Beale's attorney complained that this move by the sheriff was not legal, for according to Section 243 of the Mississippi Constitution, "no criminal proceedings shall be allowed to enforce the collection of the poll tax"; and under Section 241, penalty for nonpayment "is loss of citizens' rights of suffrage during the period of delinquency." Moreover, the attorney added, according to Article 12 of the constitution, the intent was to make the poll tax a way of regulating "a large class of voters . . . [for] to forgo the privilege of exercising the rights of suffrage, [was] the only penalty for the non-payment of the poll tax."[31] Just to be sure the court understood the issue, the attorneys added that under this approach the state had gained "a large majority of intelligent and competent white electors." If Beale's meager goods could be confiscated, then the poll tax would be compulsory, "the consequence of which will be an enormous increase in the number of negro voters throughout the state, thereby impairing if not destroying the franchise scheme advised by the Constitutional Convention of 1890."³² Solomon Calhoon was even less measured in his handwritten response, arguing that the convention refused to make the poll tax compulsory, for its "purpose was to exclude <u>ignorance</u> not <u>niggers</u>" (Calhoon's emphasis).³³

In the brief filed for Beale on appeal, the attorneys continued their argument that "there was no concealment of the purpose of the convention to make the payment of the poll tax a condition of the suffrage." Specifically, they argued, the purpose of the tax was to "disfranchise the illiterate and non–tax paying negro voters and to give the state a majority of white voters." They pointed out that Senator George had admitted as much on the floor of the Senate when questioned by Senator Hoar about the Mississippi Constitution. The attorneys further added that it was idle to argue that the tax's primary purpose was to support the schools, for the convention had removed the poll tax from the education section and just to be clear had placed it under the franchise. Why did the constitution specifically say that "no criminal proceedings shall be had for the collection of the poll tax"? The answer: to ensure that people had no incentive to pay.³⁴

The final brief presented to the Mississippi Supreme Court from the appellant's attorneys reiterated most of the earlier arguments, but it went further in its argument regarding the benefits of the poll tax being left as it was. They argued that the percentage of illiteracy among African Americans was falling and that within a few years, if literacy were the only restriction, African American voters would once again outnumber white voters. The poll tax would help to ensure lack of registration on the part of African Americans: "On the other hand, if the payment of the poll tax is made compulsory, as it will be if a voter's bed and blankets may be seized for tax, it will be but a short time before the State is again cursed with a negro majority, with all the evils and perils that follow in the train of so disastrous an event." Since the advent of the constitution, "the violence and frauds that attended former elections have ceased, and . . . all elections are peaceable and honest and the former conflicts between the races have stopped, let us hope forever."³⁵

For the state, Judge J.A.P. Campbell argued that the convention should have used plain language if counsel for the defendant were correct in their interpretation. Campbell said the real issue of the case was Section 243, which referred to "said tax to be a lien only upon taxable property." He went into extensive argument on the history of liens but then pointed out that perhaps the word was not even an issue. Rather, if the tax is to be "in aid of the common schools . . . to be an aid, it must be collected." Why should the convention have determined where the money would go if it was not to be collected? If the convention had not intended for nontaxable property not to be subject to a lien, why did it not say so? "One thing is certain," he argued, "if schools are to be aided, the poll tax is to be collected, and if nontaxable property is not liable, the tax is a sham and a delusion." If there were no reason for anyone to pay, including those who were solvent, few would. The schools would suffer and other citizens would have to shoulder the burden of educating the state's children.[36]

The Mississippi Supreme Court decided against Nash. The poll tax remained optional. In consequence, "no state spent less on black education" than Mississippi.[37]

The arguments in the briefs and records of the case were frank and unequivocal. So, too, had been the comments and verification as to the purpose of the constitution itself. The intent of the convention, not to mention the constitution, was plain. In the face of such bluntness, Mississippi African Americans were split as to their appropriate reaction. Though many whites continued to point to Isaiah Montgomery's speech as indicating that the African American community was complicit and in support of disfranchisement, by no means were all African Americans willing to acquiesce.[38] Certainly there were a few who did because conformity was easier than protesting. For others, however, the alternatives were political opposition or fighting through the courts. The national political stage was closing quickly, given the demise of the Elections Bill and the subsequent repeal of the Reconstruction Acts. For African Americans, the demise of the Elections Bill was a clear indication that Congress was not going to help and that a remedy to the problem of the franchise was not forthcoming. In all fairness there had been those in Congress who had tried valiantly to effect change, but clearly the country was in no mood to continue Reconstruction or reform of the South. In order to resist, either there had to be a concerted political effort or the remedy would have to come from the courts.

Politics proved not to be an answer. First, the effects of the voting restrictions were catastrophic to African American voters, and without the power of the ballot box, their influence was waning. Second, the political leaders of the Republicans in Mississippi were sorely divided. This division was not simply between the accommodationists (as Isaiah Montgomery and his friend Booker T. Washington) and the protestors (John Roy Lynch and W.E.B. Du Bois). Rather, the problem was local and lay between James Hill and John Roy Lynch.

The breach between the two men had reached an impasse in 1884. Since then Lynch had spent more time in Washington, DC, and in consequence, more Republicans in the state, especially African Americans, began to view

Lynch as an outsider.[39] Lynch, of course, did not see the situation that way. He was, however, out of touch with the realities of the hardening color line and the attendant violence in the state. Both Lynch and Hill knew the white leaders in the state, but Lynch approached these men as equals; that Hill did not, irritated Lynch. Hill did not publicly oppose the state constitution of 1890, but Lynch did and very vocally. The difficulty for historians in understanding the issues involved comes from the lack of evidence on the Hill side. Unlike Lynch, Hill wrote no autobiography to clarify his positions. Most of the extant material supporting the breach appears in white newspapers of the time, but the material is just as biased as Lynch's account. Although some of the narrative has been uncovered, the story within the state must be placed within the national political context.

A growing number of national Republicans viewed the party in the South as representing "rotten boroughs" in which (primarily) African American party members were acknowledged as leaders of states and districts that did not create votes. Certainly the census indicated the potential for voters in these districts, but the realities, whether from fraud, intimidation, or quasi-legal means, were few counted Republican votes in these districts. Other parts of the country began to question allowing representation for the Republican convention to these districts, not to mention granting patronage in a Republican administration.[40] African American loyalists fought to keep this system, though the arrangement invited corruption. Both Lynch and Blanche Bruce had benefited handsomely from patronage, as had their organizations back in the state. It therefore was to Hill's advantage to fight for control of the state Republicans. Recognition from the national party translated into patronage, both for him and his men. These were real jobs that allowed not only cash to a strapped and increasingly marginalized group of people but also a securing of class position in stratified society.

The system of patronage benefited African Americans in Mississippi only if the Republicans remained in power. Thus, when Cleveland was reelected in 1892, Lynch lost his position as auditor of the treasury.[41] After some reflection, Lynch decided to return to Mississippi and join the bar. According to his autobiography, Lynch had already been practicing law in DC and therefore thought admission to the bar in Mississippi would be a simple exercise. There were, however, new rules typical of the period for admission to the bar.[42] Lynch had to pass a lengthy written exam and failed the first attempt, but, characteristically, he went to call on the chief justice of the Mississippi Supreme Court to ask why he failed. Justice T. E. Cooper explained that the primary reason was Lynch's limited knowledge of Mississippi statutes. Lynch went home, studied, retook the exam, and passed. He did not stay in the state, however, but rather returned to DC to set up a practice with Robert Terrell.[43] In spite of his years of continuing residence in Washington, and subsequently in Chicago, Lynch retained several plantations near Natchez.[44] A wealthy man, he returned many times to run his political organization, although during the decade of the 1890s he slowly sold off much of his real estate.

In 1896 Lynch was unduly cautious in announcing his support for William McKinley. His explanation is lengthy, but in simple terms he feared that acknowledging his support for McKinley too early might push Hill into an opposing camp. That he understood there was a possibility of a division in the state leadership is enlightening. The division was real and profound. Mark Hanna, who was coordinating McKinley's drive to the presidency, took advantage of the split. He promised Hill verification from the party as well as patronage. Lynch claimed that Hanna later realized the deal had been a mistake; the split was only local in nature and did not affect the McKinley nomination. Nevertheless, some damage had been done to the Lynch and Bruce machine.[45]

The subsequent fight between Lynch and Hill was, according to Lynch, "a life-and-death struggle."[46] Hanna was supplying Hill with the means necessary to make the fight. Following the earlier struggle in 1892, the compromise in the state had been to give the chairman of the party to the Lynch faction and the vice-chairman to the Hill faction—in 1896, Isaiah Montgomery. The rest of the coordinating committee was equally divided. When three of the Lynch men died, the chairman replaced them with individuals from the same faction. According to the rules, though, the appointments had to be confirmed, but since the new appointees could not vote until seated, the committee was in the hands of the Hill men. They did not confirm the appointments and instead replaced the Lynch appointments with ones from the Hill faction. The resulting Hill-tilting committee called for state elections for delegates. The only avenue Lynch had was to have his men voted in by a substantial margin.[47]

For Lynch to win his majority, he needed money, money that the Hill men then controlled. Lynch realized that he would receive no help from Bruce and so mortgaged two of his plantations near Natchez. Ultimately he lost them both as the depression of the 1890s deepened. Lynch later claimed that he gladly resorted to mortgage to regain control of the organization.[48]

Hill retaliated by approaching the Democratic governor of the state for help. They agreed on ways of gaining control of the state convention. The vice-chairman was to arrive a half hour ahead of time and call the convention to order and take possession of the gathering; admission to the convention was to be by ticket and administered only by those who knew. The police were to be set at the entry to allow admission only to those with tickets. With this fait accompli the Lynch group simply left the convention and retired to a new location to elect their own delegates. The "result was two conventions and two sets of delegates to the national convention from the state at large."[49]

The next stage of conflict was the national convention in Chicago. Lynch assumed that the Hill delegation would be recognized and seated, for Hill served on the very committee that would evaluate his own delegation. Moreover, Lynch asserted that Hill's deal with Hanna included the promise that Hill's delegation would be seated. McKinley asked Lynch to come to see him in Canton, Ohio, to explain the situation from his perspective. Despite this meeting, the agreement between Hanna and Hill remained in effect. Hill's delegation from the state at large was seated, as well as those from four of the districts. The other three went to the Lynch delegation. One of Hill's delegates, however, stubbornly supported his candidate, Senator Quay, rather than McKinley. Hanna was not pleased.[50]

Hill was pleased, however, with the results of the convention, for twelve of the eighteen delegates from Mississippi were from the Hill faction. Hill chartered a Pullman car for him and his friends to return to Jackson. Lynch noted that Hill did not realize the temporary nature of the support, nor did he reach out to the Lynch faction. But according to Lynch, Hill "maintained an independent and a defiant attitude as long as he could."[51] Hill even suggested that the Lynch faction disband. Although some of this faction considered the suggestion, Lynch called his supporters together in Jackson when the delegates returned from Chicago. They agreed to his suggestion that their faction put out their own ticket with himself at the head, and they did. Under the new constitution, Hill had an opportunity to check Lynch. He argued that having practiced law for many years in Washington, DC, Lynch was no longer a resident of the state and therefore could not vote or run for office.[52] The Lynch ticket won a majority of Republican voters in five of the seven districts, in spite of the counting having been controlled by the Democrats, whom Lynch believed supported Hill.[53]

Lynch may have been out of touch with the political realities in the state when the heated controversy began in the 1890s, but Hill was even more out of touch with the political realities in Washington. President McKinley asked Lynch for comment on a list of six postmaster appointments for Mississippi, three of whom would have been Lynch supporters. Lynch knew enough to be firm about his own men but kind regarding the others. Hill, however, did not understand political reality. He tried to undermine the Lynch men and therefore managed to offend McKinley.[54] McKinley then moved systematically to appoint representatives from each faction in equal terms, a move that undermined Hill's new position as head of the Mississippi Republican caucus. Moreover, as head of his organization, Hill did not receive the patronage appointment he wanted but had to settle for receiver of public moneys at Jackson. Bruce, who had remained aloof from all the infighting, was appointed registrar of the US Treasury Department, a plum of an appointment.[55] To his eternal astonishment, upon the advent of the Spanish-American War, Lynch was appointed a major and additional paymaster of volunteers. Lynch found that he enjoyed the experience in the military and stayed with it for years after the war ended.[56]

Lynch maintained his connections with the Republican Party in Mississippi, while Hill found himself in trouble. Hill admitted to Lynch that his actions at the 1896 convention were a mistake, for their skirmish for control destroyed what they had built. The result was that the Republican Party in Mississippi was run by white men thereafter, and patronage flowed through them.[57] Moreover, because Hill did not acquit himself well in his appointment in Jackson, he was left without national backers. Hill's successor in office was Isaiah Montgomery, who Hill had assumed was loyal to him. When pressed on the issue, Montgomery said that, since he had not sought the office but had been offered it, he would accept the position. Hill was devastated and ruined.[58]

The consequence of this infighting was a diversion among the Republicans. When they should have been resisting the Democrats and joining together to seek change and justice, they were fighting each other. Hill knew his state and he knew the Democrats in charge. Lynch and Bruce knew the powers in Washington; they were eloquent, had a following, and were solidly networked within the Republican Party. Lynch, Bruce, and Hill should have been a formidable team. Whether they could have effected change is debatable. Yet the split itself meant that no meaningful resistance was offered to the overwhelming dominance of the political conservatism within the state.

◆ ◆ ◆

Despite the devastating split within the state's Republican Party, arguments over the poll tax, and the decline in voter registration and participation, there were still a few African Americans who continued to vote and exercise their access to the polls, particularly in the Delta. This part of the state had a long history of accommodation through fusion between the dominant white leaders and the extremely large African American population in the area. One black lawyer, Cornelius J. Jones, took on the incumbent state Democrat, Thomas C. Catchings, for a seat in Congress. Jones was backed by the Hill wing and probably had money that he needed from Isaiah Montgomery. This campaign caught the imagination of African Americans in the Delta, and many turned out to hear him speak. To no one's surprise, Jones lost, but he contested the election in a well-versed appeal that engendered conspiracy theories. Jones also lost the appeal because he was backed only by the Hill group, a situation that further undermined the state Republicans.

Cornelius Jones was also an African American attorney in the Delta. A native of Mississippi, he spent his childhood in Vicksburg, the largest city in the state at that time. At the age of fifteen he entered Alcorn College and took business courses. After graduation he worked for two years as a purchasing agent for the New Orleans Cotton Seed Association and by all accounts did well. He then followed the practice of the time by reading law. In his case, he began under a former chief justice of Louisiana (a Republican), but when the judge died before he finished, Jones returned to Mississippi and completed his studies under W. L. Sharkey, the grandson of a former Republican governor of Mississippi. Admitted to practice in Vicksburg in 1888, the following year he was elected to the Mississippi legislature. There he objected strongly to the calling of a state constitutional convention. On January 28, 1890, following acrimonious debate and having listened to strong racist sentiment (including words from future governor Vardaman), Jones defended his race. He pointed out that the proposal was a violation of the Fifteenth Amendment to the Constitution and that if the state passed such legislation, he would fight it.[59]

There were few options for attorneys to contest the new constitution and many fewer alternatives to helping their clients in a climate of growing threats to African Americans in the state. Jones and others like him needed to get their cases removed from a state trial and before a federal judge and jury; as long as the case was before a Mississippi jury, he concluded there was no hope for his clients. There was one precedent that provided a ray of hope: *Strauder v. West Virginia*.[60] In 1879 the US Supreme Court decided that the explicit provision in West Virginia stating "All white male persons . . . shall be able to serve as jurors" violated the constitutional rights of the defendant, and that therefore the original verdict should be quashed and the case shifted to a federal court.[61] During the intervening years there had been several cases that narrowed the decision. For instance, the discrimination had to be overt, and procedurally, the motion to remove or quash a panel had to come before the trial commenced.[62]

Anyone who sought to challenge a state's constitutional or statutory provisions was therefore faced with severe constraints on the possibility of success. In spite of these restrictions, Jones sought the US Supreme Court review of the state's constitution. Like so much else of the time, Jones's actions were indirect. He undoubtedly realized that the constitution's language lacked the specificity required for it to be struck down. Jones therefore chose to argue that the *effect* of the constitution was the same as if it specifically declared that no African American could be a voter. To establish that point, Jones pointed to the fact that there were no African Americans on the jury panel selected for two trials in which his clients were convicted of murder. Jurors were selected from rolls of voters. Thus the absence of African American jurors meant that African Americans had been excluded from the voting rolls, a fact that violated both the Equal Protection Clause of the Fourteenth Amendment and the voting provision of the Fifteenth Amendment.

In making those arguments, Jones also seemed to realize that he needed to show that his client was disadvantaged by not having any members of his race on the jury panel. He therefore included in his briefs extensive information about the facts of the crime as well as about the social and economic setting for those involved in the case.

While representing Charlie Smith, a black defendant under indictment for murder, Jones made the argument that the lack of African American representation on juries selected in the state was a violation of the Fourteenth Amendment.[63] The facts of the case were simple, but at the same time were convoluted in detail. A group of drunken African American men were at a dance; they got into a fight and started shooting at each other. When the firing stopped, some men went back into the house; but then two more shots were fired into the building, killing Wiley Nesbit. The next morning Smith fled the scene after allegedly claiming to a friend that he had shot a few men the evening before. Smith was located a year later, brought to trial, and convicted.[64] The case was first challenged before the Mississippi Supreme Court, which upheld the conviction, but then the case reached the US Supreme Court in 1895. Jones presented his argument before the Court, the first African American lawyer to do so.[65] Jones had to make his case connect to a violation of the Constitution for the Court to hear him; if successful, Smith could possibly be either retried in a federal court or have the judgment quashed. The issues turned on questions of a violation of the state's rules on the composition of the grand jury that indicted Smith and of a violation of the Fourteenth Amendment's due process clause because there were no black men on the jury. Jones pointed out that Bolivar County, the site of the case, had 1,300 African American men registered as voters but only 300 white men. If the rules were followed, an all-white jury was statistically improbable.[66] Justice Harlan, writing for the unanimous Court, ruled against Smith.[67] Harlan pointed out that the violation of the state's rules was not a federal issue; the composition of the jury, though, might have been. The justice stated that Jones had not produced enough evidence to back his claim that there was actual damage done because of the lack of diversity on the jury. Sadly, part of the request had been to grant subpoenas to gather evidence, and without that ability evidence was going to be very difficult to accumulate.

The same day that Jones argued *Gibson* before the Court (December 13, 1895), the Court heard a second case from Mississippi, this one argued by Emanuel M. Hewlett and assisted by Jones.[68] Jones had brought the cases to the Supreme Court and had asked Hewlett for assistance.[69] Jones had not been the original attorney at the trial, and it is not clear when he received the case. The facts, though muddled, provide colorful insight into the conditions in the state. The controversy turned over the question of twenty cents owed to John Gibson, a laborer on a plantation in the Delta. Gibson's claim was that the manager of the plantation, Robert Stinson, short-changed him twenty cents for the week's work when payday came on Saturday at the general store. Gibson complained and, according to witnesses, threatened the manager, and then went to the plantation to ask the owner to make Stinson pay him. The owner refused to get involved. Stinson and Gibson met at the front gate of the house and got into a tussle that resulted in Stinson's death. The question was whether it was murder or self-defense, especially since one of the witnesses testified that he saw Stinson beating Gibson with a cane.[70] Hewlett argued that a lack of diversity on the grand jury made the indictment and the subsequent conviction of his client a violation of the Fourteenth Amendment.[71] Again, Justice Harlan wrote the opinion. This one turned not only on the jury question as with *Smith* but also on the assertion that the case was in violation of the constitutional prohibition of ex post facto laws.[72] Because the procedural rules in the new Mississippi Code of 1892 (produced to coincide with the new constitution) were passed after the commission of the crime, Jones claimed that Gibson should have been prosecuted under the old rules of procedure. In his opinion Justice Harlan determined that the jury question was unproven to have been a factor in the verdict; in addition, he pointed out that the motions to remove the trial or to quash it had not been made before the trial; thus the remedy would then have to come from the state courts. Moreover, the ex post facto question was moot. Any legislature at any time can create rules about procedure, which has no bearing on a crime. Therefore the fact that the new Mississippi Code (1892) came into effect after the murder also had no effect on the outcome. Both Mississippi cases were unanimous decisions written by Justice Harlan. That he did not see this issue as a Fourteenth Amendment rights violation is noteworthy, for the justice was known as the "Great Dissenter" because of his sharp dissents in *Plessy* and in the *Civil Rights Cases* (1883).

Cornelius Jones had not given up on this type of appeal to the Supreme Court. He found two other cases in the summer of 1896. Both made it to the

Mississippi Supreme Court and one before the US Supreme Court. Both, as the two previous ones, were murder cases and therefore serious. Unlike the facts presented in the previous cases, the guilt of the defendants appeared probable given the testimony; but Jones took his charge gravely. He decided to defend his clients by arguing that the grand jury, which had brought the indictment, was composed of only white jurors (based on the Mississippi constitutional provisions and tied directly to the new constitution). Therefore his defendants had been denied their constitutional rights of due process. This time the motions had been made at the correct point in the proceedings, although denied by the trail judge.[73]

The facts of the first case, *John Henry Dixon v. State of Mississippi*, were these: John Henry Dixon had been seeing Felina (no last name), whom he thought was promised to him in marriage. Her relatives disapproved of him, particularly because of his temper, and began to interfere. One afternoon Dixon, with a loaded gun, came storming down the street to find Felina and deal with her relatives. Angry, he shot two warning blasts at Jake, a child staying with Eliza Minor, Felina's great aunt. The shots brought Lavinia Higgins to her porch to admonish Dixon. Dixon responded by pointing his gun at her and shooting her in the leg. While she survived, his next shot through Eliza's front door killed Nancy Minor, who was simply sitting by the hearth. The jury found John Henry Dixon guilty, and the judge sentenced him to life in prison.[74]

The last of the quartet of cases in which Jones was involved is the most celebrated, *Williams v. Mississippi*. Here Jones brought all of his arguments before the Court. Here in particular he presented far more facts than the Court would consider; but once again Jones seemed to be attempting to make the Court realize that the lives of African Americans in Mississippi were so unique that no one other than an African American could provide a "peer," essential if there was to be even hope for a fair trial.

The facts of the *Williams* case were equally as simple as those in *Dixon*. The grand jury had brought an indictment against Henry Williams for strangling Eliza Brown, "a human being."[75] A few days after Christmas, Theophilus Brown, Eliza's brother, found her body under a pile of dirty clothes. Eliza had been a laundress. In the days before washing machines, a laundress was an important part of any town; the work was difficult, exhausting, and not particularly well paid. According to his testimony, Brown had gone to Eliza's home, a three-room house where she lived with Williams, to retrieve his favorite pair of pants but found Eliza instead.[76] Eliza had last been seen the day after Christmas in the company of Henry Williams near the railway station and then at Wray's saloon. According to testimony by Addie Brown,

Eliza's sister-in-law, Williams was suspicious of Eliza's behavior. He had heard rumors that she had started seeing someone else, and he was angry. Addie further claimed that Eliza was to return that evening but never came.[77]

When the body was discovered two days later, no one could find Williams. Weeks later, Ike M. Muckle, an African American bounty hunter, found Williams hiding up in the rafters of the barn on Dr. Mason's plantation. According to Muckle, Williams confessed to him that he had killed Eliza in self-defense when she threatened him with a gun. He had come to the house to get money from her, claiming that she held the $15 he had earned picking cotton, but she had only fifty cents to give him. When he arrived, he discovered another man, whom he did not recognize, scooting out the back.[78]

At this point the testimony became a bit more garbled. Lou Gay Coleman, a friend of Henry's, testified that he was with Henry and Muckle after Henry was under arrest and was waiting at the Leland rail station for a train to return them to Greenville. According to Coleman, Muckle never confessed; rather, he said he would report that Henry had confessed so that a reward would be paid. Under oath Henry stated that he had never confessed and agreed with Coleman's account of the wait at the rail station. In a variation on Muckle's testimony, Henry claimed that he did confront Eliza about the fleeing man that evening. When she pointed a pistol at him, he retaliated by hitting her beside the head, grabbed the falling pistol, hit her again, and cast her down. He threw the pistol on the bed and left her alive. Moreover, he said he had not fled the scene of a crime, but rather had been seeking work. When arrested, he was simply in the barn eating pecans.[79]

In his closing statement, the district attorney referred to the state of Eliza's body, which was found hidden beneath dirty clothes and had no bruises other than strangle marks on her neck and the stocking of her left leg around her ankles. He further stipulated that Eliza had kept her money in that stocking but had no money on her when found.[80] Like the Dixon trial, the jury found Henry Williams guilty of murder. Unlike the Dixon trial, the judge sentenced Williams to hang on July 30.[81] Williams's only hope was appeal.

Cornelius Jones, attorney for both Dixon and Williams, used the same plan for both cases. The motions, included within the trial records, are nearly verbatim with each other. As soon as the trial convened and before a plea was entered, he asked the court to quash the indictments, "because the laws by which the grand jury was selected, organized, summoned and charged, which presented the said indictment, are unconstitutional and repugnant to the spirit and letter of the [federal] constitution."[82] He pointed out that Section 241 of the state constitution, which states that only electors can be jurors, "is but a scheme on the part of the framers of that Constitution to abridge the suffrage of the colored electors, in the State of Miss [sic], on account of the previous condition of servitude by granting a discretion to said officers."[83] In addition, he pointed out that doing so "denied [to them] the right to equal protection and benefit of the laws, of the State of Miss, on account of their color and race."[84] He further complained that the convention had only one African American delegate among the 134; that the resulting constitution, which disfranchised, was never given to the people to ratify; and that the "enforcement of the provisions ... resulted in discrimination against the race of the defendant being that of Negro."[85] Jones argued that "the defendant's race" should have been "represented impartially on the Grand Jury which presented this indictment" and that therefore "the accused is deprived of that equal protection of the laws of the State, because of the discrimination against the members of his race."[86]

In both cases, Jones had the defendants from each case swear affidavits that the facts in the motion were true. And he included these affidavits in the briefs for both cases so that Henry Williams showed up in the Dixon case and John Henry Dixon in the Williams case. When the trial court refused in both cases to quash the indictment, Jones requested that the cases be moved to federal district court on the same grounds as the motion for quashing the indictment: Mississippi's constitutional provisions denied due process to both men on the grounds of their race and previous condition of servitude. In each case, the motion was denied, and the trial went forth with predictable results.[87]

Both cases were appealed to the Mississippi Supreme Court. The record in *Williams* includes a flowery brief signed by Cornelius Jones and addressed to the honorable Thomas N. Woods, chief justice of the Mississippi Supreme Court. Jones admitted that Williams had been convicted and sentenced to hang.[88] This conviction should not stand, he argued, because the grand jury had been improperly convened with no African American jurors. Moreover, the grand jury was convened based on laws derived from the Mississippi Constitution of 1890, which had been enacted "with the express purpose of effecting a denial to the negroes of the state the right of elective franchise, because of their race[,] color and previous condition of servitude." Both cases upheld the convictions and did not consider the constitutional issues.[89]

Having exhausted review by the Mississippi courts, Jones turned to the US Circuit Court for the Southern District, arguing that the court of origin should have quashed the indictment or granted the motion for removal to federal court. Grounds were that Williams's "rights as a Citizen of the United States as guaranteed under the Federal Constitution were abridged and denied in the circuit court of Washington County, Mississippi, and ultimately the judgment of the Supreme Court of the State."[90]

Eventually the case reached the Supreme Court of the United States. Justice Joseph McKenna wrote the unanimous decision of the court. The opinion began with a reminder of the facts of the case but then turned to the central issue: "The question presented is, are the provisions of the constitution of the State of Mississippi and the laws enacted to enforce the same repugnant to the Fourteenth Amendment to the United States?"[91] The Court had recognized that discrimination by the "General Government, or by the States, against any citizen because of his race" would be in violation of the Fourteenth Amendment; but "the denial must be the result of the constitution or laws of the State, not of the administration of them."[92] Although the Court acknowledged that the Mississippi constitutional convention intended to disfranchise, as was argued before the Mississippi Supreme Court in *Ratliff v. Beale*, Justice McKenna asserted that "nothing tangible can be deduced from this," for the characteristics of sloth and shiftiness, cited by the attorneys, could be applicable to anyone: "They reach weak and vicious white men as well as weak and vicious black men, and whatever is sinister in their intentions, if anything, can be prevented by both races by the exertion of that duty which voluntarily pays taxes and refrains from crime."[93]

Justice McKenna therefore concluded, "It cannot be said ... that the denial of the equal protection of the laws arises primarily from the constitution and laws of Mississippi, nor is there any sufficient allegation of an evil and discriminating administration of them."[94] He continued that there was "nothing direct and definite in this allegation either as to means or time as affecting the proceedings against the accused," for the plaintiff entered no charge against the officers who created the jury lists. As for the allegation that the convention meant to disfranchise, the Court was not concerned "unless the purpose is executed by the constitution or laws or by those who administer them." The plaintiff must state this argument directly, if it was an issue, rather than simply allude to it.[95] The Court was "not obliged to reason from the probable to the actual, and pass upon the validity of the ordinances complained of as tried merely by the opportunities which their terms afford of unequal and unjust discrimination in their administration." McKenna did admit, however, that "though the law itself be fair on its face and impartial in appearance, yet, if it is applied and administered by public authority with an evil eye and an unequal hand, so as practically to make unjust and illegal discriminations between persons in similar circumstances, material to their rights, the denial of equal justice is still within the prohibition of the Constitution."[96] Just to be sure everyone understood, McKenna added: "This comment is not applicable to the constitution of Mississippi and its statues. They do not on their face discriminate between the races, and it has not been shown that their actual administration was evil, only that evil was possible under them." Thus the Court affirmed the lower court decision. Williams was hanged on September 28, 1899.[97]

Local newspapers ignored the case completely. Had the decision been different, they would most likely have taken note. As it was, the decision slipped by the public. Jones tried twice more to get the Supreme Court to reverse its opinion, but the fact that the Court determined that these cases had to involve not only overt discrimination but also that the *administration* of the law could not be a part of the appeal on constitutional grounds closed off this approach to the courts.[98] Some historians have blamed Cornelius Jones for not doing a better job; they insist that once his cases were before the Supreme Court, he should have worked harder to present better supporting evidence.[99] Jones, however, was one of the few African American lawyers who got *any* cases to the Court, much less a multiple number. Other attorneys had the benefit of a college or university law degree, for legal education was shifting from reading law to university training.[100] Other attorneys would eventually follow his lead, but Cornelius Jones was in the vanguard of attorneys fighting back against the rising tide of discrimination. He had no one to guide him through the campaign.

Jones did not give up after losing *Williams*. He continued his fight through other cases, but he also did not ignore the political option.[101] He was the Republican nominee for the Third Congressional District in Mississippi against Thomas Catchings. He appealed to the House and Senate when, not surprisingly given the attitudes of the time, he lost.[102] He moved to Memphis, Tennessee, for several years, where he brought a class action suit against William McAdoo, then US secretary of the treasury, for punitive damages on behalf of African Americans. Although he claimed that the United States had been enriched through the tax levied on raw cotton that slaves had picked, the case failed on procedural grounds. On closure of the case, the Justice Department brought an indictment against Jones for fraud. He had appealed to African Americans for financial help; for a contribution of $1.75, Jones promised a share of the monetary judgment. In 1918 Jones then left for Muskogee, Oklahoma, where he maintained a successful legal practice for his remaining years.[103]

People have overlooked this case of *Williams v. Mississippi* for years, which is not surprising given the significance of *Plessy* issued only the year earlier. Yet the case is very important. The question, then, is whether the case is the pivot from which other southern states saw either an acquiescence on the part of the Supreme Court in disfranchisement or a pronounced hesitancy in getting involved in constitutional questions.[104] During this period the federal courts had little discretion in the types of cases they were to hear. They were required to take cases in which a state statute or a state constitution violated the US Constitution. Because of this requirement, they were hesitant to deal with constant judicial review and therefore defined their parameters in a narrow fashion. Certainly the decision in *Williams* fits this interpretation. The Court admitted that Mississippi's constitutional provisions could be in violation of the Fourteenth Amendment, particularly regarding the wide latitude granted election officials. Possibility or even probability of misbehavior did not mean that violations had happened. The plaintiff would have to prove the direct connection, which was a challenging requirement. That the Court's construct was difficult was exactly the narrow approach the Court wanted.

Journal articles and books printed in the period agreed with the decision. For example, a 1904 book on the Constitution and its interpretations discusses the issues surrounding the Fourteenth Amendment. The author acknowledges that a state constitution that sets an educational standard for voters is not "repugnant" to the Constitution, even though "administrative officers may avail themselves of it to discriminate against negroes."[105] According to Charles Wallace Collins, in a book printed in 1912, as long as a legal provision does not prohibit specifically on the basis of race, "it is practically impossible for a negro to prove on what ground he has been excluded."[106]

After the Scottsboro case (1931), an article appeared in the *Mississippi Law Journal* to discuss its relevance to jury restrictions in Mississippi. According to the author, Alabama's law was not well crafted and thus left open to judicial review. In contrast, he claimed Mississippi was less likely to be a "problem" since jurors must come from electors. He reasoned that the "ratio of Negro qualified electors to white qualified electors is variously estimated as between one to five hundred and one to fifteen hundred. One to one thousand may be taken as a generous estimate." He attributed this small number of African American voters as "largely through the foresight and sagacity of the late Hon. J. Z. George, [that] the Mississippi Constitution of 1890 securely guards against the registration of Negroes in large numbers"[107] The ones who had registered successfully were in the professional classes, which were excused from jury duty (ministers, doctors, dentists, and government workers such as postal employees).[108] As late as 1950, even following shifts on the Court, legal analysis assumed that the burden of proof regarding discrimination lay with the defendant.[109]

To argue that *Williams* is not important to the minds of southern jurists misses the point, although people have tried. McKenna was not actively confirming the provisions of the Mississippi Constitution of 1890. What the Court was doing was defining when it could or would act. The fact that the decision established a narrow parameter for intervention suited the Supreme Court well. The case also suited other southern states—but, unlike the Court, they acted.

◆ ◆ ◆

Back in Mississippi, however, the ruling appeared to grant permission to handling the race problem as white men of the state wished. Though the number of lynchings fell a bit in this decade, it still was astonishingly high compared to the rest of the country. Historians have located descriptions of lynchings in this period, which are horrifying in their straightforward accounts of torture. No one is certain whether this development was a new addition to the ritual of lynching, indicating a further spiraling into depravity, or whether it had always been there. While the rest of the country endured lynchings with a majority of white victims, in Mississippi a large percentage of the 195 documented cases were directed at African Americans.[110]

In addition to the sadly more familiar race riots in Mississippi, there was also a rise of systemic and institutionalized intimidation. This new form of terror had its roots in the Ku Klux Klan of the Reconstruction period, but no evidence exists that it was directly related or that the old Klan membership had never dissolved. Historians are not even certain why this new group was called whitecappers, other than to speculate that old memories of white-robed figures of the Klan resurfaced and gave the new group its common name. No one even knows if these groups had other names, though here there appears to be some correlation between dirt farmers' secret clubs and the rise of whitecappers in an area. What is apparent is that the depression of 1893 was the catalyst that pushed the violence into the open and exposed the class jealousy underlying the problems.[111] From the African American side of the issue, Isaiah Montgomery argued that those people targeted by the vigilantes were the most industrious, those who were pulling ahead economically and therefore threatened the perceived economic and social order.[112]

Most of the documented whitecapping incidences of this period happened in the southwest section of the state. Enough reports of intimidation and murder created wariness among northern investors at a time the state desperately needed money. Governor Stone, under pressure from merchants and railroad executives, made it clear that the state would not tolerate the behavior of the whitecappers and even went to the extent of offering a reward for information or capture.[113] In 1894, frustrated by northern reaction, Stone published an article in the *North American Review* that explained the problems behind lynching. He argued that the unique circumstances in the South following the war had led to "problems" that had now been addressed by the new suffrage provisions of the new constitution, which he believed would alleviate the tensions and lynching would cease. Surprisingly, some thought that Stone was correct, for even the editors of the *Washington Post* found his article "illuminating and carefully constructed."[114]

Judge J. B. Chrisman, prominent in the constitutional convention, was magistrate in one of the courts trying whitecappers in Brookhaven.[115] When a mob of whitecappers rode into town, right up to the courthouse, Judge Chrisman adjourned court and went out to stop the men. He found, though, that they had little regard for his position as judge, and they threatened to shoot him unless he released the men on trial. Only the fortuitous arrival of the sheriff and his men alleviated the threatening situation.[116] The firm response by the old guard helped to tamp down the rise of these vigilante groups, but they reemerged early in the next decade.

Lynching was more difficult to stop, and even the old guard was of two minds about the practice. Historians have long argued about the causes of lynching and have debated why it arose in this period. The most novel hypothesis, from historian Edward Ayers, is that, wherever there was a substantial increase in African American population, the social order was threatened. Since strangers were unknown in the community and had no one to speak on their behalf, whenever trouble erupted, the stranger became the inevitable culprit in the minds of many. This interpretation certainly resonates in places like the Delta, which saw a large increase in African American population during the period and also suffered from a lack of governmental control. For some white citizens, lynching was a way to keep control of a "threatening" population.[117] Therefore little opposition appeared until the numbers rose to threaten what little law and order there was. Provoked, Governor Stone used the militia to protect a black man accused of murder, and following his conviction, several prominent white men in the area intervened with a mob to allow justice to be served through the courts.[118] This time it worked. Stone was not always so successful, but the number of lynchings did fall in the 1890s.[119]

By the end of the decade and the turn of the century, Mississippi had reached a sense of stability, but more violence and upheaval were yet to come. The old guard, those who had served the Confederacy, passed. Supreme Court justice L.Q.C. Lamar died in 1893, Senator George in 1897, and Senator Walthall in 1898. Governor Stone wanted a Senate seat, but he was not selected by the state legislature because of his hard money position; members of the state legislature were silverites.[120] In 1899 the state elected Governor Longino, the last of the old guard. To everyone's surprise, he began his inaugural speech expressing his dismay over lynching, and he proposed a program to stop it.

The legislature would not countenance the bill, and nothing came of the proposal other than to ensure that Longino would never again be elected to state office. Over the years, each time he attempted to run for office, his proposal to stop lynching resurfaced in state newspapers, none of them in support of his efforts.[121]

Among African American leaders, Blanche Bruce died in 1898; James Hill made it to the next century, dying in 1901.[122] John Lynch reinvented himself and became army paymaster during the Spanish-American War. Isaiah Montgomery traveled in his position as a business leader among African Americans, but as mayor of Mound Bayou he was noted as "well-spoken, but old-fashioned in dress and manners" when he visited Salt Lake City. A reporter there stated Montgomery saw the irony in the lynching of black people (as a barbaric way of treating those society viewed to be uncivilized). Ever the believer in the quality of the elites, Montgomery stated that "better minds" were pushing the South to change this violence.[123]

Why Montgomery should cling so stubbornly to his trust in the paternalist leaders of Mississippi is open to question. By the time he was interviewed in Salt Lake City, he had seen the state through the Civil War, Reconstruction, Restoration, and control by the Bourbons. He had known anarchy, violence, economic struggles, and racial violence. By the end of the decade following the constitutional convention, the white citizens of the state no longer fought each other over the provisions of the constitution, but rather banded together to defend it against bills in Congress and before the US Supreme Court. The vigorous defense was far more successful than they had hoped, for the national government (for the most part) turned its attention away from Mississippi and the South. The state could run its affairs the way it wanted, but the future was uncertain. No longer needing to defend themselves against outsiders, or even against African Americans, citizens began turning on each other to fight for control of the economic, political, and social issues unsolved by the dying generation.

So ended the nineteenth century.

CHAPTER 11

Conclusion

In 1910 Robert E. Wilson, former secretary of the convention of 1890, and a group of former delegates decided to hold a reunion celebrating the twentieth year of the constitution's adoption. Specifically they wanted to "renew old acquaintances, recall past times and events and to engender and awake feelings of friendship and fellowship between the survivors of that historic convention."[1] By that time 63 of the original 136 delegates were still living.[2] Wilson found them all.

As they planned the reunion, the letters among the delegates were sad, for the passage of time was obvious. A number mentioned illness—paralysis, feeble old age, brain fever, or no specifics at all but simple reference to general ill health.[3] Two died in the weeks preceding the event.[4] Others had left the state and found the distance too onerous to travel.[5] R. G. Hudson grieved that he could not make the long trip, for he thought "my experience as a member of that memorable body was the most interesting and valuable I ever had."[6] Only one expressed some reservation, Pat Henry (who had voted against the constitution); he could "see no good to be accomplished save the pleasant meeting together of those yet living, which doubtless all would enjoy."[7]

Most of the men were proud of their participation in the convention. Most believed they had tried their best to solve a very difficult issue. Based on the historical record, apparently the majority were God-fearing, churchgoing people. That they purposely circumvented the provisions of the Fourteenth and Fifteenth Amendments to the US Constitution, that they lied on the floor of the US Senate, that they assumed that a whole swath of Mississippians (black and white) had no business exercising the franchise, that they purposely took it upon themselves to do "wrong" so that "right" might prevail—few among the delegates questioned this history.

To a large extent the source of the problem concerning their self-congratulation was a rewriting of history to make their efforts palatable, if not noble. This was not unusual in the period, for the notion of a Lost Cause became the pervading metaphor of the Civil War and Reconstruction, not only in the South but also in academia.[8] In Mississippi, this story included the 1890 constitutional convention. In 1902 Dunbar Rowland, the new head of the state archives, gave a speech to the alumni at Ole Miss about the history of the state during the previous forty years. He asserted that Mississippians had viewed the "experiment" of universal suffrage with misgivings but "made an honest effort to give [African Americans] a fair trial." Northerners, he added, simply did not understand African Americans as those in South did, particularly the ones who held a strong bond with their former slaves.[9]

Rowland set out the argument to be used for generations to come as he shifted blame to malevolent outsiders. He asserted that "carpetbaggers" took advantage of naive freedmen; radicals in Congress "poisoned" the attitudes of freedmen and "taught him to mistrust and hate his former masters." Though he admitted wrongs committed by southerners, he emphasized that African Americans were "unworthy of suffrage" and that their "rule" was ruinous to the state. In other words, African Americans had their chance but failed, but that failure had come through the machinations of "carpetbaggers" (outside influence). Therefore, to Rowland and his colleagues, something had to change.[10]

According to Rowland, a list of southern heroes emerged, including L.Q.C. Lamar and James Z. George, and redeemed the state. This state of affairs might have continued but for a "period of mild intimidation." Leaders in the state feared that "continued suppression of the negro vote would promote a feeling among the whites to use the same methods on each other and promote a low tone of political morality."[11] Why leaders needed to create a new organic law to respond to "mild intimidation" and the subsequent threat of a "low tone of political morality" Rowland never explained; and of course the well-documented reality of violent intimidation was not acknowledged. Rowland openly admitted that the "avowed and confessed object of the convention was to eliminate the ignorant vote, whether white or black." He excused his way of thinking by arguing that good government could not exist where 60 percent of the voters were illiterate.[12] The resulting disfranchisement was "good," for it allowed African Americans to work for the franchise: "The whites who were disfranchised accepted the situation without a murmur."[13]

The resulting constitution, Rowland added, was so good that it had withstood the onslaughts of Congress (the Force Bill debates) and review by the US Supreme Court in *Williams v. Mississippi*, which he argued "forever settled the question of negro suffrage."[14] Rowland went further, though, and stated that the efforts of the convention had also settled the race issue. Though there were some who did not want to educate African Americans and wanted to keep them in a state of ignorance, "their following is small." Most people in Mississippi wished the race well, and he erroneously emphasized that "there is no persecution of the negro in Mississippi."[15]

Rowland, like others of the time, was rewriting the history of the events following the war to suit his agenda. He cannot have truly believed "there was no persecution of the negro in Mississippi." Yet he was correct in emphasizing the role of race in disfranchisement at the convention. Though there were other issues, the acknowledged purpose of calling the constitutional convention had been twofold: to disfranchise and to broker the power struggle between the black and white counties and therefore gain some political and social stability. Of the two, efforts to disfranchise worked.[16] Voting by African Americans did not entirely cease after the new constitution, but it did decrease substantially. In 1892 only 8,615 African Americans registered to vote in the state, but that was enough to ensure that some minor public offices in the Delta could be theirs. Voting strength also declined for white voters, who either did not have the money for the poll tax, had not established residency, or simply could not read or explain provisions of the constitution. The number of white voters dropped from 120,000 in 1890 to around 68,000 in two years.[17]

In comparison, the late nineteenth century was nationally a time of big voter turnout.[18] Every other southern state at least exceeded 50 percent participation in the franchise. According to one expert, "Most southerners, both black and white, voted during the late nineteenth century until the enactment of poll taxes, literacy tests, and other restrictive legislation curtailed mass electoral participation."[19] Mississippi was the exception, having moved far ahead of the others in the frontline of disfranchisement.

The process of disfranchisement proceeded from a mixed bag of motives, though all were based on what the delegates thought would be reform for the better. The problems they had identified were the race question, a dismal economy, and a nonfunctioning government. Provisions of the new constitution were included to fix the problems they had identified. Reform does not always mean improvement, but it does mean that is what they thought they were doing. Of their measures, ironically one of the most effective restrictive changes came with a degree of reform, for "in a brief span of five years from 1887 to 1892, thirty-eight of the forty-four states adopted Australian ballot legislation which provided for an official, state-printed, consolidated ballot."[20] According to elections expert Walter Dean Burnham, "The adoption of the secret ballot deprived political parties of their function of printing and distributing ballots; personal voter registration procedures favored the more politically involved middle-class citizen over those of lower socio-economic status."[21] In spite of the "success" of the Australian ballot, it was not the only measure used to create disfranchisement, particularly in Mississippi, where citizens had endured the poll tax, the Understanding Clause, and residency requirements. The combination proved lethal to suffrage.

Race in the form of disfranchisement, however, was not the only issue addressed at the convention, for class had also become a contentious issue under the guise of white counties versus black counties. Both sides strove for power in the state, as they sought political prowess to control the struggling economy. The black counties thought they had worked out a compromise for not letting too much power go through reapportionment. What they wanted most of all was to be sure that the white counties did not tax them "unfairly." To that end they gave up some representation within the legislature, a choice they thought did not matter.

In the long run reapportionment was not an effective strategy for the black counties. As long as citizens did not think African Americans needed representation within the legislature (and therefore could be ignored), apportionment accomplished little to address the inequalities of representation between white and black counties. White population in the black counties was substantially smaller than in the white ones, but following the adoption of the new constitution, the black counties still claimed sixty-eight seats in the state legislature, compared to fifty-two for the white counties.[22] The compromise within the convention, brokered by Senator George, had been to reset representation based on actual voters. But since the resetting was based on voting patterns before the convention, when African Americans had a bit more access to the polls, the "miss-allocation" of representatives continued. The "remedy" came only with a constitutional amendment in 1906 that divided the state into three equal sections, regardless of population, and awarded equal representatives to each section.[23]

Further revisions in the constitution came with the revocation of party conventions through the Primary Election Law of 1902.[24] Previously the party conventions were dominated by delegates who were apportioned on the basis of the state legislature, which was under control of the black counties and in which dirt farmers in the white counties had little power or say. Reoccurring scandals generated a push for reform. Though the claim had been that the new constitution would clean up issues over the ballot, the Delta at least had not found the reform to have worked. At one point, Issaquena County, which had 169 white men, cast 182 ballots in the local election; only 84 had been cast the previous election. People began to feel that these problems were "too glaring" and could not be ignored any longer.[25]

With the passage of the primary law, an idea that was popular throughout the nation, the white counties gained more power.[26] With few African Americans voting, and even with a reduced number of white men voting, still the number of white dirt farmers outnumbered the elites in the state. In consequence, the "direct primary not only undermined the party's leadership's control over the nomination of candidates, but also denied the out party its position as the only available alternative." The Democratic Party may have controlled the state, but it was subject to fracture between the different factions and class divisions. Admittedly elections were more honest, but they had consequences regarding party structure.[27] The populist yearnings of earlier decades came to fruition in the state.

Fraud at the ballot box was not the only problem of political corruption within the state. Certainly animosity toward moneyed interests, especially banks, continued. Corruption and general ineptness also reappeared. During the Longino administration (1900–1904), over $100,000 disappeared from the state treasury. J. R. Stower, the state treasurer, "lent" the money to a railroad through an intermediary. Stower and others were arrested. Only six months later charges of forgery of state bonds by the new treasurer, G. W. Carlisle, emerged and horrified citizens.[28] Little wonder that state voters were ready for a change.

◆ ◆ ◆

With the advent of the Primary Election Law of 1902, candidates could now ignore the Delta and concentrate on the more numerous registered voters in white counties. James K. Vardaman was the first of the candidates to recognize this fact. Vardaman had run for the gubernatorial position twice before, each time losing to a Delta-anointed politician.[29] His family was originally from Mississippi but left for Texas after the war and then returned. By 1900 he had served in the legislature, practiced law, and was editor of a couple of different papers.[30] From that pulpit he had become well known for his decidedly racist views, but he did not start that way. He changed into someone espousing rabid bigotry.[31] Most historians have concluded that Vardaman assumed the white counties were composed of virulent racists and therefore crafted his comments and positions to attract them. He also appealed to their pocketbooks by arguing that white-paid taxes should go to white schools and African Americans' taxes to their schools.[32] That African Americans had little and therefore paid little in taxes mattered not to him. Rather, Vardaman pointed out that if the state had seen fit to disfranchise these voters, why should the state then pay to educate African Americans so that they could vote?

More specifically, Vardaman believed that educating African Americans was a waste. In a 1905 interview published in the *Hawaiian Star*, Vardaman was reported as stating that the African American "has no social or political rights that a white man is bound to respect, and so far as I am concerned he never will have any. He will never vote in this state again, because he is utterly incapable of understanding the genius of self-government." Specifically referring to industrial schools on the line of Tuskegee, Vardaman added, "I don't believe in educating negroes. Their place is in the field, and when they leave it they are out of place. When you educate a negro you spoil a good field hand."[33] Vardaman also warned that if educated, African Americans would soon be pushing for social equality, which to many minds at the time threatened to "pollute" the race.[34] Later, as governor, in a letter explaining his veto of money allocated to an African American college in the state, Vardaman stated that education not only did not benefit African Americans, but rather that the effect was "pernicious." He then added that at some time in the future African Americans might evolve enough so that education could be a "positive factor for good, rather than a menace to our civilization, a blessing rather than a curse."[35]

This proposal to deny or substantially reduce funding of African American education was not the only racist demagoguery to which Vardaman resorted. On the matter of lynching, Vardaman was blunt. He claimed he did not understand why any white man would oppose it. He based his argument on the belief that black men were lustful and white women should be protected from their assaults, an argument that resonated with a number of Mississippians.[36] The problem was that the argument had little basis in reality. Though the incidence of lynching was actually down in the first decade of the twentieth century, only 29 of the 152 lynching victims were accused of rape.[37]

Vardaman was abundantly clear about his positions on white supremacy. Symbolically, he took to wearing white suits and a large-brimmed white hat, drove a team of white oxen, and took the name of the Great White Chief. He won the election in November 1903 and served as governor from 1904 to 1908.[38] His tenure proved to be as tempestuous as people feared, for his outspokenness on racial bigotry unleashed a resurgence of whitecapping.[39]

Whitecapping had generally died down until Vardaman came into office, for previous governors had taken a firm stance against it. Vardaman quickly discovered that, as governor, he, too, had to react and that he could not ignore the vigilante groups. Whitecapping took on a new level of violence and added murder to the list of lawlessness. The previous decade's incidences of whitecapping had been robust in the southwestern counties and were closely tied to the "Farmers Industrial" secret societies.[40] By the start of the Vardaman administration, whitecapping had spilled into the Delta because of reports that African Americans were banding into their own secret societies to protect their homes and livelihoods.[41] Governor Longino's quick action in 1903 helped to quell the violence; investigation by the governor had revealed membership in the farmers' leagues in these counties of over 700 men.[42] Immediately following the election of Vardaman in 1903 and just before he took office in January 1904, whitecappers murdered two African American men in Lincoln County and attacked a couple of others. Local law enforcement proved ineffective, and so not unexpectedly a large number of African Americans packed up and started to leave the area, in one town over fifty people in just one evening.[43] Labor shortages loomed, and Vardaman knew he had to act.[44]

The national reputation of the state fell further. Money for investment was no longer trickling into the state, and some bankers actually were leaving. With the support of the state legislature, Vardaman hired Albert Hoyt, a Pinkerton detective, to investigate white violence directed at African Americans, particularly the murders in Lincoln County. Hoyt was so effective that the investigation uncovered the extent of the membership in the county and exposed who was involved in the murders.[45] The consequence was not only court cases that produced convictions but also the squashing of the movement in the county. Campaigns in other counties produced similar results. In Franklin County, Hoyt produced 198 signed confessions, and a grand jury indicted over 300 for intimidation. The convictions and sentences were commuted, but the outcome was to dismantle the organization.[46]

Even worse were the situations in Kemper and Neshoba Counties in eastern Mississippi. An African American newspaper in Baltimore reported that two conductors on the Mobile and Ohio Railway had been killed, which triggered a race riot. It started in the little town of Wahalak but soon spread to Scooba. More than a dozen African Americans eventually lay dead, and a number of others were hurt. The sheriff of Kemper requested the state militia, and Vardaman complied.[47]

How popular were Vardaman's positions on race? Race was not the only issue on his agenda, but it was the one that tended to polarize the electorate. Certainly in the white counties he was popular. There were those in the state who opposed him, for the very reasons of race-baiting and his engendering race hatred; cynically, some opposition was based on the undermining of the labor supply as African Americans fled the state. Even the *Atlanta Constitution* noted the upswing in race riots, lynching, and whitecapping, and laid this increase in violence specifically at the feet of Vardaman and his kin. The paper noted that the state had recently been in the "clutch of frenzied passion, which of all the ghastly evils generated in the nethermost hell of weak human nature, is the most deadly, the most devastating, the most terribly deviant of the laws of man and of God- race prejudice." It noted that this "reign of terror" had "interrupted the peaceful lives of these little villages," and it advocated miscreants, white or black, needed to be dealt justice under the law. This upheaval they ascribed to Vardaman, who "whipped the prejudice of the Caucasian against the Negro to a white heat; appealing to the lowest most debasing instincts which must sadden the Almighty when He looks upon the human soul."[48]

Other efforts to institutionalize and legalize the system of segregation continued into the Vardaman period. In June 1904 a new state law took effect segregating trolleys in towns. What is remarkable is that during a period of strong pressure to segregate and demoralize African Americans, at least in this incident of new discrimination they pushed back. The effort began among the upper crust of the African American population, who did not appreciate being lumped together on the basis of race, for they saw themselves belonging to a class rather than self-identifying on the basis of race.[49] Not only in Mississippi but throughout the South, African Americans began a boycott of the streetcars. There is an indication that the source of the effort in the state came from black churches. Little information, however, remains to determine what sort of coordinated effort this was across states; but even if grassroots, it was remarkable. It was also ineffective, and segregation on the streetcars moved forward.[50]

The problem with blaming racism for most of Vardaman's support is that he was also a spokesman for the common man, albeit the white ones. Surprisingly, he was viewed by outsiders as a radical who opposed the standard order of society and the economy.[51] White farmers loved that he spoke directly to their concerns. He came from the Frank Burkitt wing of the Mississippi Democratic Party, and he never forgot his supporters. To that end, he backed equalization of tax assessments in the state, fair deposits of state funds in banks, higher pay for judges (to forestall temptation of bribery), sale of the governor's mansion (which did not happen), an increase in state education funds for lower schools and for white students, regulation of child labor, and improvement at the brutal state penitentiary at Parchman. In fact, he was remarkably strident in his defense of the rights of prisoners. In a letter to a judge in Brandon, Vardaman argued that even a convict was "entitled to the protection of the law against unjust and inhuman treatment. He is a human being, and the person who would take advantage of the convict's unfortunate condition to wreak personal revenge upon such convict is a very bad man and deserves the severest punishment prescribed by law."[52]

He also took on the moneyed interests, including regulation of insurance, railroads, utilities, and manufacturing. He moved on public health issues, attacking the spread of tuberculosis; placed a quarantine during a yellow fever epidemic in 1905 (offending the governor of Louisiana in the process); and improved facilities for those with mental disabilities.[53] In short, Vardaman can be classified with the progressives of the period, but he was a complex figure, just as was the state itself at the turn of the twentieth century.

♦ ♦ ♦

Mississippi was not alone in the experience of the rise of the demagogues who played on race hatred and stirred up animosity. Ben Tillman came to power earlier in South Carolina, followed by Jeff Davis in Arkansas, Napoleon Bonaparte Broward in Florida, and Tom Watson and Hoke Smith in Georgia.[54] Whipping up base emotions was far easier than dealing with the real problems of the time. The South had not repaired itself or caught up with the rest of the nation during the Gilded Age or the Progressive Era. In particular, Mississippi struggled to pull itself out of the bottom of the economic standings of the nation. Agriculture remained the foundation of the economy, but it was based on cotton. The price for cotton had fallen dramatically during the decades following the Civil War. Farmers, once independent, with plans for their futures, were reduced to tenancy and the devastating cycle of crop liens. And then in 1907 the boll weevil made its appearance in the state and brought massive devastation with it. In the long run, the damage from the boll weevil made farmers diversify, but in the short run people's lives were ruined.

Diversification included a nascent industry, but even burgeoning commerce produced only short-term solutions. Lumber became the king of "industry," but that dominance also had a cost. The lumber itself was good and in high demand, but the industry stripped acreage and left only stumps behind as the lumbermen moved to new areas. Towns grew up like mushrooms and disappeared just as fast. For many, though, it was a salvation from the problems of growing cotton. It allowed a bit of dignity to families trying to scratch out a living. Others fled to towns, making the areas south of the lumber fields, like Gulfport, grow.

Even the lumber industry fought a profound problem in the state—its grim transportation infrastructure. In spite of the good roads movement in the rest of the country, Mississippi did not have many paved roads. Automobiles were few and far between, and the demand for transportation for industry, much less for individuals, was not a priority. In fact, by 1910 there were only 10 miles of stone-surface roads in the state, 125 miles of gravel roads, and 185 miles total of "improved" roads. Unimproved roads of the public highways totaled 38,698 miles. The first legislation to create real highways did not come in the state until 1914, long after other states enacted such legislation. Even then the proposal was underfunded and more of an acknowledgment that something needed to be done.[55]

The Mississippi demagogues, such as Vardaman and Theodore Bilbo (yet to come), addressed some of the economic concerns of the electorate. Just as twenty years earlier, Mississippians assumed there would be a limited amount of growth. It would be easier to be generous and share and be inclusive when there was enough. When there would always be scarcity—and they reckoned this conclusion was the case—they were more cautious, if not actually miserly. They wanted no taxes, but in consequence they got no roads. They wanted industry, but they had no roads to ship goods. They wanted schools but were not able adequately to support teachers on what little they paid or keep schools open long enough to allow progress. Thus literacy remained a problem, and poverty was endemic.[56]

Mississippi had tried to improve in the area of education, for it actually allocated a higher percentage of taxes to education than any other state. The problem was that amount was so low that only South Carolina supported state education less. A lack of money for education was not the only problem. According to a study by the state department of education in 1903, over 90 percent of teachers had no professional training, and most had not finished high school.[57] The census in 1910 concluded that illiteracy, at least among whites, had fallen to only 8 percent, although there is some question as to the veracity of this number. Given these problems, as well as the prevalent racism, legislatures began to move toward further restricting money allocated to African American schools.[58]

Money in all its forms remained an issue. Taxable income was too small across the state. Physical handling of money remained a challenge because the distribution of specie and bills was erratic and often bypassed the state. Banks expanded quickly in the first decade of the new century, fertilized by loosened regulations. These underfunded institutions failed in record numbers from 1907 to 1914 and generated further belt-tightening within the state. There was nothing to stimulate an economy—there were no super-rich as in the East and Midwest, no swaths of industry, no growing pools of investment. Instead, the state remained stubbornly agricultural, believing that it allowed Mississippi to remain independent. But droughts, floods, and the arrival of the boll weevil in 1907 made even agriculture problematic.

Despite all of these difficulties, to some extent Mississippi did improve economically. It did have a few roads paved, and the dirt roads were an improvement on those twenty years previous. It had solvent banks, at least until the national banking collapse in 1907, when unfortunately Mississippi suffered in the panic more than most. It also had more students in school than before. Towns were beginning to get electric lighting, and more people within the towns were installing them.[59] Nevertheless, Mississippi lagged behind every state in the Union except for South Carolina. At times national comparisons were remarkable and devastating. For a state that craved respect, the people found themselves used as the example of the worst excesses of government fraud, inadequate education, poor roads, and violence.[60] It was far easier to keep telling themselves that everything was good and that they were moving upward and that people like Vardaman, who told them they had the right set of beliefs, would provide the help they needed. In reality, to outsiders, he became a representative of the worst of the South, particularly as he opened his senatorial stint campaigning to repeal the Fifteenth Amendment.[61]

◆ ◆ ◆

In retrospect, given the state's history over twenty years, the delegates at the 1890 convention reunion should have questioned their "success," but they did not. Perhaps it was too much for them to have recognized the inherent problems of disfranchisement that affected the social fabric, the government, and the economy, for restriction of the franchise and social Darwinism were accepted nationally. Their second goal, though—creating stability in the state between white and black counties—had not happened. The power of the white counties was rising and destabilizing the economy and rule of law. The first trickles of the Great Migration of African Americans from the Delta had already started and by the end of World War I would become a flood. Vardaman's intemperate language encouraged African Americans to leave, unleashed violent vigilantes, and discouraged outside investment. Farmers in the eastern part of the state did not want to pay taxes to build levees in the Delta, and so the area faced disabling floods, which would eventually include the one that in 1927 covered a fifth of the state. Education and transportation suffered from a lack of investment, a problem that can be traced not just to Mississippi being a poor state but also to the compromises in the state constitution that delicately balanced the power of taxation to prevent a shift in the taxing power away from the black counties. The result was a stalemate as both sides vied for power. Leadership was lacking, particularly leadership that would be honest about the real problem and about how the state compared to the other states in the period.

Pat Henry may well have had a clear picture of the reunion when he admitted he saw no real reason to have one, other than to renew old ties and to reminisce. Had it just been a gathering of old men to retell ancient narratives, the reunion may have been only a footnote in history. Certainly the event did not receive front-page coverage in the *Clarion-Ledger*. In fact, notice of the event appeared next to a story about the Ringling Brothers circus coming to town. The delegates, however, viewed the importance of their reunion differently.

Though they had originally planned an August event, the climate and the age of the invitees made an autumn event more sensible.[62] They met at noon on November 1, exactly twenty years from when they had adjourned the convention, and they gathered in the New Capitol. Back in 1890 the convention delegates had debated the need for new construction and balked at its requisite expense, but by the turn of the century the legislature saw the wisdom in erecting a new building.[63] In addition, the state was able to avoid the expense of construction. Though it had passed legislation authorizing the issuance of $1 million in bonds, the state attorney general brought suit against the railroads for back taxes, and the state was able to recoup the exact amount needed for the building. In addition, using the site of the old penitentiary meant no expense in land purchase. The Beaux-Arts building was completed in 1903 and dedicated on Jefferson Davis's birthday at a gathering.[64] The building was lit with electric lights, a wonder to many and unusual for its time.[65]

At the last moment, Robert Wilson, the convention secretary who had organized the event, was unable to attend, and his brother took minutes in his place. The delegates sat down to letters read from missing delegates, most of whom were ill; then, following parliamentary rules, they elected presiders. Before they adjourned to dinner at the Edwards Hotel, two of the members made important addresses, both of which were recorded in the proceedings.[66]

The first was from Mayre Dabney, who spoke in glowing terms of the convention and the constitution. Dabney had been a delegate from Vicksburg in Warren County and was a strong supporter of the provisions to disfranchise. In the speech he was blunt about the reasons for the convention, stating that the "primary purpose of it was to adopt some provision in our organic law which would secure to the State a good and stable government, freed from the incubus of Republican or negro rule from which we had suffered since the adoption of the 1869 Constitution by the carpet-bag." Even more specifically he asserted that "all understood and desired that some scheme would be evolved which would effectually remove from the sphere of politics in the state the ignorant and unpatriotic negro." To effectively disfranchise, he said there were two strands of thought: one was that the poll tax would be effective, and the other was that the Understanding Clause would be better. Dabney claimed that given the astuteness of these men, they chose to do both.[67]

Dabney then asked, given the advantage of time, which of these options was the more effective. He thought he had the answer, since he had done some research on the issue. As explained in chapter 10, in 1896 Cornelius Jones, a Republican and the attorney for the defendant in *Williams v. Mississippi*, had run against General T. C. Catchings in the Third Congressional District. When Jones lost, he contested the election, arguing that the Understanding Clause of the Mississippi Constitution violated of the provisions of the US Constitution. If the clause had not been in effect, Jones argued, he would have won, for it prohibited access to the polls by African Americans. Catchings hired Dabney to investigate.

In one sense, Dabney was thorough. In his investigation he went to each county seat in the districts and examined the "records of the circuit clerk's offices, and the poll books, and tax lists." He found that few African Americans had paid their poll taxes. Upon asking the circuit clerks directly, he found that "it was a rare occurrence for any person, white or black, to be denied the right to register when he applied. One clerk said the he had refused to register only one man on account of the understanding clause; others said they had refused very few for any cause."[68] In addition, he found that most younger African Americans could read and write, so that the Understanding Clause was not an issue.[69] Dabney concluded that the poll tax was by far the more effective of the two restrictions on the franchise. He also referred to earlier efforts to require payment of the tax and warned that stipulation would undermine the effectiveness of the provisions of the constitution.[70]

In spite of these efforts, in reality Dabney's investigation was only superficial. For instance, he did not question whether the general atmosphere of the time indicated to African Americans it would be safer not to pay their poll tax. In fact, there is no evidence at all that he interrogated any African Americans in the inquiry as to why they did not pay the tax. For Dabney, the issue appeared simple, and he concluded that the provision of the constitution instituting a voluntary poll tax was effective. This was, of course, the argument of the state in *Ratliff v. Beale* in 1896, discussed in the previous chapter. To Dabney, the point was that the goal of the convention was achieved through the poll tax, and he never questioned that goal, at least at the reunion.

Isaiah Montgomery delivered the second speech, which was formal and far more nuanced than Dabney's. Too many of the delegates did not understand the importance of his paper. Yet, unlike his notable speech at the 1890 convention, this speech was one of the two that were printed and distributed to the delegates and local libraries. It appears to have been equally well received by the delegates. He started by stating that "as the single representative of a people so largely interested in the former work of this body, I should say a few words on this anniversary occasion." As always, he started with the positive, noting that the convention laid a "foundation" for harmony with the other states in the Union in "seeking the highest and purest ideals of civil self-government." Though he claimed the tone of the document itself was "fundamentally just" and it brought "order . . . out of chaotic uncertainty, and gave peace to a confused people," he admitted the many criticisms were "based mainly on methods of administration."[71] Clearly this reference was a jab at Dabney's speech.

Montgomery acknowledged the race problems that emerged from emancipation, though he used circumlocution: "the relations between two races of diverse origin upon the ruins of established associations, which had occupied nearly two centuries in building—admittedly the most intricate ever decreed for adjudication by a civilized Christian people." The solution, he said, "was that this grave question should be dismissed from politics for one or two generations."[72]

Montgomery followed with the reminder that twenty years had now passed, or a generation, and indicated an analysis of the past twenty years was appropriate. He then turned to the good things that had happened among the African American citizens of the state, though he emphasized that "conditions still lack much of being satisfactory." Always starting with praise for the white community, he pointed to the New Capitol surroundings as showcasing the progress of the state. Then he turned to his own community, which had also made strides. He gave as example the ten African American banks in the state with resources of $750,000; in 1890 there were none. African American insurance companies collected and distributed $150,000 in 1890, but twenty years later the sum was over $1 million. Mound Bayou in 1890 had only a couple of hundred inhabitants, surrounded by forest, wolves, and panthers. Twenty years later the town had 25,000 inhabitants, schools, churches, and other institutions: "The community [owned] over 30,000 acres of land, thirty percent of which [was] improved with many neat homes and thriving farms." Farm products from the township "moved to market at a range of forty to fifty thousand dollars a week."[73]

Montgomery was laying down the gauntlet. During the 1890 convention a number of delegates, along with newspaper editors and letters to the editors, argued that African Americans were not civilized, educated, or dependable. This attitude was the reason that the delegates wanted to disfranchise a whole race, and it was the reason that the nation was willing to turn away and ignore the issue. Here, one generation later, Montgomery was pointing to the strides made by his people in only twenty years. He was also signaling to his people that, as difficult as those years had been, they had excelled.

In the next paragraph, however, Montgomery returned to the laudatory theme. He acknowledged that "many of the giant intellects of that day have wrapped about themselves the mantle of peace and gone to their final reward. Those who yet remain are reminded by increasing infirmities and the immutable ravages of time... they [will] enter the shadows of the mystic beyond."[74]

Today Montgomery remains a conundrum; his attitude is difficult to explain. As noted earlier, in 1890 Montgomery had been unprepared for the recriminations he faced when he returned home from the convention. One former friend questioned how Montgomery could "surrender the rights of 123,000 Negroes upon the altar of expediency."[75] He tried to explain his position to his former friends, like Booker T. Washington and Ida B. Wells, but they were horrified. Eventually he managed to mend fences.[76] The editors of the *Washington Bee* were more blunt: "What has Mr. Montgomery done for the Republican Party and what has he done in furtherance of the interest of his race?" With emotions rising, they added, "In short while it is known that he has not given his services to his people or the party beyond what was in consonance with his inordinate ambition, it will be remembered that in the constitutional convention of Mississippi he betrayed his party and his race and voted for the disfranchisement of the brave Afro-American voters of that state."[77]

In later years Montgomery expressed regret that the state had not acted in an honorable manner with the franchise, but he never completely repudiated the constitution or his part in the convention. When he attended the twentieth anniversary of the convention, again the only African American, he gave further support to the constitution, even if he may not have intended to do so.[78] There is no record of where he stayed or what difficulty he had when attending the dinner in a very segregated Jackson.[79] He did speak to the assembled reunion, praising the work of the original convention while still noting the criticism of its administration.[80]

Montgomery's goal of protecting his town and his people in that town was successful. They were left alone. In an ironic twist, Montgomery later claimed that the town of Mound Bayou was protected by friendly white people.[81] Other black settlements across the South were not nearly so fortunate. Mound Bayou eventually fell on really hard times and barely survived, but that was not until after Montgomery's death in 1924.[82] Other African Americans in the state moved toward emphasizing economic progress while staying out of politics, a decision that was safer. And there were a number of rising professionals in the urban areas who found it more expedient to be "social realists" and who would "conduct their public lives in scrupulous conformity to the racial code."[83]

The conundrum of Isaiah Montgomery's participation in the Mississippi constitutional convention of 1890 can be explained through understanding the parameters of his worldview: that of paternalism and the responsibilities of an upper class in which he included himself. Certainly in 1890 the leadership of the larger African American community in the South and the nation was farther along compared to Mississippi in creating a horizontal network based on race rather than class. What this explanation does not do is excuse. White supremacists in the state pointed in 1890 and in 1910 to his participation and support as evidence that this constitution was not only good for African Americans, but was created with friendly motives.[84] Certainly Montgomery did not know what the future held, and his experience led him to believe that the better people would win this cultural struggle.[85] Where blame can be attached to Montgomery is his reluctance to speak out later.[86] Moreover, he did not have to attend the twentieth anniversary ceremony, as many African Americans might view this action as a form of unspoken support for disfranchisement. Montgomery's presence did make a statement, and he should have known it would be used to hurt the very people he had hoped to protect.

For the rest of the state, it, too, had a chance to turn from the demagoguery of Vardaman. At the reunion, a number of the delegates were interviewed by a reporter from the Laurel paper, and they voiced strong opposition to Vardaman.[87] Back at the start of the year, the legislature had endured a lengthy caucus over the new appointment of a senator to represent Mississippi in Washington. Vardaman and his supporters were energetic in support of his candidacy, but the opposition, which was split early on, galvanized around the idea of anyone but Vardaman. LeRoy Percy, a grandee of the Delta, won the seat, to the horror of the white county political forces, for it seemed to undo the growing political strength of the white counties and return it to the Delta. The foundation for the opposition to Vardaman was based primarily on a repugnance to his racial intemperance. The respite from virulent racism, though, was brief, for the announcement of the death of Senator McLaurin coincided with the lengthy voting process for Percy; the passing of the old guard indicated a bleak future for the political elites.[88] In 1910 Vardaman supporters were bitter, and they worked hard for this senatorial appointment. In the meantime, they began to promote the idea of direct election of senators, arguing that the people should decide.[89] The votes for the popular Vardaman lay in the white counties, whose voters certainly outnumbered the white voters in the black counties, and a shift to popular vote for senator would surely put their candidate into office.[90] By 1913 Percy was not able to hang on to the seat, and Vardaman became the new senator, a position that provided a national audience for his brand of racism.

To a certain extent, though, the last hurrah by the old delegates of the constitutional convention lay in their opposition to Vardaman. The *Greenville Democrat* editors, certainly representing the Delta side of the issues, ironically argued that since these were the very men who "solved" the race problem, they should be listened to: "The opinions of men of this type are worthwhile. They present a sharp and pleasing contrast to the crops of spellbinders, agitators, fulminators and hired substitutes who are frantically endeavoring to stir up hate, passion and prejudice in every nook and corner of Mississippi, and to keep alive Vardaman's dying cause."[91] To understand this reaction to Vardaman, a return to the concepts of paternalism and hard-liners is necessary. These divisions did not go away with the promulgation of the new constitution, but instead gave voice and credence to the hard-liners and to Vardaman himself.

◆ ◆ ◆

That the authors of the Mississippi Constitution of 1890 became the symbols of moderate, civilized, and temperate statesmen only reveals the nature of the pivotal swing in power from the black counties to the white. Control shifted. What happened was not the stability they craved, but the beginning of an earthquake. Attributing this situation to Vardaman and his successors is missing the point. Vardaman would never have achieved his success without the changes put in force by the constitutional convention.

When the editors of the *Atlanta Constitution* wrote an editorial to castigate Vardaman for his virulent racism, they ascribed to him the worst sort of political manipulation. White supremacy, the editors argued, was "established beyond peradventure," so this race-baiting was senseless. They asked, "Does the man expect he can engrave deep into his incendiary views on susceptible minds, without an inevitable and a dreadful aftermath?" In consequence, they said he was "*sowing dragon's teeth throughout Mississippi*." To further emphasize its danger, not only in Mississippi, but throughout the South, they said, "Each outbreak like those in Mississippi breeds its fellow—larger, more bloody, perhaps with less provocation—near at hand, sometimes in far distant states." The editors ended with an appeal: "What the South needs ... is sober-headed, conscientious, scrupulous leaders capable of transquilizing [sic] those agencies that lie like dormant dynamite beneath conditions in this section."[92]

The readers of the *Atlanta Constitution* knew their Greek mythology. The story of Jason and the Argonauts and the myth of Cadmus were familiar to them. Both Jason and Cadmus had slain dragons and sowed the teeth, which grew into armed warriors. Like dragons, though, these warriors could not be trusted, for they turned on each other. This analogy of dragon teeth, however, works far better when explaining the source of the rise of the demagogues: the constitution of 1890. In giving up some control of the state, but retaining the ability to tax, the black counties had not understood the dissension they had unleashed and the struggles that were yet to come. Though the delegates claimed to be God-fearing men who knew virtue and integrity, they were willing to lie to each other, to Congress, and to their own people to ensure the passage of this constitution. The end was not what they wanted; yet because they had sold the idea that disfranchisement of African Americans was the raison d'être for the convention, when that provision proved successful, there was no room to renegotiate. The long-term effect was dissension, parsimoniousness, and racial hatred. These delegates had sown dragons' teeth and would reap the armed warriors and fomented disputes that were inevitable. The civil rights era was preordained.

Notes

Prologue

1. *Clarion-Ledger*, May 6, 1890, p. 1. A portion of the letter is also quoted in David Marsh Silver, "In the Eye of the Storm: Isaiah Montgomery and the Plight of Black Mississippians, 1847–1924" (Honors thesis, Amherst College, 1993).

Chapter 1. Introduction and Overview

1. Albert Dennis Kirwan, *Revolt of the Rednecks: Mississippi Politics, 1876-1925* (Lexington: University of Kentucky Press, 1951), particularly 65–70.

2. For comparison, see V. O. Key, *Southern Politics in State and Nation* (New York: Albert A Knopf, 1949); C. Vann Woodward, *Origins of the New South, 1877–1913* (Baton Rouge: Louisiana State University Press, 1951); Morgan Kousser, *The Shaping of Southern Politics: Suffrage Restriction and the Establishment of the One-Party South* (Chapel Hill: University of North Carolina Press, 1974); Kirwan, *Revolt of the Rednecks*; Steven Edward Cresswell, *Rednecks, Redeemers, and Race: Mississippi after Reconstruction, 1877–1917* (Jackson: University Press of Mississippi, 2006); Michael Perman, *Struggle for Mastery: Disfranchisement in the South, 1888-1908* (Chapel Hill: University of North Carolina Press, 2001). Perman does an excellent job in reviewing earlier analyses of disfranchisement (1–8).

3. Stephen Edward Cresswell, *Multiparty Politics in Mississippi, 1877–1902* (Jackson: University Press of Mississippi, 1995), 86–92.

4. Neil R. McMillen, *Dark Journey: Black Mississippians in the Age of Jim Crow* (Chicago: University of Illinois Press, 1990), 293–95.

5. These terms will be discussed at length in later chapters.

6. This was not true of other states. See Joel Williamson, *The Crucible of Race: Black-White Relation in the American South since Emancipation* (New York: Oxford University Press, 1984), 111–39. Compare this with the argument of C. Van Woodward in *The Strange Career of Jim Crow* (New York: Oxford University Press, 1966), 44–59. Woodward uses Mississippi as an example, but then extrapolates across the region.

7. Williamson, *Crucible of Race*, 111–19.

8. C. Van Woodward, *Origins of the New South, 1877–1913* (Baton Rouge: Louisiana State University Press, 1951), 176–86; Paul H. Buck, *The Road to Reunion* (Boston: Little Brown, 1937), 144–50.

9. William F. Holmes, "The Leflore County Massacre and the Demise of the Colored Farmers' Alliance," *Phylon* 34 (1973): 267–74; Omar H. Ali, *In the Lion's Mouth: Black Populism in the New South, 1886–1900* (Jackson: University Press of Mississippi, 2010), 58–64.

10. *Clarion-Ledger*, January 31, 1889, p. 1.

11. S. S. Calhoon, "The Causes and Events That Led to the Calling of the Constitutional Convention of 1890," *Publications of the Mississippi Historical Society* 6 (1902): 107; Calhoon was the president of the convention. See also James P. Coleman, "The Origin of the Constitution of 1890," *Journal of Mississippi History* 19, no. 2 (April 1957): 85.

12. Timothy B. Smith, *J. Z. George: Mississippi's Great Commoner* (Jackson: University Press of Mississippi, 2012), 100. Smith presents George as a moderate here, rather than a chameleon. See also Dunbar Rowland, *Courts, Judges and Lawyers of Mississippi, 1798–1935* (Jackson, MS: Hederman Brothers, 1935), 99–103.

13. Among those calling for ratification were the *Clarion-Ledger, Tupelo Ledger, Oxford Eagle, Brandon Republican, Yazoo Sentinel*, and *Aberdeen Sentinel*. For a discussion, see *Clarion-Ledger*, September 4, 1890, p. 4; October 9, 1890, pp. 2–4; and October 30, 1890, p. 4.

14. *Congressional Record Containing the Proceedings and Debates of the Fifty-First Congress, Second Session*, Vol. 22 (Washington, DC: Government Printing Office, 1891), selections from 602–895; George H. Ethridge, *Mississippi Constitutions* (Jackson, MS: Tucker Printing, 1928), 617–749; Heather Cox Richardson, *The Death of Reconstruction: Race, Labor, and Politics in the Post–Civil War North, 1865–1901* (Cambridge, MA: Harvard University Press, 2001), 210–24; Thomas Adams Upchurch, *Legislating Racism: The Billion Dollar Congress and the Birth of Jim Crow* (Lexington: University Press of Kentucky, 2004).

15. Charles W. Calhoun, *Conceiving a New Republic: The Republican Party and the Southern Question, 1869–1900* (Lawrence: University Press of Kansas, 2006), 259, 260; Paul H. Buck, *The Road to Reunion: 1865–1900* (Boston: Little, Brown, 1937), 280; Richardson, *Death of Reconstruction*, 210–12.

16. *Williams v. Mississippi* 170 US 213 (1898); *Williams v. Mississippi*—error to the supreme court of the state of Mississippi, No. 531, argued and submitted March 18, 1898, decided April 25, 1898 (213–25).

17. *Proceedings of a Reunion of the Surviving Members of the Constitutional Convention of 1890* (Jackson, MS: Premier Printing, 1910).

18. For a quick overview of the economy of the state, see Cresswell, *Rednecks*, 98–146; and Kirwan, *Rednecks*, 40–49.

19. Loren Schweninger, *Black Property Owners in the South, 1790–1915* (Urbana: University of Illinois Press, 1990), 205.

20. McMillen, *Dark Journey*. See also Vernon Lane Wharton, *The Negro in Mississippi, 1865–1890* (Chapel Hill: University of North Carolina Press, 1947). Both books are excellent resources, but McMillen's is a cultural history, and Wharton's is more of a social history. Somehow Wharton had some access to papers in the 1940s that are no longer available.

21. John Roy Lynch did not like him. By 1890 Lynch was living in DC, but maintained a fiction that he was still in charge of the Mississippi Republican Party. Hill, who did live in the state, was his opposition. See John Roy Lynch, *Reminiscences of an Active Life: The Autobiography of John R. Lynch*, ed. John Hope Franklin (Chicago: University of Chicago Press, 1970), 358–417.

Chapter 2. The Bourbon Elites

1. This is the building presently known in Mississippi as the Old Capitol, which stands at the head of Capitol Street in downtown Jackson.

2. *Journal of the Proceedings of the Constitutional Convention of the State of Mississippi* (Jackson, MS: E. L. Martin, printer to the Convention, 1890), 242.

3. Ibid., 378.

4. "The Constitutional Convention," *Clarion-Ledger*, August 13, 1890, p. 4. Throughout the discussion of the convention in the next three chapters, I have used the *Clarion-Ledger* extensively. As the largest newspaper in the capital, the editors daily sent men to report verbatim the speeches in the convention. Because of this reporting, at times the paper had better accounts than the official minutes. The news reports, however, were lengthy and covered many columns and pages. They are all listed as "The Constitutional Convention," but often the title is lost among the columns. Therefore, I have omitted titles in the references from the *Clarion-Ledger* concerning only the convention.

5. The convention minutes give the number as 166, but that is undocumented elsewhere; Convention Minutes, see list of delegates. Compare that to 134 delegates claimed by Frank Johnson in "Suffrage and Reconstruction in Mississippi," *Publications of the Mississippi Historical Society* 6 (1902): 212. The information in this article is helpful, but one needs to exercise care in reading, remembering the particular point of view of Frank Johnson, which was particularly supportive of those who would disfranchise. Johnson lists the two Republicans as Montgomery and Judge Simrall. He lists former governor Alcorn as an independent.

6. *Clarion-Ledger*, October 30, 1890, p. 4. Other authors have identified two college presidents, along with four members of the congressional delegation. See John W. Winkle, *Mississippi State Constitution: A Reference Guide* (Westport, CT: Greenwood Press, 1993), 11. Senator Walthall did not participate. I have found reference to a delegate from Coahoma County, a J. W. Cutrer, who did not make it to the convention on time because he was under arrest in Colorado for murdering editor Chew of Friars Point. The election had been vicious, with editor Chew calling Cutrer a man with "negro" blood; during the subsequent dual, both men fired, but Cutrer hit his target and Chew died. The sheriff arrested Cutrer, but primarily to get him away from "hot heads" in the county. Eventually Cutrer was released to attend the convention, and he joined the other delegates only a couple of days late. See "Mississippi's Constitutional Convention," *Evening Star* (Washington, DC), August 14, 1890; and *Daily Commercial Herald* (Vicksburg), July 31, 1890, p. 1.

7. Judge Calhoon was a circuit court judge who eventually served on the Mississippi Supreme Court. He beat R. C. Patty to the position by only one vote. See Kirwan, *Revolt*

of the Rednecks, 65. According to Kirwan, Patty was a member of the Farmers' Alliance in Noxubee County (which he mistakenly identifies as a white county). See John Knox Bettersworth, *Mississippi: A History* (Austin, TX: Steck, 1959), 377; "Convention," *Daily Commercial Herald* (Vicksburg), August 12, 1890, p. 1. Bettersworth, a professor at Mississippi State, wrote the high school text on the history of Mississippi used for years in the state. While it is not an academic history, it is suitable for a quick reference to numbers, state legislative committees, lists of state officers, and such.

8. *Proceedings*, 10. See also *Clarion-Ledger*, August 13, 1890, p. 1. Compare this to an editorial in an African American paper in Richmond, Virginia: "Mississippi's Constitution," *Richmond Planet*, August 16, 1890, p. 4. The editor specifically stated that the convention intended to circumvent the constitution, but such perfidy would not last because "Right is eternal."

9. *Clarion-Ledger*, August 13, 1890, p. 1, written by E. H. Bristow from Aberdeen on August 7. The caps of the word "race" are his. See also a letter from "Senex" published in the *Clarion-Ledger*, January 31, 1889. For a gentler explanation of the issues, see a letter written by ex-governor Alcorn to an editor in South Carolina: *Keowee Courier*, September 11, 1890.

10. This chapter and the next give only a cursory overview of Reconstruction in Mississippi, with emphasis on important issues that appear later. For a thorough examination of the period, see William C. Harris, *The Day of the Carpetbagger: Republican Reconstruction in Mississippi* (Baton Rouge: Louisiana State University Press, 1979).

11. Don Doyle, *Faulkner's County: The Historical Roots of Yoknapatawpha* (Chapel Hill: University of North Carolina Press, 2001), 315. Compare to Willie D. Halsell, "The Bourbon Period in Mississippi Politics, 1875–1890," *Journal of Southern History* 11 (1945): 519–37, particularly the first page, where she writes of the origins of the term and whether it applies to Mississippi. Halsell was the reference librarian at Mississippi State.

12. For a rundown of the political powers in Mississippi right after the restoration, see "Mississippi," *Memphis Daily Appeal*, July 31, 1871, p. 1; Bettersworth, *Mississippi*, 337; Doyle, *Faulkner's County*, 315. James Chalmers, listed above, was also a brigadier general.

13. Eric Foner, *A Short History of Reconstruction, 1863–1877* (New York: Harper and Row, 1990), 62, 63.

14. Harris, *Day of the Carpetbagger*, 296–300; Bettersworth, *Mississippi*, 321, 322.

15. Ali, *In the Lion's Mouth*, 122.

16. Steven Hahn, *A Nation under Our Feet: Black Political Struggles in the Rural South from Slavery to the Great Migration* (Cambridge, MA: Belknap Press of Harvard University Press, 2003), 242. See also Wharton, *The Negro in Mississippi*, 158–59.

17. Hahn, *Nation under Our Feet*, 243.

18. Bradley G. Bond, *Political Culture in the Nineteenth Century South: Mississippi 1830–1900* (Baton Rouge: Louisiana State University Press, 1995), 170–74; Bettersworth, *Mississippi*, 323, 326; Kenneth M. Stamp, *The Era of Reconstruction, 1865–1877* (New York: Alfred Knopf, 1966), 199–201. See Robert Bowman, "Reconstruction in Yazoo County," *Publications of the Mississippi Historical Society* 7 (1903): 127, which states: "The people of Yazoo county had groaned under Radical misrule and the heavy weight of burdensome taxation and official corruption. The negroes were the controlling power in elections."

19. So many left, in fact, that the tax rolls of the period include an abbreviated notation—GTT (Gone to Texas). J. Mills Thornton III, "Fiscal Policy and the Failure of Radical

Reconstruction in the Lower South," in *Region, Race, and Reconstruction: Essays in Honor of C. Vann Woodward*, ed. J. Morgan Kousser and James M. McPherson (New York: Oxford University Press, 1982), 349–94. Thornton argues that economic issues are too often ignored in the switch to the Democratic Party by white small farmers in the 1875 and 1876 elections.

20. For a list of raised taxes per county, see J. S. McNeily, "War and Reconstruction in Mississippi, 1863–1890," *Mississippi Historical Society* Centenary Series 2 (1918): 410.

21. Foner, *Reconstruction*, 185.

22. W. H. Hardy, "Recollections of Reconstruction in East and Southeast Mississippi," *Publications of the Mississippi Historical Society* 7 (1903): 207.

23. See Doyle, *Faulkner's County*, 282–87; Bettersworth, *Mississippi*, 371, for reference to popularity of secret organizations of all kinds.

24. Florence Warfield Sillers (Wirt Williams edited the DAR compilation), *Bolivar County, Mississippi: Its Creation, Pioneer Days and Progress in the Heart of the Mississippi Delta* (1948; repr., Spartanburg, SC: Reprint Company, 1976), 168. The Sillers book is local history and is certainly "unreconstructed history" at that. Because of that, it does provide a view into the motivations of the Delta elites during that period. For more information, see Harris, *Day of the Carpetbagger*, 371–405.

25. See Bradley Bond, *Mississippi: A Documentary History* (Jackson: University Press of Mississippi, 2003), 129–34, for account of testimony before Congress over a beating that resulted in the original "bloody shirt." Foner, *Reconstruction*, 184, 185. For details on Klan activity in this period, see Blanche Ames, *Adelbert Ames, 1835–1933* (New York: Argosy Antiquarian, 1964), 350–69, including a reproduction of an etching of arrested Klan members from Tishomingo County (361). An account in Sillers, *Bolivar County*, 161, in which the writer refers to "heroic" actions by the Klan in the "dark days," reveals how warped these perceptions of the Klan were locally.

26. Walter Sillers, "Reconstruction," in *History of Bolivar County, Mississippi: Its Creation, Pioneer Days and Progress in the Heart of the Mississippi Delta*, ed. Florence Warfield Sillers. (Spartanburg, SC: Reprint Company, 1976), 158. For an explanation for the mistrust, see "General Gordon Carpetbaggers," *Memphis Daily Appeal*, September 24, 1875, p. 2.

27. J. Z. George to L.Q.C. Lamar, May 13, 1874, Lamar Letterbooks, Lamar Papers, Mississippi Department of Archives and History. His behavior so impressed the North that in 1875 he was nominated for the vice-presidency under the little known American Union Party, which also nominated General N. P. Banks for president. "Political," *Northern Tribune* (Cheboygan, MI), August 28, 1875, p. 2. See also "Washington: The Sumner Eulogies" *New York Times*, April 28, 1874, p. 1. Lamar made a good appearance to both sides of the aisle. See "Washington Notes," *New York Times*, December 10, 1872, p. 1, in which Lamar refers to himself as thoroughly reconstructed.

28. James G. Revels, "Redeemers, Rednecks and Racial Integrity," in *A History of Mississippi*, ed. Richard Aubrey McLemore (Hattiesburg: University and College Press of Mississippi, 1973), 597, 598.

29. Sillers, *Bolivar County*, 162–65.

30. Harris, *Day of the Carpetbagger*, 653, 680. For a reference to the rise of the Democrats, see "Mississippi," *Memphis Daily Appeal*, September 5, 1875, p. 1. Lamar is usually portrayed as a moderate. African American papers were uncertain what to make of him. See "Secretary

Lamar," in *Washington Bee*, October 2, 1886, and October 30, 1886, for an examination of the problem and the split among African Americans. For another take on this split, see Ames, *Adelbert Ames*, 413–22. Ames quotes a story that questions how "moderate" Lamar was (436). Especially note the letter from Lamar to Charles Reemelin, August 25, 1875, in Edward Mayes, *L.Q.C. Lamar: His Life, Times, and Speeches, 1825–1893* (Nashville, TN: Methodist Episcopal Church, 1896), 258–59. Mayes was Lamar's son-in-law.

31. Smith, *J. Z. George*, 100. Smith presents George as a moderate here, rather than a chameleon. George asked for "equality of benefits," but he was also specific about those benefits accruing to the white race. Compare this to the brief report in Skates, *Mississippi*, 117.

32. Smith, *J. Z. George*, 136, 137. This biography of George is the first in many decades. Smith notes several times George's nickname, and he points out the common aspect to the man, including a habit of chewing tobacco, which resulted in a tongue cancer in 1892. His lack of polish, though, should not be equated with a lack of intellect or education, for George was politically astute and a sharp lawyer. For further analysis of the problem of labeling George, see Smith's discussion on p. 173. See also May Spencer Ringold, "Senator James Zachariah George: Bourbon or Liberal?" *Journal of Mississippi History* 16 (July 1954): 164–82.

33. For testimony as to the effects, see Bond, *Mississippi*, 135–43; Stephen Cresswell, *Mormons & Cowboys, Moonshiners & Klansmen: Federal Law Enforcement in the South and West, 1870–1893* (Tuscaloosa: University of Alabama Press, 1991), 29; Stamp, *Reconstruction*, 201–10. There were some odd efforts to entice African American voters to their side; see *Clarion*, October 18, 1876, p. 1, in which the editors suggested it was time for "colored voters" to "throw off the degrading chains of party slavery."

34. For an example, see Wharton, *The Negro in Mississippi*, 191; "Agitated Mississippi," *National Republican*, October 12, 1875, p. 1.

35. Quotations come from Francis Butler Simkins and Robert Hilliard Woody, *South Carolina during Reconstruction* (Chapel Hill: University of North Carolina Press, 1932), 564–69. See also Wharton, *The Negro in Mississippi*.

36. "Morton Forestalled," *Memphis Daily Appeal*, January 14, 1876, p. 2; Johnston, "Conference," 68.

37. See "Mississippi," *Memphis Daily Appeal*, October 19, 1875, p. 1; Bettersworth, *Mississippi*, 332; and Smith, *J. Z. George*, 108, 109, for accounts of this meeting. John Ray Skates, *Mississippi: A Bicentennial History* (New York: W. W. Norton), 118, has a rather inoffensive account of the election.

38. Sillers, *Bolivar County*, 159, 160. Compare this account to one on Kemper County; see Hardy, "Recollections," 209.

39. "Why Ames Refused to Fill Davis Place," *Memphis Daily Appeal*, March 31, 1876, p. 1; "Mississippi," part of a speech from General Chalmers in which he blames Ames for the political problems of the 1876 election, *Memphis Daily Appeal*, June 13, 1876, p. 2; Smith, *J. Z. George*, 109.

40. "The Ames Impeachment," *National Republican* (Washington, DC), February 28, 1876, p. 1; "United States Senatorship," *Weekly Clarion*, January 28, 1880, p. 1. The editors of the *Weekly Clarion* must have considered the election pretty secure; although they often ignored criticism of the state from outside, they did reprint a column from the *Cincinnati Commercial* that identified George as the "man who conducted the rifle-club and shot-gun

Democratic campaign in Mississippi in 1875." "An Outside Republican View," *Weekly Clarion*, February 4, 1880, p. 1.

41. Bettersworth, *Mississippi*, 33.

42. Sillers, "Reconstruction," 158.

43. Johnson, "Suffrage and Reconstruction," 203. Also found in Alfred H. Stone Collection, Mississippi Department of Archives and History, Vol. 17, no. 4.

44. Lynch, *Reminiscences*, 182.

45. Johnson, "Suffrage and Reconstruction," 205. Lest there be any doubt about the continuation of intimidation, see "No Intimidation," *Memphis Daily Appeal*, December 27, 1884, p. 1; "Southern Lawlessness," *Bismarck (North Dakota) Weekly Tribune*, January 18, 1889, p. 1. The Jackson paper reported some, but denied others. "Bloody Affair at Marion," *Weekly Clarion*, November 10, 1881, p. 2, is an example of a reported outrage, but the following are denials of intimidation and fraud: editorial, *Weekly Clarion*, September 15, 1881, p. 2; "Insane Cry of Intimidation and Fraud," *Weekly Clarion*, September 29, 1881, p. 2; "The False Cry of Bulldozing and Ballot Cheating," *Weekly Clarion*, October 27, 1881, p. 2.

46. Wharton, *The Negro in Mississippi*, 200.

47. Calhoon, "Calling of the Constitutional Convention," 109.

48. Sillers, *Bolivar County*, 163–65. For more references to the local reaction to the federal law that permitted use of federal marshals, see "Bayonet Rule of the Federal Government," *Weekly Clarion*, July 23, 1879, p. 1; "The Democratic Position," *Weekly Clarion*, September 17, 1879, p. 2; "Federal Election Laws," *Weekly Clarion*, April 7, 1880, p. 2; "Troops at the Polls," and "Absurd Regulations as to Ballots," *Weekly Clarion*, April 28, 1880, p. 3; "Deputy Marshalls in Elections," *Weekly Clarion*, May 26, 1880, p. 2, in which the editors claimed the "Constitution guaranteed to the States the exclusive control over elections." Sheer frustration by the editors resulted in "Unadulterated Partisan and Sectional Malignity and Misrepresentation," *Weekly Clarion*, July 22, 1880, p. 2.

49. Johnson, "Suffrage and Reconstruction," 202–3.

50. The eleventh census compared 1860 to 1890 in farm valuations in Mississippi. The valuation of farms (land, fencing, and buildings) in 1860 was $190,789,662 and by 1890 had finally climbed back up to $127,423,157. This number was not adjusted for inflation. Department of the Interior, Census Office, *Abstract of the Eleventh Census, 1890* (Washington, DC: Government Printing Office, 1894), 68 (hereafter cited as *Eleventh Census*).

51. Bettersworth, *Mississippi*, 334.

52. Kenneth Greenberg, *Honor & Slavery* (Princeton, NJ: Princeton University Press, 1996), xi–xiv. "Paternalism" is a term with conflicting interpretations and emotions, which historians have examined repeatedly over the last century. It is fraught with difficulties, but it would also be impossible to ignore. For example, see Ulrich Bonnell Phillips, *Life and Labor in the Old South* (repr., Boston: Little Brown, 1963); Stanley M. Elkins, *Slavery: A Problem in American Institutional and Intellectual Life* (Chicago: University of Chicago Press, 1976); Eugene Genovese, *Roll Jordan Roll: The World the Slaves Made* (New York: Pantheon Books, 1974); Lacy Ford, *Deliver Us from Evil: The Slavery Question in the Old South* (Oxford: Oxford University Press, 2009).

53. Yvonne Jones, "Black Leadership Patterns and Political Change in the American South" (41–54); and Kay Young Day, "Kinship in a Changing Economy: A View from the Sea

Islands" (11–24), both in *Holding Onto the Land and the Lord: Kinship, Ritual, Land Tenure and Social Policy in the Rural South*, ed. Robert Hall and Carol Stack (Athens: University of Georgia Press, 1982).

54. The Davis family is a good example. Joe held the title to all the Davis holdings, which was the eventual issue in who owned the land and whether Jefferson was the presumptive heir to lands already sold to the Montgomery family.

55. An interesting but strained interpretation is that of Bond, *Political Culture*, 218–19. Middle class, which he tries to define, is even more difficult to define than upper class. Certainly, though, with the advent of a consumer class, a professional class, and a merchant class, one can find vestiges of the middle class. More work needs to be done on these social distinctions. I have elected not to discuss all the permutations of class distinctions that appear in literature (historical, sociological, or anthropological), for such inclusion would overtake the narrative. Suffice it to say most people know these classes existed, but find them hard to define, probably because it is highly dependent on who is defining the group—those within or those without.

56. Historians have written on the antebellum free black community, and some have observed that some African Americans in the period did very well economically, a number owning slaves of their own. Ira Berlin, *Slaves Without Masters: The Free Negro in the Antebellum South* (New York: New Press, 1974).

57. Janette Thomas Greenwood, Bittersweet Legacy: The Black and White "Better Classes" in Charlotte, 1850–1910 (Chapel Hill: University of North Carolina Press, 1994), 22; Lawrence Otis Graham, Our Kind of People: Inside America's Black Upper Class (New York: Harper Collins, 1999), 5–15.

58. In short, William Faulkner's novels were fictional, but based on enough reality to resonate. My mother grew up in Holly Springs, Mississippi, where the stories were often told about families who had lost everything in the war, but were still "fine families." Everyone knew who they were.

59. Kirwan, *Revolt of the Rednecks*, 27–39; Bettersworth, *Mississippi*, 335.

60. Kirwan, *Revolt of the Rednecks*, 40.

61. "Railroads, Their Great Value," *Weekly Clarion*, November 30, 1881, p. 1. Railroads grew, but they came from a deficit. For instance, in 1890 Mississippi had only 2,332 miles of track, almost double that of ten years earlier. If one compares that to Georgia, which had 4,557 miles, then the problems begin to appear. South Carolina had slightly less miles of track than Mississippi. Further comparisons are difficult because the newly formed states in the West were just beginning their push, and northern states were far ahead. Proper comparisons would have to include square miles in the states, population needs, and so forth. See *Eleventh Census*.

62. Bettersworth, *Mississippi*, 352. The difficulty was that this offer was only good for a year. Companies would have to move quickly.

63. Ibid. Even Jefferson Davis worked for and on behalf of railroads. See Letter from Jefferson Davis, *Weekly Clarion*, February 5, 1879, p. 2; for other examples, see "Natchez and Jackson Railroad," *Weekly Clarion*, March 2, 1879, p. 1.

64. "The Governor's Message," *Weekly Clarion*, January 4, 1882, p. 3 (subtitle "Railroad Matters"); Edward L. Ayres, *Promise of the New South: Life after Reconstruction* (New York:

Oxford University Press, 1992), 9–11. For a brief analysis of the pull of the railroad and its imaginative connections, see also John M. Giggie, *After Redemption, Jim Crow and the Transformation of African-American Religion in the Delta 1875–1915* (New York: Oxford University Press, 2008), 32–33.

65. Cresswell, *Rednecks*, 100–102. Justice J.A.P. Campbell (chief justice of the Mississippi Supreme Court) and Judge H. H. Chalmers were caught up in this debate; they enter this narrative in chapter 4.

66. For reference to the African American committee leader of the Knights, see "Stealing a March: Barry's Friends Give Powderly a Little Surprise," *Atlanta Constitution*, November 11, 1888, p. 1.

67. Cresswell, *Rednecks*, 156, 157,

68. Revels, "Redeemers, Rednecks, and Racial Integrity," 596. The issue continued over the next decades; see "Legislative Supervision over Railroad Corporations," *Weekly Clarion*, September 17, 1879, p. 2.

69. Bettersworth, *Mississippi*, 338.

70. McLemore, *History of Mississippi*, 602. Part of Lowry's problem was his aristocratic bend. For instance, he upheld the law against prize fighting (bare-knuckled); therefore he sought to prosecute John L. Sullivan, who fought Kid Kilrain in Marion County in 1889. For the story and consequences, see "Slugger Sullivan Arrested," *Los Angeles Daily Herald*, July 12, 1889, p. 4; series of untitled columns in *Fort Worth (Texas) Daily Gazette*, July 12, 1889, p. 2; "Sullivan a Winner," *Pittsburg Dispatch*, July 12, 1889, p. 1.

71. Burkitt pointed to an item that ran in a number of newspapers that reported Lowry's son had used the governor's pass for the railroads. *Wichita Eagle*, March 30, 1888, p. 4. See also "Is This Democracy," *San Antonio (Texas) Light*, November 22, 1883, p. 2; McLemore, *History of Mississippi*, 2; Kirwan, *Revolt of the Rednecks*, 56.

72. Revels, *Redeemers*, 597.

73. Halsell, "Bourbon Period," 527. She identifies Walthall as not only aristocratic but also wealthy for the time and place. He was a railroad lawyer and not trusted by the farmers. See "An Outside Republican View," *Weekly Clarion*, February 4, 1880, p. 1.

74. Timothy Smith quotes a Republican in the state who suggested that George was more liberal and Barksdale was more conservative. It really depended on the context, for Barksdale was an agrarian. Smith, *J. Z. George*, 99. See also Harris, *Day of the Carpetbagger*, 674–77; Kirwan, *Revolt of the Rednecks*, 51, 52.

75. Halsell, "Bourbon Period," 526–28. She indicates that Stone was more of a self-made man, but certainly had more polish than George. An early thesis suggests that the heavy reliance on the old aristocracy in the state led to growing suspicions in the North about the long-term plans of the old planter class. See Oscar Dooley, "The Disfranchisement of the Negro in the South—the Changing Sentiment of the North from 1870 to 1910" (Master's thesis, University of Mississippi, 1936), 67.

76. James W. Garner, "The Senatorial Career of J. Z. George," *Publications of the Mississippi Historical Society* 7 (1903): 261, 262.

77. Ibid., 262.

78. Ibid., 246.

79. Ibid., 247.

80. Revels, "Redeemers," 600. In 1880 Lamar had come to Mississippi to lobby the legislature to appoint his friend Walthall to the Senate. George was appointed instead, and some editors of the time thought this indicated a reduction of support in the state for Lamar. "Senator Lamar," *Weekly Clarion*, February 4, 1880, p. 4.

81. The party had its own splits between the farmers and planters. According to Halsell, the House was controlled by the farmers, and the Senate, by the planters. Her case, though, is not coherently argued and so is not included in the body of this chapter. That there was a split between the two sides was convincing.

82. "Facts and Figures for the People," *Weekly Clarion*, October 6, 1881, p. 1; "The Triumph of the Conservative Democracy," *Weekly Clarion*, November 16, 1881, p. 2; Bettersworth, *Mississippi*, 335.

83. Revels, "Redeemers," 590. See also Stone Papers in Mississippi Department of Archives and History. The story is also reported in David G. Sansing and Carroll Waller, *A History of the Mississippi Governor's Mansion* (Jackson: University Press of Mississippi, 1977), 72. This push for economy went so far as to suggest that the governor's salary was reasonable only if he became responsible for the upkeep of the deteriorating mansion. Ibid., 74.

84. Bettersworth, *Mississippi*, 336. See also Revels, "Redeemers," 591. Revels argued in 1973 that few historians used the term anymore; it, however, continues, and for the governors of the period, the term fits pretty well.

Chapter 3. Opposition to the Bourbons

1. "From Major Barksdale," *Clarion-Ledger*, July 4, 1889, p. 1. See also Department of the Interior, Census Office, *Abstract of the Twelfth Census of the United States, 1900* (Washington, DC: Government Printing Office, 1904), 85, which gives a breakdown of occupations in the state. In 1900 Mississippi had 490,582 in agriculture. The problem with this number is that it is counting males over the age of ten, and it is not clear about a female count. For reference to hopes for agricultural revival, see "How to Increase Southern Wealth and Prosperity," *Weekly Clarion*, October 13, 1881, p. 1. For a wider discussion, see Doyle, *Faulkner's County*, 296–303.

2. Walter Nugent, *Structures of American Social History* (Bloomington: Indiana University Press, 1981), 87–120, for a full discussion.

3. Between 1870 and 1900, the number of Mississippi farms grew from 68,023 to 220,803. Acreage of improved land went from 4,209,146 in 1870 to 7,594,428 by 1900; and the value of those farms rose from $92,890,758 in 1870 to $204,332,027. *Eleventh Census*, 65; Dunbar Rowland, *History of Mississippi: The Heart of the South* (Chicago: S. J. Publishing, 1925), 530. The number of farms is controversial. The census counted landowners and sharecroppers as separate farms. Compare this to numbers given of males in agriculture. Department of the Interior, Census Office, *Census Report*, Vol. 5, *Twelfth Census of the United States Taken in the Year 1900, Agriculture* (Washington, DC: Census Office, 1902), Table LXXIV (hereafter cited as *Twelfth Census*, Vol. 5). Gilbert Fite, "Southern Agriculture since the Civil War: An Overview," *Agricultural History* 53 (1979): 7.

4. John M. Barry, *Rising Tide: The Great Mississippi Flood of 1927 and How It Changed America* (New York: Simon and Schuster, 1997), 103. Barry attributes the whole idea of sharecropping to W. A. Percy, planter in Washington County, Mississippi. For further discussion of the subject, see Fite, "Southern Agriculture," 5, 6; Doyle, *Faulkner's County*, 308–12; and Kirwan, *Revolt of the Rednecks*, 43–45.

5. Cresswell, *Rednecks*, 98. For more on the development in the Delta, see Willis, *Forgotten Time*, 35–40; and Doyle, *Faulkner's County*, 311. Depressing statistics from the census of the period refer to a slow rise in value of farms, but compared to other states, it was dismal. See *Twelfth Census*, Vol. 5, Tables cvi, cii. See also Table LXXIV for farms classified by ownership or tenancy.

6. For the text of the lien laws during this period, see J.A.P. Campbell, *The Revised Code of the Statute Laws of the State of Mississippi* (Jackson, MS: J. L. Power, State Printer, 1880), 388–90; and Woodward, *Origins*, 180, 181. For a thumbnail sketch, see Dun and Bradstreet & Co., *Reference Book: And Key Containing Ratings of Merchants, Manufacturers and Traders Generally* (New York: R. G. Dun, 1912), appendix, Mississippi.

7. Woodward, *Origins*, 184; Kirwan, *Revolt of the Rednecks*, 46. For a lively account, see Thomas Hughes, *G.T.T. Gone to Texas: Letters from Our Boys* (London: McMillan Press, 1884).

8. Halsell, "Bourbon Period," 533.

9. *Eleventh Census*, 65. This same census notes an increase in the number of renters for farms, from 17,440 in 1880 to 30,366 in 1890. Mississippi was in trouble. The 1910 census breaks down the numbers further. Among white farmers in the state, 66,628 were owners and 41,572 were tenants. Among African American farmers in the state, 25,626 were owners and 139,605 were tenants. Department of Commerce and Labor, Bureau of the Census, *Abstract of the Thirteenth Census of the United States, 1910* (Washington, DC: Government Printing Office, 1913), 297 (hereafter cited as *Thirteenth Census*).

10. In 1900 fully 73.9 percent of farm income in the state derived from cotton, more than from any other state. *Eleventh Census*, 119.

11. Roland, *History of Mississippi*, 510. Rowland notes that indigo had a brief reign as cash king in the state, long before the time of this study. What is noteworthy is that farmers were always tied to a market in some ways. These were not subsistence farmers, but rather were looking to make their fortunes.

12. By 1890 only two states grew more cotton than Mississippi (Georgia and Texas). Both of those states, though, had more acreage under cultivation. In 1890 Mississippi produced 1,154,725 bales of cotton from 2,883,278 acres of cotton cultivation; Georgia produced 1,191,846 bales from 3,345,101 acres, and Texas produced 1,471,242 bales from 3,934,525 acres. Mississippi had fertile soils that could produce bumper crops. See *Eleventh Census*, 91, 92; and Rowland, *History of Mississippi*. Rowland notes that by 1895 it cost more to grow cotton than farmers received at harvest. See "A Voice from Mississippi," *Atlanta Constitution*, November 23, 1883; and "Mississippi: The Condition of the Planter and Laborer," *Atlanta Constitution*, December 11, 1887. See Department of the Interior, Census Office, *Census Reports*, Vol. 6, *Twelfth Census of the United States Taken in the Year 1900, Agriculture* (Washington, DC: Census Office, 1902), Table 10.

13. Nationally, farmers received less for the total return on all the cotton planted in 1894 on over 23 million acres than was received in 1873 on over 9 million acres planted—and 1873 was the year of the panic. The actual drop in price was 11.1 to 5.8 cents per pound Woodward, *Origins*, 185. See also Bond, *Political Culture*, 254, 255.

14. Ayres, *Promise of the New South*, 201.

15. "Yazoo Bottom Region," *Weekly Clarion*, September 29, 1881, p. 2. As late as 1879, according to one author, the Delta was only 10 percent developed. Barry, *Rising Tide*, 98. Those elderly persons writing memories for the Bolivar County history made frequent references to the wildness of the Delta, including panthers and bears (which Teddy Roosevelt hunted in the Delta during his presidency). For an account written by an early settler of the region and reprinted some years later, see J. C. Burris, "My Recollections of the Early Days of Bolivar County," in Sillers, *Bolivar County*, 102–10. See note on the use of this book in chapter 2. On p. 103 Burris refers to a complete wilderness in his childhood (before the war), which included bears, wolves, turkeys, beavers, cougars, and spotted panthers.

16. A. H. Whitfield et al., *The Mississippi Code of 1906 of the Public Statute Laws of the State of Mississippi* (Nashville, TN: Brandon Printing, 1906), 501–3; see also Rowland, *History of Mississippi*, 537.

17. Whitfield, *Code of 1906*, 901; Rowland, *History of Mississippi*, 219, 220. The original members of the commission were well known, indicating the importance placed on it by Congress: Benjamin Harrison, James Eads, and Morton Harrod. "The Mississippi Rising," *Atlanta Constitution*, February 27, 1890. See also Willis, *Forgotten Time*, 45–50.

18. "Mississippi Levees," *Clarion-Ledger*, July 18, 1889, p. 2.

19. In this instance, cattle included sheep. See "Sheep Raising and Cotton Planting," *Weekly Clarion*, October 6, 1881, p. 4. For a comparison with the rest of the South, see Steven Hahn, *The Roots of Southern Populism: Yeoman Farmers and the Transformation of the Georgia Upcountry, 1850–1890* (New York: Oxford University Press, 2006), 60. See also Fite, "Southern Agriculture," 8. As for fencing, at first the state thought that railroads should fence off their track, but eventually the concept moved to fencing pasture. "Killing of Stock by Railroad Trains," *Weekly Clarion*, February 4, 1880, p. 1.

20. Mississippi grew corn, wheat, and a little oats and wheat. The state, as did many southern states, pretty much dropped wheat production during this period. *Eleventh Census*, 81. See Fite, "Southern Agriculture," 8. The New Orleans Exposition of 1885 displayed a number of Mississippi products that were not of the usual variety: "timothy grass, Japanese clover, water grass, wild millet, white clover, red clover, burr clover, crab-grass, bear grass, Bermuda grass, chicken corn, red top, peavine, milo, maize, velvet grass, rice straw and sassafras." Rowland, *History of Mississippi*, 529. Yes, crabgrass was grown as a crop! Compare this with the census records for other foodstuffs grown in the state: sugar fell in production during the late nineteenth century; poultry and egg production double in the decade between 1880 and 1890. *Eleventh Census*, 81, 92, 100. For an example, see "Bermuda Grass," *Weekly Clarion*, November 27, 1878, p. 4. No longer was foraging the norm, but rather pasturing, which required suitable crops for cattle grazing. Thus forage became an important part of agricultural production in the 1880s. According to state records, acreage devoted to forage in 1879 was only 9,319, and by 1889 it was 66,159. By 1899 it had increased yet another 50 percent to 99,261.

21. Local boosterism refers to truck farming and its growth in Crystal Springs and Hazlehurst; see "Mississippi Press" under *Coffeeville Times, Clarion-Ledger*, October 3, 1889, p. 1. For analysis of the soil in the area, see James Burgess, *Soil Survey of the Crystal Springs Area, Mississippi* (Washington, DC: Government Printing Office, 1905).

22. The *Eleventh Census* reported a rise in fisheries on the coast, but for oysters in particular. See *Eleventh Census*, 149, 150. For reference to peach farming, see *Princeton Union*, April 30, 1879, p. 3. For canning factory references, see *Dallas Daily Herald*, June 26, 1883, p. 7; *Dallas Daily Herald*, June 14, 1883, p. 6; Cresswell, *Rednecks*, 146.

23. An example of this class division and suspicions, as well as racist attitudes, can be found in the discussion of the membership of the Loyalist Clubs during Reconstruction. Though the clubs were later identified with secrecy among Republicans and African Americans, early on Leake County had a large number of poor white farmers as members, who were attracted by the club's position on agricultural issues. See Michael W. Fitzgerald, *The Union League Movement in the Deep South: Politics and Agricultural Change during Reconstruction* (Baton Rouge: Louisiana State University Press, 1989), 25. Fitzgerald argues that the number of poor white farmers in Mississippi as members in the clubs was fewer than in Alabama because they were more geographically disbursed throughout the state. He never gives numbers to back up this assertion.

24. "Mississippi Press," *Clarion-Ledger*, July 11, 1889, p. 1. The paper quotes the New Albany *Watchman* as suggesting that if a local candidate did not support repeal of the lien law, do not vote for him. The opposition had been growing for some time to the lien law. For instance, see McMillen, *Dark Journey*, 134–40.

25. Ayres, *Origins*, 229.

26. R. H. Henry, *Editors I Have Known since the Civil War* (New Orleans: E. S. Upton Printing, 1922), 243–44. Unfortunately, none of Mollison's papers have survived. At the turn of the century, he migrated to Chicago.

27. A. M. Muckenfuss, "The Development of Manufacturing in Mississippi," *Publications of the Mississippi Historical Society* 10 (1909): 163.

28. From 1880 to 1890, the value of the timber from the state leaped from $1,920,335 to $5,670,774. The timber industry continued to grow. By 1909 Mississippi ranked third in the nation in lumber production. Rowland, *History of Mississippi*, 548; Bond, *Political Culture*, 61–62; Department of the Interior, Census Office, *Census Reports*, Vol. 8, *Twelfth Census of the United States Taken in the Year 1900, Manufacturers* (Washington, DC: Census Office, 1902), 464 and Table 3 (hereafter cited as *Twelfth Census*, Vol. 8).

29. *Eleventh Census*, 149, 150. Not only did total value increase, but so did wages. As early as 1879 the numbers involved were noteworthy. A South Carolina newspaper reported that 1,000 persons in two counties in Mississippi were involved in the turpentine industry. *Anderson Intelligencer*, October 16, 1879, p. 4. The story was also picked up in the Dakota Territories: *Bismarck Tribune*, December 26, 1879, p. 3, and *Wichita City (Kansas) Eagle*, January 1, 1880, p. 4. The value to the state increased in 1900; see *Twelfth Census*, Vol. 8, which gives a number of $1,472,835. See also Rowland, *History of Mississippi*, 545; and Bond, *Political Culture*, 63. Skilled turpentine workers were in demand. For a story on the exodus of African American workers from North Carolina to the Mississippi fields, see *Richmond Dispatch*, November 10, 1889, p. 6.

30. Wesson Industry Vertical File, Mississippi Department of Archives and History; Rowland, *History of Mississippi*, 541; Bond, *Political Culture*, 256. For photograph of the mill, see Online Electronic Resource, Mississippi Department of Archives and History. "Cotton Mills," *Weekly Clarion*, July 23, 1879, p. 2.

31. This factory was owned by Edmund Richardson at the time. Richardson was the largest landowner in the state and the originator of convict leasing. After he died, his son, John Richardson, took over. One newspaper incorrectly claimed that he married Winnie Davis (of Jefferson Davis descent) in 1891, but they never did marry. See *Brenham (Texas) Weekly Banner*, March 26, 1891, p. 2. A laudatory column can be found in *Milan (Tennessee) Exchange*, June 5, 1879, p. 2. See Bettersworth, *Mississippi*, 349; and Cresswell, *Rednecks*, 143.

32. "Advantages of the South Over the North for Cotton Manufacturing," *Weekly Clarion*, November 10, 1881, p. 1; "Cotton Manufacturing in the South," *Weekly Clarion*, November 10, 1881, p. 1; Rowland, *History of Mississippi*, 540. In spite of growth, Mississippi still lagged behind other states in textiles. See Halsell, "Bourbon Period," 535.

33. I. A. Newby, *Plain Folk in the New South: Social Change and Cultural Persistence, 1880–1915* (Baton Rouge: Louisiana State University Press, 1989), 556. Newby bases his information on a letter from R. M. Sasser to Terence V. Powdley, August 12, 1886, in Terence Powderly Papers, microfilm edition, Georgia State University Library.

34. Ibid., 554, 555. Newby notes the union was weak; its members were men, in spite of a large number of women and children working at the plant. The presence of women and children added to the reluctance of the union to call a strike.

35. "Mississippi Press," *Clarion-Ledger*, July 11, 1889, p. 1, quotes the *East Mississippi Times* in suggesting that farmers need working capital and will elect those who work for it. The editorial does not suggest how that would happen.

36. Woodward, *Origins*, 312.

37. Patrons of Husbandry, Mississippi State Grange Papers, Box 1, Mississippi Department of Archives and History. See also Frank Burkitt, Vertical File, Mississippi Department of Archives and History.

38. W. Scott Morgan, *History of the Wheel and Alliance and Impending Revolution* (St. Louis: C. B. Woodward, 1891), particularly 55, 96, 130, 155, 302.

39. Bettersworth, *Mississippi*, 346. Farm mortgages in the state doubled in that decade. Fite refers to five-cent cotton ("Southern Agriculture," 12).

40. Ayres, *Origins*, 219.

41. Ibid., 218, 219. The issue of silver was hotly debated in the state during this period, though the lack of understanding of basic economics was a fundamental problem. See "The Silver Dollar Question," *Weekly Clarion*, September 22, 1881, p. 2.

42. Ayres, *Origins*, 220. See also "Mississippi Press," *Clarion-Ledger*, May 30, 1889, p. 1, which quotes the *Tupelo Lodger* on the connections between the Grange and the Alliance.

43. Ayres, *Origins*, 221; "Emigration and the Lien Law," *Weekly Clarion*, January 18, 1881, p. 1; letter to editor, *Weekly Clarion*, February 1, 1882, p. 2, in which the writer points out that the collateral in a lien law is fictitious.

44. Ayres, *Origins*, 234.

45. See chapter 5.

46. "Legislative Supervision over Railroad Corporations," *Weekly Clarion*, September 17, 1879, p. 2.

47. The Greenback Party began in 1874; the party platform had a number of planks, but its primary goal was to keep paper money, issued during the Civil War, in circulation.

48. Cresswell, *Rednecks, Redeemers, and Race*, 125; Doyle, *Faulkner's County*, 316.

49. Some have even argued that John R. Lynch was the mastermind behind the run. Cresswell, *Multiparty Politics*, 60; Bond, *Political Culture*, 273–74.

50. "Facts from the Record: Greenbackers and Democrats," *Weekly Clarion*, September 22, 1881, p. 2. The editors argue that if Greenbackers were serious about reform, they would not align themselves with the Republican Party, which they called corrupt. Cresswell, *Multiparty Politics*, 59.

51. "The Recent Elections: A Lesson to Greenbackers," *Weekly Clarion*, October 22, 1879, p. 2; "The Situation on the Eve of the Election," and "Have We Forgotten?" *Weekly Clarion*, October 29, 1879, p. 2; "The False Cry of Bulldozing and Ballot Cheating," *Weekly Clarion*, October 27, 1881, p. 2. Cresswell, *Multiparty Politics*, 65 (Creswell quotes Kousser, *Shaping of Southern Politics*, 28); Johnson, "Suffrage and Reconstruction," 204.

52. "Bloody Affair at Marion," *Weekly Clarion*, October 27, 1881, p. 2; Cresswell, *Multiparty Politics*, 70. Doyle points out that some of the violence was directed at merchants (*Faulkner's County*, 317). One of the more intriguing examples was in Yazoo County, where there was a shoot-out between Henry Dixon, a supporter of the Greenbackers who was running for sheriff, and Jared Barksdale, the brother of Ethelbert Barksdale. The paper openly insinuates that Dixon was agitating the African American population to get out to vote, and therefore he was a threat. See the following issues of the *Weekly Clarion* for a number of articles: August 27, 1879; September 3, 1879; September 10, 1879.

53. Johnson, "Suffrage and Reconstruction," 218; "Greenback Party" and "Startling Exposure," *Weekly Clarion*, August 4, 1880, p. 1.

54. "The Morning's News," *Sacramento Daily Record-Union*, July 15, 1884, p. 4; Cresswell, *Multiparty Politics*, 75. Why the Democrats did not nominate anyone is open to conjecture.

55. Chalmers's yearly political swings were known and acknowledged. "General Chalmers in Tate County," *Weekly Clarion*, September 29, 1881, p. 1. Lynch saw this maneuver as unprincipled and disloyal. Halsell sees Chalmers's shifts as an indication that the control by the Bourbons was slipping. Such an interpretation would assume, however, that the Bourbons always had firm control, which was not the case. See Halsell, "Bourbon Period," 533; Kirwan, *Revolt of the Rednecks*, 9; *Weekly Clarion*, July 5, 1882, p. 1, which argued, "we are asking to preserve the civilization of our State; he who is not with us is against us."

56. Untitled column, *Daily Astorian* (Oregon), November 21, 1882, p. 2; Cresswell, *Mormons*, 37; Cresswell, *Multiparty Politics*, 77; Kirwan, *Revolt of the Rednecks*, 10.

57. Kirwan, *Revolt of the Rednecks*, 11, 12.

58. Willie D. Halsell, "Republican Factionalism in Mississippi, 1882–1884," *Journal of Southern History* 7 (1941): 85; Kirwan, *Revolt of the Rednecks*, 13, 14.

59. For more on this inner-party struggle, see Willie D. Halsell, "Chalmers and Mahoneism in Mississippi," *Journal of Southern History* 10 (February 1944): 37–58. Chalmers did contest the election of 1886. See "At Harrison's Home," *Omaha (Nebraska) Daily Bee*,

November 30, 1888, p. 1; "Observed as a Holiday," *St. Paul (Minnesota) Daily Globe*, November 30, 1888, p. 1. For reference to the national issues over Chalmers and his political shifts, see "Speakership," *Louisiana Capitolian* (Baton Rouge), December 6, 1881, p. 2.

60. See letter to the paper by John Lynch, "Mississippi Politics," *National Republican* (Washington, DC), September 3, 1883, p. 3. There was no love lost between Lynch and Chalmers, even after Chalmers switched parties. Cresswell, *Multiparty Politics*, 86–92. For more on the issue of fusion (which refers to a star chamber meeting), see "Appeal Specials," *Memphis Daily Appeal*, October 7, 1884, p. 1. There is a reference here to the nomination of Isaiah Montgomery as an elector.

61. Blanche K. Bruce Vertical File, Mississippi Department of Archives and History.

62. For a definition of better class for African Americans during this time period, see Greenwood, *Bittersweet Legacy*, "Introduction." Greenwood's definitions apparently influenced Schweninger. See Schweninger, *Black Property Owners in the South*, 128–29.

63. Revels did not take the seat without controversy; the Senate debated for three days. See George Alexander Sewell and Margaret L. Dwight, *Black History Makers* (Jackson: University Press of Mississippi, 1984), 7–48; Wharton, *The Negro in Mississippi*, 7–11; "Congress," *New York Times*, February 26, 1870, p. 1. Locals painted Revels in a scurrilous light, and it is difficult to tell now what is true, whether he really had fights and was guilty of embezzlement in his church in St. Louis. The charges were so mixed with racial slurs that it is hard for a historian to piece together truth or fiction. See McNeily, "War and Reconstruction," 387.

64. Sewell and Dwight, *Black History Makers*, 11–14, Skates, *Mississippi*, 115. The name was changed to Alcorn Agricultural and Mechanical College in 1878.

65. Lawrence Otis Graham, *The Senator and the Socialite: The True Story of America's First Black Dynasty* (New York: Harper Collins, 2006).

66. This lust for learning was not unusual among a people long denied. For more information on education, see Christopher M. Span, *From Cotton Field to Schoolhouse: African American Education in Mississippi, 1862–1875* (Chapel Hill: University of North Carolina Press, 2009), 3–4, 23–48.

67. Graham, *The Senator and the Socialite*, 1–86. See also Wharton, *The Negro in Mississippi*, 161.

68. Sillers, "Reconstruction," 157; Sillers, *Bolivar County*, 165; "New Colored Senator," *New York Times*, February 8, 1874, p. 5.

69. Sillers, "Reconstruction," 157.

70. "Washington," *New York Times*, March 6, 1875, p. 1.

71. Sewell and Dwight, *Black History Makers*, 16–22. See also "The Mob in Mississippi Politics," *Daily Constitution* (Atlanta), August 14, 1879.

72. Sewell and Dwight, *Black History Makers*, 22.

73. Ibid., 23.

74. He served as registrar of the treasury and recorder of deeds for the District of Columbia. Ibid., 24, 25.

75. Revels trained as a barber but served as a minister. Lynch trained as a photographer and spent years working in the government as a civilian and in the regular army. Following Reconstruction, Hill was appointed Internal Revenue collector in Vicksburg and continued to lead Mississippi Republican politics. All of these men made their names in relative urban

settings: Bruce in DC, Revels in Natchez and as college president in Holly Springs, Hill in Vicksburg and Jackson, and Lynch in Natchez and Chicago. While Holly Springs is not Chicago, it is also not rural, certainly not in the nineteenth century. See Sewell and Dwight, *Black History Makers*, 7–48; Wharton, *The Negro in Mississippi*, 160–72.

76. Cresswell, *Mormons & Cowboys*, 31.

77. Sewell and Dwight, *Black History Makers*, 32.

78. Ibid., 33

79. Chalmers was part of the restoration of the Democrats in the state. See "Mississippi," *Memphis Daily Appeal*, September 5, 1875, p. 1; "About Congressmen," National Republican, December 16, 1880, p. 2; Editorials, *Saline County Journal* (Kansas), December 2, 1880, p. 2. See also Bond, *Political Culture*, 274–75. For more on Chalmers's earlier political history in which he appeared solidly Democratic, see "Letter of Hon. J. R. Chalmers on Political Issues," *Weekly Clarion*, July 16, 1879, p. 1; "General Chalmers on the Kemper Trial," *Weekly Clarion*, October 8, 1879, p. 1; and "Speech of Hon. J. R. Chalmers," *Weekly Clarion*, October 29, 1879, p. 1. For fusion issues, see *Clarion*, July 11, 1883, p. 1, which includes a letter to the editor from Frank Johnson.

80. John Hope Franklin, "Introduction," in Lynch, *Reminiscences*, xx; Kirwan, *Revolt of the Rednecks*, 9, 10. See "The Mississippi Plan: The Contest of Lynch vs Chalmers in the House of Representatives," *Atlanta Constitution*, April 27, 1882; *Belmont (Ohio) Chronicle* April 20, 1882, pp. 1, 2; "Government News," *New York Tribune*, March 23, 1881, p. 1; "The Contested Cases," *Salt Lake Herald*, June 4, 1882, p. 1. Especially note the *Weekly Clarion*'s comment that James Hill was the "best" of the African American leaders of the age (March 5, 1879, p. 2).

81. McMillen. *Dark Journey*, 60, 61. Hill saw the realities in a way that Bruce and Lynch did not. He was quoted as stating the Democrats controlled election machinery and therefore could "count them out," in spite of having a "40,000 Republican majority in Mississippi." "James Hill," *Weekly Clarion*, June 12, 1880, p. 1. The *Weekly Clarion* identified Lynch as an "agitator." See issue of February 26, 1879, p. 1.

82. Johnston, "Conference," 67.

83. Foner, *Short History of Reconstruction*, 235; Johnston, "Conference," 67; Ames, *Adelbert Ames*, 435; Harris, *Day of the Carpetbagger*, 688–89.

84. Ali, *In the Lion's Mouth*, 68; Cresswell, *Mormons*, 29; Nicholas Lemann, *Redemption: The Last Battle of the Civil War* (New York: Farrar, Strauss and Giroux, 2006), 111–15. The numbers in this massacre, which went on for a couple of days following the barbeque, are unknown. Lemann includes a number of personal and horrifying accounts.

85. Lemann, *Redemption*, 115; Hahn, *Nation under Our Feet*, 299. For a different account, giving only the white Clinton side, see *Memphis Daily Appeal*, September 7, 1875; *Jasper (Indiana) Weekly Courier* September 24, 1875, p. 2. The numbers of injured or dead vary dramatically, and only victims' names from the white side are given and none for the African Americans. Equally frustrating is the account given in the *National Republican* (Washington, DC), September 7, 1875. Both accounts, though, blame the use of intoxicating beverages. See also "The Clinton Riot," *State Journal* (Jefferson City, Missouri), September 17, 1875; "White Leaguers' War," *National Republican* (Washington, DC), September 7, 1875.

86. "Mississippi," *Memphis Daily Appeal*, June 13, 1876, p. 1; Ames, *Adelbert Ames*, 483.

87. Johnston, "Conference," 67.

88. Needless to say, this procedure was not typical of slave auctions. No information exists as to the life of Ben and Mary before their sale to Joe, but the note indicates not only literacy, but a sense of self-worth and innate dignity.

89. See Gladys B. Shepperd, "The Montgomery Saga, From Slavery to Black Power," p. 9 (manuscript labeled Baltimore 1971, found in Benjamin Montgomery Papers, Library of Congress, hereinafter cited as BMP); and Janet Sharp Hermann, *Pursuit of a Dream* (New York: Oxford University Press, 1981), 3–34. Hermann identifies Ben Montgomery and indeed Joe Davis as exceptional people; she does not have the same view of Isaiah Montgomery. Although there have been some historians who have called into question the treatment of slaves on the Davis plantation because of a lack of data, Hermann, who did extensive research on the subject, has concluded the validity of this claim.

90. Isaiah T. Montgomery, Autobiographical Notes, folder at Mississippi Department of Archives and History (hereinafter cited as Isaiah's story).

91. Ibid. See also Hermann, *Pursuit of a Dream*, 3–34.

92. It is debatable whether Isaiah Montgomery continued to work as the traditionally defined house-servant.

93. BMP, 19.

94. Joe Davis bought property near Bolton (between Vicksburg and Jackson), but even this area proved to be too close to Union troop movements. Eventually he rented property in Alabama during the war, first in Choctaw County and then near Tuscaloosa. He took most of his slaves with him.

95. Hermann, *Pursuit of a Dream*, 19–20.

96. For a detailed analysis of this written code of the nineteenth century, see John. F. Kasson, *Rudeness & Civility: Manners in Nineteenth-Century Urban America* (New York: Hill and Wang, 1990), 34–69, particularly p. 54 regarding African Americans of the period.

97. Oberlin was often the college of choice for upper- and middle-class African Americans in this period. See Graham, *Our Kind of People*, 15.

98. BMP, 17.

99. The confusion after the war for many freedmen was similar. See Ira Berlin et al., *Slaves No More: Three Essays on Emancipation and the Civil War* (Cambridge: Cambridge University Press, 1992), 77–186; and BMP, 20. Stamp did not have the full story about Davis Bend, although he tried to use it as an example of the "might have beens" of the war effort. Stamp, *Reconstruction*, 125–26.

100. Jane Sharp Hermann, after extensive research, came to conclusion that the price of $75 an acre was a fair price at the time of the contract, although prices fell precipitously following those years. According to Hermann (*Pursuit of a Dream*, 43), Ben Montgomery had buried his money before fleeing to Cincinnati. When he needed to purchase the land he unearthed $30,000, $10,000 of which he used for working capital and $20,000 for a down payment. Schweninger, *Black Property Owners*, 196.

101. In 1870 the family received an award for the best bale of cotton at the St. Louis fair, and in 1876 the Montgomery & Sons concern received a medal at the International Exhibition in Philadelphia for the best raw cotton. See WPA Slave Narratives, account of Isaiah Montgomery collected after his death (BMP).

102. Mary died in 1885. Both Ben and Mary were buried in the old plantation cemetery close to the graves of Joe Davis and his wife. Hermann, *Pursuit of a Dream*, 45–55.

103. Ibid., 143, 157.

104. This number is noted in Wharton, *The Negro in Mississippi*, 42; and in Sewell and Dwight, *Mississippi Black History Makers*, 160. See also Schweninger, *Black Property Owners*, 195.

105. Hermann, *Pursuit of a Dream*, 83–91. In *Bittersweet Legacy*, Greenwood gives the worth of John Schenck, a carpenter, the richest African American man in Charlotte in 1870, as $2,500 (Table A-5, p. 248), a far cry from the wealth of the Montgomerys.

106. For more discussion, see Greenberg, *Honor & Slavery*, xi–xiv.

107. In 1867 Joe was ill and short of food. Ben worried about him and sent produce from the plantation. Joe had a granddaughter who stayed on the plantation and refused to move; both families accepted the situation. See Shepperd manuscript, p. 38, in BMP; and Hermann, *Pursuit of a Dream*, 146.

108. The Montgomery family enjoyed the help of some of the best attorneys in the state: Wiley P. Harris, J. Z. George, and Thomas Marshall. Harris and George, as well as Isaiah Montgomery, were heavily involved in the constitutional convention of 1890. Frank E. Everett, *Brierfield: Plantation Home of Jefferson Davis* (Hattiesburg: University and College Press of Mississippi, 1971), 102–3.

109. Isaiah's own story does not place blame on Jefferson Davis and his family, but some historians do. Eric Foner and Joshua Brown, *Forever Free: The Story of Emancipation and Reconstruction* (New York: Alfred A. Knopf, 2005), 80. See also Hermann, *Pursuit of a Dream*, 202; and Maurice Elizabeth Jackson, "Mound Bayou: A Study in Social Development" (Master's thesis, University of Alabama, 1937). Sewell and Dwight refer to Jefferson Davis as "depressed but determined to repossess Davis Bend." George Alexander Sewell, *Mississippi Black History Makers* (Jackson: University Press of Mississippi, 1977), 159.

110. Hermann, *Pursuit of a Dream*, 209.

111. Ibid., 204, 219–25. See also Willis, *Forgotten Time*, 71–75.

112. Isaiah reported in 1890 that he started the settlement with 600 residents. By that time he had a "business of $30,000 per annum, exclusive of cotton shipments which amount to 250 bales. [His] real estate interests [were] worth about $20,000." See Isaiah's story.

113. Sewell and Dwight, *Mississippi Black History Makers*, 161.

114. Compare Mound Bayou to Cameron, Alabama, which was also an African American community with a similar structure. Sydney Nathans, "Fortress without Walls: A Black Community After Slavery," in Hall and Stack, *Holding Onto the Land*, 55–68.

115. Mississippi, Vol. 21, p. 81E, Dun &Co. Collection, Baker Library Historical Collections, Harvard Business School. These records normally include blunt assessments, such as under another person: "regarded unreliable, tricky and not very honest" (Mississippi, Vol. 2, p. 10, or in the same volume, "Debts very large. Conditions doubtful," 107). I was not able to find the African American political leaders of the time in these volumes: Hiram Revels, John Lynch, James Hill, or Hiram Revels. Schweninger does note the wealth of John Roy Lynch, Dr. E. P. Brown of Natchez, and George Bowles of Natchez. Schweninger, *Black Property Owners*, 299.

116. Mississippi, Vol. 21, p. 170, Dun & Co.

117. The concept of public virtue, more typically understood in the eighteenth century, is explained in Gordon S. Wood, *The Radicalism of the American Revolution* (New York: Vintage Books, 1991), 104–7.

118. Sewell, *Mississippi Black History Makers*, 158.

119. "The Montgomery Saga: From Slavery to Black Power," manuscript in BMP. The Davis brothers, who heavily influenced Isaiah, certainly viewed involvement in the public sphere as a responsibility.

120. Jackson, "Mound Bayou," 44, 55.

121. Sewell and Dwight, *Mississippi Black History Makers*, 160.

122. See Isaiah's story.

Chapter 4. Calling the Convention

1. For example, see letters to the editor regarding the calling of a constitutional convention, *Clarion-Ledger*, August 1, 1889, p. 1, which claim the Reconstruction constitution was "foisted" upon them. For examples of other pushes, see "Constitutional Convention," *Weekly Clarion*, February 1, 1882, p. 2. The state legislature considered this issue in 1880. See "State Senate," *Weekly Clarion*, January 14, 1880, p. 2; "Constitutional Convention," and on the same page, "The Report Against Calling It," *Weekly Clarion*, February 11, 1880, p. 2; see also *Daily Clarion*, February 3, 1884, editorial page, in which the editors suggest Mississippi was the only former Confederate state still operating under a Reconstruction constitution and therefore should consider a constitutional convention.

2. Federal elections in this period were for congressmen. Election of senators came later with the passage of the Seventeenth Amendment in 1913, but at this point they were appointed by state legislatures. Voting for the president meant voting for electors, which is the same as today. Therefore, the important area affected by a federal law over elections was the election of congressmen.

3. Calhoun, *Conceiving a New Republic*; Dooley, "Disfranchisement," 138.

4. Perman, *Struggle for Mastery*, 38. See also Buck, *Road to Reunion*, 277.

5. Calhoun, *New Republic*, 229. Harrison also spoke on the same issue in Detroit on Washington's Birthday, before the inauguration. Buck, *Road to Reunion*, 276.

6. Calhoun, *New Republic*, 233.

7. Ibid., 234. According to Calhoun, the number in 1888 was 18, mostly from the South. This compares with 200 since the war.

8. Ibid., 233. The problems were widespread. See Kousser, *Southern Politics*, 25, 26.

9. Dewey W. Grantham, *The South in Modern America: A Region at Odds* (New York: Harper Collins, 1994), 9; the South also connected education to empowerment of African Americans: Dooley, "Disfranchisement," 100–104. See also the *Daily Democrat* (Natchez), September 15, 1888, which printed a speech given by Judge A. A. Gunby at Louisiana State University concerning the problems of education, and the resulting chaos on an uneducated citizenry. He did not differentiate between races or gender. African Americans, including the Afro-American League, supported Blair's measure, although they had reservations on the acquiescence to segregated schools. Calhoun, *New Republic*, 231. The Afro-American League

was founded in 1887 to provide support and help to the African American community and to fight lynching. It changed its name two years later to the National Afro-American League. The Jackson paper finally noted this issue as one of segregated schools and suggested that African Americans did not approve of integration. See "Don't Like It," *Clarion-Ledger*, December 13, 1888.

10. Calhoun, *New Republic*, 230. For more on this issue, see Upchurch, *Legislating Racism*, 46–65.

11. Upchurch, *Legislating Racism*, 115–118; *Congressional Record*, 21:2153–54.

12. Still one of the best examinations of social Darwinism during this period is Richard Hofstadter, *Social Darwinism in American Thought* (repr., New York: Beacon Press, 1992).

13. The best recent examination of this issue is in Richardson, *Death of Reconstruction*, 203–9; see also Dooley, "Disfranchisement," 17, 18, 95.

14. "Harrison's Wedge," *Clarion-Ledger*, April 25, 1889, p. 2.

15. "Mississippi Press," *Clarion-Ledger*, June 13, 1889, p. 4, quoting the *Winona Times*. This allegation became a familiar refrain when papers pointed out the hypocrisy of northerners about this issue. See "Mississippi Press," *Clarion-Ledger*, April 11, 1889, p. 4, quoting the *Grenada Sentinel*.

16. Cresswell, *Mormons*, 43. See also "Senator George of Mississippi," *Atlanta Constitution*, October 10, 1888.

17. Calhoun, *New Republic*, 234. For a contrarian view of the proposal, see McNeily, "War and Reconstruction," 533, 534.

18. Calhoun, *New Republic*, 237. The state took note. See "Nothing to Fear," *Clarion-Ledger*, March 21, 1889, p. 1; and "The Negro Alarmed," *Clarion-Ledger*, April 4, 1889, p. 1.

19. Several bills were introduced, but there was division among the Republicans. John Roy Lynch identified them with four sections, but in reality he divides them into those with principles and those without. See Lynch, *Reminiscences*, 333–35.

20. Not until the passage of the Seventeenth Amendment in 1913 were senators elected by the people. See Article I, Sections 4 and 5, regarding congressional oversight of elections.

21. Senator John C. Spooner, newly elected from Wisconsin, proposed the bill, which was sent to Senator Hoar's committee. The proposal was worked into the bill with the help of John Davenport, who had served as head of the elections board in New York City. One might wonder about the use of New York as an example of rectitude in the Gilded Age. See Calhoun, *New Republic*, 236–39. The number of requests required for intervention range from 100 to 500. Buck, *Road to Reunion*, 279, 280; Perman, *Struggle for Mastery*, 39; Upchurch, *Legislating Racism*, 85–97.

22. Perman argues that the bill had three areas of innovation: "expansion of the role of the supervisors, the centrality of the federal courts rather than state election officials in the voting proceedings, and the creation of a three-man board of canvassers" (*Struggle for Mastery*, 38, 39). See *Clarion-Ledger*, June 19, 1890, p. 1.

23. William H. Rehnquist, *Centennial Crisis: The Disputed Election of 1876* (New York: Alfred A. Knopf, 2004), 94–98. Compare to David Dudley Field, *The Electoral Votes of 1876: Who Should Count Them, What Should Be Counted, and the Remedy for a Wrong Court* (New York: D. Appleton, 1877), 19.

24. For an explanation of the issue, see Field, *Electoral Votes*, 20–22.

25. Quoted in Calhoun, *New Republic*, 240. The *Clarion-Ledger* simply labeled Ingalls as hating the South. See June 5, 1890, p. 1. See also *Washington Bee*, February 21, 1891.

26. Calhoun, *New Republic*, 241. The *Federalist Paper* is that of Alexander Hamilton, number 59.

27. For a better, but similar, chart, see "Petition of Ezra Nat. Hill for the Passage of a National Election Law" Mis. Doc., No. 244, in the Senate of the United States, 51st Congress, 1st Session. Dooley, certainly bigoted on race matters, admitted that some of the proponents of the bill were "actually sincere in their conviction that the negro vote should not be suppressed because it was legally and morally wrong." Dooley, "Disfranchisement," 112.

28. Calhoun, *New Republic*, 236.

29. Ibid., 242.

30. Ibid., 243.

31. "Elections in the South." *Washington Post*, February 20, 1890.

32. *Journal of the House of Representatives of the United States*, 51st Congress, 1st session (Washington, DC: Government Printing Office, 1890), 807–21. This committee became a standing one in 1893 and lasted until 1947.

33. The concern over a perception of a return to the old times of Reconstruction was sensed in both parties. The Republicans were not united on the bill. Buck, *Road to Reunion*, 279. See also McNeily, "War and Reconstruction," 535, 536.

34. Calhoun, *New Republic*, 246.

35. "Senators Will Fight," *Clarion-Ledger*, May 8, 1890, p. 1.

36. McNeily, "War and Reconstruction," 534.

37. Johnson, "Suffrage and Reconstruction," 204.

38. "Negro Resolutions," *Clarion-Ledger*, July 4, 1889, p. 2.

39. Ibid.

40. "Negro Education: An Expensive Luxury to the State of the Mississippi," *Clarion-Ledger*, July 4, 1889, p. 3.

41. "Republican Convention," *Clarion-Ledger*, September 26, 1889, p. 1. Rumors had been persistent that the Republicans intended to nominate a complete ticket. See "Mississippi Press," *Clarion-Ledger*, March 21, 1889, p. 1, quoting the *Pascagoula Democrat-Star*; and the same column on March 28, 1889, p. 1, quoting the *Water Valley Progress*.

42. Creswell notes that moderate Democrats had warned Republicans not to hold public meetings lest they provoke violence. Creswell, *Mormons*, 40, 41.

43. "General Chalmers," *New York Times*, September 26, 1889. A brief note of the convention gives the numbers as 254 delegates, of which 60 were white—which would be about one in four rather than one in six.

44. "Republicans," *Daily Democrat* (Natchez), August 15, 1889, p. 1; Creswell, *Mormons*, 40.

45. Both Chalmers and Mollison were not supporters of Lynch, which is a clear indication of the problems brewing in the state Republican Party.

46. Sewell and Dwight, *Mississippi Black History Makers*, 75.

47. Wharton, *The Negro in Mississippi*, 209. The story is entirely missing from John Roy Lynch's autobiography. See also *Los Angeles Daily Herald*, October 20, 1889, p. 1. This paper acknowledged how bad things were for the party.

Notes   233

48. "The Chalmers Contest," *Clarion-Ledger*, September 19, 1889, p. 1. On September 26 the newspaper identified him as "Gen. James B. Chalmers of Memphis."

49. "Chalmers Resigns," *Clarion-Ledger*, October 10, 1889, p. 4.

50. *Los Angeles Daily Herald*, October 20, 1889, p. 4. This paper claimed that the reason the slate was withdrawn was because of threats of violence, though no details were given other than to say, "We can do no more."

51. "More Race Troubles," *Clarion-Ledger*, September 19, 1889, p. 4. For more on the movement, see Omar H. Ali, "Reconceptualizing Black Populism in the New South," and Lewie Reece, "Creating a New South," both in *Populism in the South Revisited: New Interpretations and New Departures*, ed. James M. Beeby (Jackson: University Press of Mississippi, 2012), 128–76.

52. Ali, *In the Lion's Mouth*, 47, 48. See also p. 52 for reference to farming methods.

53. Ibid., 52. Historians differ as the total membership of the organization, ranging from 250,000 at the low, to over one million.

54. Ibid., 50.

55. Ibid., 62; William F. Holmes, *White Chief: James Kimble Vardaman* (Baton Rouge: Louisiana State University Press, 1970), 35.

56. More of the story can be read in Willis, *Forgotten Time*, 132–36. No one knows whether the Oliver Cromwell of Leflore County and the Oliver Cromwell of the Clinton Riot of 1874 were the same, related, or unconnected.

57. Ali, *In the Lion's Mouth*, 67, quoting the *New Mississippian*, September 4, 1889.

58. Hahn, *Nation under Our Feet*, 422.

59. Ayers, *Promise of the New South*, 236. Certainly whites blamed Cromwell. "No Bloodshed," *Daily Commercial Herald* (Vicksburg), September 5, 1889, p. 1. See also Ali, *In the Lion's Mouth*, 67, 68; and Hahn, *Nation under Our Feet*, 423. See letter from the Leflore County sheriff to Governor Lowry, December 25, 1890, Governors Papers, Robert Lowry, Correspondence Box. The sheriff, L. T. Baskett, referred to "two thousand alliance men who were spoiling for a fight." He also claimed the men had barricaded themselves, were armed, and were threatening to kill white men and then despoil white women.

60. Outsiders had poured into the area to "help" local posses. Hahn, *Nation under Our Feet*, 223; Holmes, "Leflore County Massacre," 271; "Race Troubles in Leflore County," *Grenada Sentinel*, September 7, 1889, p. 2; "No Bloodshed," *Daily Commercial Herald* (Vicksburg), September 5, 1889, p. 1.

61. With one exception, in a brief cryptic quotation from the *Boston Herald*, so see "A Severe Lesson," *Daily Commercial Herald* (Vicksburg), September 10, p. 2; and "Won't Play Charles I," *Clarion-Ledger*, September 19, 1889, p. 6. For an in-depth commentary on the tradition of silence, see Richard Rubin, *Confederacy of Silence: A True Tale of the New Old South* (New York: Atria Books, 2002). Silence and secrets are themes woven throughout the book.

62. Leflore, in the Delta, had only in July nominated James K. Vardaman for the legislature. Though he did not start out as the virulent racist he became, he was known for his conservative views even then. See *Clarion-Ledger*, July 11, 1889, p. 4.

63. Holmes, "Leflore County Massacre," 270–72. For more, see "Twenty-Seven Lives: The Total Killing in the Mississippi Rioting," *Washington Bee*, September 21, 1889, p. 2.

64. Holmes, "Leflore County Massacre," 273; "Race Troubles in the South," *Evening Star* (Washington, DC), September 2, 1889, p. 1.

65. Ali, *In the Lion's Mouth*, 68. Holmes reported that Cromwell had probably escaped, which is also noted in the *Evening Star* (see previous note). See also Holmes, "Leflore County Massacre," 272–79; Hahn, *Nation under Our Feet*, 423.

66. Holmes, "Leflore County Massacre," 267–74.

67. Johnson, "Suffrage and Reconstruction," 211. See also Coleman, "Origin," 81, who quotes Johnson. More than fifty years ago Governor Coleman wrote this article to encourage his constituents to approve a call to write a new constitution.

68. For example, see *Brandon Republican*, undated, clipping found in J. Z. George Papers, Scrapbook, pages unnumbered, Box 3, Mississippi Department of Archives and History (hereinafter cited as George Papers).

69. Coleman, "Origin," 72; see also Lynch, *Reminiscences*, 340. Lynch identifies the Lamar-Walthall group as the "liberal" wing and the George group as the radical wing.

70. See Smith, *J. Z. George*, 147. For more, see "Constitutional Convention," *Daily Clarion*, February 25, 1886, and February 26, March 2, and March 3, 1886.

71. Johnson, "Suffrage and Reconstruction," 211. See also "The Mississippi Plan," *Atlanta Constitution*, March 5, 1890.

72. Coleman, "Origin," 73

73. Ibid., 74, 75. This was not the first suggestion of a prohibitive cost. See "The Cost of a Constitutional Convention," *Daily Clarion*, January 19, 1886.

74. Coleman, "Origin," 78.

75. Ibid., 79; Smith, *J. Z. George*, 147.

76. McNeily, "War and Reconstruction," 523, 533.

77. Johnson, "Suffrage and Reconstruction," 206.

78. Coleman, "Origin," 81.

79. The *Yazoo Herald* spoke specifically on this point. See reference in "Mississippi Press," *Clarion-Ledger*, March 21, 1889, p. 1; and reference to the *Neshoba Democrat* in same column, April 4, 1889, p. 1.

80. Editorial snippet, *Clarion-Ledger*, June 6, 1889, p. 4.

81. "The Mississippi Press," *Clarion-Ledger*, June 6, 1889, p. 4. There were still papers that thought they only needed amendments. See "Mississippi Press," *Clarion-Ledger*, July 4, 1889, p. 1, quoting the *Magnolia Gazette*; and same column, May 23, 1889, p. 1, quoting the *Brandon Republican*; as well as May 16, 1889, p. 1, quoting the *Carroll County Democrat*, the *Aberdeen Examiner*, and the *Kosciusko Star*, which thought a convention would only benefit the lawyers.

82. Coleman, "Origin," 85.

83. Johnson, "Suffrage and Reconstruction," 208. See "Senator George," *Clarion-Ledger*, October 24, 1889, p. 1.

84. Coleman, "Origin," 85, 86. See also Johnson, "Suffrage and Reconstruction," 209.

85. *Clarion-Ledger*, October 24, 1889; Coleman "Origin," 86. See also Smith, *J. Z. George*, 147; and J. S. McNeily, "History of the Measures Submitted to the Committee on Elective Franchise, Apportionment and Elections in the Constitutional Convention of 1890," *Publications of the Mississippi Historical Society* 6 (1902): 129, 130.

86. "Republican Executive Committee," *Clarion-Ledger*, October 24, 1889, p. 8.

87. "Unkindest Cut of All," *Clarion-Ledger*, October 31, 1889, p. 1.

88. Guy B. Hathorn, "Suffrage, Apportionment, and Elections in the Mississippi Constitutional Convention of 1890" (Master's thesis, University of Mississippi, 1942). Johnson points out that the power in the legislature lay to the west of the Illinois Central Railroad (the Delta). Johnson, "Suffrage," 221. In contrast, Morgan Kousser argues that the turnout for voting for the delegates was so small (at 15 percent of eligible voters) that the conclusion is that only the elites supported a convention. There can be a number of reasons for a small turnout, including the agricultural calendar or the fact that it was a by-election (which are notoriously low in voter participation). See Kousser, *Southern Politics*, 142.

89. Lucy Rice Eckford, "The Personnel and Proceedings of the Mississippi Constitutional Convention of 1890" (Master's thesis, State College, Mississippi [now Mississippi State], 1935), 8.

90. *Clarion-Ledger*, July 31, 1890. The *Daily Commercial Herald* (Vicksburg) August 8, 1890, p. 1, noted the allegations of murder in the northern press, which claimed Cook was killed because he was a Republican. The *Herald* said he was simply killed by a "bad man" and that it had nothing to do with the election; it was merely a coincidence. See also Wharton, *The Negro in Mississippi*, 210, 211; and R. Volney Riser, *Defying Disfranchisement: Black Voting Rights Activism in the Jim Crow South, 1890–1908* (Baton Rouge: Louisiana State University Press, 2010), 39. Riser notes that one other African American cast his candidacy into the pools of Natchez, but withdrew quickly on the grounds that it was "not wise." Riser quotes from the *New Orleans Crusader*.

91. Cresswell, *Multiparty Politics*, 104. Cresswell identifies the turnout as the lowest in the state since the Civil War. Cresswell also covered the murder of Cook; see pp. 102, 103. For comparison, see also "Another White Man Murdered in Mississippi," *Cleveland Gazette*, June 20, 1890, in which the editors voiced frustration that maybe the death of a white man will count more and the nation will finally pay attention.

92. The Australian ballot is explained in chapter 5. For the poll tax, see "Mississippi Press," *Clarion-Ledger*, June 6, 1889, p. 4, quoting the *Water Valley Progressive*; for the Australian ballot or Dortch law (where the government prints the ballot, which requires reading), see "The Australian Ballot," *Clarion-Ledger*, February 21, 1889, p. 3; and "Reform in Balloting," *Clarion-Ledger*, April 25, 1889, p. 3; for the grandfather clause, see letter from R. G. Rives of Macon, *Clarion-Ledger*, March 14, 1889, p. 6.

93. See letter from R. G. Rives of Macon, *Clarion-Ledger*, March 14, 1889, p. 6. Notice of this issue emerged even among noted lawyers and academics in the North, but they admitted no court would touch the problem. See William Gillette, *Right to Vote: Politics and the Passage of the Fifteenth Amendment* (Baltimore: Johns Hopkins University Press, 1965), 98–104; and John H. Mathews, *Legislative and Judicial History of the Fifteenth Amendment* (Baltimore: Johns Hopkins University Press, 1909), 75.

94. For example, see "Negro Problem," *Clarion-Ledger*, February 2, 1889, p. 2. The other alternative was to amend the Constitution to get rid of the Fourteenth and Fifteenth Amendments. "The Race Problem," *Clarion-Ledger*, June 13, 1889.

95. Winkle, *Mississippi State Constitution*, 2–6. Whether or not the 1832 constitution included property qualifications is open to some debate, but certainly that document moved toward the typical "Jacksonian" view of democratization of the polity.

96. *Clarion-Ledger*, April 3, 1890, p. 1.
97. "Dual Voting Plan," *Clarion-Ledger*, April 10, 1890, p. 1.
98. *Clarion-Ledger*, May 1, 1890, p. 1.
99. Ibid.
100. "The Campbell Plan," *Clarion-Ledger*, May 8, 1890, p. 1.
101. "Judge Campbell's Plan," *Clarion-Ledger*, May 15, 1890, p. 4.
102. "The Campbell Plan," *Clarion-Ledger*, May 22, 1890, p. 1.
103. The spelling of Calhoon is sometimes listed in local papers as Calhoun. I have chosen to use the more frequent Calhoon.
104. "A Public Calamity," *Clarion-Ledger*, June 5, 1890, p. 1.
105. "Judge Calhoun's Views," *Clarion-Ledger*, July 24, 1890, p. 4.
106. "Unite for White Rule," *Clarion-Ledger*, June 12, 1890, p. 2.
107. "The Suffrage Question," quoted in the *Clarion-Ledger*, June 19, 1890, p. 1.
108. *Clarion-Ledger*, June 26, 1890, p. 1.
109. "The Suffrage Question," *Clarion-Ledger*, July 3, 1890, p. 4.
110. "The Campbell Plan," *Clarion-Ledger*, July 10, 1890, p. 1.
111. Editorial, *Clarion-Ledger*, July 17, 1890, p. 4.
112. Smith, *J. Z. George*, 147.
113. "Consider Two Points," *Clarion-Ledger*, July 24, 1890, p. 3; see also Smith, *J. Z. George*, 150.
114. "The Great Problem," written to C. E. Wright, esq., editor of the *Daily Commercial Herald* (Vicksburg), from Senator George, June 27, 1890, (n.p.), George Papers.
115. Ibid. There were other ideas, but most did not get far. One was prescient of the grandfather clause eventually used in other states, but not Mississippi. Letter to editor from R. G. Rivas, *Clarion-Ledger*, January 24, 1889, p. 2.
116. "Franchise: Senator George's Speech in Support of the Committee Report," George Papers, Box 3. The newspaper clipping does not give a paper, a location, or a date. It does refer to the convention as meeting at the time, so it would be early fall of 1890.
117. Undated clipping, George Papers, Box 3.

Chapter 5. The Convention Debates the Franchise

1. The *Atlanta Constitution* editors thought it was a question of race. See "The Race Problem in Mississippi," July 21, 1890.
2. Perman is cautious about the use of the terms "black" and "white" counties as a method of analysis. I have chosen to use them, however, because the delegates used the terms themselves and they drew lines of difference between the groups with that nomenclature.
3. Paternalists in Mississippi were not much different from those in South Carolina. See George Tisdall, "The Campaign for the Disfranchisement of Negroes in South Carolina," *Journal of Southern History* 15 (May 1949): 218.
4. Galloway is even today remembered in Jackson. The downtown Methodist church still bears his name.

5. The split was acknowledged even outside of the state; see "Mississippi Constitution," *Fort Worth (Texas) Daily Gazette*, September 18, 1890, p. 2.

6. Johnson, "Suffrage and Reconstruction," 213. Johnson says the two who brought the objection were Col. E. H. Moore and W. L. Pearson.

7. See ibid., 205.

8. Montgomery is discussed at length in the next chapter. For further information on Melchior, see Sillers, *Bolivar County*, 160.

9. "Convention," *Daily Commercial Herald* (Vicksburg), August 14, 1890, p. 1. The majority report suggested seating the delegates from Pearl River, but the minority report, written by Smith of Vicksburg, objected. After discussion, the vote was in favor of the minority report, and the delegate was not seated.

10. *Proceedings*, 67; see also "Complexion of the Convention," *Clarion-Ledger* August 13, p. 4, which was the editorial page. The editors noted that Montgomery was the only "negro" and Republican, but they identified three other Republicans: former governor Alcorn, Melchior, and Judge Simrall. The *Daily Commercial Herald* noted the problem even before the convening of the convention but also suggested that the Republicans had an advantage in that their election had been certified by the secretary of state. *Daily Commercial Herald* (Vicksburg), August 5 and 12, 1890.

11. *Proceedings*, 67. The pages of the *Clarion-Ledger* covering this event, which should have been August 21, are missing from the microfilm at the Library of Congress, as well as other copies requested through interlibrary loan. This issue picks up on p. 9, which the paper calls section 2, unlike any other edition. The seating was controversial, and a few historians have concluded that Montgomery cut a deal with Senator George. There is no evidence that this took place. See *Daily Commercial Herald* (Vicksburg), August 21, 1890, p. 1; and Kirwan, *Revolt of the Rednecks*, 65, note 4. In fact, the *New York World*, later covering Montgomery's controversial speech, referred to this incident and reported that Montgomery took to the floor and eloquently defended his own seating. *New York World*, September 27, 1890, p. 1.

12. *Proceedings*, 75.

13. John Roy Lynch stated that the question was never called. See Lynch, *Reminiscences*, 343. Lynch is one of the people who claimed an undercover agreement between Montgomery and George had ensured the seating of Montgomery and Melchior. The *Natchez Democrat*, August 23, p. 1, refers to a long speech by Montgomery the day of the vote, though it includes no details; the *Daily Commercial Herald* (Vicksburg) referred to the speech on August 21, and then on September 4, 1890, p. 2. The paper called it a beautiful speech and noted that the *Boston Journal* referred to the speech and the seating of Montgomery as an indication of the fairness of the proceedings. An editorial by the Vicksburg paper reiterated that claim the following day.

14. *Proceedings*, 76. Noxubee County had over 75 percent African American population, but it was located on the eastern side of the state. It was the only county in the east that had that large a population of freedmen. For the best, readily available map of population distribution, see Perman, *Disfranchisement*, 71.

15. "The Colored Alliance," *Clarion-Ledger*, September 1, 1890, p. 3.

16. *Proceedings*, 113.

17. Johnson, "Suffrage and Reconstruction," 216. See also letter to C. H. Jones from Senator George, dated September 26, 1890, in George Papers, Scrapbook, pages unnumbered, Box 3. See also "Mississippi's Rights," *Atlanta Constitution*, September 1, 1890. For a copy of the bill of readmission, see *Congressional Globe and Appendix, Second Session, Forty-First Congress*, Part VII, 636.

18. *Clarion-Ledger*, August 28, 1890, p. 1; compare to "Washington," *New York Times*, February 4, 1870, p. 1. See *Congressional Globe* (debates on January 14, 1870), p. 485, for the specifics in the bill: "That the constitution of said State shall never be so amended or changed as to deprive any citizen or class of citizens of the United States of the right to vote or hold office in the said State ... or prevent any person on account of race, color, or previous condition of servitude from serving as a juror, or participating equally in the school fund or school privileges." On p. 483, the senators refer to the idea that a state cannot change this compact alone, but must be agreed on by both parties.

19. Congressional Globe and Appendix, Second Session, Forty-First Congress, Part VII, 636.

20. *Clarion-Ledger*, August 28, 1890, p. 3. For discussion of *United States v. Cruikshank* 92 US 542 (1876), see Kermit L. Hall et al., eds., *The Oxford Companion to the Supreme Court of the United States* (New York: Oxford University Press, 1992), 209.

21. Johnson, "Suffrage and Reconstruction," 218. Harris was the law partner of Senator George. See Kirwan, *Revolt of the Rednecks*, 67; Smith, *J. Z. George*, 93.

22. *Proceedings*, 85, 86

23. This issue was noted as far away as Utah, which was also watching with interest. For a reprise of the Utah editor's conclusion as to why Mississippi should not have to lose its representative, see *Salt Lake Herald*, December 30, 1892, p. 4. According to the *Herald*, Mississippi's restrictions were similar to those of other states. In contrast, see the San Francisco *Morning Call*, December 13, 1890, which thought Mississippi in violation.

24. Clearly this argument was more of a stretch.

25. Peter Onuf, *Statehood and Union* (Bloomington: Indiana University Press, 1987), 117–25.

26. Johnson, "Suffrage and Reconstruction," 216.

27. *Clarion-Ledger*, August 28, 1890, p. 3.

28. Ibid.

29. Sean Wilentz, *The Rise of American Democracy: Jefferson to Lincoln* (abridged college edition) (New York: W. W. Norton, 2009), 195–205.

30. *Proceedings*, 303, 304.

31. Ibid., 340.

32. Note the wording of this section, also on p. 340.

33. Ibid., 341.

34. Winkle, *Mississippi State Constitution*, 2–6.

35. *Clarion-Ledger*, April 3, 1890, p. 1. See also "George and Campbell," *Daily Commercial Herald* (Vicksburg), n.d., George Papers, Box 3.

36. *Clarion-Ledger*, April 10, 1890, p. 1.

37. Coleman, *Origin of the Constitution*, 89. Another delegate was violently killed after being elected to the convention. It is not clear as to the motive.

38. The same is true of the issue of apportionment of the legislature. Both issues, however intimately related to racial issues before the Convention, took on a life of their own and as such will be dealt with in a subsequent chapter.

39. *Proceedings*, 77; *Clarion-Ledger*, August 28, 1890, p. l; *Daily Commercial Herald* (Vicksburg), August 28, p. 1. Balloting in the nineteenth century was often a raucous affair, even when race was not a factor. Not by chance were the political associations called "parties," for often voters partied the night before with their fellow voters and imbibed large quantities of liquor. A number of people feared this would offend the sensibilities of females. See Michael McGerr, *The Decline of Popular Politics: The American North 1865–1928* (New York: Oxford University Press, 1988).

40. *Clarion-Ledger*, August 28, 1890, p. 3.

41. Charles Chauncey Binney, "American Secret Ballot Decisions," *American Law Register and Review* 41 (1893): 101–12, in particular 102–3. See also Numan Bartley and Hugh D. Graham, *Southern Politics and the Second Reconstruction* (Baltimore: Johns Hopkins University Press, 1975), 8.

42. Examples of tissue ballots can be found in the South Carolina State Archives. These were numerous ballot-printed tissues stuck together. When cast as one ticket, they came apart and produced scores of tissue ballots, which would be counted as many votes.

43. George E. Hill, "The Secret Ballot," *Yale Law Journal* 1 (October 1891): 26–29; Jerrold G. Rusk, "The Effect of the Australian Ballot Reform on Split Ticket Voting: 1876–1908," *American Political Science* Review 64 (1970): 1220–38.

44. The addition of the poll tax among the provisions is attributed to Judge Calhoon. See Kirwan, *Revolt of the Rednecks*, 70. The poll tax was an idea with a long history in the state; see "A Poll Tax," *Weekly Clarion*, November 23, 1881, p. 2. The inaugural address given by Governor Robert Lowry called for consideration of a poll tax, printed in supplement, *Clarion*, January 11, 1888.

45. *Proceedings*, 134, 135.

46. Winkle, *Mississippi State Constitution*, 5–9.

47. As to whether the poll tax was actually required became the source of controversy some years later. See chapter 10.

48. *Proceedings*, 230.

49. Ibid., 245.

50. Ibid., 229–31.

51. The *Daily Commercial Herald* (Vicksburg), August 24, 1890, p. 4, notes that Senator George was chair of a subcommittee on franchise. The committee itself was chaired by Patty, who had lost the bid for president of the convention. Though the committee discussions were supposed to be secret, the *Herald* had a source; the paper knew that early on, the Franchise Committee supported woman suffrage. *Daily Commercial Herald* (Vicksburg), August 30, 1890, p. 1.

52. *Proceedings*, 23.

53. Ibid., 234.

54. Ibid., 236.

55. Ibid., 237.

56. Ibid., 229, 230.

57. See *Clarion-Ledger*, October 25, 1890, p. 4, in which J. S. McNeily refused credit but laid it at the feet of Senator George. Johnson does the same; see "Suffrage and Reconstruction," 222. See also Kirwan, *Revolt of the Rednecks*, 70. More on the Understanding Clause is in chapter 6.

58. "Ability to Read," *Clarion-Ledger*, September 1, 1890, p. 4. To increase the size of the paper, there had to be money, from subscriptions, purchases, and advertising. Hints indicate all three were factors, and advertising space certainly increased in these weeks. The *Clarion-Ledger*, with only a brief hiatus, stayed with a daily edition from then on.

59. E. S. Watson, "Watching the Convention," *Clarion-Ledger*, September 11, 1890, p. 1. So, too, were northern papers. See reference in *Keowee (South Carolina) Courier*, September 11, 1890, p. 4.

60. Although a number of speeches were reported in the paper, there is no record of which speeches went unreported when a delegate turned in a copy. Montgomery's speech, later reported in the *News of the World*, was only partially printed in the *Clarion-Ledger*. See next chapter.

61. Opponents of the Australian ballot neglected to mention an obvious issue: it cost the state money to print. Given the parsimonious nature of the state in this period, an oversight of a budget consequence is surprising. For notes on the cost to government, see Alan Ware, "Anti-Party and Party Control of Political Reform in the United States: The Case of the Australian Ballot," *British Journal of Political Science* 30 (2000): 14.

62. "Two Good Speeches," *Clarion-Ledger*, September 11, 1890, p. 1.

63. "Well Taken," *Clarion-Ledger*, September 4, 1890, p. 4.

64. There is an assumption on the part of a number of delegates that illiterate whites were farmers rather than those living in the towns. "Honorable W. A. Boyd's Speech," *Clarion-Ledger*, September 11, 1890, p. 1.

65. "Interesting Colloquy," *Clarion-Ledger*, September 11, 1890, p. 4. This conflict continues between Fewell and George over other issues. There is not enough information to determine whether this was based on a philosophical or a personal difference.

66. *Clarion-Ledger*, September 11, 1890, p. 5.

67. Ibid. For an earlier example of this concern, see "The Negro Problem," *Clarion-Ledger*, January 31, 1889, p. 1.

68. Ibid.

69. Ibid.

70. Ibid.

71. The secrecy of the meetings was noted in Texas. See *Fort Worth (Texas) Daily Gazette*, August 18, 1890, p. 2.

72. *Clarion-Ledger*, September 18, 1890, p. 5.

73. Compare this to Coleman, "Origin," 71, in which he stated that 12 percent of white citizens and 60 percent of African Americans could not read or write in 1890. He further identified about that slightly less than half the eligible white children and only about a third of the African American children attended school then.

74. *Clarion-Ledger*, September 18, 1890, p. 1.

75. Ibid., 2.

76. Ibid., 3. Calhoon never explains why he wanted African Americans to remain; given his strong prejudice, it is a clear question. One may only surmise from this material that he wanted workers.

77. Ibid. See comments from delegates C. S. Coffey of Jefferson County and Gore of Webster. Citizens' rights refer only to white voters.

78. Ibid.

79. *Clarion-Ledger*, September 18, 1890, pp. 2, 3.

Chapter 6. The Convention Adopts the Understanding Clause

1. The advocates of adoption of the report met in the House chamber, and opponents in the Senate chamber. Clearly the divide was still deep, as indicated by the debates themselves.

2. *Clarion-Ledger*, September 18, 1890, p. 4.

3. Ibid.

4. For example, see Matthew Holden, ed., "What Answer? Speech in Support of the Franchise Committee Report," Isaiah Montgomery Studies Project, 2004, Mississippi Department of Archives and History; Hermann, *Pursuit of a Dream*, 230. This argument is not unlike that of Robert Norrell's apology for Booker T. Washington in *Up from History: The Life of Booker T. Washington* (Cambridge, MA: Belknap Press of Harvard University Press, 2009), 421–42. Isaiah Montgomery's comments in his speech certainly lend credence to that argument, when he stated that his "mission here is to bridge a chasm that has been widening and deepening for a generation."

5. "A Noble Speech," *New York World*, September 27, 1890, p. 1.

6. In a recent book, Volney Riser paints Montgomery as impotent in the convention, which is certainly another step in the analysis, beyond that of pragmatism, but the comment is only in passing and is backed by little evidence. See Riser, *Defying Disfranchisement*, 39, 40.

7. Apparently the speech was delivered when the convention met as a committee at large, which did not require inclusion in the minutes.

8. The speech has been a source of controversy ever since it was given and subsequently published. Those issues will be discussed in the subsequent chapters. "A Noble Speech," *New York World*, September 27, 1890, p. 4. See reference in Johnson's article, wherein he holds Montgomery's acquiescence as a tribute to his race and to the appropriateness of the report. Johnson, "Suffrage and Reconstruction," 224. For brief references, see *Daily Democrat* (Natchez), September 16, 1890, p. 1. The *Daily Commercial Herald* (Vicksburg) ignored the speech altogether. For a discussion of the use of the slur, see J. Saunders Redding, *The Lonesome Road: The Story of the Negro's Part in America* (New York: Doubleday, 1958), 18. Montgomery attributed the lack of publication and acknowledgment of his speech to racism on the part of the *Clarion-Ledger*. "That Colored Orator," *New York World*, October 1, 1890, p. 1.

9. "A Noble Speech," *New York World*, September 27, 1890.

10. Ibid.

11. Ibid.

12. Ibid. He repeated that supposition later in the speech, referring more bluntly to "our race has not yet attained the high plane of moral, intellectual and political excellence common to yours."

13. Ibid. The *New York World* viewed the speech in a favorable light. Senator J. Z. George kept a clipping of the speech in his scrapbook. See George Papers, Box 4; "A Noble Speech," *New York World*, September 27, 1890. The speech is printed in total, and followed by a comment.

14. "That Colored Orator," *New York World*, October 1, 1890, p. 1.

15. For instance, see August Meier, *Negro Thought in America, 1880–1915* (Ann Arbor: University of Michigan Press, 1963), 38; Hermann, *Pursuit of a Dream*, 231; Lynch, *Reminiscences*; Alfred M. Dustin, ed., *Crusade for Justice: Autobiography of Ida B. Wells* (Chicago: University of Chicago Press, 1970); and Wharton, *The Negro in Mississippi*, 211–12.

16. Sewell and Dwight, *Mississippi Black History Makers*, 162. While their paragraph on this issue indicates an endnote, nothing exists by that number in the endnotes. The *Washington Bee* named him a traitor and gave two full columns to taking him to task. See "Betrayed the Colored Race," *Washington Bee*, December 24, 1890.

17. In contrast, Sewell and Dwight believed that Montgomery's vote was part of a deal with the Senator J. Z. George faction. Sewell and Dwight, *Mississippi Black History Makers*, 162.

18. Redding, *Lonesome Road*, 18, 98–99.

19. "The Situation in Mississippi," *New York World*, September 27, 1890, p. 1.

20. For a discussion of these concepts in simple terms, see Paul G. Fuller, "E. P Thompson and American History: A Retrospective View," *History Teacher* 28, no. 1 (1994): 31–36.

21. For a discussion of the intergenerational aspects of family structure, see Betty G. Farrell, *Elite Families: Class and Power in Nineteenth Century Boston* (Albany: State University of New York Press, 1993), 1.

22. Brian M. DuToit, *Configurations of Cultural Continuity* (Rotterdam, Netherlands: AA Balkema, 1976), 93–108; Max Gluckman, ed., *The Allocation of Responsibility* (Manchester: Manchester University Press, 1972), 51–54, 257–58.

23. Shortly after Montgomery moved to Bolivar County, he became involved with local Republican politics. According to him, much of the impetus to surface politically was the need to press for coordination of levees. He represented the area Republicans in 1890 when he lobbied for federal assistance in flood control and levee building and testified before the Senate Committee on Commerce. Hermann, *Pursuit of a Dream*, 230.

24. Washington, *Up from Slavery*. Some years later Washington wrote to Charles Waddell Chesnutt and argued that "you place too much reliance upon the ballot to cure evils that we are at present suffering." While he admitted the ballot was "valuable and should not be surrendered," he pointed out that the Atlanta riots took place in a state that had not yet disfranchised voters. He appears to have some ambivalent feelings, which, given the circumstances of the era, one can understand. See Booker T. Washington, Louis Harlan, and R. W. Smock, *Booker T. Washington Papers*, vol. 9 (Urbana: University of Illinois Press, 1972), 112 (re: October 29, 1906) (hereafter cited as Booker T. Washington Papers).

25. Foner and Brown, *Forever Free*, 206, 207.

26. Sheppard, "Montgomery Saga," 187; Redding, *Lonesome Road*, 26, 95.

27. Johnson, "Suffrage and Reconstruction," 211. He also believed that the federal government would not allow a faulty application of the restrictions; see *New York World*, September 27, 1890, p. 1.

28. See Hermann, *Pursuit of a Dream*, 243, for Montgomery's reaction to the election of Vardaman.

29. *Clarion-Ledger*, September 18, 1890, p. 5. Redding argues that Montgomery thought a property qualification would be best, for it was forthright and African Americans could and were gaining land. See Redding, *Lonesome Road*, 19.

30. *Clarion-Ledger*, September 18, 1890.

31. Ibid.

32. *Proceedings*, 275.

33. "A Negro Problem: A Solution Suggested by a Correspondent," *Clarion-Ledger*, October 2, 1890, p. 1. A return to Africa, whether voluntary or involuntary, had been debated for years. The idea was not new, but was quickly met with a reaction to assure African American workers that they were welcome to stay. See below.

34. Ibid.

35. Ibid.

36. Ibid., 2. See also editorial comment on p. 4, where the *Clarion-Ledger* quoted the *St. Louis Republican* and other Democratic journals and agreed that the Understanding Clause should be repealed: "It cannot be defended North or South."

37. The *Baptist Record* pointed out the inconsistency here from an ethical standpoint. See "Plain Talk," *Clarion-Ledger*, October 2, 1890, p. 6.

38. For a specific reference to a fear of returning to Reconstruction, see "Convention," *Daily Commercial Herald* (Vicksburg), September 12, 1890, p. 1.

39. "Section Five," *Daily Commercial Herald* (Vicksburg), September 12, 1890, p. 4.

40. Ibid., 1.

41. "Don't *Like* It, But Takes It," *Daily Commercial Herald* (Vicksburg), September 12, 1890, p. 1.

42. "Appeal of the Press: Expunge the Fraud and Save the Honor of the State," *Daily Commercial Herald* (Vicksburg), September 12, 1890, 1. Muldrow gave notice on October 2. The convention was under Roberts Rules of Order, and the delegates had also voted to not reconsider the franchise section without a large vote. This was to curtail grandstanding, but it closed off legitimate debate.

43. *Proceedings*, 378.

44. Ibid., 372.

45. Ibid., 492, 493.

46. Ibid., 503.

47. Ibid., 542, 548.

48. *Clarion-Ledger*, October 9, 1890, p. 1.

49. Ibid., 2. This article quotes support from the *Aberdeen Weekly* and the *Columbus Index*. See also *Salt Lake City Herald*, October 3, 1890, p. 4. These editors noted the provision as providing "serious possibilities of evil."

50. *Clarion-Ledger*, October 9, 1890, p. 4.

51. Ibid., 2.

52. Ibid., 4.
53. "The Franchise Question," *Clarion-Ledger*, October 9, 1890, p. 4.
54. "He Has the Power," *Clarion-Ledger*, October 9, 1890, p. 4.
55. "In a Nutshell," *Clarion-Ledger*, October 16, 1890, p. 1. See also "Cost of the Convention" on p. 2, from the *Greenville Democrat*, which decried the ever-increasing cost of the convention as well as the provisions passed by the convention delegates.
56. "In a Nutshell," *Clarion-Ledger*, October 16, 1890, p. 1.
57. Ibid., 2; *Daily Democrat* (Natchez), October 16, 1890, p. 2.
58. "Expunge the Clause," *Daily Democrat* (Natchez), October 16, 1890, p. 4.
59. Roberts Rule of Order.
60. *Clarion-Ledger*, October 16, 1890, p. 4.
61. "Finds Little Favor," *Clarion-Ledger*, October 16, 1890, p. 3.
62. Ibid., 4.
63. *Clarion-Ledger*, October 23, 1890, p. 2.
64. "A Negro Paper's Advice," *Clarion-Ledger*, October 23, 1890, p. 1.
65. Ibid., 2.
66. "The Negro Again," *Clarion-Ledger*, October 23, 1890, p. 1.
67. Ibid. Many of the newspapers that the *Clarion-Ledger* quoted can no longer be found in any archive; these are our only examples. A few, such as the *Greenwood Enterprise*, have some poorly preserved copies, but by no means a full run.
68. Ibid. The extension of the terms of office became a subject of debate. See chapter 7.
69. Ibid.
70. Ibid., l, 6. One of these was the *Daily Commercial Herald* (Vicksburg). See "Editorial," October 4, 1890, p. 2, for a statement of its support.
71. *Clarion-Ledger*, October 30, 1890, p. 1.
72. Ibid., 4.
73. Ibid., 2.
74. Ibid., 3.
75. Ibid.
76. Ibid., 5.
77. Ibid.
78. *Proceedings*, 617–21.
79. *Clarion-Ledger*, October 30, 1890, p. 5.

Chapter 7. The Convention Considers Reform Agendas

1. In the beginning, the committee supported the idea, at least according to inside sources quoted by the *Daily Commercial Herald* (Vicksburg), August 30, 1890, p. 1. The *Herald* reported that the committee passed the proposal 17 to 11. It never explained the later report from the committee, which rejected the proposal. More interesting was the article in the same paper on September 3, 1890, which reported that the committee had voted against woman suffrage by the same numbers, 17 to 11. The correspondent reported that Patty believed support was waning for the idea.

2. Ayers, *New South*, 317–20; Marjorie Spruill Wheeler, *New Women of the New South: The Leaders of the Woman Suffrage Movement in the Southern States* (New York: Oxford University Press, 1993), 112–14. See also Mark Lawrence Kornbluh, *Why America Stopped Voting: The Decline of Participatory Democracy and the Emergence of Modern American Politics* (New York: New York University Press, 2000), 112.

3. Kornbluh, *Why America Stopped Voting*, 114. Blackwell later wrote that if Mississippi had only had a suffrage movement in 1890, women probably would have received the vote in the state. The statement is certainly one of the great what-ifs in history, but there is some logic to his reasoning.

4. Wheeler, *New Women of the New South*, 112–14. See also reference in Perman, *Struggle for Mastery*, 79; and Kornbluh, *Why America Stopped Voting*, 112.

5. *Clarion-Ledger*, August 28, 1890, p. 3.

6. Ibid., 1.

7. Ibid.

8. Ibid., 6.

9. Ibid., 5.

10. *Daily Commercial Herald* (Vicksburg), September 2, 1890, p. 1.

11. *Clarion-Ledger*, September 4, 1890, p. 1. According to Perman, *Struggle for Mastery*, 79, the vote on woman suffrage within the committee was tied at 16 to 16, with Patty casting the deciding vote to oppose. Perman references the convention reports for this detail, but his citation appears to be incorrectly given and therefore not possible to verify. Patty was from Noxubee County.

12. *Clarion-Ledger*, September 4, 1890, p. 2.

13. Ibid.

14. Ibid., 4. Compare this to the *Atlanta Constitution*'s stance, "The Women of Mississippi," September 6, 1890, in which the editors argued that women did not want the ballot. "Convention," *Daily Democrat* (Natchez), September 6, 1890, p. 1.

15. *Clarion-Ledger*, September 11, 1890, p. 2.

16. Ibid. Interestingly, the editors of the *Daily Democrat* (Natchez) agreed with him on the principle, but not the logical conclusion. They argued that if women should be granted suffrage, it should be done because it was right, and not because it was expedient. "Editorial," *Daily Democrat* (Natchez), September 3, 1890, p. 2.

17. Ibid., 4; *Daily Democrat* (Natchez), September 11, 1890, p. 1. See debates in chapter 5, in which a number of delegates, as well as letters to the editor, argued that African Americans could never get enough education to be appropriate electors. The Fewell-George dispute can be found in Timothy B. Smith's biography of George, but Smith does not examine the woman suffrage issue. See Smith, *J. Z. George*, 153, 154.

18. "Convention," *Daily Democrat* (Natchez), September 11, 1890, p. 1.

19. *Clarion-Ledger*, September 11, 1890, p. 5.

20. *Clarion-Ledger*, September 18, 1890, p. 1.

21. Ibid.

22. Compare this plea for unity to a clipping from the *Natchez Democrat* included in the George Papers, in which the editors worry that prospects were not good when the two "giants" of the age, Campbell and George, were arguing over ideas.

23. "Convention," *Daily Democrat* (Natchez), September 13, 1890, p. 1.

24. *Clarion-Ledger*, September 18, 1890, p. 3.

25. Ibid., 4.

26. *Proceedings*, 122, 168.

27. Ibid. For example, see p. 214 and the removal on p. 505.

28. Perman notes that the proposal never made it out of committee. See Perman, *Struggle for Mastery*, 81.

29. Ayers, *Promise of the New South*, 160–186, particularly 167 on interdenominational dating.

30. For more on the early struggles of Tougaloo College, see "Tougaloo College, 1860–1899," Vertical File, Mississippi Department of Archives and History; "Inaugural Address," January 7, 1880, p. 2., in which the governor advocates some state money for Tougaloo's normal school function. For Shaw, see pamphlet, "Tenth Annual Report of the Freedman Support of the Methodist Episcopal Church," Cincinnati, Ohio, 1878, Mississippi Department of Archives and History.

31. For references to the importance of the churches in the area, see "The Great International Council of Methodists," *Weekly Clarion*, September 15, 1881, p. 1; untitled notes on Methodist meetings, *Weekly Clarion*, September 22, 1881, p. 3; "The Methodists," *Weekly Clarion*, October 13, 1881, p. 1; "Mississippi Baptist Convention," *Weekly Clarion*, October 27, 1881, p. 2. These examples are typical of the period. Dunbar Rowland gave the African American Baptist membership in the state in 1923 as 400,000, which differed with the census. In addition, this number did not include the peripheral Baptist groups, such as the Free Will Baptists, Colored Primitive Baptists, and so forth. Rowland, *History of Mississippi*, 604.

32. The connection between the church and temperance, as well as the secular and political opposition to it, can best be illustrated by the debates between Jefferson Davis and Bishop Galloway (see chapter 4 for his identification). *Clarion*, January 11, 1888, p. 1.

33. "The Liquor Question," *Weekly Clarion*, January 18, 1882, p. 1, ties temperance directly to religious values. See also the little pamphlet written by A. Burwell: "Dramshops, Industry, and Taxes: An Address to the People of Mississippi" (New York: National Temperance Society and Publication House, 1875), in Mississippi Department of Archives and History. Bettersworth, *Mississippi*, 364. The first community to go dry was Old Greensboro, known for its law breaking. See also Cresswell, *Rednecks*, 103.

34. Sillers, *Bolivar County*, 211.

35. W. H. Patton, "History of the Prohibition Movement in Mississippi," *Publications of the Mississippi Historical Society* 10 (1909): 181. Her visit went unreported in the *Weekly Clarion*. See also "Temperance Proceedings," *Weekly Clarion*, August 4, 1880, p. 1.

36. The Gulf Coast counties and cities remained wet and refused to vote dry. Some of this opposition may have been influenced by the position of Jefferson Davis, who was living on the coast at the time and who was a strong opponent of prohibition. Bolivar was not the only county with pressure to proceed with local option; see untitled entry on Copiah County in *Wichita Daily Eagle* (Kansas), July 16, 1886, p. 2. The Prohibition Party was making inroads into the state; see "Jackson, Mississippi," *Memphis Daily Appeal*, July 30, 1884, p. 1.

37. Cresswell, *Rednecks*, 103.

38. Patton, "Prohibition Movement," 184, and editor's note on 182.

39. Cresswell, *Rednecks*, 105, 106. For general comment on violence over temperance in Mississippi, see untitled column, *National Republican* (Washington, DC), August 11, 1886, p. 2.

40. Indeed, Senator George presented some of these petitions on the floor of Congress. See "Congress," *Omaha (Nebraska) Daily Bee*, January 12, 1882, p. 1.

41. These counties were on the coast or in the river towns along the Mississippi. See Patton, "Prohibition Movement," 187, 201.

42. Cresswell, *Rednecks*, 106.

43. *Daily Commercial Herald* (Vicksburg), September 2, 1890, p. 2.

44. Cresswell, *Rednecks*, 88, 94.?

45. Ibid., 253.

46. "Convention," *Daily Commercial Herald* (Vicksburg), September 24, 1890, p. 1. See also *Daily Democrat* (Natchez), September 2, 1890, p. 1.

47. "Convention," *Daily Democrat* (Natchez), September 29, 1890, p. 1.

48. "Temperance," *Daily Commercial Herald* (Vicksburg), September 27, 1890, p. 1.

49. "Convention," and "Saloon Question," *Daily Democrat*(Natchez), September 27, 1890, pp. 1, 2.

50. Alfred Benjamin Butts, "Public Education," *Publications of the Mississippi Historical Society* (1919): 20–156; see especially 150. In addition, see Doyle, *Faulkner's County*, 346.

51. Span, *Cotton Field to Schoolhouse*, 48; Bettersworth, *Mississippi*, 355. No one complained about the lack of tax payments from white citizens, and in some counties there were large numbers who were not taxable.

52. Cresswell, *Rednecks*, 99.

53. For example, see "Educational Facilities for Blacks in Mississippi," *Weekly Clarion*, September 15, 1881, p. 1; Bettersworth, *Mississippi*, 357.

54. An advertisement for the college in the Jackson paper stated the charges for room and board in 1881 would be $137 for the year. *Weekly Clarion*, September 29, 1881, p. 1. Rowland, *History of Mississippi*, 486–88; Doyle, *Faulkner's County*, 341–46. Not all was well, for some saw the college as a destructive influence. See "Our State University," *Weekly Clarion*, June 25, 1879, p. 1.

55. Rowland, *Heart of the South*, 498, 499. See also "Inaugural Address," *Weekly Clarion*, January 7, 1880, p. 2, in which the governor refers to Alcorn specifically as an Agricultural and Mechanical School. Some reports indicated that Revels had worked for the Democrats in the 1876 election. See *Cairo (Illinois) Bulletin* November 2, 1876, p. 2. Revels had also been a successful farmer. See untitled note in *Opelousas (Louisiana) Courier*, January 1, 1887, p. 1; the same entry is in "The South," *Iola (Kansas) Register*, January 7, 1887, p. 6; *Barton County Democrat* (Kansas), January 6, 1887, p. 2.

56. Apparently the citizens of the state were uncertain as to the permanence of the college: see "Agricultural and Mechanical College," *Weekly Clarion*, September 29, 1881, p. 1, which asks for a clarification of the purpose of the college; and "The Governor's Message," *Weekly Clarion*, January 4, 1882, p. 2, which specifically claims the college is no longer an experiment, but a success. *Report of Joint Select Committee of the Mississippi Legislature, Appointed to Inquire into the Present Condition, General Management, Discipline, Adaptation to the End for Which Created, and Present Usefulness and Prospects of the Agricultural and Mechanical College of Mississippi* (Jackson: J. L. Power, State Printer, 1882); *Class of 1908*,

Mississippi Agricultural and Mechanical College (Atlanta: Ruralist Press, 1964). This little book includes accounts of the experiences of the 1908 graduates (including my grandfather). Rowland, *Heart of the South*, 494–98.

57. Mississippi State College for Women 1884–1956, Vertical File, Mississippi Department of Archives and History. This file is marginally helpful. For the building pressure to create the college, see "A State Female College," *Weekly Clarion*, October 6, 1881, p. 2; "A Plea for Higher Education for the Women of Mississippi," *Weekly Clarion*, November 30, 1881, p. 1; letter to editor, *Weekly Clarion*, February 1, 1882, p. 2. See also an untitled note in *Weekly Clarion*, September 22, 1881, p. 3, which noted a speaker on the rights of women regarding education and inviting all to attend, including women. Bettersworth, *Mississippi*, 360; Rowland, *Heart of the South*, 488–93.

58. The close connection between education, religion, and the local press is evident in many advertisements and notices for events, openings, and changes at the local colleges. See, for instance, *Weekly Clarion*, September 15, 1881, p. 4.

59. Rowland, *Heart of the South*, 501–3. A photograph of Major R. W. Millsaps can be found at the Mississippi Department of Archives and History [PI/1999.0001].

60. The Lowry family owned and ran the college. See reference in *New Ulm (Minnesota) Weekly* May 6, 1885, p. 3; Rowland, *Heart of the South*, 504; "Tourists," *San Francisco Call*, July 10, 1897, p. 4, which refers to students from the best families of Mississippi; "Middleton, Tennessee," *Memphis Daily Appeal*, February 28, 1885, p. 2.

61. Rowland, *Heart of the South*, 504, 505. There were a few other colleges, but most folded.

62. Ibid., 118.

63. The majority report advocated that tax and levees on alcohol be placed into the general fund for education so that no increase of taxation would result. See "Convention," *Daily Democrat* (Natchez), August 29, 1890, p. 1, and October 6, 1890, p. 1.

64. "Convention," *Daily Commercial Herald* (Vicksburg), September 15, 1890, p. 1.

65. "Convention," *Daily Commercial Herald* (Vicksburg), October 7, 1890, p. 1.

66. Coleman, "Origin of the Constitution," 70.

67. Ayers, *Promise of the New South*, 418.

68. *Clarion-Ledger*, August 28, 1890, p. 5.

69. *Proceedings*, 329; *Daily Democrat* (Natchez), October 4, 1890, p. 2; October 5, 1890, p. 1; October 7, 1890, p. 1.

70. *Clarion-Ledger*, October 2, 1890, p. 5; *Daily Democrat* (Natchez) October 4, 1890, p. 1. Child labor was rife; see Ayers, *Promise of the New South*, 416.

71. *Proceedings*, 350.

72. Ibid., 118.

73. Ibid., 122, 123; see also *Clarion-Ledger*, October 9, 1890, p. 5; and "The Work of Revision," *Daily Commercial Herald* (Vicksburg), October 8, 1890, p. 1. The delegates do make provisions for schools for those who were blind and deaf.

74. *Proceedings*, 356, 357. In fact, the state had allocated monies in the past to be paid through the counties. This was particularly true of the Chickasaw school fund, which derived from the rental income of lands allocated to the state from the federal government at the point of Indian Removal during the Jackson administration. The convention

discovered that some of these lands had been illegally sold, and thereby would no longer give income to the state. The issues over the ownership of the land and rental from the lands that remained became a heated part of the debate. The eventual outcome was to rent the remaining land at 6 percent per annum, which monies were to be given to the state and redirected to the counties, rather than the previous oversight by the counties. See *Proceedings*, 366, 367. See also *Clarion-Ledger*, October 8, 1890, p. 5; *Daily Commercial Herald* (Vicksburg), October 8, 1890, p. 2, and October 9, 1890, p. 1.

75. "Suffrage," *Daily Commercial Herald* (Vicksburg), September 13, 1890, p. 2.

76. *Clarion-Ledger*, September 18, 1890, p. 3. On the very next page, though, the *Vicksburg Post* argued that it supported an educational qualification because that would ensure white supremacy for some time to come. Apparently one group identified progress among African Americans, and the other did not recognize it. For more on the debate in the convention, see "Suffrage," *Daily Commercial Herald* (Vicksburg), September 13, 1890, p. 2.

77. "Section Five," *Clarion-Ledger*, October 9, 1890, p. 1. See also Meier, *Negro Thought*, 162.

78. *Clarion-Ledger*, October 2, 1890, p. 5.

79. In reality, this had more to do with the Blair Bill that the Elections Bill. *Clarion-Ledger*, October 9, 1890, p. 5.

80. "Southern Candor," *Clarion-Ledger*, October 23, 1890, p. 3.

81. *Daily Commercial Herald* (Vicksburg), October 9, 1890, p. 1.

82. J. H. Jones, "Penitentiary Reform in Mississippi," *Publications of the Mississippi Historical Society* 6 (1902): 111, 112. A quick narrative of the history can be found in Cresswell, *Rednecks*, 47–49, and Willis, *Forgotten Time*, 16–19. For information on the leasing, see "Proposals for the Leasing of Mississippi Penitentiary," *Weekly Clarion*, May 12, 1880, p. 4.

83. Jones, "Penitentiary Reform," 113. See "Leasing the State Penitentiary," *Weekly Clarion*, July 21, 1880, p. 2, in which the editors said this issue was of "deep interest and concern," for the "wrong choice could be costly to the state." They did admit that the "pecuniary interests" of the state were paramount, but the well-being of the prisoners should "also be looked into."

84. Jones, "Penitentiary Reform," 114.

85. Ibid.

86. Ibid.

87. See editor's note in ibid., 111.

88. Ibid., 116.

89. Ibid., 117.

90. Ibid., 121 (emphasis added).

91. Ibid., 123, 126.

92. Ibid., 120. Sadly, although abolished in the new constitution, vestiges continued under cover for decades to come.

93. "Convention," *Daily Commercial Herald* (Vicksburg), 1890, p. 1.

94. Ayers, *Promise of the New South*, 154–55. See also Willis, *Forgotten Time*, 17–20 in which he pinpoints the beginnings of convict leasing in the state to Reconstruction. Harris identified the practice as developed under Governor Humphrey. See Harris, *Day of the Carpetbagger*, 38–39. Also opposed to leasing was Governor Stone. "Opposed to Leasing Convicts," *Weekly Expositor* (Brockway Center, Michigan), January 23, 1890, p. 6.

95. *Clarion-Ledger*, September 4, 1890, p. 5.

96. Douglas A. Blackmon. *Slavery by Another Name: The Re-enslavement of Black Americans from the Civil War to World War II* (New York: Anchor, 2009); "Leasing of Convicts Abolished," *Evening Star* (Washington, DC), September 5, 1890, p. 6; "Convict Labor," *Great Falls (Montana) Weekly Tribune*, December 14, 1894, p. 3.

97. *Clarion-Ledger*, September 11, 1890, p. 3; "Convicts Not to Be Leased," *St. Paul (Minnesota) Daily Globe*, September 4, 1890, p. 1.

98. "Good Work," *Daily Commercial Herald* (Vicksburg), September 7, 1890, editorial page.

99. "Convention," *Daily Commercial Herald* (Vicksburg), September 5, 1890, p. 1.

100. Ibid.; "Convict Leasing," *Mt. Sterling Advocate* (Kentucky), January 21, 1896, p. 1. "Convention," *Daily Commercial Herald* (Vicksburg), September 6, 1890, p. 1.

101. "Where They Started," *Clarion-Ledger*, September 11, 1890, p. 4. See Article 10, section 223 in the Mississippi Constitution. There was a delay, however, in implementation. See "Latest News Itemized," which noted the annual leasing of convicts and how much money exchanged hands for cotton pickers. *Daily Bulletin* (Honolulu, Hawaii), January 9, 1893, p. 2.

102. *Clarion-Ledger*, September 18, 1890. p. 3. See "Mississippi's Experiment: Convict Leasing," *Atlanta Constitution*, January 12, 1896. The state did build a new capitol, however, in 1903, on the site of the old penitentiary.

103. Butts, "Public Administration," 221; Doyle, *Faulkner's County*, 303, 304; "Yellow Fever," *Wheeling (West Virginia) Daily Intelligencer*, July 30, 1878, p. 1; "Jackson: The Fever," and "Yellow Fever Scourge," *Weekly Clarion*, November 6, 1878, p. 2; "Yellow Fever," *Memphis Daily Appeal*, August 11, 1878, p. 1; "Vicksburg," *National Republican*, August 28, 1878, p. 1; "The Plague," *Little Falls (Minnesota) Transcript*, September 12, 1878, p. 2. The scourge went late into the fall, provoking a delay in the opening of Ole Miss: see "Public Health Question," *Weekly Clarion*, November 20, 1878, p. 2.

104. See Helen Craft Anderson, "A Chapter in the Yellow Fever Epidemic of 1878," *Publications of the Mississippi Historical Society* 10 (1909): 223–36. For Holly Springs specifically, see *Weekly Democratic Statesman* (Austin, Texas), September 19, 1878, p. 3; "World's Health," *Leavenworth (Kansas) Weekly Times*, October 31, 1878, p. 2; "Yellow Fever Reports," *Evening Star* (Washington, DC), September 7, 1878, p. 1. General Featherston (see earlier in this chapter) also suffered from the fever, but survived. "Local Paragraphs," *Memphis Daily Appeal*, September 25, 1878, p. 2. Yellow fever did not stop its incursions into the state; see "Yellow Fever in Mississippi," *Atlanta Constitution*, September 6, 1897.

Chapter 8. The Convention Exposes Class Divisions

1. Kirwan, *Revolt of the Rednecks*. Historian Glenn Feldman argues that at least in Alabama, class division was a mythology. He may be correct about Alabama, but Mississippi absolutely had a split. The difference may be based on the time period. Alabama's convention came during the Progressive Era, and Mississippi was caught up in the period of the Farmers' Alliance. See Glenn Feldman, *The Disfranchisement Myth: Poor Whites and Suffrage Restrictions in Alabama* (Athens: University of Georgia Press, 2004), particularly 1–14.

2. The *Lexington Advisor* placed this idea at the feet of Burkitt, whom they called Captain. The *Lexington Bulletin* also referred to the apportionment scheme as beneficial to "wool-hat-ism," a slur at the poverty of rural people. Copies of these clippings can be found in the George Papers, Box 3. They have no dates but clearly are from the period of the convention.

3. "Senator George," *Clarion-Ledger*, July 7, 1890, p. 1; Hathorn, "Suffrage," 36. For more on the senator, see "Senator George," *Daily Democrat*, September 18, 1890, p. 2.

4. Ayers, *Promise of the New South*, 148.

5. "The Protectorate Plan," *Clarion-Ledger*, August 28, 1890, p. 4. Albert Kirwan, who had remarkable insight on most of these issues, appeared to miss this point. He thought that black counties really maintained control because of the inequality of voting strength of actual voters in different counties. This mismatch was done on purpose to control the taxation of the counties. See his "Apportionment in the Mississippi Constitution of 1890," *Journal of Southern History* 14 (May 1948): 234–46, particularly 243; and Hathorn, "Suffrage," 37.

6. Kirwan, "Apportionment," 234–35.

7. "The Protectorate Plan," *Clarion-Ledger*, August 28, 1890, p. 4.

8. George Papers, Box 3, n.d.

9. William Alexander Mabry, "Disfranchisement of the Negro in Mississippi," *Journal of Southern History* 4 (August 1938): 327.

10. Ibid., 328; Kirwan, "Apportionment," 236.

11. Hathorn, "Suffrage," 39. This was McLaurin of Sharkey County. Hathorn got this information in the Mississippi Department of Archives and History from a folder entitled "Propositions Presented at the Constitutional Convention of 1890." The file no longer exists.

12. Hathorn, "Suffrage," 40.

13. Ibid., 40–41.

14. Ibid., 41; "Convention," *Clarion-Ledger*, September 10, 1890, p. 1. The committee was not really in agreement on this issue. See Martin speech in *Clarion-Ledger*, September 17, 1890, p. 1.

15. Hathorn, "Suffrage," 41; *Clarion-Ledger*, September 18, 1890, p. 2; "Hybrid and Abortion," *Daily Democrat*, September 21, 1890, p. 2.

16. "State Sectionalism," *Daily Democrat*, September 12, 1890, p. 2.

17. Mabry, "Disfranchisement," 328.

18. "Food for Thought," *Clarion-Ledger*, September 11, 1890, p. 4.

19. *Clarion-Ledger*, September 18, 1890, p. 3. The *Daily Commercial Herald* (Vicksburg) points out that black counties would lose out under this plan, but Senator George, who had always represented those counties, had proposed this for the good of the state. Of course, as senator, he was supposed to be supporting the state as a whole rather than one particular area. George Papers, Box 3.

20. *Clarion-Ledger*, September 9, 1890, p. 1, and September 11, 1890, p. 1.

21. *Proceedings*, 329.

22. "That Unjust Apportionment," *Clarion-Ledger*, September 18, 1890, p. 4. See also "The Sykes Plan" on same page for a suggested alternative. See "The George Plan" in *New Mississippian*, n.d., George Papers, Box 3. Sykes advocates a simple education qualification, which would be "clear and simple, honest and legal."

23. *Clarion-Ledger*, October 2, 1890, p. 4.

24. Ibid., 2; Kirwan, "Apportionment," 237. Compare this to the *Greenville Times*, which did support George's plan; the clipping can be found in George Papers, Box 3. The legislature also created an electoral college for governor to give more control to the white counties. According to Perman, this section was not even used until recently. See Perman, *Struggle for Mastery*, 82.

25. *Clarion-Ledger*, October 9, 1890, p. 3. The issues involved are discussed below under levees.

26. *Proceedings*, 256.

27. *Clarion-Ledger*, October 30, 1890, p. 1.

28. "Keep the Constitution Pure," *Daily Democrat*, September 14, 1890, p. 2.

29. *Clarion-Ledger*, November 8, 1890, p. 3.

30. Perman, *Struggle for Mastery*, 82.

31. Kirwan, "Apportionment," 239. Kirwan was quoting Dunbar Rowland. Kirwan disagreed with Rowland; he believed that apportionment accomplished little and that inequalities from the past decade simply continued. See ibid., 239–42.

32. *Clarion-Ledger*, August 13, 1890, p. 3. It is important to remember that the Colored Farmers' Alliance was a separate group, as previously discussed in chapter 3. The People's Party (Populists) was not yet formed, and there was no indication—yet—that its members would be anything other than loyal Democrats. The fact that it is mentioned here, though, indicates that there was some talk. Good books on the Farmers' Alliance, as well as Populism, are numerous, though they often conflict on emphasis. See especially Robert McMath Jr., *Populist Vanguard: A History of the Southern Farmers' Alliance* (Chapel Hill: University of North Carolina Press, 1975).

33. The assessed value of property in the state in 1890 was only $158 million. Coleman, "Origin of the Constitution of 1890," 69.

34. *Clarion-Ledger*, September 18, 1890, p. 2. Compare to comments by delegates Bell and Kennedy, who read letters opposing property qualifications, as well as Guyton, who read a letter from the Alliance. See ibid., 5. See also *Proceedings*, 107–14.

35. Noted as far afield as the Midwest. See *St. Paul (Minnesota) Daily Globe*, August 16, 1890, p. 5, and the next day's issue, p. 7.

36. *Proceedings*, 50.

37. "An Elective Judiciary," *Clarion-Ledger*, August 28, 1890, p. 1.

38. Compare *Proceedings*, 36, 360. Elections were reintroduced in 1910.

39. Ibid., 362.

40. "The Judiciary," *Daily Commercial Herald* (Vicksburg), October 11, 1890, p. 1; "Let Well Enough Alone," *Sentinel* (Grenada), September 21, 1890, p. 1.

41. *Proceedings*, 515.

42. "Jury Changes Needed," *Clarion-Ledger*, August 28, 1890, p. 1.

43. Ayers, *Promise of the New South*, 9.

44. *Clarion-Ledger*, August 13, 1890, p. 2.

45. *Proceedings*, 271.

46. Ibid., 225, 226.

47. Ibid., 486.

48. Ibid., 540.

49. Ibid., 469. They omitted private cars from that equation. See also "Convention," *Daily Commercial Herald* (Vicksburg), October 25, 1890, p. 1.

50. *Proceedings*, 467.

51. Ibid., 524.

52. Ibid., 488.

53. Ibid., 431.

54. Ibid., 430.

55. Ibid., 373. Meridian was an up-and-coming town in 1890 with the juncture of rail lines. The businessman is not identified.

56. Ibid., 458.

57. *Clarion-Ledger*, August 28, 1890, p. 3.

58. *Proceedings*, 484.

59. "Need Not Be Alarmed," *Daily Commercial Herald* (Vicksburg), October 24, 1890, p. 2. The editors noted that Senator George was wearing a suit made from cloth from the local Wesson Mills.

60. *Clarion-Ledger*, September 4, 1890, p. 3.

61. *Proceedings*, 487.

62. Ayers, *Promise of the New South*, 104–31.

63. *Proceedings*, 428. Final restrictions are on p. 540. George was not alone in this confusion.

64. Sillers, *Bolivar County*, 87.

65. For further descriptions of the damage in 1882, see "Mississippi Flood," *Atlanta Constitution*, February 23, 1882.

66. "The Floods of the Mississippi River: Including an Account of their Principal Causes and Effects and Description of the Levee System and Other Means Proposed and Tried for the Control of the River, with a Particular Account of the Great Flood of 1887" (New York: Engineering News, 1897). This reprint pamphlet can be found in the Mississippi Department of Archives and History. Sillers, *Bolivar County*, 87, 88.

67. See previous chapter on Montgomery; and Barry, *Rising Tide*, 21–92.

68. Kirwan, *Revolt of the Rednecks*. For reference to floods that spring in which Greenville was submerged, see "The Levees," *Clarion-Ledger*, April 3, 1890, p. 1; and "Mississippi Levees," *Atlanta Constitution*, June 23, 1890.

69. *Proceedings*, 30.

70. Ibid., 284.

71. Ibid., 480–82.

72. "Convention," *Daily Commercial Herald* (Vicksburg), September 6, 1890, p. 1. No information in the column explains the Greenwood reference.

73. Ibid.

74. *Clarion-Ledger*, September 11, 1890, pp. 4, 5; "Convention," *Daily Commercial Herald* (Vicksburg), September 6, 1890, p. 1.

75. *Clarion-Ledger*, September 11, 1890, pp. 4, 5. See Mississippi Constitution, Article 9, section 214, which allows the state legislature to determine the "manner" of the military duties, which in principle were stated as obligatory for "all able-bodied males between the ages of eighteen and forty-five."

76. "Convention," *Daily Commercial Herald* (Vicksburg), September 7, 1890, p. 1. Apparently one of the references to Leflore County was the episode discussed in chapter 3.

77. "Convention," *Daily Democrat*, September 18, 1890, p. 1.

78. "Convention," *Daily Commercial Herald*, September 8, 1890, p. 1.

79. *Clarion-Ledger*, September 11, 1890, p. 3. See also *Proceedings*, 149; and *Daily Commercial Herald* (Vicksburg), September 9, 1890, p. 1, which concluded the report that provoked much debate.

80. *Clarion-Ledger*, October 9, 1890, p. 2.

81. Ibid., 4.

82. "Should Be Submitted," *Clarion-Ledger*, September 4, 1890, p. 4.

83. "The Constitution Makers," *Clarion-Ledger*, October 2, 1890, p. 4.

84. *Clarion-Ledger*, October 9, 1890, p. 4.

85. *Clarion-Ledger*, October 30, 1890, p. 4.

86. *Sentinel*, October 11, 1890, p. 3, and October 4, 1890, p. 3; the *Examiner* edition is no longer extant.

87. *Sentinel*, November 6, 1890, p. 3.

88. Ibid.

89. Marin, Burkitt, Gore, and McLaurin of Smith County. *Clarion-Ledger*, November 6, 1890, p. 3. According to Johnson, the totals were different: the votes were 104 yes, 8 no, and 21 not voting. He points out that Alcorn, Montgomery, and Simrall voted for the constitution. Johnson, "Suffrage and Reconstruction," 223.

90. "The Farewell Address," *Clarion-Ledger*, November 6, 1890, p. 5.

91. "The Work Is Done," *Clarion-Ledger*, November 6, 1890, p. 4.

92. "The New Constitution, How Mississippi Will Be Affected by It," *Clarion-Ledger*, November 1890, p. 2.

Chapter 9. Defending the New Constitution in Congress

1. The introduction of the bill was discussed in chapter 4. As a reminder, the Elections Bill was nicknamed the Force Bill by the Democrats who hoped to tar the bill with the brush of notoriety. Both terms are used in this book, for people at the time also used both names.

2. Some historians have concluded this was when the Republican Party shifted. See Richardson, *Death of Reconstruction*, 210–24. See also Calhoun, *New Republic*, 260–88.

3. Aldrich actually wrote the Library of Congress to ask the librarians to investigate cloture rules elsewhere. Calhoun, *New Republic*, 247.

4. Perman, *Struggle for Mastery*, 40. This compromise was the suggestion of Senator Matthew Quay (R-Pennsylvania), who was under tremendous pressure from businessmen.

5. In particular, Calvin Chase of the *Washington Bee* and T. Thomas Fortune of the *Age* were unsure of the certainty of Republican support. The Afro-American Press Association was fully in support of the Lodge Elections Bill. Meier, *Negro Thought in America*, 30, 38.

6. Calhoun, *New Republic*, 249–50.

7. Ibid., 250.

8. Ibid., 251; *Clarion-Ledger*, November 13, 1890, p. 4.

9. See Fred Wellborn, "The Influence of the Silver-Republican Senators, 1889–1891," *Mississippi Valley Historical Review* 14 (1928): 462–80, particularly 478, in which the author concludes there was no secret agreement or collusion, for there did not need to be any for both sides to feel they won.

10. Calhoun, *New Republic*, 252. Even normally supportive journals opposed the bill. See Richardson, *Death of Reconstruction*, 210–12.

11. For example, see Senator Gray of Maryland and Senator Daniel of Virginia, *Congressional Record*, 22:202, 246.

12. Perman, *Struggle for Mastery*, 49; Buck, *Road to Reunion*, 280.

13. Perman, *Struggle for Mastery*, 43.

14. Calhoun, *New Republic*, 254. See also *Congressional Record*, 22:679.

15. *Congressional Record*, 22:203.

16. Ibid., 202. This was Senator Gorman (D-Maryland). The reference to a needy economy comes *before* the 1893 panic.

17. Ibid., 320.

18. Ibid., 218. This was Senator Gray (D-Delaware). On December 10 Senator Allison asked for a printing of both bills, side by side, to be distributed to the members of the Senate. Presumably this would also take time. See ibid., 297. Senator Daniel (D-Virginia) agreed that this bill would only benefit Republicans and that its expense was unknown, but he also slyly pointed out that the West might have to "endure" voting by Chinese immigrants. Ibid., 245–47.

19. Ibid., 279–83; Upchurch, *Legislating Racism*, 139–40.

20. *Congressional Record*, 22:284.

21. Ibid., 285.

22. Ibid., 286–92. George claimed the bill that prescribed the regulations for holding elections was very one-sided. When Senator John Spooner (R-Wisconsin) pressed George on this issue, the senator from Mississippi had to admit that he was using language from the House bill rather than the one from the Senate.

23. Ibid., 332.

24. Ibid., 324. The exchange appears to confirm further the prevailing belief in the nation of social Darwinism and its resulting racism; too often people assumed that a mixed-race person would have innate capabilities that a pure-blood people would not. For Montgomery's views on the Elections Bill, see "That Colored Orator," *New York World*, October 1, 1890, p. 1.

25. *Congressional Record*, 22:451–53.

26. Ibid., 455.

27. Ibid., 456.

28. Ibid., 457.

29. Ibid., 459.

30. Ibid., 460.

31. Ibid., 504; "Federal Elections Bill, *Clarion-Ledger*, December 4, 1890, p. 5.

32. *Congressional Record*, 22:511.

33. Ibid.

34. Ibid., 514.

35. Ibid., 521.

36. Ibid., 524–28.

37. Ibid., 571. The source of the copy of the *Clarion-Ledger* remains a mystery. The *Clarion-Ledger* simply sees this as the last vestige of hatred directed toward the South. "South and the Force Bill," *Clarion-Ledger*, January 8, 1891, p. 1.

38. *Congressional Record*, 22:572; "A Republican Speech," *Clarion-Ledger*, January 8, 1891, p. 3.

39. *Congressional Record*, 22:620.

40. Ibid., 630.

41. Ibid., 679.

42. Ibid., 683. In simplest terms the Stalwarts supported strong Reconstruction in the South and patronage. The Anti-Stalwarts (or Half-Breeds as they were often known) mostly supported civil service reform. For a brief explanation, see Allan Peskin, "Who Were the Stalwarts? Who Were Their Rivals? Republican Factions in the Gilded Age," *Political Science Quarterly* 99 (1984): 703–16. Often Mugwumps were confused with the Half-Breeds. See Gerald W. McFarland, "The New York Mugwumps of 1884: A Profile," *Political Science Quarterly* 78 (1963): 40–58.

43. *Congressional Record*, 22:713.

44. Ibid., 727.

45. Ibid., 728. See chapter 2 for more on the Chisholm story.

46. Ibid., 730.

47. Ibid., 731.

48. Ibid., 732, 733. The *Clarion-Ledger* articles are to be found in that paper on the dates as listed above. See chapter 5.

49. Ibid., 763–73.

50. Ibid., 804, 806.

51. Ibid., 820, 835.

52. Ibid., 853.

53. Ibid., 857.

54. Perham, *Struggle for Mastery*, 41.

55. *Congressional Record*, 22:861.

56. Ibid., 872; Calhoun, *New Republic*, 254.

57. *Congressional Record*, 22:865.

58. Ibid., 867.

59. Ibid., 869. Senator George spoke the next day and stated that the murder was a personal matter between individuals and was not a racial problem. See ibid., 896.

60. Calhoun, *New Republic*, 255. George's speech was not in the *Record*, having been reserved for editing. It is difficult to find other than in reprints.

61. Speech can be found in the *Congressional Record*, as well Ethridge, *Mississippi Constitutions*, 617–749. Portions are also quoted in Smith, *J. Z. George*, 156.

62. Ethridge, *Mississippi Constitutions*, 622; Smith, *J. Z. George*, 157.

63. Ethridge, *Mississippi Constitutions*, 626.

64. Ibid. 650; Smith, *J. Z. George*, 159.

65. Ethridge, *Mississippi Constitutions*, 633.

66. Ibid., 636, 637.
67. Ibid.
68. Ibid., 650.
69. Ibid., 652.
70. Ibid., 654.
71. Walter Nugent, *Into the West: The Story of Its People* (New York: Alfred A. Knopf, 1997), 60, 78.
72. Calhoun, *New Republic*, 256. See also "A Republican Speech," *Clarion-Ledger*, January 8, 1891, p. 3. The paper changes the spelling of Wolcott to Walcott several times in the article.
73. Perman, *Struggle for Mastery*, 40; see also "It Will Rest Awhile," *Clarion-Ledger*, December 18, 1891, p. 1.
74. Ethridge, *Mississippi Constitutions*, 667, 669.
75. Ibid., 676.
76. Ibid., 684.
77. Ibid., 685.
78. Ibid., 688.
79. Ibid., 689–92.
80. Ibid., 694. See also Smith, *J. Z. George*, 159, 160. According to the *Washington Bee*, Walthall was more blunt than recorded in the *Record*. He argued that Mississippi had the right to "protect itself from negro rule." See supplement in the *Bee*, February 21, 1891.
81. Ethridge, *Mississippi Constitutions*, 695.
82. Ibid., 696.
83. In an effort to explain that he knew exactly what the Understanding Clause was meant to be, George admitted in this section that the clause was his. Ibid., 697.
84. Ibid., 702; see also Smith, *J. Z. George*, 161.
85. The *Clarion-Ledger* took George to task for this statement, calling him "unjust and incorrect," and they listed the papers that opposed the clause. *Clarion-Ledger*, January 8, 1892, p. 1. For more on the subject, see also *Clarion-Ledger*, January 15, 1891, pp. 1, 3.
86. Calhoun, *New Republic*, 254.
87. Ibid., 256.
88. "The Scene Shifts," *Clarion-Ledger*, January 15, 1891, p. 4; also in "Cloture Laid Aside," *Clarion-Ledger*, January 29, 1891, p. 2; "Federal Election Supervision," January 26, 1893, *Clarion-Ledger*, p. 4. See Perman, *Struggle for Mastery*, 41, for a discussion as to why Stewart changed his mind. Cameron of Pennsylvania was another Republican whose overriding concern was business. Buck, *Road to Reunion*, 280.
89. Calhoun, *New Republic*, 259.
90. Buck, *Road to Reunion*, 280.
91. Ibid., 281. The southern view of the issues became the accepted one. During this time, Alabama congressman H. A. Herbert published a book, *Why the Solid South*, that influenced interpretations of Reconstruction for generations to come. Widely received, it questioned northern strategy and motives. Hillary Abner Herbert, *Why the Solid South?* (Baltimore: R. H. Woodward, 1890).
92. See Democratic pamphlets for 1892, microfilm ZH9, New York Public Libraries.

93. Richardson, *Death of Reconstruction*, 210–12. Richardson does an excellent job of pulling together strands of this story that, while previously known, had been left unconnected.

94. Calhoun, *New Republic*, 270.

95. Paul Finkelman, *Dred Scott v Sanford: A Brief History with Documents* (Boston: Bedford Series, 1997), 58, 59.

96. Reference letter from South Carolina.

97. Calhoun, *New Republic*, 271.

98. Federalist Papers, 59–61.

99. Calhoun, *New Republic*, 271

100. Quoted in ibid., 272.

Chapter 10. Defending the New Constitution in the Federal Courts

1. *Guide to U.S. Elections*, vol. 1, 6th ed. (Washington, DC: CQ Press, a division of SAGE, 2010), 772. In 1892 the total number of votes cast in Mississippi was 52,519; compare to the total in 1876 of 164,776, although the use of tissue ballots makes that total questionable. In 1903 the total was 58,721. Taking it from another angle, in 1892 Mississippi the turn-out of potential voters was only 18.4 percent and in 1904 only 15.5 percent. See Jerrold G. Rusk, *A Statistical History of the American Electorate* (Washington, DC: CQ Press, a division of the Congressional Quarterly 2001), 51, 70–72.

2. *Nation* 54 (1892), 139; also quoted in Woodward, *Origins of the New South*, 344. See also "Disfranchisement," *Clarion-Ledger*, February 19, 1891, p. 6; "*Clarion-Ledger* Endorsed," *Clarion-Ledger*, February 26, 1891, p. 5. Perman references numbers from the Mississippi secretary of state's records of the congressional elections of 1892 as 69,905 white voters and 9,036 African American voters. I looked, but I did not find his reference, which may be my fault and not his. See Perman, *Struggle for Mastery*, 89.

3. Subsequently the state has amended the constitution innumerable times, producing an unwieldy tome that is still used as organic law in Mississippi. Reforms not passed in the original form were eventually added.

4. Even Frederick Douglass thought Isaiah Montgomery had been swayed by the threats and intimidation when he supported the franchise restrictions in the constitution; he said, "I hear the plaintive eloquence of his marvelous address a groan of bitter anguish born of oppression and despair." See "Douglass to His Race," *Plaindealer*, November 14, 1890. See also "A Surrender That Failed," *Colored American*, November 26, 1898.

5. See chapter 8.

6. Volney Riser argues that the decision was not so very important, but it certainly was to Mississippi. Riser, *Defying Disfranchisement*, 46–73.

7. Populism in the West was more of a threat to Republicans, when fusion joined Populists to Democrats. In the South, fusion was more typical between Populists and Republicans. See Woodward, *New South*, 275–76; and Lawrence Goodwyn, *The Democratic Promise: The Populist Moment in America* (New York: Oxford University Press, 1976), 430–35.

8. "Senator Walthall Interviewed," *Clarion-Ledger*, November 19, 1891, p. 4. For a discussion of Populism, see Ayers, *New South*, 249–82; and Goodwyn, *Democratic Promise*, 270–72.

9. "The Mississippi Fight," *Atlanta Constitution*, July 12, 1891; the election was thoroughly covered in the *Clarion-Ledger*. The problems started immediately after the convention; see "Judge Campbell for Senator," *Clarion-Ledger*, November 6, 1890, p. 5; and letter to editor, *Clarion-Ledger*, November 13, 1890, p. 4; "Kemper Speaks," *Clarion-Ledger*, November 27, 1890, p. 2.

10. Ayers, *New South*, 255. Goodwyn identifies Burkitt as state treasurer of the Alliance and editor of the *Choctaw County Messenger* (*Democratic Promise*, 254–56); for an example of his writing, see "Evils of Concentrated Wealth," *Barbour County Index* (Kansas), June 14, 1899, p. 2. Burkitt became the president of the National Reform Press Association. "Reform Press Convention," *Little Falls (Minnesota) Weekly Transcript*, April 3, 1900, p. 1. Both George and Walthall were under threat as well from the Populists, but they survived. See "The Fall Elections," *Washington Bee*, November 7, 1891; *Clarion-Ledger*, May 14, 1891, p. 4. Burkitt commanded some power and prestige in the Populist Party; see *San Francisco Call*, July 25, 1896, p. 3, for reference to a strong run by Burkitt for the vice-presidential nomination from the Populist Party.

11. Calhoun, *New Republic*, 273; Bond, *Political Culture*, 278–83.

12. Woodward, *New South*, 344. For a different set of numbers, see *Guide to U.S. Elections*, 772. This publication by the Library of Congress gives 52,519 as a total, with 40,030 going to Cleveland; 1,398 to Harrison; and 10,118 to Weaver, the Populist candidate.

13. "Will Sell Out Bodily," *Sedelia (Kansas) Weekly Bazoo*, July 26, 1892, p. 1; Ayers, *New South*, 268, 269. Ayres (278) argues that Mississippi and Arkansas are the only two states where a strong farmers' alliance was hindered by disfranchisement. See also letter from Frank Burkitt at his home in Okolona, Mississippi, to a "Walter" (unidentified), July 21, 1894, in John M Stone Papers, Private Manuscripts, Box 1, Mississippi Department of Archives and History. Bradley Bond identifies Walter as Walter Barker, but it is not clear as to why. See Bond, *Mississippi*, 153. Burkitt was a leader among the Democrats; he was a state at-large elector for the presidential election for the Democrats in 1892. See "National Democratic Ticket," *Biloxi Herald*, June 25, 1892, p. 1; "From Mississippi," *Advocate*, August 10, 1890, p. 13.

14. Woodward, *New South*, 259; "Mississippi: What the Democrats of the State Are Doing," *Atlanta Constitution*, July 19, 1892. In addition, see "The Campaign in Mississippi," *Atlanta Constitution*, October 8, 1894; "A Street Fight," *Memphis Daily Appeal*, July 15, 1880, p. 1.

15. Ali, *In the Lion's Mouth*, 85. Ali is quoting a letter from Powell to the *National Economist*.

16. Ibid., 91. Ali suggests that several African American farmers sold their votes in this period, for labor was cheap and times were hard, but he offers no proof. He does point to James Lynch as supporting some white Democrats in the mid-1890s for expediency. See ibid., 121.

17. The story covers the front page of the *Clarion-Ledger*, December 4, 1890. Woodward, *New South*, 70. Woodward includes references to other states that had similar problems at this time. For reference to the pardon, see "Gov. Stone Pardons Col. Hemingway," *Chicago*

Daily Tribune, June 17, 1894. Hemingway was master of the state Grange. See McLemore, *History of Mississippi*, 602. See also *Biloxi Herald*, February 22, 1890, p. 1. The story broke across the country: *St. Paul (Minnesota) Daily Globe*, February 22, 1890, p. 5. See note in the *Lafayette (Louisiana) Advertiser* June 23, 1894, p. 5, which notes the pardon but also states that although Hemingway could not say where the money had gone, few people thought he actually stole the money, and 15,000 people signed a petition for his pardon.

18. One paper explained that the warrants were of the same size, were on the same paper, had the same border, and that the reverse had a similar design of a stag's head. These would "pass for a current $5 bill," and doubtless these warrants were intended to go into general circulation at the time they were issued. *Evening Star* (Washington, DC), July 28, 1894, p. 17. See also "The Mississippi Case," *Atlanta Constitution*, September 14, 1894. Confusion over money and warrants was understandable and had been an issue for some time. See letter from Frank Johnson to John Ayers, *Clarion-Ledger*, March 16, 1893, p. 1.

19. John M. Stone Papers, Private Manuscripts, Box 1, Mississippi Department of Archives and History. An excellent description of the problem can be found in "Hazen Demands Mississippi Script," *Chicago Daily Tribune*, July 16, 1894. See also "Mississippi's New Warrants," *Washington Post*, July 17, 1894.

20. "Mississippi May Decline: A Demand from the Governor to Cease Issuing Certain Warrants," *New York Times*, July 15, 1894. The warrants were to be issued until 1896, with an interest rate of 3 percent per annum; about $200,000 was in circulation at the time of the arrests. The *Chicago Daily Tribune* article noted in the note above gives the interest rate at 2 percent.

21. "For the Arrest of Gov. Stone," *New York Times*, September 11, 1894.

22. Stone Papers, Private Manuscripts. Making sure the case stayed in Mississippi paid off. A grand jury refused to indict the governor and his cabinet, although the US attorney general approved indictment. See *Biloxi Herald*, September 1, 1894, p. 5, and November 17, 1894, p. 5. Corruption issues continued with the next governor, Anselm McLaurin, who some argued was aware of and participated in kickbacks with levee construction. See Kirwan, *Revolt of the Rednecks*, 109, 117.

23. During the Harrison administration, Lynch had been appointed as fourth auditor for the United States, a job that he lost when Cleveland returned to power. A few African American papers thought this an insult to Lynch, but it probably was an indication of a slip in influence. See *Washington Bee*, November 16, 1889, p. 1. See also *Washington Bee*, October 19, 1889.

24. See "Their Day of Freedom," *American Non-Conformist*, January 9, 1896.

25. Lynch was frustrated with both parties, but by 1890 he had no brook at all with Democrats. In a speech in Columbus, Ohio, that year, he expressed the belief that any African American who was a Democrat was untrue to his wife, family, race, and country. See *Washington Bee*, October 4, 1890, p. 2, which is quoting from an article in the *Columbus Evening Post*. The *Post* took exception to the speech. See also "A Proper Solution," *Clarion-Ledger*, January 29, 1891, p. 5. For note of the dispute, see *Washington Bee*, February 15, 1896, p. 2.

26. Hill continued to try a number of vocations: he had been postmaster in Vicksburg, though there was rising opposition to his appointment, especially under Cleveland. "Jim Hill Will Hold the Vicksburg Post Office," *Biloxi Herald*, August 27, 1892, p. 1. He was the "negro

agent" for a "negro display" (unclear as to what that meant); see *Biloxi Herald*, September 21, 1895, p. 8. See also "Mississippi's Proposition," *Atlanta Constitution*, November 24, 1895. The feud continued to split the Republicans in the state. *Colored American*, July 7, 1900, p. 9.

27. Nash was an activist. He threatened suit against insurance companies that declared support for the tariff, arguing that violated state law against trusts and combines. See *St. Paul (Minnesota) Globe*, December 29, 1899, p. 1. He also trained under L.Q.C. Lamar. See subject file (Wiley N. Nash) at the Mississippi Department of Archives and History. The question regarding the poll tax and liens had come up before, under Governor Stone. See *Clarion-Ledger*, March 9, 1893, p. 7, which quotes a letter between then attorney general Frank Johnston and Governor Stone.

28. The subject file at the Mississippi Department of Archives and History does not mention that Nash was attorney general, although he was identified as having studied law under L.Q.C. Lamar, clerked for Judge Hill in the US District Court, was admitted before the US Supreme Court in 1881, and served as district attorney from 1875 to 1880 and in the legislature in 1880. He also had practiced law with Colonel H. L. Muldrow (of the convention) in Starkville. *Clarion-Ledger*, October 24, 1889, p. 4.

29. *W. T. Ratliff v. Ambus Beale*, Mississippi Supreme Court case of 1896, notes and briefs found in the Mississippi Department of Archives and History, pp. 1, 2. These are handwritten briefs.

30. The use of the chancery court here helps to emphasize that this is a test case.

31. *Ratliff v. Beale*, p. 3.

32. Ibid., 5.

33. Ibid., Solomon Calhoon brief. Notes are handwritten and difficult to read.

34. Ibid., Brief in reply for appellee, Supreme Court, October term, 1896.

35. Ibid. For an opposing view regarding frauds, see *Clarion-Ledger*, December 4, 1890, p. 1, in which the editors made the astounding statement that "some have even suggested that when the peaceful methods of fraud are made impossible they may supplant by intimidation all laws intended to secure to the citizen his constitutional rights."

36. *Ratliff v. Beale*, Brief for the appellant by J.A.P. Campbell.

37. McMillen, *Dark Journey*, 73. For a perspective on why the state spent so little on African American education, see "Progress for the Negro," *Clarion-Ledger*, February 16, 1893, pp. 2, 4, 5.

38. McMillen, *Dark Journey*, 23–28, 49. For examples, see "Who Are Our Friends?" *Broad Ax*, October 5, 1898.

39. McMillen, *Dark Journey*, 49.

40. Ibid., 58.

41. Lynch, *Reminiscences*, 358.

42. Robert H. Wiebe, *The Search for Order: 1877–1920* (New York: Hill and Wang, 1967), 117.

43. Lynch, *Reminiscences*, 365–68; see also Robert Terrell Papers, Library of Congress, Reel 1.

44. Lynch, *Reminiscences*, xxvi–xxvii.

45. Ibid., 371–78.

46. Ibid., 381.

47. Ibid., 381–82.
48. Ibid., 384.
49. Ibid., 386.
50. Ibid., 388.
51. Ibid., 390.
52. Ibid., 393.
53. Ibid., 392.
54. Ibid., 397.
55. McMillen, *Dark Journey*, 61. Bruce died shortly thereafter.
56. Lynch, *Reminiscences*, 399–406.
57. McMillen, *Dark Journey*, 60.
58. Lynch, *Reminiscences*, 417.
59. A. E. Patterson. *The Possibilities of the American Negro: With Illustrations and Biographies of Some of the Leading Negroes in America* (Cairo, IL: Cairo Standard Publishing, 1903), 154–59. Jones represented Issaquena County in the Delta.
60. *Strauder v. West Virginia*, 100 US 303 (1879).
61. "Quash" has a specific meaning in legal terms, essentially meaning to void. Because the term is used extensively in the opinions and briefs, I have chosen to retain its usage in this chapter.
62. Benno Schmidt, "Juries, Jurisdiction, and Race Discrimination: The Lost Promise of *Strauder v West Virginia*," *Texas Law Review* 61 (May 1983): 1460–62. For other cases, see *Ex parte v. Virginia*, 100 US 339; *Strauder v. West Virginia*, 100 US 303; *Neal v. Delaware*, 103 US 370.
63. *Charlie Smith v State of Mississippi*, trial minutes, Mississippi Department of Archives and History, and *Smith v. State of Mississippi*, 162 US 592 (1896), on writ of error. Many of the handwritten pages in the archival notebook are unnumbered. Jones noted that in Washington County, the one in the case, had 7,000 African American citizens suitable for jury duty and only 1,500 white citizens. Not one was on the jury rolls. See J. Clay Smith, *Emancipation: The Making of the Black Lawyer, 1844–1944* (Philadelphia: University of Pennsylvania Press, 1993), 293.
64. Brief of evidence can be found in *Smith v. Mississippi*, trial minutes, pp. 40–45, followed by extensive testimony.
65. A. E. Patterson claims that Jones was the first African American to argue before the Court. Patterson, *Possibilities of the American Negro*, 159. See also *Washington Bee*, December 21, 1895, p. 1.
66. *John Gibson v. State of Mississippi* 162 US 565 (1896), on writ of error.
67. Smith, *Emancipation*, 294. The case was *Gibson v. Mississippi*. See *Washington Bee*, December 21, 1895, p. 1.
68. *Gibson v. Mississippi*, trial minutes, Mississippi Department of Archives and History; and Schmidt, "Juries, Jurisdiction, and Race Discrimination," 1462.
69. Hewlett was an outspoken advocate for African American rights in DC, and he eventually became a justice of the peace there. See *Washington Post*, December 7, 1887, p. 8; September 9, 1891, p. 2; August 3, 1902, p. 11; September 7, 1902, p. 9; May 25, 1903, p. 9; and October 16, 1904, p. 11.

70. The details here are important. Stinson was white, and Gibson was black. Knowing the racial attitudes of the all-white jury, the trial minutes include questions by the defense and prosecution attorneys asking jurors if they could arrive at a fair decision in a case such as this. See *Gibson v. Mississippi*, trial minutes, pp. 1–6 and p. 88 for reference to the beating (which is unmentioned in the type-written trial minutes to the Mississippi Supreme Court).

71. Hewlett pointed out that, as in *Smith v. Mississippi*, the numbers involved made the probability of an all-white jury nearly impossible (Washington County had 7,000 African American voters to 1,500 white ones). *Gibson v. Mississippi*, 162.

72. Ibid.

73. Ibid.

74. *John Henry Dixon v. Mississippi*. Mississippi Supreme Court case of 1896, minutes, notes, and briefs found in the Mississippi Department of Archives and History. Testimony is recorded in the notebook of the minutes of the trial, pp. 25–34. Both Dixon and Williams were tried in Greenville, Mississippi. See also Riser, *Defying Disfranchisement*, 63.

75. *Henry Williams v. State of Mississippi*, briefs and minutes of Mississippi Supreme Court records, Mississippi Department of Archives and History, p. 2 in trial minutes (as they were called).

76. Testimony by Theophilus Brown and Ella Hicks in trial minutes (as they were called), pp. 21–29. Under oath, Ella Hicks refers to a previous trial (p. 28), but the specifics are never given. This may have been the inquest referenced on p. 35. Interestingly, Brown claimed Williams lived with Ella because she did his laundry (p. 28).

77. *Williams v. Mississippi*, minutes, 33.

78. Ibid., 35–38.

79. Ibid., 41–46.

80. Ibid., 46, 47. Reference to the state of the stocking was testified on p. 27, but not to the fact that it was where Ella kept her money.

81. Ibid., 49.

82. Ibid., 3.

83. Ibid., 4.

84. Ibid., 5.

85. Ibid.

86. Ibid., 9.

87. Ibid., 12–20.

88. The dates for the hanging differ in the appeal; Jones says December 10. A respite had been granted by the governor for the appeal, but this is the only information about the change in date for execution.

89. Ibid., appeal addressed to Justice Woods for the Mississippi Supreme Court.

90. Ibid., handwritten appeal to the Circuit Court of the United States, Southern District of Mississippi.

91. *Williams v. Mississippi* 170 US 213 (1898). *Williams v. Mississippi*—error to the supreme court of the state of Mississippi, No. 531, argued and submitted March 18, 1898, decided April 25, 1898 (213–25).

92. Ibid., 219.

93. Ibid., 222; Schmidt, "Juries, Jurisdiction, and Race Discrimination," 1467–68.

94. *Williams v. Mississippi*, 222.

95. Ibid., 223.

96. Ibid., 224.

97. Ibid., 225.

98. Schmidt, "Juries, Jurisdiction, and Race Discrimination," 1468–69.

99. See Riser, *Defying Disfranchisement*, 67–69. What more evidence could have been given is problematic, especially since the appeal process in this period rested on procedural issues rather than fact (which would have been covered in the trial).

100. Wiebe, *Search for Order*, 117; Smith, *Emancipation*, 290.

101. *Washington Post*, January 30, 1899, p. 8. Jones continued to be a voice in the Republican Party. *Washington Post*, April 22, 1898, p. 5.

102. *Washington Post*, March 20, 1897, p. 3; January 18, 1899, p. 7; January 19, 1899, p. 7. See *The Colored American*, April 7, 1900, for a photograph of Jones on the front page, noting his appeal regarding the congressional seat. Further information can be found on p. 8 of that issue. There is a reference that Jones was suggested for appointment as an insular judge, but I can find no confirmation that it happened. *The Colored American*, March 8, 1902, p. 1.

103. Smith, Emancipation, 294–95; *Washington Post*, July 14, 1915, p. 14; *Chicago Defender*, July 24, 1915, p. 1; July 25, 1915, p. 4; September 16, 1916, p. 12; *Atlanta Constitution*, March 22, 1922, p. 2.

104. For example, see Malcolm Cook McMillan, *Constitutional Development in Alabama, 1798–1901: A Study in Politics, the Negro, and Sectionalism* (Spartanburg, SC: Reprint Company, 1978), 287–88.

105. William A. Sutherland, *Notes on the Constitution of the United States: Showing the Constitution and Operation of the Constitution as Determined by the Federal Supreme Court and Containing References to Illustrative Cases from the Inferior Federal Courts and State Courts* (New York: Bancroft-Whitney, 1904).

106. Charles Wallace Collins, *Fourteenth Amendment and the States: A Study of the Operation of the Restraint Clauses of Section One of the Fourteenth Amendment to the Constitution of the United States* (Boston: Little, Brown, 1912), 75. He specifically footnotes both *Williams* and *Gibson*. Compare this to Mathews, *Legislative and Judicial History of the Fifteenth Amendment*, 123.

107. J. F. Barbour Jr., "Note and Comment, Constitutional Law—Equal Protection of Laws, Exclusion of Negroes from Jury Service, Effect on Defendant's Right to a New Trial," *Mississippi Law Journal* 8 (1935–1936): 201.

108. Ibid., 204.

109. Herbert Saul Rovner, "The Effect of Racial Discrimination in the Indictment State," *Wyoming Law Journal* 5 (1950): 97–100.

110. *Clarion-Ledger*, February 16, 1893, p. 4, in which the paper suggested lynchings helped to keep down the prison population. "A Negro Fiend Lynched," *Clarion-Ledger*, September 10, 1891, p. 3; Julius E. Thompson, *Lynchings in Mississippi: A History, 1865–1965* (Jefferson, NC: McFarland, 2007), 35. In comparison, the nation had 1,709, so 11 percent of the total in the decade were in Mississippi. During the period 1882–1889, Mississippi had 280 documented lynchings and the nation had 1,216, giving the state a full 23 percent of the national total (p. 20). The numbers slipped even farther down in the first part of the next

decade, to 152; but out of a national total of 904, that gave Mississippi a startling percentage of just under 17 percent (p. 48). See also Doyle, *Faulkner's County*, 323–26, for a disturbing account.

111. See "White Cap Sympathizers Take Possession of the Town," *Clarion-Ledger*, May 11, 1893, p. 1; "White Capism," *Clarion-Ledger*, May 11, 1893, p. 4; "More Whitecaps," *Clarion-Ledger*, 1893, p. 1; Cresswell, *Rednecks*, 58. Cresswell quotes the *Magnolia Gazette* of 1893, which reported a resolution by one of these clubs that directly connected the depression and farmer resentment toward the economic elites of the state. See also Hahn. *Nation under Our Feet*, 424; and William F. Holmes, "Whitecapping: Agrarian Violence in Mississippi, 1902–1906," *Journal of Southern History* 35 (1969): 166.

112. McMillen, *Dark Journey*, 120.

113. Holmes, "Whitecapping," 167; *Mt. Sterling (Kentucky) Advocate*, January 17, 1893, p. 4.

114. Alfred H. Stone, "The Suppression of Lawlessness in the South," *North American Review* (April 1894): 500–506; see also *Washington Post*, April 15, 1894.

115. See chapter 5. During the convention Judge Chrisman proposed a property qualification for voting and he referred to illiterate white voters as "ignoramouses [sic]." This was not a man who had much time for the poor white farmer. For details, see "Judge J. B. Chrisman Is Dead at Canton," *Clarion-Ledger*, February 3, 1910, p. 8.

116. See reports in the *Clarion-Ledger*, May 11, 1893, pp. 3, 4; May 18, 1893, pp. 1, 5; and June 1, 1893, p. 1; Cresswell, *Rednecks*, 60, 61.

117. Ayres, *Promise of the New South*, 156. Compare this to a letter by Jefferson Davis to a paper in Anderson, South Carolina, in which he argued that race riots in the state were rare, but tended to be in areas with *fewer* African Americans than more. He argued that his plantations were in areas where African Americans completely outnumbered whites, but the incidences of violence were nearly unknown. His assertion is counterintuitive, but much research remains to be done on the issue. "Jefferson Davis on Race Riots," *Anderson (South Carolina) Intelligencer*, February 14, 1889.

118. Wharton, *The Negro in Mississippi*, 226.

119. See, for instance, "Rewards for Mississippi Lynchers," *New York Times*, November 27, 1895. Stone offered a $500 reward for their capture. See also editorial, *New York Times*, December 1, 1895. It has long been believed that the turn toward the radical racist position gave permission to the lynchers to behave as they did; the problem with this interpretation is that the number of lynchings fell in the 1890s. See C. Vann Woodward, *The Strange Career of Jim Crow*, 2nd ed. (New York: Oxford University Press, 1966), 67–110.

120. "The Case of Mississippi," *St. Louis Post-Dispatch*, July 23, 1895; "Gov. McLaurin a Candidate," *Washington Post*, January 8, 1896. See "Mississippi Test," *Atlanta Constitution*, January 26, 1894. Stone was not the only one who opposed silver; see *Clarion-Ledger* editions of January 1, 1891, p. 1. This issue had been brewing for a while: "In Mississippi," *Advocate* (Kansas), March 14, 1894, p. 7.

121. Cresswell, *Rednecks*, 63, 64. The old guard had not acquitted themselves well in the early campaigning. Both Lowry and McLaurin announced their candidacies, but both began to accuse each other of drunkenness and using young girls for "immoral purposes." The electorate did not approve. Both men had previously been governor. Lowry's friends had tried to nominate him as ambassador to Mexico under the Cleveland administration. Over

time, Longino suffered accusations that he had African American blood and that he had a brother-in-law who was a Republican (which was true). Kirwan, *Revolt of the Rednecks*, 105, 156. See also Governors' Papers, Robert Lowry, Mississippi Department of Archives and History.

122. "The Register of the Treasury Banqueted by His Friends," *Evening Star* (Washington, DC), May 20, 1898, p. 16. The story is about the celebration of the appointment of Judson Lyons to succeed Bruce when he died. Attendees noted were John Lynch and Cornelius Jones.

123. For noting pride, see "Race Gleanings, an Exclusively Negro Town," *Afro-American*, September 17, 1898, p. 3; "The Business League Progress Is Great," *Afro-American*, August 21, 1909, p. 1; and "Mississippians Attracted to Mound Bayou," *Afro-American*, July 2, 1910, p. 1. "Metropolitan Life," *Salt Lake Herald*, March 27, 1892, p. 10.

Chapter 11. Conclusion

1. Robert Wilson, *Proceedings of the Reunion of the Survivors of the Constitutional Convention of 1890: on the Twentieth Anniversary of the Adoption of the Constitution* (Jackson, MS: Premier Printing, 1910), 7. The original letter from Wilson called for meeting in August, but the group decided that November 1, the date of promulgation, was better. Certainly Mississippi weather in the days before air-conditioning was better in November; see p. 8. See also, "Twenty Years Later," *Clarion-Ledger*, November 3, 1910, p. 4.

2. For lists, see Wilson, *Proceedings*, 9, 10.

3. See Robert E Wilson papers, Mississippi Department of Archives and History, letters from G. W. Dryer, August 8, 1910; George Dillard (n.d.); John H. Reagan (n.d.); John R Baird, April 30, 1910; Frank Burkitt (n.d.); and E. O. Sykes (n.d.).

4. Robert Wilson papers, letter from H. M. Street, October 30, 1910.

5. Robert Wilson papers, letters from R. G. Hudson, October 25, 1910, from Tacoma, Washington, and from J. G. Hamilton, from Pasadena, California (n.d.). Both men were attorneys and still practiced.

6. Robert Wilson papers, letter from Pat Henry, May 14, 1910.

7. Ibid.

8. A good example of this is William Archibald Dunning, *Essays on the Civil War and Reconstruction and Related Topics* (New York: Macmillan, 1898); another example of this genre would be Claude Bowers, *The Tragic Era: The Revolution after Lincoln* (New York: Houghton Mifflin, 1929).

9. Dunbar Rowland, "A Mississippi View of Race Relations in the South," read before the Alumni Association of the University of Mississippi, June 3, 1902 (Jackson, MS: Harmon Publishing, 1903), 3, 4.

10. Ibid., 6–9.

11. Ibid., 10, 11.

12. He gave no numbers here and no reference for this number.

13. Ibid., 12, 13. Compare this with an article in the *Atlanta Constitution* that attributed falling numbers of white voters in Mississippi to apathy. "Too Much Apathy They Say," *Atlanta Constitution*, September 4, 1902.

14. Rowland, "Race Relations," 14, 15.

15. Ibid., 18, 19.

16. "Twenty Years Later," *Clarion-Ledger*, November 3, 1910, p. 4. In this column the editors preferred a euphemism: "chief political features of this constitution legally eliminated ignorance from the body politic."

17. Bettersworth, *Mississippi*, 379. According to Adam Faircloth, following disfranchisement African American voting strength fell from 190,000 to 8,000 in two years. See Adam Faircloth, *Better Day Coming: Blacks and Equality 1890–2000* (New York: Viking Press 2001), 6. See also Wharton, *The Negro in Mississippi*, for other references.

18. Kornbluh, *Why America Stopped Voting*, 15. For an in-depth account of northern voting during this period, see Michael McGerr, *The Decline of Popular Politics: The American North 1865–1928* (New York: Oxford University Press, 1988).

19. Kornbluh, *Why America Stopped Voting*, 45.

20. Ibid., 45.

21. Barley and Graham, *Southern Politics*, 8.

22. Bettersworth, *Mississippi*, 379.

23. Ibid., 381.

24. Kirwan, *Revolt of the Rednecks*, 132. For another state's take on the law, see "The Mississippi Primary," *Times Dispatch* (Richmond, Virginia), July 7, 1903, p. 4. The state had been toying with the idea for years. See "Mississippi Politics," *Atlanta Constitution*, February 17, 1895.

25. Kirwan, *Revolt of the Rednecks*, 125, 126.

26. Bettersworth, *Mississippi*, 385. The primary quickly became a *white* primary, which was seen only in the South. It did not start out that way. This had been debated for some years, for the constitution had given the legislature the power to create a primary. See Kirwan, *Revolt of the Rednecks*, 115, 123.

27. Bartley and Graham, *Southern Politics*, 8. In fact, the general election became inconsequential. See Kirwan, *Revolt of the Rednecks*, 131.

28. Kirwan, *Revolt of the Rednecks*, 143.

29. Bond, *Political Culture*, 290–95.

30. Bettersworth, *Mississippi*, 394–96.

31. Holmes, *White Chief*, 38, particularly 58–62. Holmes identifies an unreconstructed rebel who influenced Vardaman. See also Cresswell, *Rednecks*, 193.

32. "Governor of Mississippi Urges Voters to Stop Educating Negro Children," *Daily Press* (Newport News, Virginia), August 5, 1906, p. 1.

33. "Governor Vardaman," *Hawaiian Star*, April 28, 1905, 2nd ed., p. 6. Compare this to a letter from a supporter from South Carolina who argued that Vardaman saw little use in educating African Americans in the classics, but an industrial education was more suitable. "Governor Vardaman's Veto," *Watchman and Southron* (Sumter, South Carolina), April 13, 1904, p. 4; Cresswell, *Rednecks*, 198.

34. "Against Negro Education," *Seattle Republican*, January 22, 1904, p. 6; "Fifteenth Amendment Doomed by Vardaman," *Arizona Republican*, October 19, 1905, p. 1; Kirwan, *Revolt of the Rednecks*, 147.

35. Letter to the Mississippi House of Representatives, March 14, 1904, Vardaman papers, Mississippi Department of Archives and History.

36. Holmes, *White Chief*, 36. The expressed fear was miscegenation, but neither he nor the others mention white men with black women. Holmes acknowledges this paradox. See also *Biloxi Daily Herald*, January 3, 1899.

37. Thompson, *Lynchings in Mississippi*. Another historian puts the number of lynchings during the Vardaman years at 92. This was bad enough, but in the years between 1889 and 1945 Mississippi accounted for 476 verified lynchings, which was a full 13 percent of the total in America. McMillen, *Dark Journey*, 229–31. This issue of rape connected strongly to white supremacy arguments, though less publicly acknowledged in Mississippi than in other states. See Glenda Elizabeth Gilmore, *Gender and Jim Crow: Women and the Politics of White Supremacy in North Carolina, 1896–1920* (Chapel Hill: University of North Carolina Press, 1996), 67–73.

38. McLemore, *History of Mississippi*, 42–44. See also Ayers, *Promise of the New South*, 412.

39. One newspaper, the *Herald* (Vicksburg), that supported Vardaman claimed the problems had nothing to do with Vardaman, but had erupted because Longino had failed to control violence and African Americans. Kirwan, *Revolt of the Rednecks*, 154. For comparison, see Holmes, "Whitecapping," 174. "Judge F. A. Critz Runs for Office," *Atlanta Constitution*, September 15, 1902.

40. Holmes, "Whitecapping," 168. No apostrophe given on "Farmers." How this group might have been related to the Farmers' Alliance is unknown.

41. Holmes, *White Chief*, 135. The resurgence of whitecapping actually started in 1902, but came to notice in its virulence in 1904. Verification of whitecapping atrocities is scanty in Mississippi newspapers, but is strongly evident in papers in other states.

42. Holmes, "Whitecapping," 170, Cresswell, *Rednecks*, 199.

43. Holmes, "Whitecapping," 175.

44. A shortage of labor had previously galvanized Governors Stone and Longino. See ibid., 172.

45. See Vardaman papers. Copies of his letters as governor on onionskin, Mississippi Department of Archives and History. Letters to the agency regarding Hoyt and the subsequent bills can be found from May 4, 1904; July 13, 1904; October 14, 1904; February 24, 1905; and March 27, 1905. See Holmes, "Whitecapping," 177–84, for a complete narrative.

46. Holmes, *White Chief*, 138–42. Kirwan adds a reference to a similar situation in Washington County, but it is not clear whether he is really referring to this situation. Kirwan, *Revolt of the Rednecks*, 163.

47. "Nine Men Dead in Race Riots: Mississippi Mob Still Slaying Negroes," *Afro-American*, December 29, 1906, p. 2. See also selections in *Times Dispatch* (Richmond, Virginia), December 26, 1906, p. 1; and *Minneapolis (Minnesota) Journal*, December 26, 1906. For references to Vardaman's protection of prisoners under threat of lynching, see letters in the Vardaman papers: letter to Hon. Sam Cook, Clarksdale, Mississippi, March 31, 1904; letter to W. D. Beecham, Felder, Mississippi, May 19, 1905; letter to Messrs. Corely and Sharbrough, Collins, Mississippi, April 5, 1906; letter to John F. Bush, Vicksburg, Mississippi, May 29, 1906 (which notes copies sent to twenty state officials and supreme court judges).

48. "Where at Least Much of the Blame Rests," *Afro-American*, January 5, 1907, p. 4, which the editors claim is quoting from the *Atlanta Constitution*. Compare this to "The Brutal White," *Appeal*, April 9, 1904, p. 2.

49. Richardson, *Death of Reconstruction*, 222, 223.

50. McMillen, *Dark Journey*, 294.

51. Kirwan argues that Vardaman's race-baiting was not really so bad and that his work on behalf of the poor in the state deserves credit rather than censure. Kirwan, *Revolt of the Rednecks*, 163.

52. Letter to Judge J. R. Enochs of Brandon, Mississippi, May 16, 1905, in Vardaman papers. In another incident Vardaman sent a special prosecutor to help with a case against men charged with inhuman treatment of a convict. Letter to W. D. Beacham, Felder, Mississippi, May 19, 1905.

53. There were other areas he tried to improve as well, for this is only a short list. See Kirwan, *Revolt of the Rednecks*, 164–76. Also Cooper and Terrill, *American South*, 548.

54. Tisdall, "Campaign for the Disfranchisement of Negroes," 219–33.

55. McLemore, *Mississippi*, 285, 286. Bolivar County had no gravel roads until 1914, and grading for dirt roads by the county only began in 1910. See Sellers, *Bolivar County*, 64.

56. The 1910 census reported the illiteracy rate among African Americans in Mississippi had fallen from 49.1 percent in 1900 to 33 percent in 1910. Among white children, the census reported an illiteracy rate of only 5.4 percent in 1910, compared to 8.1 percent in 1900. *Thirteenth Census*, 238. Cresswell, *Rednecks*, 189.

57. Kirwan, *Revolt of the Rednecks*, 137. Most rural areas did not even have a high school, but that was true of much of the nation at the turn of the twentieth century.

58. What triggered the issue, though, was the realization that African American children dropped out of school earlier than white children. That meant black counties received more money for schools that would be dedicated to the remaining white children. Governor Longino suggested that state money be allocated to enrolled students to make to make the system more fair. Further complicating the problem was that school attendance was improving across the board, though it ranged depending on the age of children. See *Thirteenth Census*, 238; Kirwan, *Revolt of the Rednecks*, 138–40.

59. A census chart showed that in 1900 Mississippi had only forty-three power stations. The state produced only 7,660 total horsepower from engines and water and 6,841 in dynamos. Compare that to 21,305 and 17,950, respectively, for South Carolina the same year. Department of the Interior, *Abstract of the Twelfth Census*, 413.

60. For example, see Gordon Martin, *Count Them One by One: Black Mississippians Fighting for the Right to Vote* (Jackson: University Press of Mississippi, 2010), 8. Martin quotes the *Chicago Defender*, in which the editors referred to Mississippi as "the most brutal community in history."

61. "South Loses in House," *New York Daily Tribune*, January 14, 1908; "Williams and Vardaman," *Times Dispatch* (Richmond) July 9, 1907, p. 6; "Fifteenth Amendment Doomed by Vardaman," *Arizona Republican*, October 19, 1905, p. 1; "Satan's State," *Cleveland Gazette*, June 16, 1894, p. 11; "Advocates Repeal of the Fifteenth Amendment," *Bisbee Daily Review*, October 19, 1906. For analysis of this problem, see James W. Silver, "Mississippi: The Closed Society," *Journal of Southern History* 30 (1964): 3–34, especially 3 and 4.

62. Robert Wilson papers, see original letter from Robert Wilson, indicating an August event, April 28, 1910; letter from E. J. Marett, August 10, 1910, asking why; and Wilson, *Proceedings*. 8. See also "Reunion of the Members of the Convention of 1890," *Laurel (Mississippi) Chronicle*, July 8, 1910.

63. "Mississippi Awards Her New Capitol Contract," *Atlanta Constitution*, December 14, 1900. The old building was ignored for a while, until the women of the state began a movement to refurbish it and repair its roof. See a little pamphlet issued and written by Eron Opha Moore Rowland, "An Appeal to the Legislature of the State of Mississippi for the Preservation of the Old State House" (Jackson, MS: Tucker Printing House, 1914). A copy of this pamphlet can be found at the Mississippi Department of Archives and History.

64. McLemore, *Mississippi*, 31, 32; Bettersworth, *Mississippi*, 390, 391. Sadly, even here the issues of corruption remained. Governor Longino issued a warrant for the arrest of the contractor (J. E. Gibson) of the new capitol on charges of bribery. See Kirwan, *Revolt of the Rednecks*, 142.

65. Some of the lightbulbs are still the originals.

66. Robert Wilson papers, letter from R. F. Abbey, April 30, 1910, in which he suggested a dinner at the Edwards not to cost over $5 to $10 a plate. That price would have been rather large for the time and place.

67. Wilson, *Proceedings*, 12. Dabney gave specific numbers on p. 14.

68. Ibid., 13.

69. Ibid., 14.

70. Senator Money also agreed with this conclusion. See "Disfranchisement in Mississippi," *Atlanta Constitution*, December 24, 1905.

71. Wilson, *Proceedings*, 16, 17.

72. Ibid., 17.

73. Ibid., 19.

74. Ibid., 10.

75. Letter from Henry Downing to Booker T. Washington, September 27, 1890, Booker T. Washington Papers. Downing was the president and manager of the United States African News Company in New York.

76. Norrell, *Up From History*, 417.

77. *Washington Bee*, March 8, 1902, p. 1.

78. For an example of white men using Montgomery for their own purposes, see "Who Are Our Friends?" *Broad Ax*, October 5, 1898.

79. Letter from Isaiah Montgomery in Robert E. Wilson papers, Mississippi Department of Archives and History. The letter refers to the reunion: "I heartily coincide with the movement (reunion)."

80. "Paper Read by Isaiah Montgomery," Wilson, *Proceedings*, 16–20.

81. *World's Work*, July 14, 1907. Redding connects this with Walter Sillers Sr., a friend of Montgomery's and his lawyer. See Redding, *Lonesome Road*, 72. In addition, Redding also questions why Montgomery went to the reunion, but gave no satisfactory answer (99).

82. McMillen, *Dark Journey*, 300–392.

83. Ibid., 298.

84. Johnson, "Suffrage and Reconstruction," 213.

85. See *Salt Lake City Herald*, March 27, 1892, p. 10, in which Montgomery referred to his hope that the "better minds in the South" would push for change. The editors noted Montgomery saw the irony in the lynching of black people as a barbaric way of treating those viewed to be barbarians.

86. See Isaiah Montgomery's letter to Booker T. Washington, September 6, 1904, and letter from Washington to Montgomery, September 14, 1904. Both refer to the whitecapping problem in Mississippi under Governor Vardaman. See Booker T. Washington Papers, Vol. 8, pp. 61, 69. In addition, see McMillen, *Dark Journey*, 299, which quotes Montgomery as stating that he has to keep a low profile and not get involved.

87. "Opinions Worthwhile," *Greenville Weekly Democrat*, November 10, 1910, p. 1.

88. "The Caucus Vote," *Clarion-Ledger*, January 13, 1910, p. 4. See notice of McLaurin's death on the same page. See also Cresswell, *Rednecks*, 202.

89. "Somewhat Slabberdastical," *Clarion-Ledger*, March 3, 1910, p. 4.

90. "Caucus Drawing Along," *Clarion-Ledger*, January 20, 1910, p. 4.

91. "Opinions Worth While," *Greenville Democrat*, November 10, 1910, p. 1.

92. "Where at Least Much of the Blame Rests," *Afro-American*, January 5, 1907, p. 4, which is quoting from the *Atlanta Constitution* (emphasis added). Compare this to "The Brutal White," *Appeal*, April 9, 1904, p. 2.

Bibliography

Ali, Omar H. *In the Lion's Mouth: Black Populism in the New South, 1886–1900.* Jackson: University Press of Mississippi, 2010.
Ames, Blanche. *Adelbert Ames, 1835–1933.* New York: Argosy-Antiquarian, 1964.
Ashworth, John. *Slavery Capitalism, and Politics in the Antebellum Republic.* Vol. 1, *Commerce and Compromise, 1820–1850.* Cambridge: Cambridge University Press, 1995.
Ayers, Edward L. *The Promise of the New South: Life after Reconstruction.* New York: Oxford University Press, 1992.
Barley, Numan, and Hugh D. Graham. *Southern Politics and the Second Reconstruction.* Baltimore: Johns Hopkins University Press, 1975.
Barry, John. *Rising Tide: The Great Mississippi Flood of 1927 and How It Changed America.* New York: Simon and Schuster, 1997.
Berlin, Ira. *Slaves without Masters: The Free Negro in the Antebellum South.* New York: New Press, 1974.
Berlin, Ira, et al. *Slaves No More: Three Essays on Emancipation and the Civil War.* Cambridge: Cambridge University Press, 1992.
Bettersworth, John Knox. *Mississippi: A History.* Austin, TX: Steck, 1959.
Blackmon, Douglas. *Slavery by Another Name: The Re-enslavement of Black Americans from the Civil War to World War II.* New York: Anchor, 2009.
Bond, Bradley G. *Political Culture in the Nineteenth Century South: Mississippi 1830–1900.* Baton Rouge: Louisiana State University Press, 1995.
———. *Mississippi: A Documentary History.* Jackson: University Press of Mississippi, 2003.
Bowers, Claude. *The Tragic Era: Revolution after Lincoln.* New York: Houghton, Mifflin, 1929.
Buck, Paul H. *The Road to Reunion: 1865–1900.* Boston: Little, Brown, 1937.
Burton, Vernon. *The Age of Lincoln.* New York: Hill and Wang, 2007.
Calhoun, Charles W. *Conceiving a New Republic: The Republican Party and the Southern Question, 1869–1900.* Lawrence: University Press of Kansas, 2006.
Campbell, J.A.P. *The Revised Code of the Statute Laws of the State of Mississippi.* Jackson, MS: J. L. Power, State Printer, 1880.
Cobb, James C. *The Most Southern Place on Earth: The Mississippi Delta and the Roots of Regional Identity.* New York: Oxford University Press, 1992.
———. *Away Down South: A History of Southern Identity.* New York: Oxford University Press, 2005.

Collins, Charles Wallace. *Fourteenth Amendment and the States: A Study of the Operation of the Restraint Clauses of Section One of the Fourteenth Amendment to the Constitution of the United States.* Boston: Little Brown, 1912.

Cooper, William J., Jr., and Thomas E. Terrill. *The American South: A History.* 2nd ed. New York: McGraw Hill, 1996.

Cresswell, Stephen. *Mormons & Cowboys, Moonshiners & Klansmen: Federal Law Enforcement in the South & West, 1870–1893.* Tuscaloosa: University of Alabama Press, 1991.

———. *Multiparty Politics in Mississippi, 1877–1902.* Jackson: University Press of Mississippi, 1995.

———. *Rednecks, Redeemers, and Race: Mississippi after Reconstruction 1877–1917.* Jackson: University Press of Mississippi, 2006.

Currie, James T. *Enclave: Vicksburg and Her Plantations, 1863–1870.* Jackson: University Press of Mississippi, 1980.

Doyle, Don. *Faulkner's County: The Historical Roots of Yoknapatawpha.* Chapel Hill: University of North Carolina Press, 2001.

Dun and Bradstreet & Co. *Reference Book: And Key Containing Ratings of Merchants, Manufacturers and Traders Generally.* New York: R. G. Dun, 1912.

Dunning, William Archibald. *Reconstruction, Political and Economic, 1865–1877.* New York: Harper Brothers, 1907.

Dustin, Alfred M., ed. *Crusade for Justice: Autobiography of Ida B. Wells.* Chicago: University of Chicago Press, 1970.

DuToit, Brian M. *Configurations of Cultural Continuity.* Rotterdam, Netherlands: AA Balkema, 1976.

Eckford, Lucy Rice. "The Personnel and Proceedings of the Mississippi Constitutional Convention of 1890." Master's thesis, State College, Mississippi (now Mississippi State), 1935.

Elkins, Stanley M. *Slavery: A Problem in American Institutional and Intellectual Life.* Chicago: University of Chicago Press, 1976.

Ethridge, George H. *Mississippi Constitutions.* Jackson, MS: Tucker Printing, 1928.

Everett, Frank E. *Brierfield: Plantation Home of Jefferson Davis.* Hattiesburg: University and College Press of Mississippi, 1971.

Faircloth, Adam. *Better Day Coming: Blacks and Equality 1890–2000.* New York: Viking Press, 2001.

Farrell, Betty G. *Elite Families: Class and Power in Nineteenth Century Boston.* Albany: State University of New York Press, 1993.

Field, David Dudley. *The Electoral Votes of 1876: Who Should Count Them, What Should Be Counted, and the Remedy for a Wrong Count.* New York: D. Appleton, 1876.

Finkelman, Paul. *Dred Scott v Sanford: A Brief History with Documents.* Boston: Bedford Series, 1997.

Foner, Eric. *A Short History of Reconstruction, 1863–1877.* New York: Harper and Row, 1990.

Foner, Eric, and Joshua Brown. *Forever Free: The Story of Emancipation and Reconstruction.* New York: Alfred A. Knopf, 2005.

Ford, Lacy. *Deliver Us from Evil: The Slavery Question in the Old South.* New York: Oxford University Press, 2009.

Franklin, John Hope. *Reconstruction: After the Civil War.* Chicago: University of Chicago Press, 1961.

Garner, James W. *Reconstruction in Mississippi.* Reprint, Baton Rouge: Louisiana State University Press, 1968.

Genovese, Eugene. *Roll Jordan Roll: The World the Slaves Made.* New York: Pantheon Books, 1974.

Giggie, John M. *After Redemption, Jim Crow and the Transformation of African-American Religion in the Delta 1875–1915.* New York: Oxford University Press, 2008.

Gluckman, Max, ed. *The Allocation of Responsibility.* Manchester: Manchester University Press, 1972.

Goodwyn, Lawrence. *Democratic Promise: The Populist Moment in America.* New York: Oxford University Press, 1976.

Graham, Lawrence Otis. *Our Kind of People: Inside America's Black Upper Class.* New York: Harper Collins, 1999

———. *The Senator and the Socialite: The True Story of America's First Black Dynasty.* New York: Harper Collins, 2006.

Grantham, Dewey W. *The South in Modern America: A Region at Odds.* New York: Harper Perennial, 1995.

Greenberg, Kenneth. *Honor & Slavery.* Princeton, NJ: Princeton University Press, 1996.

Greenwood, Janette Thomas. *Bittersweet Legacy: The Black and White "Better Classes" in Charlotte, 1850–1910.* Chapel Hill: University of North Carolina Press, 1994.

Guide to U.S. Elections. Vol. 1. 6th ed. Washington, DC: CQ Press, a division of SAGE, 2010.

Hahn, Steven. *A Nation under Our Feet: Black Political Struggles in the Rural South from Slavery to the Great Migration.* Cambridge, MA: Belknap Press of Harvard University Press, 2003.

———. *The Roots of Southern Populism: Yeoman Farmers and the Transformation of the Georgia Upcountry, 1850–1890.* New York: Oxford University Press, 2006.

Hall, Kermit L., et al., eds. *Oxford Companion to the Supreme Court of the United States.* New York: Oxford University Press, 1992.

Hall, Robert, and Carol B. Stack, eds. *Holding Onto the Land and the Lord: Kinship, Ritual, Land Tenure, and Social Policy in the Rural South.* Athens: University of Georgia Press, 1982.

Harris, William C. *The Day of the Carpetbagger: Republican Reconstruction in Mississippi.* Baton Rouge: Louisiana State University Press, 1979.

Hathorn, Guy B. "Suffrage, Apportionment, and Elections in the Mississippi Constitutional Convention of 1890." Master's thesis, University of Mississippi, 1942.

Herbert, H. A. *Why the Solid South?* Baltimore: R. H. Woodward, 1890.

Hermann, Janet Sharp. *The Pursuit of a Dream.* New York: Oxford University Press, 1981.

Hofstadter, Richard. *Social Darwinism in American Thought.* Reprint, New York: Beacon Press, 1992.

Holden, Matthew, Jr., ed., *"What Answer?" Speech in Support of the Franchise Committee Report, Mississippi Constitutional Convention, 1890.* Charlottesville, VA: Isaiah T. Montgomery Project, 2004.

Holmes, William F. *The White Chief: James Kimble Vardaman*. Baton Rouge: Louisiana State University Press, 1970.
Hughes, Thomas. *GTT Gone to Texas: Letters from Our Boys*. London: McMillan Press, 1884.
Jackson, Maurice Elizabeth. "Mound Bayou: A Study in Social Development." Master's thesis, University of Alabama, 1937.
Journal of the Proceedings of the Constitutional Convention of the State of Mississippi. Jackson, MS: E. L. Martin, printer to the Convention, 1890.
Kantrowitz, Stephen. *More Than Freedom: Fighting for Black Citizenship in a White Republic 1829–1889*. New York: Penguin Press, 2012.
Kasson, John F. *Rudeness & Civility: Manners in Nineteenth Century Urban America*. New York: Hill and Wang, 1990.
Key, V. O. *Southern Politics in State and Nation*. New York: Albert A. Knopf, 1949.
Kirwan, Albert D. *Revolt of the Rednecks: Mississippi Politics, 1876–1925*. Lexington: University of Kentucky Press, 1951.
Kornbluh, Mark Lawrence. *Why America Stopped Voting: The Decline of Participatory Democracy and the Emergence of Modern American Politics*. New York: New York University Press, 2000.
Kousser, J. Morgan. *The Shaping of Southern Politics: Suffrage Restriction and the Establishment of the One-Party South*. Chapel Hill: University of North Carolina Press, 1974.
Kousser, J. Morgan, and James M. McPherson. *Region, Race, and Reconstruction: Essays in Honor of C. Vann Woodward*. New York: Oxford University Press, 1982.
Lemann, Nicholas. *Redemption: The Last Battle of the Civil War*. New York: Farrar, Strauss and Giroux, 2006.
Loewen, James. W. *The Mississippi Chinese*. Cambridge, MA: Harvard University Press, 1971.
Lynch, James D. *Kemper County Vindicated and a Peep at Radical Rule in Mississippi*. New York: E. J. Hale & Son, 1879; reprint, New York: Negro Universities Press, 1969.
Lynch, John R. *Reminiscences of an Active Life: The Autobiography of John R. Lynch*. Ed. John Hope Franklin. Chicago: University of Chicago Press, 1970.
Martin, Gordon. *Count Them One by One: Black Mississippians Fighting for the Right to Vote*. Jackson: University Press of Mississippi, 2010.
Mayes, Edward. *L.Q.C. Lamar: His Life, Times, and Speeches, 1825–1893*. Nashville, TN: Methodist Episcopal Church, 1896.
McLemore, Richard Aubrey, ed. *A History of Mississippi*. Hattiesburg: University and College Press of Mississippi, 1973.
McMath, Robert, Jr. *Populist Vanguard: A History of the Southern Farmers' Alliance*. Chapel Hill: University of North Carolina Press, 1975.
McMillen, Neil R. *Dark Journey: Black Mississippians in the Age of Jim Crow*. Chicago: University of Illinois Press, 1990.
McPherson, James. *Battle Cry of Freedom*. New York: Oxford University Press, 1988.
Meier, August. *Negro Thought in America, 1880–1915*. Ann Arbor: University of Michigan Press, 1963.
Miller, Mary Carol. *Lost Landmarks of Mississippi*. Jackson: University Press of Mississippi, 2002.

Money, Hernando. "Election of Senators by Direct Vote." Washington, DC: Senate, Government Printing Office, April 11, 1902.
Montgomery, Isaiah T. Autobiographical Notes, folder at Mississippi Department of Archives and History.
Morgan, W. Scott. *History of the Wheel and Alliance and Impending Revolution*. St. Louis: C. B. Woodward, 1891.
Newby, I. A. *Plain Folk in the New South: Social Change and Cultural Persistence, 1880–1915*. Baton Rouge: Louisiana State University Press, 1989.
Norrell, Robert. *Up from History: The Life of Booker T. Washington*. Cambridge, MA: Belknap Press of Harvard University Press, 2009.
Nugent, Walter. *Structures of American Social History*. Bloomington: Indiana University Press, 1981.
———. *Into the West: The Story of Its People*. New York: Alfred A. Knopf, 1997.
Oakes, James. *The Ruling Race: A History of American Slaveholders*. London: W. W. Norton, 1998.
Onuf, Peter. *Statehood and Union*. Bloomington: Indiana University Press, 1987.
Patterson, A. E. *The Possibilities of the American Negro: With Illustrations and Biographies of Some of the Leading Negroes in America*. Cairo, IL: Cairo Standard Publishing, 1903.
Perman, Michael. *Struggle for Mastery: Disfranchisement in the South 1888–1908*. Chapel Hill: University of North Carolina Press, 2001.
Phillips, Ulrich Bonnell. *Life and Labor in the Old South*. Reprint, Boston: Little, Brown, 1963.
Proceedings of a Reunion of the Surviving Members of the Constitutional Convention of 1890. Jackson, MS: Premier Printing, 1910.
Redding, Saunders. *The Lonesome Road: The Story of the Negro's Part in America*. New York: Doubleday, 1958.
Rehnquist, William H. *Centennial Crisis: The Disputed Election of 1876*. New York: Alfred A. Knopf, 2004.
Richardson, Heather Cox. *The Death of Reconstruction: Race, Labor, and Politics in the Post–Civil War North, 1865–1901*. Cambridge, MA: Harvard University Press, 2001.
Riser, R. Volney. *Defying Disfranchisement: Black Voting Rights Activism in the Jim Crow South, 1890–1908*. Baton Rouge: Louisiana State University Press, 2010.
Rowland, Dunbar. *History of Mississippi: The Heart of the South*. Chicago: S. J. Publishing, 1925.
———. *Courts, Judges, and Lawyers of Mississippi, 1798–1935*. Jackson, MS: Press of Hederman Brothers, 1935.
Rubin, Richard. *Confederacy of Silence: A True Tale of the New Old South*. New York: Atria Books, 2002.
Rusk, Jerrold G. *A Statistical History of the American Electorate*. Washington, DC: CQ Press, a division of the Congressional Quarterly, 2001.
Sansing, David G., and Carroll Waller. *A History of the Mississippi Governor's Mansion*. Jackson: University Press of Mississippi, 1975.
Sewell, George Alexander. *Mississippi Black History Makers*. Jackson: University Press of Mississippi, 1977.

Sewell, George Alexander, and Margaret L. Dwight. *Mississippi Black History Makers*. Jackson: University Press of Mississippi, 1984.
Shepperd., Gladys B. "The Montgomery Saga, From Slavery to Black Power." Manuscript in Ben Montgomery Papers, Library of Congress.
Sillers, Florence Warfield (Wirt Williams edited the DAR compilation). *History of Bolivar County, Mississippi: Its Creation, Pioneer Days and Progress in the Heart of the Mississippi Delta*. 1948. Reprint, Spartanburg, SC: Reprint Company, 1976.
Silver, David Mark. "In the Eye of the Storm: Isaiah T. Montgomery and the Plight of Black Mississippians, 1847–1924." Honors thesis, Amherst College, 1993.
Simkins, Francis Butler, and Robert Hilliard Woody. *South Carolina during Reconstruction*. Chapel Hill: University of North Carolina Press, 1932.
Skates, John Ray. *Mississippi: A Bicentennial History*. New York: W. W. Norton, 1979.
Smith, J. Clay. *Emancipation: The Making of the Black Lawyer, 1844–1944*. Philadelphia: University of Pennsylvania Press, 1993.
Smith, Timothy B. *J. Z. George: Mississippi's Great Commoner*. Jackson: University Press of Mississippi, 2012.
Span, Christopher. *From Cotton Field to Schoolhouse: African-American Education in Mississippi, 1862–1875*. Chapel Hill: University of North Carolina Press, 2009.
Stamp, Kenneth M. *The Era of Reconstruction, 1865–1877*. New York: Alfred Knopf, 1966.
Summers, Mark Walgreen. *Era of Good Stealings*. New York: Oxford University Press, 1993.
Sutherland, William A. *Notes on the Constitution of the United States: Showing the Constitution and Operation of the Constitution as Determined by the Federal Supreme Court and Containing References to Illustrative Cases from the Inferior Federal Courts and State Courts*. New York: Bancroft-Whitney, 1904.
Thompson, Julius E. *Lynchings in Mississippi, a History, 1865–1965*. Jefferson, NC: McFarland, 2007.
Waldrop, Christopher, and Donald G. Nieman. *Local Matters: Race, Crime, & Justice in the Nineteenth Century South*. Athens: University of Georgia Press, 2001.
Washington, Booker T. *Up from Slavery: With Related Documents*. Ed. W. Fitzhugh Brundage. Boston: Bedford/St. Martin's Press, 2003.
Washington, Booker T., L. R. Harlan, and R. Smock. *The Booker T. Washington Papers*. Urbana: University of Illinois Press, 1972.
Wayne, Michael Stuart. "Ante-Bellum Planters in the Post-Bellum South: The Natchez District, 1860–1880." PhD diss., Yale University, 1979.
Wells, James B. *The Chisolm Massacre: A Picture of "Home Rule" in Mississippi*. Washington, DC: Chisholm Monument Association, 1878.
Wharton, Vernon. *The Negro in Mississippi: 1865–1890*. Reprint, New York: Greenwood Press, 1984.
Wheeler, Marjorie Spruill. *New Women of the New South: The Leaders of the Woman Suffrage Movement in the Southern States*. New York: Oxford University Press, 1993.
Whitfield, A. H., et al. *The Mississippi Code of 1906 of the Public Statute Laws of the State of Mississippi*. Nashville, TN: Brandon Printing, 1906.
Wiebe, Robert H. *The Search for Order: 1877–1920*. New York: Hill and Wang, 1967.

Wilentz Sean. *The Rise of American Democracy: Jefferson to Lincoln* (abridged college edition). New York: W. W. Norton, 2009.
Williamson, Joel. *The Crucible of Race: Black-White Relations in the American South since Emancipation.* New York: Oxford University Press, 1984.
Willis, John C. *Forgotten Time: The Yazoo-Mississippi Delta after the Civil War.* Charlottesville: University Press of Virginia, 2000.
Wilson, Robert. *Proceedings of the Reunion of the Survivors of the Constitutional Convention of 1890: On the Twentieth Anniversary of the Adoption of the Constitution.* Jackson, MS: Premier Printing, 1910.
Winkle, John W. *The Mississippi State Constitution: A Reference Guide.* Westport, CT: Greenwood Press, 1993.
Wood, Gordon. *The Radicalism of the American Revolution.* New York: Vintage Books, 1991.
Woodward, C. Vann. *Origins of the New South: 1877-1913.* Baton Rouge: Louisiana State University Press, 1951.
———. *The Strange Career of Jim Crow.* 2nd ed. New York: Oxford University Press, 1966.

Articles and Chapters in Books

Anderson, Helen Craft. "A Chapter in the Yellow Fever Epidemic of 1878." *Publications of the Mississippi Historical Society* 10 (1909): 223–56.
Barbour, J. F., Jr. "Note and Comment, Constitutional Law–Equal Protection of Laws, Exclusion of Negroes from Jury Service, Effect on Defendant's Right to a New Trial." *Mississippi Law Journal* 8 (1935-1936): 196–204.
Binney, Charles Chauncey. "American Secret Ballot Decisions." *American Law Register and Review* 41 (February 1893): 101–12.
Braden, W. H. "Reconstruction in Lee County." *Publications of the Mississippi Historical Society* 10 (1909): 135–46.
Bowman, Robert. "Reconstruction in Yazoo County." *Publications of the Mississippi Historical Society* 7 (1903): 115–30.
Butts, Alfred Benjamin. "Public Education." *Mississippi Historical Society Centenary Series* 3 (1919): 20–156.
Calhoon, S. S. "The Causes and Events That Led to the Calling of the Constitutional Convention of 1890." *Publications of the Mississippi Historical Society* 6 (1902): 105–10.
Coleman, Edward Clarke. "Reconstruction in Attala County." *Publications of the Mississippi Historical Society* 10 (1909): 147–61.
Coleman, James P. "The Origin of the Constitution of 1890." *Journal of Mississippi History* 19, no. 2 (April 1957): 69–92.
Day, Kay Young. "Kinship in a Changing Economy: A View from the Sea Islands." In *Holding Onto the Land and the Lord: Kinship, Ritual, Land Tenure and Social Policy in the Rural South*, ed. Robert Hall and Carol B. Stack, 11–24. Athens: University of Georgia Press, 1982.
Fite, Gilbert. "Southern Agriculture since the Civil War: An Overview." *Agricultural History* 53 (1979): 3–21.

Fuller, Paul G. "E. P. Thompson and American History: A Retrospective View." *History Teacher* 28, no. 1 (1994): 31–36.
Garner, James W. "The Senatorial Career of J. Z. George." *Publications of the Mississippi Historical Society* 7 (1903): 245–62.
Halsell, Willie D. "Republican Factionalism in Mississippi, 1882–1884." *Journal of Southern History* 7 (1941): 84–101
———. "Chalmers and Mahoneism in Mississippi." *Journal of Southern History* 10 (1944): 37–58.
———. "Bourbon Period in Mississippi Politics, 1875–1890." *Journal of Southern History* 11 (1945): 519–37.
Hardy, W. H. "Recollections of Reconstruction in East and Southeast Mississippi." *Publications of the Mississippi Historical Society* 7 (1903): 199–215.
Hill, George E. "The Secret Ballot." *Yale Law Journal* 1 (October 1891): 26–29.
Holmes, William F. "The Leflore County Massacre and the Demise of the Colored Farmers' Alliance." 34 *Phylon* (1973): 267–74.
———. "Whitecapping: Agrarian Violence in Mississippi, 1902–1906." *Journal of Southern History* 35 (May 1969): 165–85.
Johnson, Frank. "The Conference of October 15th, 1875, Between General George and Governor Ames." *Publications of the Mississippi Historical Society* 6 (1902): 65–78.
———. "Suffrage and Reconstruction in Mississippi." *Publications of the Mississippi Historical Society* 6 (1902): 144–241.
Jones, J. H. "Penitentiary Reform in Mississippi." *Publications of the Mississippi Historical Society* 6 (1902): 111–28.
Jones, Yvonne V. "Black Leadership Patterns and Political Change in the American South." In *Holding Onto the Land and the Lord: Kinship, Ritual, Land Tenure and Social Policy in the Rural South*, ed. Robert Hall and Carol B. Stack, 55–68. Athens: University of Georgia Press, 1982.
Kirwan, Albert D. "Apportionment in the Mississippi Constitution of 1890." *Journal of Southern History* 14 (May 1948): 234–46.
McFarland, Gerald W. "The New York Mugwumps of 1884: A Profile." *Political Science Quarterly* 78 (1963): 40–58.
McNeily, J. S. "History of the Measures Submitted to the Committee on Elective Franchise, Apportionment and Elections in the Constitutional Convention of 1890." *Publications of the Mississippi Historical Society* 6 (1902): 129–40.
———. "War and Reconstruction in Mississippi: 1863–1890." *Mississippi Historical Society Centenary Series* 2 (1918): 165–535.
Muckenfuss, A. M. "The Development of Manufacturing in Mississippi." *Publications of the Mississippi Historical Society* 10 (1909): 163–80.
Patton, William Hinkle. "History of the Prohibition Movement in Mississippi." *Publications of the Mississippi Historical Society* 10 (1909): 181–201.
Peskin, Allan. "Who Were the Stalwarts? Who Were their Rivals? Republican Factions in the Gilded Age." *Political Science Quarterly* 99 (1984): 703–16.
Revels, James G. "Redeemers, Rednecks, and Racial Integrity." In *A History of Mississippi*, ed. Richard Aubrey McLemore, 588–600. Hattiesburg: University and College Press of Mississippi, 1973.

Ringold, May Spencer. "Senator James Zachariah George, Bourbon or Liberal?" *Journal of Mississippi History* 16 (July 1954): 164–82.

Roberts, W. B. "After the War Between the States." In *History of Bolivar County, Mississippi: Its Creation, Pioneer Days and Progress in the Heart of the Mississippi Delta*, ed. Florence Warfield Sillers. Spartanburg, SC: Reprint Company, 1976.

Rovner, Herbert Saul. "Note: The Effect of Racial Discrimination in the Indictment Stage." *Wyoming Law Journal* 5 (1950): 97–100.

Rusk, Jerrold G. "The Effect of the Australian Ballot Reform on Split Ticket Voting: 1876–1908." *American Political Science* Review 64 (December 1970): 1220–38.

Saller, Richard P. "Pater Familias, Mater Familias, and the Gendered Semantics of the Roman Household." *Classical Philology* 94 (April 1999): 182–98.

Sillers, Walter. "Reconstruction." In *History of Bolivar County, Mississippi: Its Creation, Pioneer Days and Progress in the Heart of the Mississippi Delta*, ed. Florence Warfield Sillers. Spartanburg, SC: Reprint Company, 1976.

Silver, James. "Mississippi: The Closed Society." *Journal of Southern History* 30 (February 1964): 3–34.

Stone, Alfred H. "The Suppression of Lawlessness in the South." *North American Review* (April 1894): 500–506.

Ware, Alan. "Anti-Party and Party Control of Political Reform in the United States: The Case of the Australian Ballot." *British Journal of Political Science* 30 (January 2000): 14.

Wellborn, Fred. "The Influence of the Silver-Republican Senators, 1889–1891." *Mississippi Valley Historical Review* 14 (March 1928): 462–80.

Witty, Fred M. "Reconstruction in Carroll and Montgomery Counties." *Publications of the Mississippi Historical Society* 10 (1909): 115–34.

Government Documents

"Alleged Election Outrages in Virginia and Mississippi." Speeches of Senators John Sherman and William Mahone, delivered in the Senate of the United States, January 29, 1885, Washington, DC.

Burgess, James. *Soil Survey of the Crystal Springs Area, Mississippi*. Washington, DC: Government Printing Office, 1905.

"Chalmers v. Manning" Speech of Hon. John H. Rogers of Arkansas, in the House of Representatives, February 15, 1884.

Department of Commerce and Labor, Bureau of the Census. *Abstract of the Thirteenth Census of the United States, 1910*. Washington, DC: Government Printing Office, 1913.

Department of the Interior, Census Office, *Abstract of the Eleventh Census: 1890*. Washington, DC: Government Printing Office, 1894.

———. *Census Reports*. Vol. 1, *Twelfth Census of the United States Taken in the Year 1900, Population*. Washington, DC: Census Office, 1902.

———. *Census Reports*. Vol. 5, *Twelfth Census of the United States Taken in the Year 1900, Agriculture*. Washington, DC: Census Office, 1902.

——. *Census Reports*. Vol. 6, *Twelfth Census of the United States Taken in the Year 1900, Agriculture*. Washington, DC: Census Office, 1902.

——. *Census Reports*. Vol. 7, *Twelfth Census of the United States Taken in the Year 1900, Manufacturers*. Washington, DC: Census Office, 1902.

——. *Census Reports*. Vol. 8, *Twelfth Census of the United States Taken in the Year 1900, Manufacturers*. Washington, DC: Census Office, 1902.

——. *Census Reports*. Vol. 13, *Twelfth Census of the United States Taken in the Year 1900, Occupations*. Washington, D.C.: Census Office, 1902.

——. *Abstract of the Twelfth Census of the United State: 1900*. 3rd ed. Washington, DC: Government Printing Office, 1904.

Memorial Address of Hon. A. F. Fox Upon the Life and Character of Hon. James Z. George of Mississippi. Delivered in the House of Representatives, May 25, 1898, Washington, DC.

Memorial Address of Hon. John S. Williams Upon the Life and Character of Hon. James Z. George of Mississippi, May 25, 1898. Delivered in the House of Representatives, Washington, DC.

Report of the Hawaiian Commission in Senate Documents, 35 Cong., 3 Sess., no. 16, 149–50.

Speech of Hon. William C. Oates of Alabama, March 24, 1884, in House of Representatives, "Mississippi Overflow: A Speech for the Constitution."

Archives

Mississippi Department of Archives and History

Broadside Politics. Vertical File
Bruce, Blanche. Vertical File
Burkitt, Frank. Vertical File
Davis, Jefferson. Papers
Dixon, Harry St. John. Papers
George, James Z. Papers
Lamar, L.Q.C. Papers
Montgomery, Isaiah T. Papers
Online Electronic Resource: turpentine photographs; political broadsides
Patrons of Husbandry, Grange Papers
Stone, Alfred Holt. Collection
Wells, Allison. Vertical File
Wesson Industry. Vertical File
Wilson, Robert. Papers

Briefs of cases: *John Henry Dixon v. State of Mississippi*; *John Gibson v. State of Mississippi*; *W. T. Ratliff v. Ambus Beale*; *Charlie Smith v. State of Mississippi*; *Henry Williams v. State of Mississippi*

Bibliography

Caroliniana/University of South Carolina

Montgomery Family. Papers

Harvard University Libraries

Dun & Co. (selected years and regions)
Harvard University, Harvard Business School, Baker Library Historical Collections

Library of Congress

Ben La Bree Chapter, No. 118, United Daughters of the Confederation. Membership Booklet. Jackson, Mississippi. Louisville, Kentucky: Courier Journal Job Printing Company, 1897
Montgomery, Benjamin. Family Papers
Terrell, Robert. Papers
Walthall, General Edward Cary. 1831–1898 Papers

Newspapers

Clarion-Ledger (Mississippi) 1889–1894 and selected years thereafter
Selections from Chronicling America/Pro-Quest
Weekly Clarion (Mississippi) 1874–1888

Index

Abbay, R. F., 117
Aberdeen Examiner, 98–99, 102, 142
Abolitionism, 51, 106, 150
Adams County, 129, 140
Africa, 95–96, 142
African Methodist Episcopal Church (AME), 36
Afro-American News Company, 146
Agrarianism, 23, 25, 33–35
Agricultural Wheel, 4, 32
Agriculture, 4–5, 10–11, 20, 24, 27, 29–32, 43, 45, 115–16, 119, 131, 134–37, 165
Alcorn (College) University, 36, 115, 181
Alcorn, James, 13, 113, 118, 122, 140, 143
Alcorn County, 97
Aldrich, Nelson, 146
Alliance. *See* Colored Farmers' Alliance; Farmers' Alliance
American Missionary Association, 115
Amite County, 82, 118
Anglo-Saxons, 12, 153, 155, 162
Anthony, Susan B., 110, 154
Antitrust. *See* Sherman Antitrust Act
Appointment, 37, 50, 133, 178–80
Apportionment, 7, 52, 66, 70, 81, 84, 87, 102, 117, 124–25, 129–31, 138, 196. *See also* Reapportionment
Arkansas, 32, 49, 133, 152
Article 12 (MS), 174
Article I (US), 51, 151, 167
Article IV (US), 74–75

Atlanta Constitution, 199, 209, 210
At-large delegates, 10, 63, 72, 76, 83, 94, 97, 106–7, 109, 118, 120, 122, 179, 204
Attala County, 93, 118
Attorney general, 49, 71, 120
Australian ballot, 81, 85, 87, 94, 98–99, 102, 126, 130, 132, 195, 196

Ballot box, 18, 19, 35, 47, 49, 51, 53, 80, 82, 88–89, 94, 100, 130, 176, 197
Ballots: access, 64–65, 150, 176; fraud, 17–19, 34–35, 47, 49, 51, 53, 55, 60, 71, 82, 94, 100, 130, 156, 166, 197; reform, 70, 80–81, 83, 88–89, 94, 103, 107, 130, 139, 151, 155, 196; tickets, 55. *See also* Australian ballot; Ballot box
Banks, 20, 28, 43, 135–37, 171, 197, 200–203, 206
Barksdale, Ethelbert, 16, 25, 30
Barry Railroad Regulation Bill, 24, 137
Baskett, L. T., 58
Bell, Thomas P., 82, 129
Beulah, MS, 17
Bilbo, Theodore G., 169, 202
Bill of Rights (US), 75, 104
Black Codes, 42
Black counties, 21, 23, 25, 70–72, 105, 116, 125–30, 138, 140–42, 154, 196, 203
Blackwell, Henry, 106–8
Blair, Henry, 49, 54, 82, 148
Blair Bill, 49, 54

Bland Allison Silver Bill, 16
Blevins, F. G., 50
Blue Mountain Female College, 108
Board of Public Works, 119
Bolivar County, 16–19, 36–37, 45, 71–72, 77, 90, 94, 112, 137–38, 155, 182, 215n24
Boll weevil, 201–2
Bolton, MS, 41
Boothe, J. B., 84, 128
Boundaries, 34, 129, 159
Bourbons, 5, 10–46, 60, 192
Boutwell Committee, 37
Boyd, W. A., 81–82, 128
Brandagee, Frank, 161
Brandon Republican, 98, 102, 141
Brierfield Plantation, 42–44, 137
Brigadier Generals, 12, 24
Brookhaven, MS, 191
Brookhaven Leader, 98–99, 102
Brotherhood of Specific Skills, 24
Bruce, Blanche, 17, 35–38, 55, 177–78, 180, 192
Burkitt, Frank: background, 24, 30, 32, 59–61, 76; constitutional convention, 79, 93, 103, 107, 116, 131, 133–34, 141–42; Populist Party, 170–71, 200, 259n10, 259n13
Butler, Matthew, 152–53

Calhoon, Solomon Saladin, 11, 18, 65–66, 70–72, 76, 81–85, 100, 110, 128–29, 133, 142, 156, 164, 174–75
Calhoon Plan, 85, 110
Calhoun County, 141
Call, Wilkinson, 154–55
Campbell, J. A. P., 64–67, 75–76, 83–85, 100, 110, 172, 174–75
Campbell Plan, 65–67, 75–76, 83–85, 100, 110
Campbell's Codes, 33
Candidates, 25, 33, 35, 40, 49, 51, 62–63, 77, 121, 165, 179, 197
Canton, MS, 179
Capital Light Guard, 58
Capitol: new, 123, 204; old, 10, 87, 100, 123
Carlisle, G. W., 197

Carlisle, John G., 172
Carpetbaggers, 14–16, 61, 68, 152, 163, 194
Carroll County, 58, 123
Carrollton, MS, 62, 100, 156
Catchings, Thomas, 180, 188, 205
Caucasians, 95, 149, 200
Census, 5, 28, 36, 61, 84, 177
Chalmers, James Ronald, 34–35, 38, 55–56, 62
Chancery court, 55, 174
Chandler, William, 167
Cheadle, Joseph, 49
Chickasaw County, 109
Chickasaw Messenger, 30, 59
Chinese Exclusion Act, 25
Chinese immigrants, 136, 145, 150–52, 160, 162
Chisholm, W. W., 153
Chrisman, J. B., 80–82, 84, 93, 100–101, 113, 118, 129, 191
Christianity, 111, 155
Churches, 11, 111, 115, 171
Cincinnati, 41, 171
Circuit Court (US), 186
Citizenship, 53, 73, 103, 118, 151, 161, 165
Civil Rights Cases, 169, 183
Civil service reform, 145
Civil War, 4, 5, 8, 11, 20, 22, 28, 32, 41, 48, 50, 67, 74, 89, 96, 106, 136, 159, 165, 167, 169, 192, 194, 201
Civilization, 31, 34, 61, 90, 109, 142, 149–50, 155, 162, 198
Clarion (Jackson), 102
Clarion-Ledger (Jackson), 8, 10–11, 55–56, 64–66, 72–73, 75, 80, 82, 87–88, 94–96, 98–103, 107–8, 123, 127, 129, 131, 133, 139, 141, 143, 151, 153–54, 159, 213n4
Class structure, 16, 21–22, 27, 30–31, 34–46, 52–53, 64–65, 66, 69–73, 76, 81–82, 85–88, 91–93, 105–6, 110, 117–18, 124–43, 147, 157, 165, 169, 177, 188–90, 195–97, 200–201, 208, 218n35
Cleveland, Grover, 48, 50, 52, 165, 166, 167, 177

Clinton, MS, 39, 62
Coinage, 20, 25, 32, 160
Colored Farmers' Alliance, 48, 56–58, 72, 171
Colquitt, Alfred H., 147, 149
Commerce, 25, 32–33, 201
Commercial Herald (Memphis), 65–66
Committee of the Whole, 81–84
Committee on Corporations and Internal Improvements, 138
"Commoner," 6, 16, 40, 126. *See also* George, James Zebulon
Confederates/Confederacy, 6, 12–13, 15–17, 26, 35, 38, 41, 48, 55, 64, 104, 152, 166
Constitution (US), 48, 74, 87, 94, 97, 104, 141, 163, 189, 193, 205
Constitutionality, 51, 117, 167
Convicts, 111, 118–23, 137, 200; convict leasing, 30, 112, 118–23
Cook, F. M. B. (Marsh), 63
Copiah County, 35, 61–62
Corinth Herald, 97, 100
Corporations, 61, 70, 79, 105, 121, 132–35, 138, 143
Coverture, 110
Cromwell, Oliver, 39, 57–58
Crop liens, 28, 33, 201
Crystal Springs, MS, 29
Cullom, S. M., 152
Currency, 31, 136, 171–72

Dabney, Mayre, 73, 103, 204–6
Daily Commercial Herald (Vicksburg), 107, 113, 133, 139
Daily Democrat (Natchez), 128, 130
Davis, Jefferson, 7, 13, 22, 40–44, 92, 204
Davis, Joseph, 7, 40, 41–44, 92
Davis Bend, MS, 40–45, 92
Dawes, Henry, 25
Dean, R. A., 76, 107
Delta (Mississippi), 6, 13–16, 21, 23, 29, 30, 34, 37–38, 44, 56, 58, 63, 71–72, 83, 92, 102, 105, 108, 116, 119, 122, 127, 130, 136–38, 141, 171, 180–83, 191, 195–97, 199, 203, 208–9

Democracy, 68, 78, 132, 156, 164, 167
Democratic Party, 4, 8, 11–14, 15–18, 16–19, 23, 25–26, 33–39, 48, 50–51, 53–55, 61, 62, 64, 66, 67, 69, 77, 83, 93, 95, 99, 108, 125, 128, 130–31, 141, 142, 145–47, 149–53, 154–56, 159–60, 162, 164, 165–68, 170, 173, 178, 179–80, 197, 200
Department of Treasury, 171
Desoto County, 85, 107, 117
Dillard, George, 104, 114, 128, 142
Dirt farmers, 4, 5, 6, 8, 11, 21, 23, 30, 33–34, 40, 114, 190, 196, 197
Discrimination, 73, 118, 159, 166, 181, 186–89, 200
Disfranchisement, 3–4, 6–7, 11–12, 33, 39, 48, 52, 59, 64–65, 69, 72–73, 76, 80, 84, 87–90, 93–95, 97, 100–101, 104–9, 117, 126–29, 132, 141–43, 154, 157, 164, 168–69, 173, 175–76, 186–88, 194–97, 203–4, 206–8, 210–11
Dixon v. Mississippi, 184–86
Dolph, Joseph, 150–52, 156–57
Dortch Law, 77, 82–83, 85. *See also* Australian ballot
Douglass, Frederick, 146
Dry Grove, MS, 39
Du Bois, W. E. B., 91, 176
Dun Reports, 44
Durant, MS, 57–58
Durant Commercial Company, 58

Edmunds, George, 150, 154
Education, 5, 20–21, 25, 36–37, 40–42, 49, 55, 62, 64, 73, 78, 80, 85, 91–93, 96, 98–99, 101, 104, 106, 110, 114–18, 132, 157, 159, 162, 172–73, 175–76, 188, 198, 200
Education Committee, 115
Education qualifications, 65, 79–82, 87, 93, 99, 103, 109, 132, 133
Edwards Hotel, 204
Election, 6–8, 17, 19, 25, 33–35, 37–38, 45, 47–51, 53–55, 59–65, 68, 70–71, 77, 79–82, 90, 93–95, 97–98, 100, 102, 106–7, 112–13,

130, 132, 143–51, 153–55, 160–61, 164–67, 170, 175–76, 178, 181, 189, 195–99
Elections Bill. *See* Lodge Elections Bill
Elective franchise, 73, 81–82, 100, 157, 186
Elective Franchise Committee. *See* Franchise Committee
Elective judiciary, 132–33
Electorate/electoral body, 34, 60, 61, 78, 148, 170, 195, 199
Electors, 59, 66, 83, 86, 97, 106–7, 128, 133, 174, 185–86, 189
Elites, 4–27, 29–30, 33–35, 40, 42, 52, 71–72, 91, 106, 114, 125, 169, 192, 197. *See also* Upper class
Emancipation, 22, 110, 158
Eminent domain, 138
Employees, 134, 189
Employers, 57, 121
Enfranchisement, 15, 64, 83, 101, 104–8, 112, 148–49
Engle, J. C., 58
Epidemics, 123–24
Episcopalians, 36, 111
Equal Protection Clause (US), 182, 186–87
Equality, 89, 152, 155, 161, 198
Equalization, 116, 200
Eskridge, H. S., 154
Eskridge, W. S., 83–84, 109, 136
Ethics, 59, 96
Eustis, James, 151–52
Ex parte Siebold, 167
Ex parte Yarbrough, 51, 167
Exemptions, 24, 79, 102–3, 134–35, 138

Factions, 6, 8, 15–16, 47, 168, 178–79, 197
Factories, 25, 31
Fair Play (Meridian), 72, 101
Farish, W. S., 71–72
Farmers, 4–6, 8, 10–11, 14–15, 20–24, 27–34, 36, 40, 48, 56–60, 65, 72, 76, 78–79, 81, 84, 93, 103, 105, 114, 125–26, 129, 131–34, 137, 141–42, 165, 168, 170–71, 190, 196–97, 199–200

Farmers' Alliance, 27–32, 56–60, 72, 76, 79, 84, 125–26, 131, 133–34, 141–42, 168, 170–71
Featherston, W. S., 122
Federalist Papers, 51, 167
Felonies, 79, 82–83, 120
Felons, 78, 172
Fewell, John W., 76, 81–84, 93, 103, 106–10, 114, 122, 139
Fifteenth Amendment (US), 3, 8, 64, 69, 73, 74, 77, 85, 94, 97, 101, 106, 107, 145, 147, 150, 155–56, 158–59, 162, 165, 181, 182, 193, 203
Filibusters, 53, 145–48
Fiscal concerns, 20, 106, 116–17, 123, 140, 172
Force Bill. *See* Lodge Elections Bill
Ford, T. S., 72, 94
Fourteenth Amendment (US), 3, 4, 73, 118, 150, 182, 183, 187, 189
Franchise, 6–7, 11, 49–50, 62–64, 67, 69–90, 92–95, 97, 99–103, 105–7, 109–10, 117–18, 125–28, 132–33, 141, 143, 149–50, 153–54, 157–58, 160, 165–68, 173, 175–76, 186, 193–95
Franchise Committee, 72, 76, 79, 81–84, 87–88, 90, 94–95, 97, 99–100, 103, 105, 107, 118, 126–27
Franklin County, 86, 100, 102, 128, 199
Fraud, 7, 16–18, 33–34, 37–38, 48, 51, 53–54, 61, 67, 77, 80, 82, 93–96, 98, 100–103, 130, 134, 143–44, 151, 153–57, 166–67, 175, 177, 188, 197
Friar's Point, MS, 39
Fry, William, 163
Fusion, 19, 33–35, 38, 54, 71, 77, 79, 162, 170, 180

Galloway, Charles, 10, 70
George, James Zebulon: background, 6–8, 12, 16–17, 22, 25, 35, 40; constitutional convention, 76, 81, 93–95, 98–101, 104, 109, 114, 126–27, 130, 135–36, 140–41;

Senate debates, 49, 61, 66–67, 144–45, 147–48, 151–54, 156–64, 170, 172, 174–75, 189, 191, 194, 196, 216n32
Gerrymandering, 18, 65, 76, 83, 87, 93, 130, 154
Gibson, Randall, 150, 156
Gibson v. Mississippi, 183, 263n70
Gold standard, 16, 32, 136, 145
Gone to Texas (GTT), 28
Gore, J. E., 85, 139
Government, 7–8, 13–14, 20, 22, 24, 26, 33–34, 46–50, 54, 60–62, 65–67, 74–75, 83, 85, 94–96, 104–5, 115, 118, 123–24, 135–37, 139, 142–43, 145, 148–52, 154–55, 157–58, 160–61, 164–67, 169, 187, 189, 192, 194–95, 198
Governors, 6, 8, 10, 12–13, 17–18, 24–26, 33, 36, 49, 55, 57, 59–63, 66–67, 71, 83, 113, 118, 120, 122, 125, 127, 140, 143, 159, 169, 171–72, 174, 178, 181, 190–91, 198–200
Grady, Henry, 48
Grandfather clause, 3, 64
Grange, 24, 32–33, 115
Grant, Ulysses S., 17, 38
Gray, George, 156
Great Agricultural Relief, 32
Great White Chief. *See* Vardaman, James K.
Green, Benjamin T., 44
Greenback Party, 4, 11, 32–35, 47, 79, 136
Greenville, MS, 61, 130, 185
Greenville Democrat, 130, 209
Greenwood, MS, 57–58, 139
Grenada, MS, 101, 124
Gulf Coast, MS, 30, 120–21
Gulfport, MS, 134, 201
Guyton, D. T., 93, 118

Habeas corpus, 152
Half-Breeds, 145
Hamilton, Alexander, 85, 167
Hamilton, Jones, 112
Hanna, Mark, 178–79
Harlan, John Marshall, 182–83

Harris, Wiley P., 65, 73, 103, 141
Harrison, Benjamin, 48–50, 54, 145–47, 160, 164
Harvard, 12
Haugen, Nils P., 52
Hawley, Joseph, 158–59, 162–63
Hemingway, William L., 171
Henderson, David, 52
Henry, Pat, 193, 204
Hewlett, Emanuel, 183, 262n69
Hierarchy, 6, 22–23, 91
Higgins, Anthony, 154, 184
Hill, Charles, 53
Hill, James, 9, 34–35, 37–38, 55, 173, 176–81, 192
Hinds County, 39, 73, 85, 112, 129, 174
Hiscock, Frank, 155
Hoar, Frisbie, 49, 53, 150, 152, 154–57, 164, 167, 175
Holland, C. K., 141
Hollendale, MS, 108
House Committee of the Election of the President and Vice-President, 53
House Journal, 53, 119
Hoyt, Albert, 199
Hudson, R. G., 193
Hurricane Plantation, 40–44, 137

Illiteracy, 4, 7, 65, 80–81, 84, 95–97, 117, 126, 162, 173, 175, 194
Immigrants, 106, 135, 145, 151, 155, 160, 162
Immigration, 136, 160, 162
Impeachment, 17
Indictments, 161, 182–86, 188, 199
Industry, 7, 75, 125, 135, 198–99
Ingalls, John James, 51, 154
Intermarriage, 158
Interstate Commerce Act, 25
Interstate Commerce Commission, 32, 33
Intimidation, 15–16, 18, 34–35, 38–39, 50–52, 54–56, 58, 60, 64, 70, 92, 95, 151, 156, 169, 177, 190, 194, 199
Issaquena County, 55, 71–72, 196

Index

Jackson, MS, 7, 10, 33, 35, 39, 54, 61–62, 63, 68, 72, 90, 97, 101–2, 112, 115, 119, 123, 156, 173–74, 179, 180, 207
Jamison, J., 74, 116
Jason and the Argonauts, 210
Jasper County, 56, 63
Jim Crow, 70, 80. *See also* Segregation
Johnson, D. S., 109
Johnston, Frank, 120–21
Jones, Cornelius J., 180–86, 188, 205
Jones, James Henry, 109, 120–22
Judicial review, 189
Judiciary, 8, 10, 73, 125, 127, 132–33
Judiciary Committee, 65, 77, 83, 141, 150
Jurors/jury, 14, 40, 54, 112, 124, 133, 153, 158, 181–87, 189, 199
Justice, 6, 19, 25, 45, 54–55, 59–60, 71, 82, 143, 151, 155, 163, 165, 172, 177, 180–83, 186–88, 91, 200

Kemper County, 62
Kerr, David, 52
King, Benjamin, 33
Knights of Labor, 24, 31–32
Kosciusko, MS, 48
Ku Klux Klan, 15, 190, 215n25

Lafayette County, 76, 107
Lamar, Lucius Quintus Cincinnatus, 6, 15–17, 22, 25–26, 35, 37, 54, 59, 191, 194
Lamar-George Wing, 35
Landowners, 28, 32–33, 65–66
Lauderdale County, 59, 85
Lawrence, MS, 111
Leake County, 84, 93, 132
Lee, S. D., 109, 115–16, 118, 123
Leflore County, 5, 57–58, 62, 139–40
Levees, 6, 20, 29, 43, 45, 75, 92, 110, 113, 122–23, 130, 136–38, 148
Lexington Advisor, 98, 99
Lincoln County, 199
Literacy, 7, 12, 62–63, 77–78, 98–99, 132, 145, 158–59, 174–75, 195

Literacy requirement, 49, 95, 117, 153
Lodge, Henry Cabot, 51
Lodge Elections Bill, 6, 8
Long, H. L., 65
Longino, Andrew, 191–92, 197, 199
Lost Cause, 8, 67, 193
Lotteries, 113, 132
Love, W. F., 82, 118, 140
Lowry, Robert, 6, 16, 24–25, 57, 59–60, 174, 265n121
Lynch, John Roy: background, 36–38, 226n75; DC connections, 53, 62, 260n23; Lynch-Hill fight, 176–80; political campaigns, 34–35, 38, 54–55, 225n55; poll tax, 173–74; Spanish-American War, 192
Lynching, 37, 139, 190–92, 198–99, 265n119

Manoway, L. W. W., 72–73
Marion, MS, 34
Marshall County, 122
Matthews, Prentice, 153
Matthews, Print, 35, 156
Mayes, Edward, 83, 115–16, 128
McClurg, Monroe, 123
McCool, MS, 50
McGaugham, William, 134
McGehee, J. H., 86, 100, 128
McKenna, Joseph, 187, 189
McKinley, William, 145, 178–79
McKinley Tariff, 145
McLaurin, H. J., 118, 122–23, 139–40
McPherson, John, 155
Melchior, George, 17, 71–72, 94
Memphis, TN, 34, 55, 188
Memphis Appeal, 95–96, 108
Memphis Commercial, 65–66
Meridian, MS, 14, 34, 56, 72, 76, 101, 106, 135, 139
Methodists, 11, 36, 70, 111, 115
Militia, 26, 39, 57–58, 124–25, 138–41, 158, 191, 199
Miller, Irvin, 84, 93, 107, 116, 122, 132, 140
Miller, Marshall, 119

Millsaps College, 115
Minority, 37, 71–72, 94, 113, 116–17, 138, 150
Missionaries, 78, 111, 115
Mississippi Agricultural and Mechanical College (Mississippi State), 11, 24, 115, 131
Mississippi Code, 33, 183
Mississippi College, 15
Mississippi Cotton Mills, 31
Mississippi Plan, 16, 59–60
Mississippi River, 43, 45, 129, 137–38
Mississippi River Commission, 37
Mollison, Willis E., 30, 55
Monopoly, 23, 57, 126, 135
Monroe County, 110, 123
Montgomery family: Ben, 40–45; Isaiah, 7, 39–41, 43–45, 70, 72, 80–94, 112, 137–38, 148, 173, 176, 178, 180, 190, 192; Mary, 41; Rebecca, 42; Thornton, 42–44; Virginia, 42
Moore, E. H., 138, 152
Morey, Henry, 52
Morgan, John, 150
Morrell Act, 115
Morris, J. L., 82, 122
Mound Bayou, MS, 44–46, 92, 192
Muldrow, H. L., 97, 99, 103, 118, 128

Nash, Wiley, 174, 176, 216n27, 216n28
Natchez, MS, 6, 18, 36, 38, 40, 63
Natchez Democrat, 67, 99, 128, 130, 142, 178
Native Americans, 78, 103, 150
Nativists, 160
Needle guns, 39
Negro (use of term in documents), 12, 15, 16, 17, 18, 34, 44–45, 54, 57, 59–61, 64–66, 73, 75, 81, 82, 89, 96, 97, 100–101, 107–10, 112, 118, 130, 143, 148–49, 152, 157, 159–62, 165, 168, 174–75, 186, 189, 194–95, 198, 200
Nesbit, Wiley, 182
Neshoba County, 199
Neshoba Democrat, 99, 108
New Harmony, IN, 40

New Orleans, LA, 29, 58
New South, 12, 48
New York World, 88, 90
Newspapers, 7–9, 18, 33–35, 47, 50, 53, 56–58, 61, 63, 65, 67, 72, 75, 80, 93, 95–96, 98–102, 108–9, 116, 119, 125, 134, 139, 141, 156, 163–64, 170, 177, 188, 192, 199
Noland, T. V., 62
Northwest Ordinance, 74
Noxubee County, 74, 128, 142

Oaths, 18, 67, 78, 94, 103, 185
Odom, J. W., 85, 107, 110, 117
Okolona, MS, 30, 59
Oktibbeha County, 109
Oligarchy, 167. *See also* Elites
Oliver, William, 31
Outsiders, 8, 11, 18, 21, 73, 108, 158, 177, 192, 194, 200
Owens, Robert, 40
Oxford, MS, 15
Oxford Eagle, 102, 141

Packwood, S. E., 135
Panola County, 34–35, 79, 84, 110, 128
Parchman, MS, 200
Paternalism, 4–5, 6–7, 12, 15, 21, 40, 69–70, 72, 92, 118, 162, 192
Patronage, 22, 34–35, 38, 50, 145, 177–78, 180
Patrons of Husbandry, 24, 32. *See also* Grange
Patty, R. C., 108, 127, 244n1
Paulding, MS, 56
Pearl River County, 71
Penitentiary, 106, 120, 200
Percy, LeRoy, 208–9
Pike County, 135
Piney Woods, 6, 29, 105
Plantations, 11, 13, 21–22, 30, 36, 40–45, 83, 92, 131, 137, 141, 148, 178, 183, 185
Planters, 5, 11, 21–23, 28, 32, 34, 42, 56, 105, 119, 125, 137, 171
Plessy v. Ferguson, 169, 183, 188

Plural voting, 64, 66, 75–76, 83, 85, 87, 99, 109
Politicians, 9, 13, 16, 20, 22, 25, 33, 36, 45, 47, 51, 67, 114, 119, 173, 197
Poll Tax, 64, 65, 78–79, 81–83, 85, 102–5, 109, 115, 130, 172–76, 180, 195–96, 205, 235, 239, 261
Populism, 105, 131, 165, 170–71, 197
Postmasters, 38, 96, 156, 179
Poverty, 9, 116
Powell, James H., 171
Precedents, 4, 159, 181
Prejudice, 19, 48, 75, 159, 162, 200
Presbyterians, 11, 111
Presbytery of Ethel, 111
Primary Election Law, 196–97
Prisoners, 58, 121–23, 200
Progressivism, 65, 105, 122, 136, 164
Prohibition, 32, 73, 77, 110–13, 132, 183, 187
Property qualification, 62–66, 75–76, 79, 80–82, 84–86, 93, 99, 103, 108, 131–32, 145, 158
Protestants, 11. *See also specific denominations*
Public schools, 13, 20, 24, 26, 78, 114–17, 173–75, 200, 202, 206

Racism/racial bigotry/racial attitudes, 4–5, 7, 9, 14, 20, 27, 30, 37, 44, 51, 54–55, 61, 69–70, 82, 89–90, 92–94, 96, 106, 112, 117, 138, 140, 156, 158, 160, 171, 181, 192, 197–98, 200
Radical racists, 4, 69
Railroad commission, 33, 120, 132, 134
Railroad commissioner, 120, 132, 134
Railroads, 14, 20, 23–25, 30–33, 38, 44, 47, 57, 70, 96, 105, 120, 122, 125–26, 132–34, 138, 184, 190, 197, 199, 201, 204, 218n61
Rankin County, 35, 117, 123, 139–40
Ratification, 7, 125, 141–42, 144, 148, 159
Ratliff v. Beale, 173–74, 187
Readmission Act of 1870, 73, 83, 109, 144

Reagan, John, 147
Reapportionment, 21, 63, 67, 76, 105, 125–31, 142, 154, 196
Reconstruction, 4–6, 8, 11, 13–15, 18–20, 22–23, 26–28, 31, 36–37, 39, 47–48, 53, 57, 59, 61–62, 64, 78, 96, 104, 114, 138–39, 144, 148–50, 152–53, 155, 157, 159–61, 163, 165–67, 169–70, 176, 190, 192, 194
Redeemers, 18, 25–26
Redemption, 55. *See also* Restoration
Rednecks, 3, 126, 168
Redshirts, 64
Reelection, 132
Reform, 11, 47, 56, 60, 64, 70, 77, 79, 81, 93, 95–96, 105–25, 132, 143, 145, 176, 195–96
Regan, C. K., 100
Registrar, 99, 163, 180
Registration, 78, 161, 170, 174–75, 180, 189, 195
Repeal, 30, 73–75, 85, 95, 97, 101, 154, 165–66, 167, 169, 176
Republican Party, 4, 8, 11, 13–15, 17–18, 25, 27, 33–35, 37–38, 45, 48–55, 57, 60, 62–63, 65, 71–72, 74, 82, 98, 102, 115, 122, 140–41, 143–48, 150–51, 153–61, 164–67, 170, 173, 176–77, 179–81, 188
Republican State Executive Committee, 62
Requirements, 28, 49, 65, 79–80, 82–83, 85, 95, 97, 103, 109, 114, 117, 126, 132, 153, 173, 189, 196
Residency/residence, 55, 65, 78, 82, 83, 85, 103, 130, 178, 195–96
Restoration, 12–13, 16, 21, 23–24, 28, 35, 39, 47, 89, 112, 119, 192
Revels, Hiram, 36–37, 115
Revenue, 113, 125, 130–31, 135, 138, 173
Reynolds, L. P., 97
Riots, 14, 34, 39, 56, 62, 139–40, 156, 160, 190, 199
Robber Barons, 45
Robinson, S. W., 117
Rowland, Dunbar, 194–95
Rust College, 115

Salary, 26, 114, 133
Scalawags, 15
Schooling, 6, 14, 41, 96, 99, 114, 116
Scooba, MS, 199
Scott v. Sanford, 165
Secession, 75, 104, 141
Secrecy, 56, 77, 83, 128
Secret Service, 171–72
Sectionalism, 99, 128, 149, 159, 164
Segregation, 4, 54, 116–17, 123, 200
Servitude, 73–75, 121, 150, 165–66, 186
Sharecroppers, 28, 32, 33
Sharkey, W. L., 181
Sharkey County, 34, 118, 139, 181
Shaw College (Rust College), 115
Sheriffs, 17, 35–37, 56–58, 62, 79–80, 138, 174, 191, 199
Sherman, John, 52
Sherman Antitrust Act, 25
Sherman Free Coinage of Silver Act, 17, 160
Sherman Silver Purchase Act, 145–46, 166–67
Shoestring District, 18, 38
Silverites, 191
Simrall, Horatio, 35, 82–83
Slaveholders, 22, 65
Slavery, 8, 65, 74–75, 91, 121–22, 149, 152, 155
Smallpox, 124
Social Darwinism, 49, 147, 149–50, 152, 156, 203
Sovereignty, 74, 85, 97, 151
Split ticket, 77
Spooner, John, 153, 157
Springer, William, 53
Stalwarts, 6, 50, 145, 153, 161
Starkville, MS, 72, 79, 131
State banks, 135, 171
State charter, 135
State Teachers' Association, 114
State Treasurer, 171–72, 197
Statehood, 27, 74
States' rights, 26, 148
Statutes, 29, 61, 132, 170, 172, 177, 189

Stewart, William, 147, 152, 160, 164
Stinson, Robert, 183
Stockholders, 23, 134, 136
Stone, John Marshall, 6, 10, 18, 24–25, 61–63, 171–72, 190–91, 217, 219n75
Stone, W. W., 172
Storis, I. W., 66
Stower, J. R., 197
Strauder v. West Virginia, 181
Street, H. M., 99
Streetcars, 4, 200
Suffrage, 6, 12, 50, 54, 59–60, 62, 64, 67, 73–78, 80–82, 84–85, 97, 99, 102, 106–10, 112, 147, 149–50, 154, 159, 161–62, 174–75, 186, 191, 194, 196
Sumner, Brooks, 151
Sumner, Charles, 15
Supervisors, 51, 117, 140, 151, 162, 167
Supremacists/supremacy, 34, 52, 56, 60–61, 65–67, 76, 85, 94–96, 107, 109–10, 113–14, 129, 131, 151, 198
Supreme Court (MS), 6, 23, 25, 71, 82, 132–33, 167, 174–76, 182, 184, 186–87
Supreme Court (US), 25, 51, 54, 134, 144, 147, 150, 155, 167, 169, 181–84, 187–88, 190–92, 194
Sykes, E. O., 110

Tallahatchie County, 83, 109, 136
Tariff, 16, 25, 31, 48, 145–46, 164
Taylor, R. H., 79, 110, 139
Teachers, 24, 101, 114–15, 173
Technology, 20, 30, 136
Temperance, 6, 70, 110–14, 118
Terrell, Robert, 178
Testimony, 15, 53, 92, 138, 148, 184–85
Thirteenth Amendment (US), 75, 91
Thomas, T. L, 121, 129, 180, 186, 188
Thompson, R. H., 128
Tippah County, 81, 128
Tougaloo College, 115
Tucker, Henry St. George, 53, 167
Tunica County, 117

Turpentine, 31
Turpie, David, 66

Unconstitutionality, 51, 165, 167, 185
Understanding Clause, 7, 80–82, 87–104, 144–45, 151, 153–54, 157, 159, 163, 168
Uneducated voters. *See* Illiteracy
United States v. Cruikshank, 73
University of Mississippi (Ole Miss), 115
Upper class, 7, 21, 36, 42, 45, 91, 208. *See also* Elites
Ursino Plantation, 43

Vardaman, James K., 169, 181, 197–200
Vest, George, 148
Veto, 24, 59, 63, 102, 198
Vicksburg, MS, 6, 14, 30, 39, 44–45, 62, 118–19, 123, 133, 135, 139, 142, 181, 204
Vicksburg Post, 81, 87, 95, 98, 102, 130
Vigilantes, 35, 58, 190–91, 198
Violations, 38, 49, 53, 71, 74, 96, 144, 148, 154, 161–62, 165–67, 171–72, 181–83, 187, 189
Violence, 4–5, 9, 14–18, 26, 34, 38, 46, 50–51, 54, 58, 64, 70, 90, 92–93, 111–12, 130, 150–51, 153, 157, 160, 164, 166, 169, 175, 177, 190–92, 198–200
Virtue, 44–45, 91, 98, 109, 115, 142, 157, 167
Voters, 4, 7, 11, 16, 18, 20, 26, 34–35, 48–50, 52–53, 55, 59, 62–67, 69, 73–74, 76–81, 83, 85–87, 89, 93, 100, 103, 106–7, 112–13, 126–28, 132–33, 143, 149, 151, 155–56, 159–63, 168, 171, 173–77, 179–80, 182, 189, 194–98

Wahalak, MS, 62, 199
Walker, Joel P., 59
Walthall, Edward: background, 6, 12, 16, 22, 25, 59, 234n69; constitutional convention, 61–62, 64; Senate debates, 144, 147, 155, 162, 191
Warrants, 26, 140, 171–72, 260n18
Warren County, 14, 36, 73
Washington, Booker T., 90–92, 169, 176, 207

Washington, DC, 6, 26, 29, 35, 37–38, 41, 45, 47, 66, 92, 96, 144, 171, 173, 176, 179, 180, 208
Washington County, 82, 109, 186
Washington Post, 53, 191
Watered stock, 134, 136
Wayne County, 82, 122
Webster County, 85, 139
Wesson, MS, 31
White counties, 4, 5, 7–8, 16, 21, 23–24, 29–30, 63, 65, 71, 76, 93, 110, 116–17, 125–31, 139–42, 154, 162, 168–69, 195–97, 199, 203, 208
White League, 156
Whitecapping, 169, 190–91, 198–99
Willard, Francis, 112
Williams v. Mississippi, 169, 184–94, 205
Wilson, Ephraim, 149
Wilson, Robert, 193, 204
Winchester, F. K., 129
Winona, MS, 112
Witherspoon, William, 85, 97, 117
Wolcott, Edward, 160
Woman suffrage, 6, 75–77, 80–81, 84–85, 106–12, 149
Woman's Christian Temperance Union (WCTU), 112
Woodville, MS, 62
Wool hat boys, 61, 171. *See also* Burkitt, Frank

Yale, 101, 156
Yazoo City, MS, 39, 62
Yazoo River, 137
Yazoo Sentinel, 102, 141
Yellow fever, 124
Yerger, W. G., 82, 129

www.ingramcontent.com/pod-product-compliance
Lightning Source LLC
Chambersburg PA
CBHW030609230426
43661CB00053B/1905